Comparative
Political
Systems

COMPARATIVE POLITICAL SYSTEMS

Political Processes in Developed and Developing States

Barbara N. McLennan

Temple University

Duxbury Press

North Scituate, Massachusetts
A Division of Wadsworth Publishing Company, Belmont, California

Duxbury Press

A DIVISION OF WADSWORTH PUBLISHING COMPANY, INC.

Comparative Political Systems: Political Processes in Developed and Developing States was edited and prepared for composition by Sheila Steinberg. Interior design was provided by Jane Lovinger and the cover was designed by Oliver Klein.

L.C. Cat. Card No.: 74-84836

ISBN 0-87872-081-2

PRINTED IN THE UNITED STATES OF AMERICA

1 2 3 4 5 6 7 8 9 10 — 79 78 77 76 75

Contents

5

Political Parties 178

6

Political Processes and Public Policy 234

7

General Assessment: Comparing Different Political Systems 267

Tables

Preface

This book is designed to be used as an introductory text in basic comparative politics. In some colleges this course may be entitled "Introduction to Political Science" or be given some other title, but the function of the course is similar in all curricula: it attempts to equip students with the concepts and approaches necessary for evaluating a variety of political systems and problems outside domestic American politics.

In the past ten years there has been a substantial transformation in basic approaches to comparative politics. Previously, a text for an introductory course in the field would have basically been an anthology of separate subjects: it would have presented simplified descriptions of politics and government in Great Britain, France, the USSR; it would have described "legislatures," "executives," "judiciaries," and "political parties"; it would have mentioned "the underdeveloped world" and would have concluded with a separate section on "world politics."

A real departure from this type of course and text was made possible by Gabriel Almond's structural-functional approach to comparative politics, which first appeared in his influential essay "A Functional Approach to Comparative Politics" in Almond and Coleman, *The Politics of the Developing Areas* (Princeton: Princeton University Press, 1960). While widely criticized for certain technical failures, the Almond essay did provide a standardized series of concepts by which political systems could be compared. The approach allowed for the comparison of developed and underdeveloped, Western and non-Western, and democratic and nondemocratic systems without an overly obvious cultural bias. It reduced political systems, regardless of geography, to relatively equivalent units ("inputs," "outputs," and "conversion processes"), which could be compared using the same concepts and language. The approach became quite widely used, especially among younger faculty, and eventually led to publication of many books utilizing these concepts, generally designed for senior level and graduate students.

The purpose of the present volume is to adapt the concepts of the structural-functional approach to a study of comparative politics on the introductory level. The book also attempts to present very different kinds of political system in a uniform framework, in order to avoid the older, more culture-bound approach which viewed all politics as European politics. A great effort was, therefore, made to include countries from every continent as well as of varying cultural backgrounds and levels of economic development. A conscious attempt was made to choose large countries, important strategically to their geographic regions, and countries that may be of special interest from a comparative viewpoint.

The result was the selection of nine countries—Great Britain, India, Chile, France, Indonesia, Zaire, Union of Soviet Socialist Republics, Egypt, and the People's Republic of China. The major European powers are therefore included, as are three great states of Asia of over one hundred million poulation—China, India, and Indonesia. Egypt, the largest and most influential middle Eastern state, is also included. Zaire (the former Belgian Congo) and Chile were selected, not only as representative of the sub-Saharan African and Latin American cultures, respectively but also because of the special character and history of each of these countries' political structures. Certainly, the final choice of each of the countries was arbitrary to a certain extent, but a great effort was made to present a balanced and diversified group of states for study.

The book is organized into seven chapters. Chapter 1, "The Political System," introduces the major concepts dealt with throughout the volume. It discusses the nature of politics, society and politics, leadership and the social system, the relationship between politics and economic development, and concludes with a discussion of political pluralism and the nature of competition in political systems. Chapter 1 also introduces three types of political system—competitive, fragmented, and noncompetitive—which serve as organizing concepts throughout the volume.

Chapter 2, "Structural and Institutional Differences Among Political Systems," presents the basic descriptive material on all nine countries relating to population, territory, and constitutional structure. This is presented early in the volume because of the introductory character of the course of study; it was found through experience in teaching this course that students could more easily understand the comparative functional concepts if they first had some basic factual information about the countries under discussion. Chapter 2, like the ensuing chapters, is organized into three sections—competitive states (Great Britain, India, and Chile); fragmented states (France, Indonesia, and Zaire); and noncompetitive states (the USSR, Egypt, and the PRC).

Chapter 3, "Political Culture and Socialization," deals with a discussion of basic cultural values as they relate to politics in the three sets of countries. The chapter also discusses varying patterns of socialization and education.

Chapter 4, "Political Participation," deals with the processes of recruitment, electoral participation, and communication in the nine countries, again organized into competitive, fragmented, and noncompetitive categories.

Chapter 5, "Political Parties," treats the different functions and characteristics of political parties in competitive, fragmented, and noncompetitive states.

Chapter 6, "Political Processes," deals with the "output" of the nine political systems—their different policies and administrative arrangements for developing and executing policies. Again the countries are subdivided into competitive, fragmented, and noncompetitive categories.

Chapter 7, "General Assessment Comparing Different Political Systems," concludes the book with an overall comparison of the characteristics of competitive, fragmented, and noncompetitive states. the links between comparative politics and an understanding of world politics are explored.

Chile is regarded as a competitive system in this book. The recent overthrow of President Allende by the military has not as yet resulted in the promulgation of new constitutional structure, and the present ruling group still appears to be transitory. Discussion of the Allende overthrow in the light of Chilean political competition is, however, included in the book.

ACKNOWLEDGMENTS

This book is the product of several years of teaching and research: its organizational framework and content were developed over four years of classroom use. Numerous students and teaching assistants at Temple University assisted in the derivation and evaluation of its content and structure at various stages. In addition, the manuscript has been reviewed, edited, and typed by numerous persons.

Particular thanks must be expressed to A. John Berrigan who, as chief teaching assistant during the first year in which the course was taught, assisted in work on the original content of the course of study. Also, Ouseph Varkey's work as teaching assistant and his contributing research on India is greatly appreciated. In addition, Carole Sussman read and edited the first draft of the manuscript, and numerous scholars at many universities reviewed and commented on it at various stages in its development. The comments of Barry Stern and Arpad Von Lazar on Chile were especially helpful. Sheila Steinberg, the final editor, has painstakingly reviewed both content and copy and must be thanked for her many comments, suggestions, and queries. Whatever flaws remain in the book are the author's responsiblitiy alone.

Chapter 1

The Political System

THE NATURE OF POLITICS

There are many definitions of politics. The word itself is derived from the Greek "polity" and linguistically can be traced to the life style of the ancient Hellenic city-states. In these communities, citizens, through direct universal participation and activity, determined their community's policies and actions. Since then "politics" has generally referred to the actions taken by and behavior patterns of citizens in attempting to arrive at joint policies and decisions.

Political decisions are normally conceived as binding on all citizens in the community. They are authoritative because they should override decisions taken by smaller segments of the community. In ancient Greece, where the communities were small, this concept offered little difficulty—whenever a small part of the community disagreed with the majority, it either went along with the greater number or staged an insurrection. Such an insurrection was, of course, another form of politics—a means by which citizens participated in community policymaking.

One of the prime problems of politics, therefore, has always been the maintenance of order. Every human community must make joint decisions; every human community must be able to reconcile differences among its members. These tasks would be very difficult to accomplish if there were not some means of maintaining order—a well-recognized system of behavior by which all persons in the community could avail themselves of the established political processes.

When we refer to politics, then, we are concerned with a particular process of human behavior that occurs at the highest level in the given community. In large political units with great complex populations, there will exist many subgroups to which human beings will maintain loyalties. These subgroups will make decisions that affect the whole political community. However, loyalty to the overall political system must override all subloyalties; in any confrontation the political authority must prevail. This, of course, implies that the political system must not only be supported in the psychological sense, but, in times of challenge, it must also have access to the dominant physical force in the community. The maintenance of order in a community as a general rule, however, must be based on the behavioral patterns of its members, not simply on coercion or threats. No small elite could maintain an orderly system without widespread support and loyalty in some sense of those terms. Permanent insurrection is equivalent to the dissolution of the political community, and while insurrections and revolutions have occurred, no human community has ever maintained this situation as the normal, permanent system of political decisionmaking.

These characterizations of the nature of politics are highly general and theoretical. The practical details of politics vary in many respects from time to time and community to community. One of the major goals of political science, dating back to the great political thinkers Plato and Aristotle, has been to create general propositions and devise theoretical explanations so that politics could be viewed in the abstract, rather than as a collection of disparate human acts having no essential relationship or connection with one another.

Theories of politics have generally been based upon fundamental assumptions about the universality of human behavior and values. Historically, many theories of politics have been invented or "discovered" in order to legitimize or support the prevailing order of the day. Thus, in the days of supreme monarchs the Western world developed the idea of the "Divine Right of Kings"; in times of republican revolution, concepts of the "Rights of Man" have been expounded and introduced. These theories are, as are many in contemporary political science, efforts to describe particular human activities in general terms. They are attempts at presenting explanations of political life in such a way that people can view their communities and their own places within these communities as logical and part of the universal order of things.

Contemporary political thought, unlike these previous concepts, attempts to be more morally neutral and objective. Rather than trying to support particular modes of political organization, efforts today are made to analyze all political systems, no matter how varied their particular frameworks, in terms as free of cultural connotations as possible. As a consequence, there has been a great increase in interest in comparative studies.

By comparing different systems, theorists are able to find similar threads, thus helping to understand the general tendencies common to political systems. In contrast, when very similar systems are compared, their special differences become evident, also aiding in refining the general concepts usually reserved for describing them. Comparative study today involves much more than theorizing about the general nature of politics. It is also concerned with gathering as much factual data as possible about all systems, so they can be compared in equal, factual terms and can contribute towards understanding patterns of environment and human behavior in equal, objective terms. The goal is thus to arrive at logical general propositions that will contribute to the basic understanding of politics and, perhaps, help us to predict its development.

SOCIETY AND POLITICS

Human beings live in communities: they are born into families; they make friends; they learn to share and transmit values; they associate themselves mentally with persons they consider to be like themselves; they organize themselves into societies. A society is a fairly large mass of persons who share enough values and characteristics that they see themselves as a group, distinct from other groups of people.

In the modern world societies have developed on a national scale. Citizens of a particular nation, especially in the highly developed Western states, see their national identification as overriding all other considerations: an American from a Northeastern state would normally feel a closer identification with an entirely different kind of American from a Southern or Western state than he would, for example, with a Canadian citizen living much closer to him, both in terms of geography and lifestyle. Social identifications are psychological; people place social significance on established geographic boundaries. This is much less true in newly established nations: in them, subnational and supranational societies often hold the loyalties of individuals rather than do the legal nations; in them, many persons prefer a religious or tribal loyalty to citizenship in a new state. Loyalties to groups both smaller and larger than the legal states often override the formal definition of nationality.

A functioning society is frequently described as a "social system" because it is more than just a collection of individuals who identify with one another. These individuals interact with each other; they produce leaders, followers, and rules by which personal and social success and failure can be measured. They collectively teach these rules to their young and thus keep their society working. The term "system" refers to the basic patterns of behavior that hold the society together. Individuals within a society divide and share their responsibilities on the basis of an understood mutual respect; sharing continues in a well-established manner over long periods of time, from generation to generation. In other words, functioning societies induct their young in an orderly manner into the operation of a social system.

Among large social groups, the social system itself must normally be organized into subgroups. Large populations are the product of relatively prosperous economic systems—they have emerged where there are large quantities of food, and this historically has occurred only with great efforts of human organization over agricultural production. For example, ancient Egypt, ancient China, and ancient India all developed large-scale agricultural production, and all three states also developed large populations and highly defined systems of political organization. Political organization was required to supervise the population in the agricultural labor pool required to produce the food supply. These ancient societies discovered that for large populations to exist at all, there must be a well-established division of labor. If cities are to exist, their citizens must be fed by surplus from the countryside; if manufacturing is to take place, the persons engaged in production must also be fed; if the arts and sciences are to thrive, artists and scientists must be fed. A society with cultural amenities such as philosophy, religion, the arts, and sciences establishes a marketplace for persons who produce the food and are willing to trade it for the values attributed to urban culture. Ancient agricultural states like Egypt, China, and India developed great cities, manufacturing industries, rich literatures and cultural traditions, great religions, and well-defined social structures to support their economic systems. Complex economic systems develop over long periods of time; they are themselves transformed by political and technological factors. Economic behavior can be affected by decisions of political leaders as well as by the social class structure. Because of these and many other relevant variables (i. e., access to transportation, natural resources, climate) no two societies and no two economic structures have developed in precisely the same manner.

All societies that have stayed together have developed subgroups—both economic and social—or social subsystems.

In dividing the labor force, societies have developed a variety of occupations and have attributed differing ranks or status to each of them. In simple societies there may exist only a few occupational subgroups—priest, soldier, and peasant, for example—but in complex systems there are many occupational and social subgroups. Individuals can belong to different groups, many of which overlap or conflict with one another. Individuals identify with their occupation, their place of residence, their family, their political party. No single subgroup claims the total identification of its members—all subgroups compete for the loyalties of individual members. The total society is held together by the competition and interaction of subgroups.

Individuals realize their social and psychological needs in small groups, where they can meet and interact with one another. When individuals belong to a variety of groups, they make it difficult for these groups to achieve domination in the total sense over their members. Groups that share the loyalties of members with other groups have to be fairly moderate in their claims against the other groups. Thus, in a social system with an efficiently distributed division of labor, the only group that in theory should be dominant is the group with the highest political authority—the government—because it is the only group that can claim the overriding loyalties of all smaller groups.

All this is, of course, highly theoretical. No government has ever been universally supported by all its citizens; on the other hand, no human society has ever permanently dissolved itself into an anarchic war among its constituent factions. In the real world social and political unity appears to be best established where economic development and the division of labor has proceeded the furthest. In many Western European countries, for example, large populations identify with their national states above any competing subgroups; in them, mutual knowledge and understanding have long been promoted by high levels of education, a common language and culture, and modern systems of communication. These states also have long histories; their political institutions—parties, interest groups, and legislatures among others—have for many years been recognized as legitimate and authoritative by the general population.

Such is not the case in many of the newer nation-states. In them, most people are barely aware of the concept of national societies: their loyalties are entirely to traditional groups—tribes, villages, and the like. In countries like Zaire, there exist few groups that share members with other groups: people live in their traditional regions; their lives are hardly touched socially and economically by persons outside their own narrow circles of acquaintances. In these states there is little national support for the new central governments, and social pluralism makes for division and disunity, rather than for moderation, compromise, and sharing.

LEADERSHIP AND THE SOCIAL SYSTEM

When we refer to politics in the modern world, we do not, as the ancient Athenians did, consider the behavior of all the citizens in the state equally. Political decisionmaking in large populations must be broken down by a division of labor, and the functions of government must be carried out by certain types of individuals with either the nominal or active support of most of the important citizens in the particular community.

Leadership, in the general sense, exists in all societies. In all cases it must rest on popular acceptance. In other words, leadership, and the system by which it is maintained, must be "legitimate"—it has to be able to promote the belief among the citizens that the existing political framework is the most appropriate for their society.[1]

A turn-of-the-century German social scientist named Max Weber, in a famous essay, discussed the sources and bases of political legitimacy in different kinds of political frameworks.[2] Weber believed that leaders emerged in particular social contexts, that they fit into prevailing norms, and that they were authoritative only so long as they could maintain their legitimacy. He categorized leaders into three types—traditional, charismatic, and bureaucratic. These categories of leadership were purely ideal or theoretical, although some historical figures approach one or another type quite closely.

Traditional Leaders

According to Weber, the traditional political system in which modes of human behavior are prescribed by custom or by written texts handed down through time and interpreted by a priestly class produced the traditional leader (see Table 1.1). The traditional system is characterized by several restrictions and limitations on the overt behavior of both leaders and followers. To become a leader in such a system, an individual normally has to be born into the proper family. To achieve the requisite legitimacy for his rule, if he seizes power by force, the leader normally insists the priests reinterpret the texts or he claims his lineage is true and pure, at least in some mythical sense.

Likewise, decisionmaking, to be accepted as legitimate in traditional systems, must be based on custom. Kings and chiefs can make important decisions, but these decisions are legitimate only insofar as they are made to appear as normal, customary, and dictated by the universally acknowledged laws of nature.

Traditional social systems are based on rigid class structures and tend to be very conservative. Leaders who wish to maintain the traditional manner of

Table 1.1.   Max Weber's Sources of Legitimacy

Source of Legitimacy	Types of Political Systems	Bases of Decisionmaking

1. Tradition:
   customs,
   mores,
   "natural law"
   "divine right"
	Hereditary monarchy,
	tribal chiefdoms
	tribal councils
		Custom, authoritative texts,
		"natural law," "divine right,"
		habitual usage

2. Charisma:
   personal mission of
     the individual leader
	Transitional and
	   revolutionary systems
		Personal understanding of
		   the self-appointed leader

3. Bureaucracy:
   rules for promotion
    and demotion,
   rules dividing responsi-
    bility and function
    by hierarchical
    levels
	Administrative structures,
	   including elective
	   and autocratic systems
	   based on routinized
	   recruitment into
	   government service
		Administrative rules

doing things are unlikely to upset their own social underpinnings. To be a real king, after all, one must have many serfs. When serfs become wage earners, they no longer subscribe in quite the same way to custom and tradition. Thus the purely traditional leader, as Weber envisioned him, exists only theoretically in the agricultural pasts of most states. However, it should be recognized that leaders everywhere, including those in modern Western countries, often claim custom and tradition as the basis for certain decisions.

Charismatic Leaders

Of all Weber's concepts, that of the "charismatic" leader has received more comment and interest than any other. At a transitional or revolutionary point in the development of the sociopolitical structure, caused perhaps by economic or military upheaval, leadership, though traditionally legitimate, can be challenged because of an apparent lack of effectiveness. Custom and tradition are no longer sufficient to legitimize the prevailing patterns of leadership, and no substitute mythology exists to serve the same purpose. Under these circumstances the charismatic leader can emerge.

The charismatic leader is not an individual who draws on sacred texts or custom but rather is a person with an inner mission, who feels compelled to "save" society according to a personal vision. His standards of right and wrong are personal; his source of legitimacy is mystical and magical; and his followers are required to recognize these special qualities. The ideal charismatic leader, according to Weber's theory, is not obligated or responsible to his society; rather the people are obligated to him because of his unique mission. He is not merely a popular man; he demands total loyalty and total submission to his person. Martin Luther probably comes as close as is historically possible to Weber's ideal charismatic figure: he challenged traditional authority and drew the source of his legitimacy from a purely personal interpretation of his mission in the world.

In the modern world, many leaders have frequently been described as being charismatic. Normally, this refers to their oratorical ability, popularity, and ability to sway crowds. Weber's definition of charisma includes much more than just this; it incorporates a sense of an inner mission in a revolutionary time and a challenge to custom and tradition. To some extent, many leaders in the world have some charismatic qualities, but very few are authentic charismatic leaders in Weber's sense of the term.

Charisma is a very unstable quality; it is revolutionary, and it lasts only as long as the revolution itself can continue. Once the revolution is over and tradition has been overturned, some method of rule or government must be instituted. This implies Weber's third source of legitimacy—the "bureaucracy."

Bureaucratic Leaders

Persons operating in a bureaucratic framework abide by rules; these are narrower restrictions than the broad sacred pronouncements that surround traditional leaders. A bureaucrat operates within a hierarchy—a framework in which there are superiors at the top and lesser ranks at the bottom. At each level, the bureaucrat is given a particular set of tasks and a system of rules by which he may perform them. To advance in the structure, he must follow the rules according to his level; he must perform his function for a particular period of time; he must please his superiors; and he must pass examinations or show educational qualifications for the higher rank. Promotions and decisionmaking are controlled by rules and must always be defended in terms of them. Bureaucracy is a source of legitimacy just as tradition and charisma are, because it endows persons with status and rank.

Significant decisionmaking in a bureaucratic system tends to be made by those in the highest ranks. Difficult and important problems are usually avoided by lower-ranking bureaucrats because they seek to improve their status and fear taking unnecessary responsibilities that they may be unable to handle. Thus they pass their most difficult problems on to their superiors, who, in turn, increase in status and power. Thus, when a bureaucrat is at the pinnacle of an organization, he can make extremely important and far-ranging decisions even though he is governed by strict rules. He has a tremendous amount of information provided by the lower ranks, and he deals with problems on a high level.

All modern states have bureaucracies, and almost all political leaders make decisions because of their positions in bureaucratic structures. However, as with the other two types of leadership, very few persons are simply bureaucratic leaders. Politicians in real life tend to draw a little from each source: they try to appear traditional; they try to project charisma; and they utilize their bureaucracies. Differences in leadership are based not only on personalities but on the condition of the social fabric in which leaders operate. It should be recognized that the three sources of legitimacy are quite contradictory to one another: a leader with a great tendency to project himself as charismatic will generally be opposed to recognizing any rules, bureaucratic or customary; likewise, a bureaucratic leader is likely to downgrade reliance on personality. The main source of legitimacy depends on the society: if bureaucrats are supported as being more legitimate than other types of leaders, this is the sort of leader who will emerge. Historically, different kinds of societies have generally produced different kinds of leaders.

Leadership: A Social Phenomenon

In every social system, leaders can maintain their authority and legitimacy only so long as they appear to be effective to their citizenry. Leaders must be able to induce people to act in support of their policies, even if these people would not voluntarily behave this way. Leaders must be able to influence and they must be able to coerce. This is why legitimacy is so important; without it, no leader could influence his following to creative action.

The ability of leaders to provide effective decisions for their societies depends on many factors. Some leaders, for example, have greater political resources than others. They can spend more money because they can tax their people more efficiently; they can promote their causes through mass media; they can command efficient military and police establishments. Leaders have much greater access to political resources in highly developed states than they do in poorly developed societies.

In addition to the availability of resources, a leader's power also depends on his own motivations and the skill with which he uses resources. Thus some leaders may be activists and popular, they may be naturally able to persuade and influence; others may be thrust into their positions by accident and be quite unable to make decisions or carry them out. Much depends on the process by which leaders are developed: traditional societies, in which leaders are born to their positions, are often quite unstable because of the extreme variability in quality of leadership despite severe controls over the education provided to would-be kings and chiefs. Similarly, different types of individuals can, by accident, become leaders in electoral or bureaucratic systems. In these latter two cases, however, persons with particular individual abilities have great advantages and are more likely to become leaders than others. Where leaders are elected their speaking ability, good looks, and ability to make and keep friends and advisors can be great advantages. In contrast, in bureaucratic systems technical accuracy and ability are greatly rewarded. In different kinds of systems, different personalities will thus be more effective and be more likely to be chosen leaders than others.

Leadership: A Psychological Phenomenon

The nature of leadership and its potential is not only a social phenomenon; it has strong psychological roots. Leaders must develop a special kind of motivation: they must willingly and actively be concerned in the pursuit of power and influence. Motivation to excel, however, is not solely a personal matter. It is often socially sanctioned and encouraged and may be more widespread in some cultures than in others.

Also, leaders must be recognized and accepted by many people before they can be effective. Persons throughout a society have to develop a mental picture of a leader and a personal sort of loyalty to him. The willingness of a society to accept authority is the result not only of different kinds of subgroup structures but also of different psychological views of political leadership that are deep and basic to most people in that society. Thus, some societies will follow any leader with even a slim claim to legitimacy; other societies have difficulty in providing enough acceptance to their leaders to allow any regime to last very long and to accomplish very much.

POLITICS AND GROUP BEHAVIOR

Every society contains subgroups from which it produces its leaders. The nature of politics is determined by the operation of this process. A major factor affecting national politics is, thus, the development of group politics and the framework for group behavior in the given society.

A group is a collection of people who are held together by a common interest, purpose, or activity. Different social systems provide different procedures by which groups are permitted to pursue their goals.

Political Groups in Competitive, Fragmented, and Noncompetitive Societies

In competitive societies (see pp. 27-29 for a definition of competitive, fragmented, and noncompetitive systems) in which public opinion is highly respected, groups are essential in the formation of all kinds of opinion, including political opinion. When a variety of often conflicting views is tolerated by society, interest groups, which are specifically oriented to particular goals, help to focus the public's attention of specific issues, articulating them for all, including politicians, to see. Thus, in representative governments, interest groups are major political actors, often more important than any politician, whatever his claims to legitimate leadership. Politicians cannot even attempt to represent constituents unless they have specific information about their needs. Interest groups inform politicians of these needs and, in turn, inform the constituencies of the actions of the politician. Thus, it is possible for an organization such as the National Rifle Association (NRA), in a competitive system such as the United States, to be influential in the elections of senators and congressmen who oppose the organization's stand on gun control. There are many hunters in the United States and they believe what the National Rifle Association says with respect to the issue of gun control. Likewise, groups interested in ecology can influence senators to defeat an attempt to build the Supersonic Air Transport (SST).

Leaders of interest groups tend to be specialists, and every government can fruitfully use the efforts of informed experts. Thus, even in fairly authoritarian systems of government, groups are established that perform similar functions to those of interest groups in the competitive structure of representative systems. In less developed states, in contrast, relatively few interest groups exist and consequently these states tend to have comparatively ineffective political systems. Politicians appear to be irresponsible in many of these countries, but this is often not because of any inherent fault or weakness of their own. Rather the people, lacking group organization, are uninformed and politicians are unable to judge what they want. The public, thus, has no basis or standard by which to judge its leaders and tends, over time, to become frustrated. Politicians, lacking accurate information, tend to rely on what their friends, relatives, and imaginations tell them. They also look to ideological formulations, because they are unable to make pragmatic, rational decisions that are based on reliable factual information.

Elite Groups Versus Mass Groups

While all societies have groups, there have been few general theories of group behavior. Gaetano Mosca[3] and Roberto Michels[4], two turn-of-the-century European social scientists, have each developed concepts of an inevitable ruling class, sometimes referred to as the "Iron Law of Oligarchy." In general, the theory holds that every group inevitably separates itself into a minority of leaders (an "elite") and an unorganized majority of followers. There have been studies of actual legislative bodies which have, to some extent, supported this theory by indicating that group size is inversely proportionate to political influence. For example, there are proportionally very few powerful politicians in the United States House of Representatives, which has 435 members; there are many powerful senators in the United States Senate, which has only 100 members. While the larger body depends almost solely on organization to accomplish its tasks, the smaller body can achieve many things on a face-to-face basis.

Although such facts appear to support the theory that most human groups divide themselves into a few leaders and many followers, oligarchies do not necessarily occur. That is, the elite of one group does not necessarily have to be identical to the elite in every other group. In societies that permit and value competition, political leaders never constitute a monolithic group that does not hear demands from below. Political power is specialized and shared by various institutions; at elections, the aggregate majority of voters can turn leaders out. Although it is true that minorities make the decisions, it is not true that a few people necessarily have all the political resources and make all the decisions all the time.[5] All individuals have some influence as part of minorities that contribute to majority rule. Indeed, even in authoritarian systems politicians must be aware of conflicting interests within society, and mechanisms must exist in order to reconcile the inevitable disagreements among politicians with conflicting views.

The Relevance of Political Ideology

These concepts of elite rule versus majority rule are important primarily because of the ideological significance different political systems attach to them. An ideology is a system of beliefs and values that organize the manner in which persons observe and evaluate their political and social systems. Ideologies grow and are passed down by social groups through both formal and informal processes. They are essential to the legitimacy of the political system.

Ideological structures exist in all political societies; all communities are held together by common assumptions about human nature and the goals of human society. Thus, for example, many of the assumptions underlying the United States Constitution are not questioned or even considered in a rational sense by most Americans. Public opinion polls, for example, have shown that large portions of the American electorate do not accept the concepts enunciated in the American Declaration of Independence and Bill of Rights when these are presented as questions for rational consideration. Many people do not really believe that "all men are created equal"; for a very long time now, we have been instructed by medical science that human beings are born with different talents and capacities. Many people also really do not believe that men "are endowed by their Creator with certain inalienable rights"; most Americans regard political rights as deriving from their political community, and not from some mythical state of nature that stands above all political organization. Despite such differences between popular belief and the philosophic assumptions on which our society is based, most Americans still accept their system of government without question.

The political systems of modern Western states, including the socialist states, are based on the theories of the eighteenth-century Enlightenment. These theories hold that a world of peace, harmony, and prosperity for all citizens is possible in the future. They assume men to be good, rational, and knowledgeable about their own interests.

This seeming agreement on goals does not imply any similarity in political organization. Indeed, political practices and the group process differ among these states because their ideological interpretations postulate different means to attain their goals. Majority rule in the Soviet Union means, in practical terms, something quite different than in the United States, but both claim to be representative states that are organized in the interests of "The People." There are great gulfs between the capitalist and socialist systems on this matter; indeed, the basic tenets of socialist ideology rest on a criticism of capitalist social and political processes. However, the common ideological assumptions of both systems have permitted movements of alliance and rapprochement, especially when confronted with alien ideologies inimical to both.

The fascist and nazi ideologies of the 1920s and 1930s were based on entirely different assumptions about human goals and human nature. They were alien and totally contrary to both capitalist and socialist thinking of that time. Fascism and national socialism were post-Enlightenment ideologies that presumed men were not primarily motivated by a will to happiness, but by a will to power. They were intensely nationalistic and viewed the world as not naturally harmonious, but as a place of combat where, as Darwin might have phrased it, the fittest survived. Thus, war was not evil but a process that produced strong men.

Fascist ideology also denied previous assumptions about the rationality of men. Sigmund Freud had discovered that, in some sense, every human being had irrational psychological drives that had to be satisfied. Fascist ideology seized upon the notion of man's irrational nature and used it to achieve maximum nationalist power by exciting the masses to their greatest heights of irrational strength. It viewed human society as inevitably governed by elites; it presumed that the leaders would be held in glory while the masses of people would be harnessed somewhat like blind beasts. In nazi Germany, this ideology coincided with racial dogmas that automatically ranked races and nationalities on the basis of their success in combat. The political goals implied by fascist ideology were a direct challenge to both capitalist and socialist systems, which viewed the future with hopes for peace. Fascism was innately warlike and aggressive; it was designed to appeal to a frightened middle class, threatened from all sides by inflation, by revolution from the urban and rural proletariats, and by the excesses of the unrestrained capitalist-aristocratic classes.

Fascist ideological goals, though relying on modern theories of Darwin and Freud, were so alien to the other states as to seem thoroughly barbaric. This was the case even though most persons in all states at the time would probably have accepted the scientific findings of both Darwin and Freud. The political interpretation given to these fairly technical scientific works unleashed a political process that threatened other states and systems of life. The concept of the national elite was turned into an excuse for subjugating and murdering all opposition; the concept of survival of the fittest implied attacks on weak nations simply because they were weak. The new ideologies lacked any presumptions about the possibility of human ability (as opposed to biological and racial determinism), mutual compromise, and peaceful growth. The political result for the fascist states was internal group chaos, over which was superimposed an authoritarian political framework with militarist goals. There were few internal mechanisms established for resolving disputes, because of the assumption that the leader knew everything and the fittest would survive anyway.

These ideologies lacked strong roots and were eliminated, at least super-ficially, when the fascist states were defeated in World War II. Elitist theories persist, however, especially in the less developed states of Asia, Africa, and Latin America, where nationalisms tend to be very intense. These states tone down the aggressive components of the prewar fascist dogmas, but they do retain a similarity in their views of the masses. It should be noted that in these poor states, where the masses are impoverished and downtrodden, the economic facts of life dictate a government by an elite.

POLITICS AND ECONOMIC DEVELOPMENT

Ancient Theory

The idea of economic influence on politics is as old as Plato and Aristotle. These ancient Athenians recognized that the distribution of wealth and the level of prosperity were related to political stability in the Greek city-state. Plato's ideal state, presented in the *Republic*, was based on a concept of justice that implied a perfect division of labor.[6] In Plato's Republic people would be chosen by merit for each occupation and would be rewarded according to Plato's concept of justice. Everyone would receive an education appropriate to the function he was to perform in society. Plato was careful in his selection of occupations for his perfect state, and he was careful in his educational prescriptions as well.

Aristotle was more concerned with describing actual states than with establishing ideal theoretical models. In observing the politics of many Greek polities, he categorized states into six types: there were three good types—kingship (rule by one man), aristocracy (rule by an elite), and polity (rule by all citizens); and three corresponding corrupt types—tyranny (rule by one selfish man), oligarchy (rule by several selfish men), and democracy (rule by mob).[7] The good states rule in the public interest, while the corrupt states serve the selfish interests of the rulers. Of all the types, Aristotle preferred the aristocracy, but in selecting the best type of state for a given society he believed economic considerations were overriding. Thus, he stated that the best kind of state was a "middle-class" state, in which most people had enough material goods to keep them satisfied. He deplored states in which a few very wealthy men were envied by a mass of very poor citizens. He viewed this as an unstable situation susceptible to revolutionary violence.

Both Plato and Aristotle would have deplored economically under-developed states of the modern world. These states are very poor. With low literacy rates, poor means of communications, and agrarian economies, these states lack the division of labor so highly valued by Plato. Most people in underdeveloped economies work very hard to produce just about enough food for themselves and their families. They do not have much leisure and few enjoy any luxuries. Their social and political views are tightly controlled by the traditional communities in which they live. They are generally subservient to a very small elite which owns most of the property and makes all decisions; a large majority of the people have little contact with the government, except when they are called upon to pay taxes or serve the elite in other ways. These states are similar to the economies that Aristotle so severely criticized; they lack a middle class, and suffer much of the instability that Aristotle predicted for such states. These generalizations are corroborated in practical and statistical terms for contemporary states in Table 1.2.

This table presents some practical economic comparisons among the nine countries analyzed in this book, including the United States. The countries are listed in declining order of per capita gross national product, a commonly used measure of the productive capacity of an economy. In general terms the first four countries listed—the USA, France, Great Britain, and the USSR—would today be considered highly developed economically; Chile would be regarded as moderately well developed; and the other five—Egypt, China, India, Indonesia, and Zaire—would be considered poor or underdeveloped. The table shows that much which has been theorized in the text in general terms is supported by statistical detail in these ten countries. The populations of the wealthy, productive nations (those with over $1,000 per capita income) are

Table 1.2. Comparison of Levels of Development of Selected Countries

Country	Population (in millions*)	Per Capita Gross National Product (in dollars)	% of Labor Force in Agriculture	Newspapers per 1000 Population	% of Population Living in Centers of over 20,000	Average Caloric Intake per Person per Day
USA	209.2	4,240	2.0	305	47.0	3,240
France	51.9	2,460	15.1	243	41.9	3,180
Great Britain	56.6	1,890	3.1	488	83.4	3,180
USSR	247.5	1,200	38.7	320	35.6	3,180
Chile	10.2	510	27.7	86	54.7	2,720
Egypt	35.9	160	56.6	28	48.0	2,690
PRC	786.1	118	80.0 (estimate)	—	8.3	1,870
India	584.8	110	72.9	13	14.6	1,900
Indonesia	128.7	100	68.0	7	9.8	1,870
Zaire	18.3	52	86.4	25	9.1	1,920

SOURCE: *United Nations Statistical Yearbook, 1972; United Nations Demographic Yearbook, 1972; ILO Yearbook of Labor Statistics 1971;* United Nations, "Total Population Estimates for World, Regions and Countries, Each Year, 1950-1985," Population Division Working Paper, no. 34. October 1970; International Bank for Reconstruction and Development, *Estimates of Gross National Product, 1969;* U.S. Department of Commerce, *Statistical Abstract of the United States,* (Washington, D.C.: Bureau of the Census, 1972). UNESCO, *UNESCO, Statistical Yearbook, 1970* (Paris, 1970); Food and Agriculture Organization, *FAO Yearbook, 1970* (Rome, 1970).

*Estimates for 1972 made by UN sources

better educated, better fed, more urban, and less agricultural. For example, while Indonesia, India, China, and Zaire all have 68 percent or more of their populations working in agriculture, their populations have the lowest caloric intake of the countries in the table. The United States with only 2 percent of its people working in agriculture makes 3,240 calories available, on the average, to every American every day. In contrast, Zaire with 86.4 percent of its people working in agriculture makes only 1,920 calories available to every person each day, or close to half that of the United States.

The table also shows the wealthy nations are more urban, with large portions of their people living in centers of 20,000 or more people, while the four poorest nations have only about 10 percent of their people living in places of this size. In addition, the wealthy countries have much higher rates of newspaper circulation, reflecting not only their higher literacy rates, but also their greater ability to distribute news and inform the public. These differences obviously can affect the political capacities of these states and their general ability to carry out policy.

Modern Theory

In the contemporary world, when people discuss the relationship of politics to economics, they generally emphasize the theories of Karl Marx. Marx was a very important contributor to modern sociological and economic theory, though his influence is undoubtedly greater in socialist than in capitalist states.

Marx, like many theorists before him, believed politics was a result of the prevailing economic system. He believed society was always ruled by one social class, which always owns the means of production (land, labor, capital, and technological know-how). Following the writings of Georg Hegel, Marx established a theory of history that was based on the progressive development of the socioeconomic class structure and the concept of inevitable class struggle. Each stage of history was characterized by the conflict of two classes (in Hegel's terminology, one class was the "thesis," the other the "antithesis"). By inevitable historical processes the more progressive class, in the socioeconomic sense, would win and establish a new social order (Hegel's "synthesis"). Marx tried to demonstrate that every ruling class, because of economic pressure, exploited people beneath it and in the process created the class that would inevitably overthrow it. Thus, he analyzed human history and categorized it into five stages: monarchy, aristocracy, captialism, socialism, and communism (see Table 1.3).[8]

The first stage (according to Marx, but disputed by contemporary historians) is the traditional period in which society is ruled over by a single monarch who owns everything within the confines of the state. Marx believed that monarchs created the feudal aristocracy because they needed it for taxes and military adventure. He regarded a feudal aristocracy as more progressive than a monarchy because it implied a larger elite and broader popular participation: an aristocratic class contains a few leaders, while a monarchical class contains only one.

Table 1.3. Marx's Theory of Political Development in History

Stages of History	*Ruling Class*		*Progressive Class*
1. Monarchy	King	is overthrown by	Nobility
2. Aristocracy	Nobility	"	Bourgeoisie
3. Capitalism	Bourgeoisie	"	Proletariat
4. Socialism	Proletariat	which leads to	
5. Communism			Classless Society

Historically, Marx's description of the early stage of history was incorrect. European monarchs emerged out of feudal competition; they became the first among equals by militarily defeating feudal competitors. Feudalism really predates monarchy in the history of Western European states. Marx, however, was not terribly concerned with ancient history and focused on the period contemporary to himself.

Marx's second stage of history is the feudal period, in which the ruling class consists of a landed, titled aristocracy. In Marx's theory the aristocracy exploits the moneyed groups in the community (merchants, traders, and manufacturers among others), whom Marx collectively labels the bourgeoisie or capitalist class. Eventually this group of people overturns feudal rule and establishes the capitalist system. Marx regarded his own era as the capitalist stage in human history. Although he believed that the capitalist stage was a progressive improvement over the feudal period, because the capitalist class constituted a wider elite than a titled, inherited aristocracy, Marx did not regard it as the final stage, but applied his historical theory to predict a new social order for the future.

Marx believed the capitalists—those who owned and controlled the business communities of nineteenth-century Europe—exploited the laborers, who would, in turn, form a class (the proletariat) that would rise to overturn the social order. This new era he termed "socialist" (the fourth stage of history), and during it the proletariat or working class would be dominant. For the first time in history the proletariat would actually be in control of their own state. Because they constituted a majority of the population, the proletariat would not produce an exploited class that would overturn it. Instead, the socialist stage would evolve into a classless society, the fifth and final stage of history, which Marx labeled "communism."

Marx regarded each stage of history as determined not only by the system of economic distribution, but by its social values as well. He believed that the ruling class, which controlled all social and political institutions—the government, the church, and the press among others—could dictate the concepts of good and bad, right and wrong to the rest of society. Indeed, he referred to the "State" (meaning all institutions of government) as an instrument of oppression used by the ruling class against its challengers. Marx believed that there would be no need for a state in the utopian communist stage of the future, because then no class would need to exploit anyone else.

Marx attributed the need for police and military forces to the natural vices of capitalism—aggressive greed, acquisitiveness, and exploitation of the weak. All classes accepted these values and this, according to Marx, led to widespread crime and international warfare. Without capitalism, Marx believed, human values could become truly international and cooperative, rather than competitive, as summed up in his dictum "Workers of the world, unite!"[9]

Marx was not a revolutionary in the military or organizational sense of the term. He believed that through natural, evolutionary processes workers would come to dominate their political and social systems. He was persuasive because he tied this theory to an elaborate and "scientific" theory of history. Marx, who lived in an age when capitalism was represented by avaricious amoral men, competing aggressively and viciously and exploiting the working class, did not foresee the age of the modern corporation, owned by and (at least to some degree) responsible to thousands of shareholders. Nineteenth-century businesses were family-owned and often were dominated by single individuals. Marx also did not envisage an age in which workers could exercise political and social power through the ballot box. He hoped this would occur and therefore supported the establishment of socialist political parties. He never foresaw that non-working-class parties would seek proletarian votes and in so doing transform their own sociopolitical basis. He also never foresaw that divisions might arise within the working class and that conflicts of interest could emerge between highly paid skilled labor and less skilled, less educated, poorer working groups. Marx had little interest in organization: he did not predict the rise of the managerial class or of the mass-based political party. He was an advanced social and economic philosopher, who was correct in some respects, but incorrect in others. For this reason his work is still an object of great controversy.

Economic Organization

Every political and social system, whether it claims to be Marxist or not, requires economic organization. The three problems to which all systems must address themselves are:

1. What is to be produced?
2. How is it to be produced?
3. For whom should it be produced?

In the modern world a variety of mechanisms for solving these problems exists.

PRICING

Western countries rely on the price system (much criticized by Marx), by which people decide what they will pay for goods in a "free market." Originally the concept of the free market assumed a state of perfect competition in which every individual was equal to every other, so that no one consumer or producer could have more impact on the price of things than any other. This was the theory of laissez-faire, often attributed to Adam Smith.[10] The basic assumption of laissez-faire theory was that man was rational. If everyone pursued his own interests, the greater good for all would ensue: buyers would buy and sellers would sell, because they shared a natural harmony of interests deriving from a complementary division of labor. In practical terms, this theory implied that government would not directly interfere in commerce: it could subsidize industries by selling land cheaply, tariffs, building roads, and other policies, but it would not fix prices or take over companies.

Modern Western states developed robust economies through the use of the unrestricted price system. By the end of the nineteenth century, however, the free market had broken down and competition was no longer free and fair to all participants. Large corporations controlled the price of their product without the restraint of real competition. This eventually led all states using the price system to regulate the economic structure through legislation. Thus some countries nationalized certain industries (e.g., railroads and banks). All established labor standards in some form or another. Large retail estab-lishments—department stores and supermarket chains—developed in response to pressure and competition from large producers and manufacturers. Today these large retailers are often more powerful than the producers who supply them. Competition among a small number of large retailers has often been effective in driving prices down, thus helping individual consumers. Also, because large stores sell so many items, they need not make so great a profit on each item they sell in order to stay in business. They benefit from what economists call "economies of scale." Obviously, this benefit, which is directly passed on to all consumers in the society through large numbers and variety of products, is made possible by the level of development of the total productive process in the economy.[11]

In contrast to the price system (now modified by many government regulations in Western states), the USSR and other socialist states have developed a system of pricing by government committee. Their economies are planned by central planning agencies, though some open pricing had been introduced in limited areas, particularly in consumer goods.

PRODUCTION AND DISTRIBUTION

In any event, the true test of the economic system is not its specific pricing mechanism, but its ability to produce and to distribute the goods it produces: thus the level of its economic development has a great and direct impact on politics.

As Aristotle realized, the greater the quantity and distribution of material goods within a society, the stronger and healthier are its people. When the people are not constantly on the verge of starvation, the country is stronger; immediate solutions do not have to be effected at the expense of long-term development strategy. The government can even make an economic mistake or two; it will not be murdering its own people by it.

Economic development means better working and living conditions. When people are working and consuming, they are less likely to be attracted by revolutionary movements. Also, in these circumstances the economy develops internally; transportation and communications media begin to link the country physically. The government can then establish a common educational program for the whole population; it can also dispense its services throughout its territory, and all its people can be informed of these activities. A famine in one area can be alleviated by a food surplus in another. All these factors help to make the political system into a functioning unit. The idea of the nation and loyalty to it can spread best when the nation's representatives, the government, can disperse its services effectively throughout the country. This enhances the government's legitimacy and its authority.

THE POLITICAL SYSTEM

We have seen that politics refers to the actions and behavior patterns taken by citizens of a political unit in attempting to arrive at joint policies and decisions. We also know that human beings normally divide themselves into groups, and that the specific configuration of groups in a state is the result of a wide variety of social and economic factors. The nature of the political process in a state is also the result of actions taken in the political system itself.

Political System Defined

There have been many definitions of the political system through the ages, just as theories of politics have changed from time to time and place to place. Today, definitions of the political system are proposed not only in the terms of traditional political theorists, but also in terms of modern theorists in the fields of political sociology, anthropology, and economics. As already noted, political units can be viewed as consisting of human groups (such as families), or as economic interrelationships, or in more general legal terms. Thus, there exists no single commonly accepted definition of the "political system," though most current definitions will overlap and many include the concept of the nation-state.

THE NATION-STATE

The nation-state, the basic unit of the contemporary political world, is also not easily defined to everyone's satisfaction. Some writers view it as primarily a cultural concept. In this view the nation-state is the political expression of a culturally united human community. In contrast, the nation-state can be viewed in entirely legal terms. One of the best formal definitions of the nation-state in international law is the statement of the Montivideo Convention, which stipulates four conditions:[12]

1. Territory. A state must have boundaries that distinguish it from other states. It must be able to specifically point out its field of jurisdiction, so that its political system is not challenged by others within it.

2. Population. The territory must contain some number of citizens. A state is a human organization; a large desert with no people on it is not a state.

3. Government. A state must be so organized that it has national leadership capable of carrying out national policy, both internally and externally. This government must be legitimate; the dissolution of the government by external or internal force also means the dissolution of the state.

4. Independent Foreign Policy. A state is independent and represents the people within it to the outside world. A unit whose foreign policy is controlled by a government other than its own is less than a state—it is a colony, or a protectorate.

PATTERNS OF HUMAN BEHAVIOR

Looked at another way, the term "political system" refers to the process of human interaction that produces political decisions, which, in turn, affect every member of the population in the territorial unit. Every person in the political unit affects and is affected by his political system. His grievances and demands, if shared by enough other members of his community, must be heard and dealt with; in turn, the actions of his government affect his opinions either in a satisfactory or unsatisfactory manner: they may induce him to either further grievances, or they may even persuade him to support the political authorities. (This general relationship of the political system to its own society is shown in Chart 1.1)

The political system can thus be broken down into (1) "inputs"—those demands and supports relating to government policymaking that come from the greater society and not from within the government itself; (2) "outputs"—those activities and policies of government that affect public support and public opinion; and (3) "conversion processes"—the actions within the government that turn inputs into outputs. This can also be described as the process of policymaking.

Chart 1.1.   The Political System

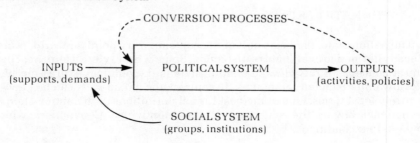

A STRUCTURAL-FUNCTIONAL DEFINITION

A subject of much recent political research has been the nature of the inputs of the political system, how they have evolved in the course of political development, and their relationship to particular political institutions and structures.[14] This has been the primary focus of the "structural-functional" school of analysis. The primary emphasis of this approach has been on the human factor in politics.

By the structural-functional method of analysis, politics is viewed as a collection of "functions." This means that for a political process to be fulfilled, certain actions (i. e., functions) must be performed. The concept also stipulates that certain kinds of activities or functions are most efficiently performed by specific kinds of institutions or structures. Indeed, one of the methods by which this approach distinguishes a politically developed from a politically under-developed state is by determining how appropriate given structures within a state are to the functions they perform.

Input Processes

Political input processes may, for example, be analyzed into separate functional activities. Human beings—through behavior patterns—produce a political culture, which affects and controls the inputs of the political system. Just as every society develops complex belief and value systems, it also develops specific patterns of thought and behavior with respect to politics. Every society develops concepts about the nature of authority and how it can legitimately be exercised. Every society also develops concepts about qualifications for leadership and about the legitimate areas of concern of the state. People everywhere have beliefs about what is right and wrong, and good and bad with respect to politics. Different political systems are thus based on very different political cultures, on different ideologies.

The development of the political culture—accomplished through the political socialization process—is basic to any society. Children are taught their political values as soon as they are able to think and understand; they are taught standards of fairness; they are taught the mark of the great leader; they are taught either to submit to authority or to participate actively in decisions. These concepts are rigorously reinforced by all institutions in a stable political system: the family, informal and formal social groups, the church, the schools, and all information media promote the same beliefs and the same values. Children are, in other words, socialized into their view of politics.

In new countries seeking to transform the nature of their politics this political socialization process may present some difficult problems. In many of these states the socialization structures do not always reinforce each other: the family and church may be very traditional, teaching submission to authority and rigid codes of behavior; in contrast, the government, the schools run by the government, and the press may be dedicated to uprooting traditional values and instituting wider political participation in the community. This kind of political system can experience great social conflict; children in school may be taught one set of values while their parents may hold contrasting beliefs. Loyalty to the state may ostensibly conflict with loyalty to church or family. Psychological problems and social turmoil could be the result of such an unbalanced socialization process.

Another feature of the input level of politics is the nature of political participation. People can participate in politics in a wide variety of ways, depending on the procedures permitted by the given political system. In a competitive political system, there may be a wide choice of approaches to political participation, which is broadly encouraged by prevailing cultural beliefs. Persons can participate individually by contacting politicians or simply by voting in elections, and they can participate indirectly by joining interest groups or political parties. They may be either very active or quite passive. In noncompetitive systems, the avenues of participation may be restricted to a single political party and its affiliated subgroups.

Every system must have some form of political participation, because it must constantly be recruiting new leaders. Political recruitment is directly influenced by the participation process: different methods of participation allow for the emergence of different kinds of political activists. Thus, a tightly organized system in which persons are inducted into specific hierarchical groups is likely to produce leaders who have a bureaucratic mentality; systems that are chaotic and permit widespread competition for political office may produce very independent leaders with strong, even charismatic personalities. Of course, much depends on the given political culture, but the process of recruitment always provides advantages to certain participants at the expense of others.

Output Processes

The conversion and output processes of the political system can also be described as "policymaking" and "policy enforcement." On the basis of information received through the input structures, the political system reaches certain decisions. Different political systems reach decisions by entirely different procedures. Thus, a highly organized bureaucratic structure may divide authority specifically and may reach decisions in a fairly bureaucratic manner; a highly competitive system may have competing elites within the political structure itself and this may result in a very chaotic, haphazard system of decisionmaking.

Policymaking, the transformation of public demands and supports into governmental action, is always a very complex process. In modern states policy is theoretically regarded as the product of the "popular will" and different procedures have been adopted in various states for achieving the appearance of popular support and representation.

Thus, even though we know that all groups are led by small groups of leaders, governmental elites in both competitive and noncompetitive systems have a wide variety of procedures by which they can reach decisions. These leaders can increase or decrease in influence, and they can change their alliances and specific reference groups. These activities occur within specific governmental institutions: the political parties, legislatures, courts, executive branches, and civil administrations. These are all supported by ideological underpinnings that state that whatever these institutions do, they "represent" the people or the public good.

The outputs or policies of a given political system result from interactions among political leaders and between segments of the political elite with groups representing interests in the general society. In some systems the function of representation is accomplished through competitive interest group activity at all levels of decisionmaking: interest groups can pressure political parties to select their candidates and support their programs; they can lobby in legislatures to present their position on specific votes; they can pressure executive agencies by presenting grievances or making public their views; and they can even appear in court to argue for clients who support their views in cases of particular interest to them. In such systems all politics can be described as interest group politics. Great Britain and the United States have well-developed interest group politics.[15]

Other systems, while still competitive, offer fewer opportunities for outright interest group conflict. Thus, some states have very strong political party structures that are able to withstand the assaults of particular kinds of special group tactics. All competitive systems, however, must be concerned with groups, because these systems seek to represent the people and all their group loyalties. All political parties that claim public support are collections of interest groups seeking to speak for the whole country. However, it is empirically true that even in competitive systems, the leaders of some political parties are more powerful and more capable of reaching decisions, despite group pressure, than many others. In noncompetitive systems leaders are extremely powerful because they can often control the interest groups.

Policymaking is always a rather formal enterprise, even though based on much informal human activity. The concepts of law, legislation, execution, and adjudication are traditional, formal, and legalistic, but they can be utilized to explain the essential features of the policymaking process. These are institutional, structural functions, now universally recognized in all nations as necessary to the activities of government.

Law. "Law" refers to the established, understood rules by which people normally live. These are rules considered necessary for human society and therefore are supported and enforced in the name of the entire community. Law in traditional times was not separated from custom, much of which was often considered to be sacred or eternal. Under such circumstances law was not often questioned; it was more commonly interpreted from traditions or sacred texts handed down through the ages by priestly figures—judges, kings, councils of elders, and the like. As the Western European nation-state began to develop, populations grew, commerce and manufacturing appeared in the form of great enterprises, and human interactions became numerous and complex. Traditional law governing human behavior had to be expanded to fit the new circumstances and to resolve new kinds of disputes. New codes of law were invented and enforced by political authorities and it gradually became evident that law could be man made, and not merely handed down from heaven or interpreted by sacred persons.

In the seventeenth and eighteenth centuries various philosophers of a
populistic bent (e. g., Jean-Jacques Rousseau[16] and John Locke[17]) came to the
conclusion that law, whether or not it existed in a "state of nature," was the
product of all human society. They concluded that for law to be legitmate it
had to represent the "popular will" and not the will of just the political leadership. Drawing on these assumptions, several states established institutions—legislatures—that were intended to represent the will of the people
through the process of election and, in so doing, could legitimately "make law"
or legislate. Executive branches and administrations were thereafter conceived
of as being "responsible" to the people via the legislature or the electoral
process: they could enforce the law, but usually only according to guidelines
established by the legislatures. Judiciaries were also conceived of as being
responsible to the people as well as to the law; they were to be appointed by
political authorities and their terms of office regulated by legislative bodies.

Such a legal system is quite formal and can easily be depicted in diagram-
matic form (see Chart 1.2). However, it is well known that law and the legal
system are not really as neatly compartmentalized as the traditional cate-
gorization would have us believe. To understand this, we must ask the practical
questions: Who makes the rules by which modern societies operatefl Who
enforces them? How are they enforced? How are they changed and challenged?

Legislation and enforcement. We know that legislatures in noncompetitive as well as in competitive systems make the law. They write the formal
documents that are given the legal seals of approval. But these documents are
not the laws that are enforced; they are merely verbal guidelines—statements of
intention. For example, no tax law in any country can be written in all its
particulars by a legislative body. The legislature can say who is to be taxed and
by what rate, but the practical qualifications, computations, exceptions, and
amendments required in any individual tax form have to be judged by
specialists. Thus any tax law normally implies the establishment of some kind of
tax administration—persons who will draw up forms and collect the revenue
according to the guidelines set up in the law. These specialists also must review
grievances and see the citizens properly adhere to the law; in so doing the
specialists interpret the law and give it specific meaning with respect to
individual cases. If we ask who makes the law—the legislature or the tax
administration—the answer in formal tax terms is the legislature wrote it, but in
terms of the individual taxpayer, the tax administration is more important.
Similarly, if a municipality passes a law stating it is illegal to park cars during
certain hours in certain locations, but the police enforce this law in only half the
stipulated locations, then the individual policemen have changed the content of
the law.

In practical terms, policy refers only to those sections of the legal formulae
that are given life by particular enforcement agencies. Most of the day-to-day
law in every state is not touched upon by the top political leadership at all; it is
enforced and interpreted by lower-level officials like police, firemen, and tax
collectors at the local level. Top political leaders are concerned mostly with new
policy initiatives and setting down new guidelines; if the guidelines are given
meaning by enforcement agencies, political leaders can forget about them. If the

Chart 1.2   The Policymaking Process: Formal Theory in Representative Government

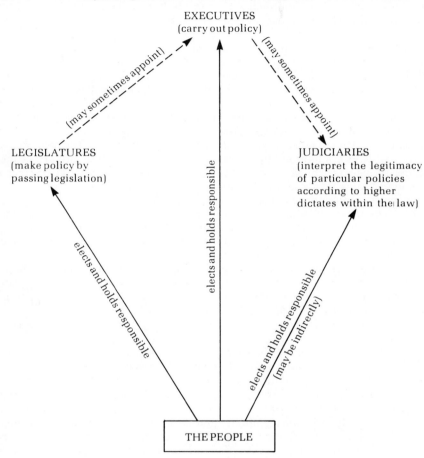

EXECUTIVES
(carry out policy)

(may sometimes appoint)

(may sometimes appoint)

LEGISLATURES
(make policy by
passing legislation)

JUDICIARIES
(interpret the legitimacy
of particular policies
according to higher
dictates within the law)

elects and holds responsible

elects and holds responsible

elects and holds responsible

(may be indirectly)

THE PEOPLE

enforcement of a law does not achieve its political objectives or excites public
criticism then the law itself will be subject to amendment by the legislative body
that originally passed it. The final enforcement of the law, not its verbal
statement, is its real test.

Specialists and bureaucrats are the enforcing agents in every political
system. In any system most legal disputes never involve courts or the open
political processes. If persons do not like a law they usually will circumvent it or
refuse to obey it. When this occurs in a well-established legal system, it is often
the law that is at fault and not the citizen. No political system imprisons persons
for refusing to obey obviously ridiculous laws, and all legal systems have such
laws on the books, either because laws become antiquated or because they were
poorly conceived by the legislature in the first place. To enforce such laws

would brand the political leadership as ridiculous itself. Rather, enforcement officials determine the legitimacy of most challenges to established law and reject or condone them on a regular day-to-day basis.

Adjudication. If enforcement agencies do most of the practical interpretation of the law, what is the function of the courts? Traditional and ancient political structures, courts are conceived of as necessary to the resolution of certain kinds of legal disputes. Most legal disputes however do not come before courts: they are settled informally, or before civil servants in other branches of government. The judicial system, like the legislative system, handles cases and controversies that are deemed important to the entire community. Crimes are legally considered to be acts against the people, and traditional crimes, such as murder, always are handled by court systems. Many so-called modern crimes, like tax offenses, are however adjudicated by executive agencies. This is true in all modern states, no matter how competitive the political system.

A court opinion like a legislative dictum speaks for the community. In some states, particularly those within the common law tradition, the statement of the highest appeals court can have the same effect as a legislative dictum. The court opinion, however, is also only a guideline and statement of intention; a court opinion must be enforced to have the effect of law.

Thus, although all traditional agencies of government perform the function of interpreting the law, the enforcement agencies give the laws their final meaning in terms of day-to-day practice. However, human society does not really depend on formal agencies for the rules by which persons behave. Most people in most systems never break the law, and they do not behave this way out of fear of violence.

People live in communities because they were trained to respect their fellows from earliest childhood and because they want to live this way. The rules of human society—politeness, civility, honesty, and the like—must be widespread or no formal legal agency could hold society together. If every person were a potential murderer there could be no community, no society, and no state. Even in the most violent, anarchic human communities crime is considered abnormal and dangerous, and it is the pressure of human cultural values and the socialization process that minimizes antisocial behavior, not the acts of formal political bodies. Thus policymaking—the output of the political system—is the product of both formal decisionmaking and informal social pressure.

Competition and Pluralism in Political Systems

We have presented a general description of the features of the political system, noting that all political systems have certain elements in common: they have social inputs because they are a part of human society; they all make policy; and they all have procedures for converting social pressures into public policy and for enforcing political decisions.

These generalizations do not, however, help us to distinguish among existing political systems. Human societies are different from one another, and so are their corresponding political structures and systems of political decision-making. The overriding factor in explaining the basic differences among systems was recognized by Plato and Aristotle: different socioeconomic relationships lead to different class structures and group arrangements. The social configuration that must be represented in a political system may have very strong tendencies toward one political direction or another.

TYPES OF POLITICAL SYSTEMS

We have noted that some political systems permit the free interplay of special groups. These we shall call "competitive" systems. In other systems, society may be divided into so many different competing and mutually hostile groups no system of competition can effectively be maintained and no authority can achieve power for very long. We shall call these "fragmented" systems. In a third type of system groups are strictly controlled and political decisionmaking occurs within a relatively small elite. These we shall call "noncompetitive" systems.

Competitive Systems

Politically competitive states in which competition is a regulated process and is understood by all participants are relatively rare. Most exist in Western Europe and North America, though some such states can be found elsewhere. In these states different political points of view are respected and even considered desirable; but only within the well-understood consensus on the rules that makes political competition possible.

In a competitive state contenders for office must have great respect for the system of leadership selection and particularly the process of popular election. A candidate or party that loses an election must feel secure from possible violence; opposition must be considered as normal and even in some sense beneficial to the system. Thus, in competitive states the function of the opposition in criticizing the government of the day is regarded as extremely important. Such an opposition must feel that it is representative of an important part of the community, and that so long as it continues to speak its views there will be a possibility for victory in the future. Oppositions are willing to wait for the next election; they will sometimes support the government on special issues. They do not see their opponents as the personifications of evil, but rather as contenders in a game or contest that has many matches; the overriding interests of all parties is to keep the game going, no matter who may be on top at the given moment.

Thus, both oppositions and governing parties in competitive systems may disagree on almost all issues, but not on procedures and understandings that make the competitive system possible. When a party wins an election it does not use its military power to put all of its critics in prison, and it does not suspend the rights of a free press and open discussion of public grievances. It does, however, reach policy decisions that it considers necessary to the strength and survival of the state. Competitive states have powerful governments that are often very efficient in decisionmaking. The fact that opposition groups in these systems support the operation of an effective government is partially responsible for this; they may criticize certain decisions, but they do not interfere in their enforcement. Loss in an election does not automatically force the losing party into revolutionary activity or rigid oppositionism.

Competitive systems rest on a precarious balance of mutual under-standings—between change and consensus—that is extremely difficult to achieve and to stabilize.[18] Systems have frequently been established with a hope of realizing stable competition, but many have not been able to sustain this over a long period of time.

Fragmented Systems

Sometimes states are unable to establish stable competition because they suffer an extreme form of social pluralism. Such states may develop fragmented political systems that attempt to represent the conflicting wills of constituent groups and are consequently unable to be effective in national policymaking. Too many groups with political aims are unwilling to compromise their special desires for the sake of a national policy; thus they stand in the way of any measure simply because they disagree with it. Such systems lack mechanisms for moderating and compromising conflicting claims. They may be legally either authoritarian or competitive, but neither formal system is capable of effective policymaking. Rather the constituent groups block each other at every stage, and weak uncertain government is the result. Such systems have existed in many countries around the world, at least for brief periods.

Noncompetitive Systems

A third type of political system—the noncompetitive system—appears when one group or collection of groups establishes itself as an ideological superior to all its opponents, at least by some standard of measurement. Sometimes such a system can arise out of fragmentation, but it must always depend on some small elite attaining preponderant power over all its com-petitors. This preponderance can derive from ideological movements or mili-tary establishments, or a combination of the two. In these circumstances, social pluralism is actually overcome by force of arms, and over time the authoritarian system becomes accepted as legitimate. This has occurred in some new states in Asia and Africa.

In other kinds of circumstances a noncompetitive state may be the result of an original lack of social differentiation and pluralism. A social structure may be innately elitist: persons may normally be trained and socialized to think of the state as a sacred or bureaucratic institution that should be governed by groups or individuals who are considered better qualified than others. Open competition in such circumstances may be seen as immoral—as an interference with the proper way in which a state may be governed.

Thus noncompetitive states that are governed by ideologically "qualified" elites often openly rule out even the possibility of criticism by outside groups. Indeed, the very formation of such groups is made impossible by the use of force and the legal system, and no criticism is permitted in the communications media or elsewhere. Such systems still claim to be operating in the public interest, and even to be representative of "The People," but politics is considered the exclusive activity of a small group who are considered better or more knowledgeable than the mass of the people. Political recruitment is rigidly controlled by this group and political decisionmaking becomes entirely private within the elite. Such a system may be very effective in making national policy, so long as it is able to learn of the social pressures that permeate its community.

Types of Political Systems and Social Consensus

Thus, the three types of political systems—competitive, fragmented, and noncompetitive—are all products of specific social and behavioral factors and reflect the group arrangement within the given societies. The fragmented system, because it is weak, often does not have a long life span: it either becomes competitive or noncompetitive, but in any event it is transformed because it seeks an effective process of decisionmaking. Effective decisionmaking must be based on a strong social consensus, which is very difficult to achieve in any truly fragmented society. Fragmented systems therefore can only achieve a kind of stable instability: they lack consensus on any forceful form of government and dislike weak forms as well. The overthrow of the immobile system in such a state therefore may result in short-lived dictatorships, for noncompetitive states also require social consensus to be effective.

All contemporary political systems have many common features. All have class structures and therefore some recognized leadership groups; all have group structures with some tendency toward fragmentation at least on certain issues. All, also, are based on some degree of common culture and therefore refuse to allow overt political competition at least in some areas or on some issues. Thus each of the three types of system can have, in some degree, the features of the other two. Also, the relative balance of forces within a community can change over time, and systems of one type can begin to resemble another. The key to understanding any political system and its possible direction of development, however, lies in understanding the forces at work in its underlying social structure.

In the modern world the social and political stability of many different political systems are being threatened by rapid and unbalanced social change and social mobility. In these systems the disaffection of groups who feel shortchanged or left-out by the policies of the established governing groups, can challenge the legitimacy of long-established institutions. Thus, legislatures and executives in widely divergent countries can find themselves under attack by disaffected youth who are unable to find employment, by rural workers who do not share in the rising standard of living of better organized urban laborers, by groups of foreign workers and ethnic groups who feel discriminated against, and by the generally poor, unskilled, and uneducated as they become politicized. Over time this kind of social disaffection can grow to such proportions that it can undermine the legitimacy and effectiveness of the ruling parties and institutions. This can cause the acceleration of fragmentation even in states that generally have been regarded as competitive or noncompetitive, and the eventual transformation of one type of political system into another. Such transformation can happen because social and political systems are not static: they have elements of competition, fragmentation, and authoritarianism within their basic social structures.

NOTES TO CHAPTER 1

1. Seymour M. Lipset, *Political Man* (Garden City: Doubleday, 1960).

2. Max Weber, "Politics as a Vocation," in H. Gerth and C. W. Mills, eds., *From Max Weber* (New York: Oxford University Press, 1946).

3. Gaetano Mosca, *The Ruling Class*, trans. H. D. Kahn (New York: McGraw-Hill, 1939).

4. Roberto Michels, *Political Parties*, trans. E. and C. Paul (New York: Collier Books, 1962).

5. Robert A. Dahl, *Preface to Democratic Theory* (Chicago: University of Chicago Press, 1956).

6. Plato, *The Republic*, trans. B. Jowett (New York: Random House, 1952).

7. Aristotle, *Politics*, trans. B. Jowett (New York: Viking Press, 1952).

8. Karl Marx, "Capital," in *Capital and Other Writings* (New York: Modern Library, 1932).

9. Karl Marx and Friedrich Engels, "The Communist Manifesto," in ibid.

10. Adam Smith, *The Wealth of Nations*, 1776.

11. John Kenneth Galbraith, *American Capitalism: The Theory of Countervailing Power* (Boston: Houghton Mifflin, 1956).

12. International law definition from the Montivideo Convention of 1933 on the Rights and Duties of States.

13. David Easton, *The Political System* (New York: Knopf, 1953).

14. In particular, see the work of Gabriel Almond, in Gabriel Almond and James Coleman, eds., *The Politics of the Developing Areas* (Princeton: Princeton University Press, 1960) and Gabriel Almond and G. Bingham Powell, *Comparative Politics* (Boston: Little, Brown, 1966).

15. Samuel H. Beer, *British Politics in the Collectivist Age* (New York: Knopf, 1965); Arthur F. Bentley, *The Process of Government* (Chicago: University of Chicago Press, 1908); David Truman, *The Governmental Process* (New York: Knopf, 1953).

16. Jean-Jacques Rousseau, *The Social Contract* (Chicago: Henry Regnery, 1954).

17. John Locke, "Second Treatise on Civil Government," quoted in F. W. Coker, ed., *Readings in Political Philosophy* (New York: Macmillan Co., 1942).

18. Lipset, *Political Man*, *op. cit.*

Chapter 2

Structural and Institutional Differences Among Political Systems

POLITICAL STRUCTURES AND INSTITUTIONS: A FRAMEWORK FOR COMPARISON

Political structures and institutions exist in all political systems. Almost all states have executives, legislatures, courts, military forces, and administrative bureaucracies. All states establish some legal leadership group, which is followed by a mass of citizens.

However, different kinds of states utilize their political structures in very different ways. In some states the executive, legislature, bureaucracy, and courts essentially share power in a well-established manner. In other states either only the executive or some other institution will be powerful and all other structures will be essentially symbolic. In other states no institution is powerful, each being able to make decisions only in a limited way for very brief periods of time. Each such system reflects the different historical and cultural patterns from which it is derived.

POLITICAL STRUCTURES AND INSTITUTIONS IN COMPETITIVE STATES

Patterns of Similarity

Political competition is a product of very special circumstances. In general, a competitive state must be conducted by political actors who have a great deal of respect for one another, feel secure, and are aware of the need for mutual trust in the conduct of their own politics. This mutual trust must be institutionalized and upheld by the legal and political processes. Many different states have been able to achieve such an institutionalization.

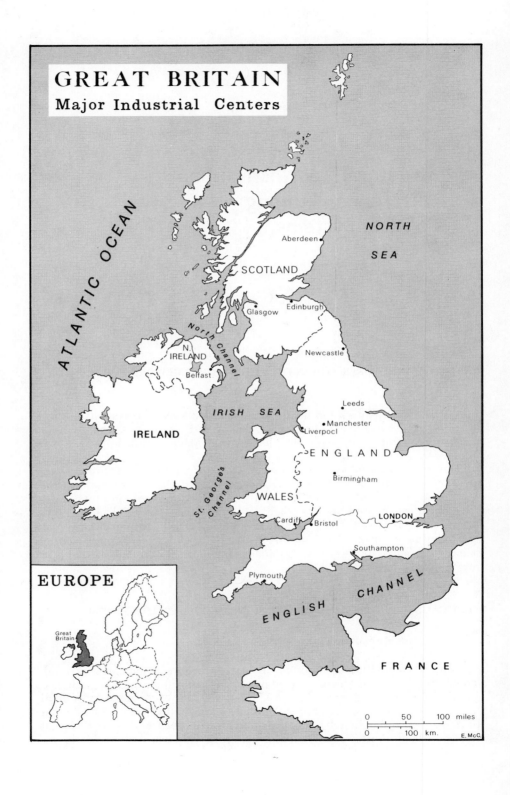

GREAT BRITAIN
Major Industrial Centers

NORTH SEA

ATLANTIC OCEAN

Aberdeen

SCOTLAND

Glasgow Edinburgh

North Channel

N. IRELAND

Belfast

Newcastle

IRISH SEA

Leeds

Manchester

Liverpool

ENGLAND

IRELAND

St. George's Channel

Birmingham

WALES

Cardiff Bristol

LONDON

Southampton

Plymouth

ENGLISH CHANNEL

EUROPE

Great Britain

FRANCE

0   50   100 miles
0   100 km.

E. McC.

Three examples of competitive states are Great Britain, India, and Chile. These states diverge in cultural background, in levels of economic development, and in size and geography. They contain different kinds of social groups and social pressures, but all have developed a political system that allows competing groups an open entry into the political structure. All moderate group conflict through similar institutional structures—interest groups, political parties, legislatures, cabinets, and judiciaries. All (with the very recent and possibly temporary exception of Chile) attempt to legitimize conflict and competition through the use of an open general electoral system. The winner of an election is the momentary leader in the competitive struggle; he is conceived of as holding the mandate of the entire nation, but only temporarily—only so long as he continues to win in elections. Political opposition is held to be legal, legitimate, and even necessary, for without such opposition in elections there can be no real test of the competence of the government.

These general similarities among the three states cloak some important differences in structure and degree—some competitive states are more competitive than others. In some systems, there are many openly competitive groups and very broad open participation in the political process. In other systems, the level of competition is restricted to relatively few persons and organizations. Such variations are a product of the different cultural, social, economic, and political factors at work in each state.

Three Case Studies: Great Britain, India, and Chile

GREAT BRITAIN

Great Britain, one of the more powerful and affluent states of Western Europe, has a highly educated and well-trained population. Historically a militarily important state, this country has, since World War II, declined in importance in world affairs vis-a-vis the United States and the Soviet Union.

Great Britain has had a unique process of political development in comparison to neighboring states on the European Continent. Geographically spread over two islands off the Continent, the country has been physically as well as psychologically separated from Europe. Great Britain has not, for example, successfully been invaded or occupied by a foreign power since 1066. The country has enjoyed tremendous military security for all of its history until the twentieth century and consequently never has developed the large prestigious standing military establishment so characteristic of other European nations, which in the past have usually been engaged in some kind of land combat.

In modern times a trading nation with strong naval commitments, Great Britain has always looked overseas for her closest economic and political ties, shying away from European relationships. In recent years because of special economic problems the British have begun to look toward Europe—a very new and controversial policy.

Because Great Britain is a country with natural boundaries, the British people developed the sense of nationhood much earlier than people in other states. A strong central government has ruled the country uninterruptedly for close to three hundred years and British political institutions have evolved gradually over a very long period of time. For example, today's British legislature, the Parliament, has evolved from a medieval institution that existed as early as the twelfth century.

Territory and Population

Legally, Great Britain includes England, Wales, Scotland, Northern Ireland, and several small outlying islands (see map, p.32). In land area Great Britain is about the size of the American state of Oregon, though with its population density of 222.5 persons per square kilometer or 573 persons per square mile (Oregon has 18.4 persons per square mile), it is ten times as densely populated as the United States, and except for the Netherlands, is the most densely populated nation in Europe. Culturally, the country is dominated by the English, who comprise about four-fifths of the total population. The breakdown of population and land area in Great Britain appears in Table 2.1.

By world standards Great Britain is an extremely homogeneous country, with few severe ethnic, religious, and language differences. Although the Protestant-Catholic controversy in Northern Ireland has become one of the most difficult religious confrontations to be found in Western Europe, with this one exception, the country appears to be extremely cohesive, though there also exist small nationalist groups in Wales and Scotland. The population is almost entirely literate, reads the same national newspapers, and is tightly drawn together by a modern communications structure centered in London. London is the preeminent center of all activity in Great Britain—social, economic, and political—and its 8 million persons comprise 20 percent of the country's total population.

Table 2.1.   Population of Great Britain

Area	Population (in millions)	Land Area (in thousand square kilometers)	Density of Population per square kilometer
England	43.5	130.3	333.8
Wales	2.6	20.8	125.0
Scotland	5.2	78.8	66.0
Northern Ireland	3.0	14.1	212.8
Outlying Islands*	0.15	.8	125.0
Total	54.5	244.9	222.5

SOURCES: *Britain, 1970* (London: HMSO, 1971); Census, *1971 Preliminary Report* (London: HMSO, 1971).

*Isle of Man and Channel Islands.

Political Structure

The British political system can be described as a parliamentary-cabinet system—a particular structural style of government that evolved gradually out of British medieval institutions. There is no single written document establishing the rights and powers of institutions in Great Britain; rather, this has become established through long-standing practice and usage.

The executive. Legally Great Britain is a monarchy. The current chief of state is Queen Elizabeth II, who inherited this position upon the death of her father, King George VI. The powers of the monarchy are severely limited in current political affairs, though informally the queen can still make her presence felt on particular kinds of issues.

The monarchy in Britain is conceived of as being above politics. The queen does not publicly state political preferences either with respect to policy or to party. She is consulted by the government on a regular basis since she must perform certain ceremonial functions. On these occasions she can make her preferences known to elected politicians, possibly with some informal effect.

The queen is the British head of state. As such she is the major representative of the nation with respect to foreign nations and both visits and receives foreign dignitaries. She presents the government's political program to Parliament in her speech from the throne and approves all bills before they can become law. She also approves all political appointments. As commander in chief of the armed forces, the queen legally declares war and makes treaties.

There are few occasions when the queen is permitted to exercise any personal discretion in public. All her major political acts are conducted on the advice and with the approval of the elected government of the day. She is able to bestow honors and titles, many on the advice of the government, but she also has some categories of title that she can bestow without the consent of Parliament. This she does rarely, and almost never with a political purpose.

An exception to this occurred in the early stages of the Rhodesian crisis of 1965. The colony of Rhodesia had been internally self-governing, though it was legally conceived of as being under the authority of Great Britain, personified by an appointed governor-general sent to Rhodesia by the British colonial office. In 1965 the internally elected government of Rhodesia was negotiating with the British government for complete independence. The British would not consent to the establishment of a constitution that would allow a white supremacist government. The Rhodesians broke off negotiations, declaring their independence of the British government; at the same time they expressed their personal loyalty to the Crown.

When independence was declared the British governor-general in Rhodesia, Sir Humphrey Gibbs, suspended the Rhodesian government on orders from London. In response, the Rhodesian government, over Gibbs's defiance, ordered him divested of his powers. The latter action took effect and for all practical purposes Rhodesia was truly independent.

In these circumstances the institution of the monarchy was openly being questioned. The Rhodesians were professing loyalty to the queen, but not to her prime minister and government. The queen thereupon decided to bestow a personal honor on her governor-general, appointing Gibbs knight commander of the Royal Victorian Order. In so doing she demonstrated support for her elected government and disapproval of the newly independent Rhodesian government. The queen thus took a personal action for political effect—a very rare occasion indeed.

The prime minister and cabinet.   Structurally and politically the British executive is vested not in the queen, but in the elected government headed by a prime minister and his cabinet. There is only one kind of election in Britain—that for local representatives to the House of Commons. The country is divided into 630 constituencies, each of which elects one member of parliament (M P). The leader of the party with a majority of seats in the House of Commons normally becomes prime minister and then names his cabinet, which is then submitted to Parliament for its almost certain approval. These elections are always accepted by the Crown.

In Great Britain, government policy is determined and executed by an administrative bureaucracy headed by the cabinet, which consists of the prime minister, a few ministers without portfolio, and the ministers who head the various departments in the administration, e. g., Foreign Affairs, Home Office, and Health among others. The ministers direct the departments and advise the whole cabinet of the affairs of their respective departments. They also speak for the government in Parliament. The cabinet sets the whole legislative program, which is debated in Parliament but not amended to any significant extent. Thus the cabinet, led by the prime minister, is supreme both in legislative decision-making and in the administration of policy.

The British cabinet consists of a variable number of persons (between fifteen and twenty-five), who are selected because of their positions as leaders of the majority party in Parliament. All are both politicians and administrators; they lead their party in Parliament and, at the same time, make the administrative decisions upon which Parliament must vote.

Cabinet deliberations are not formally and rigidly controlled, and the style of cabinet work varies as much with the personality of the prime minister as with the party in power. For example, Conservative party cabinets are notably more cohesive than Labour party cabinets, with many fewer open arguments and splits. A Conservative prime minister such as Winston Churchill or Edward Heath can usually be expected to be in much more secure command of his party supporters than is a Labour prime minister. Indeed, when Harold Wilson was the Labour prime minister (from 1963 to 1970) he was under fire almost as much from his own party's extreme elements as from the opposition.

Nevertheless, the cabinet, because it is the leading group of the Parliament, remains the major deliberative body in Great Britain, and the prime minister, no matter who he is, is the presiding chairman over cabinet meetings. It is his role to seek a consensus on policy so a uniform program can be presented to Parliament; he thus attempts to unify his party behind his own leadership.

In the past when the Conservative party was significantly more dominant in British elections, the prime minister was viewed as an extremely powerful figure who dominated cabinet meetings. Since World War II, however, many changes in cabinet proceedings have occurred and the prime minister is today subject to intense political pressure from both within the cabinet and the opposing party.

Cabinet meetings have always been held in secret, protected from public scrutiny, and cabinet members have always been collectively responsible for the total program to which they jointly agree. A political attack on an individual minister is thus made virtually impossible, because each cabinet member is only a part of the cabinet as a whole: the cabinet stands and falls together.

The cabinet is itself, however, organized into committees that specialize in areas of work and report to the prime minister, who decides the agenda. Votes are sometimes taken on policy matters, but more often a consensus is reached through informal discussion among ministers. Harold Wilson in his first term as prime minister raised the authority of cabinet committees over detailed departmental matters, thus permitting the cabinet as a whole to devote more time to important overall matters.

The legislature. The British legislature, the Parliament, derives from an ancient institution that was originally conceived of as an advisory court to the monarch. Over the ages power has shifted away from the monarch and the matter who he is, is the presiding chairman over cabinet meetings. It is his role to seek a consensus on policy so a uniform program can be presented to Parliament; he thus attempts to unify his party behind his own leadership.

House of Lords. The Parliament consists of two houses—the House of Lords and the House of Commons. The House of Lords legally consists of two categories of persons: (1) hereditary peers and peeresses, who have a seat by virtue of descent; and (2) life peers, who are appointed by the government. Among the life peers is a committee of Lords of Appeal in Ordinary, otherwise known as the Law Lords. This body consists of seventeen appointed law lords, and all previous lords chancellor, including the present one. The Law Lords constitute the highest appeals court in Britain. Also among the life peers are the Lords Spiritual, a body which consists of the two archbishops and twenty-four bishops of the Church of England. Altogether the House of Lords consists of over one thousand members, many of whom are appointed for high achievements in particular fields of endeavor. A seat in the House of Lords (except for one in the Law Lords) is in the same category as an honor or title, though on occasion, political considerations are taken into account in an appointment to the house. Thus, the House of Lords, though descended from a body exclusively representing a landed aristocracy, now includes the most honored members of all professions in Great Britain—doctors, actors, and businessmen among others.

The result has been a House with limited political power (legally, the House of Lords can only delay bills by one year, and it cannot delay money bills at all), but with some public prestige. The House debates all bills and sometimes, on touchy questions, its debates draw public attention. Of its membership only about 200 attend sessions on a regular basis, and these persons tend to become knowledgeable on political matters over time.

House of Commons.   The House of Commons is the major formal political body in the British government. As already noted, this house consists of 630 members, one drawn from from each of 630 constituencies that make up England, Scotland, Wales and Northern Ireland. These members run for election whenever a general election is called. The maximum life of any Parliament is five years, though a prime minister may dissolve Parliament in less than that time.

The House of Commons, as the only elected body in British government, is the body deemed responsible to the people. Technically, it produces all legislation and holds the executive accountable. The prime minister and his cabinet are, in general, part of the House of Commons. However, every British government usually has a few cabinet members appointed from the House of Lords; these individuals answer to the House of Lords, though their seconds-in-command are always from the House of Commons. In terms of appointment, only the House of Commons approves a new cabinet, but this is normally a formality since the prime minister has a party majority.

Because of the high level of party discipline in Britain, the actual political functions of the House of Commons are somewhat limited. The government (prime minister and cabinet) presents the legislative program, which is given public hearing in the form of debate in the House of Commons. For the most part the debate does little to change or defeat a bill.

Technically, a prime minister is held accountable for his actions to the Parliament. If he were to lose on an important bill, he would have to resign. In practice, however, the House of Commons is so strictly controlled by party organization a prime minister need not worry about losing important votes; most of his party will always support him against the opposition (see Chap. 5 for more on political parties).

This support also extends to the cabinet, which is collectively responsible to the Commons. In other words, one cabinet member will generally not be singled out and attacked for a given part of the national program. The program is conceived of as an integrated whole, defended by the entire cabinet; a defeat on one bill therefore would technically mean the resignation of the entire cabinet. In practice, because of strong party discipline, this never occurs in Britain.

The practical role of the House of Commons in political terms is to criticize the government and thus to hold it accountable for both its efficiency in administration and for its loyalty to its electoral mandate. Although this is the particular role of the minority opposition party, even members of the governing party participate in debate and make their views known to party leaders. The House of Commons is an intensely political body in which the aspirations of the voting public are most keenly felt and in which their views must be expressed. The house is a great public arena, in which debate creates public support and can indirectly influence administrative decisions.

Since 1964 some practices have been introduced to increase the potential influence of the House of Commons vis-a-vis the cabinet. The technical procedures for getting bills through the house have been simplified. Salaries for members of Parliament have also been increased so that more professionals can now remain in politics. Also, staff services in the form of library and research assistance have been greatly increased. New committees have been introduced

Chart 2.1. Great Britain: The Structure of the Government

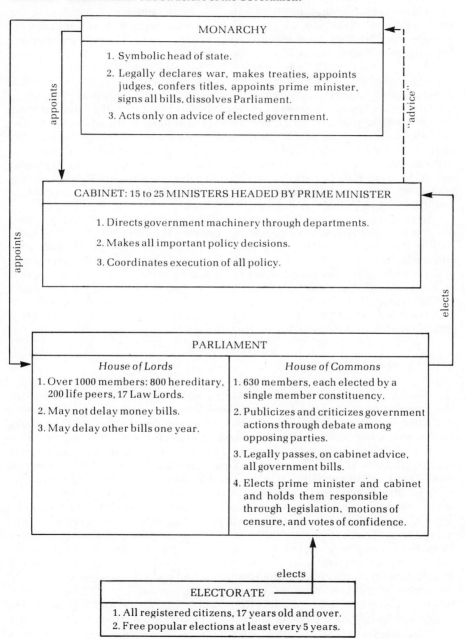

MONARCHY

1. Symbolic head of state.

2. Legally declares war, makes treaties, appoints judges, confers titles, appoints prime minister, signs all bills, dissolves Parliament.

3. Acts only on advice of elected government.

appoints

"advice"

CABINET: 15 to 25 MINISTERS HEADED BY PRIME MINISTER

1. Directs government machinery through departments.

2. Makes all important policy decisions.

3. Coordinates execution of all policy.

appoints

elects

PARLIAMENT

House of Lords

1. Over 1000 members: 800 hereditary, 200 life peers, 17 Law Lords.

2. May not delay money bills.

3. May delay other bills one year.

House of Commons

1. 630 members, each elected by a single member constituency.

2. Publicizes and criticizes government actions through debate among opposing parties.

3. Legally passes, on cabinet advice, all government bills.

4. Elects prime minister and cabinet and holds them responsible through legislation, motions of censure, and votes of confidence.

elects

ELECTORATE

1. All registered citizens, 17 years old and over.

2. Free popular elections at least every 5 years.

to deal with specialized legislative questions, and while these committees still are not powerful enough to change the essential features of legislation, the added research facilities of the house have permitted more meaningful participation by MPs in discussion and debate, as well as in investigating government activities and holding the government responsible.

The judiciary. The British judiciary is technically part of the political structure of the country, since, as already mentioned, the highest appeals court, the Law Lords, is a committee in the House of Lords appointed by the queen on the advice of the prime minister, much the same as other political appointments. While technically laws can be challenged in the courts in Great Britain, the courts have traditionally avoided cases of a political nature, ruling only on cases that fall into more settled, noncontroversial areas. In comparison to American courts, for example, the British courts do not claim the power of judicial review and do not decide whether laws are "constitutional" (a difficult concept in a country in which there is no written constitution).

In refusing to make political decisions, the courts in Great Britain support the practice of parliamentary supremacy over the law. The House of Commons is thus the only legitimate arena for discussing the law in its abstract constitutional framework. Indeed, parliamentary supremacy is a prominent feature of the British legal process and is often summed up in the traditional dictum that "if Parliament decided that henceforth all men would be women, and all women would be men, that would be the law." Presumably, even this kind of question could not be brought before a court in Great Britain. (Chart 2.1 presents a structural outline of government in Great Britain.)

INDIA

India is a very large, densely populated, and impoverished state occupying its own subcontinent on the Asian mainland. The country has an ancient history of imperial successions, violent warfare, mass movements and revolutions, as well as a rich artistic and cultural heritage. All this, however, is long past. Since the British drove the French out of the Indian subcontinent in the eighteenth century, India has generally been free from major warfare with foreign powers, though she has had some important recent skirmishes with China and Pakistan.

For about 200 years India has enjoyed a period of uninterrupted institutional development, the last 100 years of which have been characterized by a strong centralized administration under British colonial supervision. Thus many of the factors important to the development of the political structure in Great Britain can be noted in India as well. The current Indian political system, like the British, evolved over a very long period of time, though in connection with a colonial power. The system was not forced upon the country by virtue of revolution or military invasion. It developed piecemeal, at first by administrative decisions made by colonial officials, later in political and administrative bodies in which Indians participated and eventually dominated.

Topographical features—the high mountains in the North and the ocean in

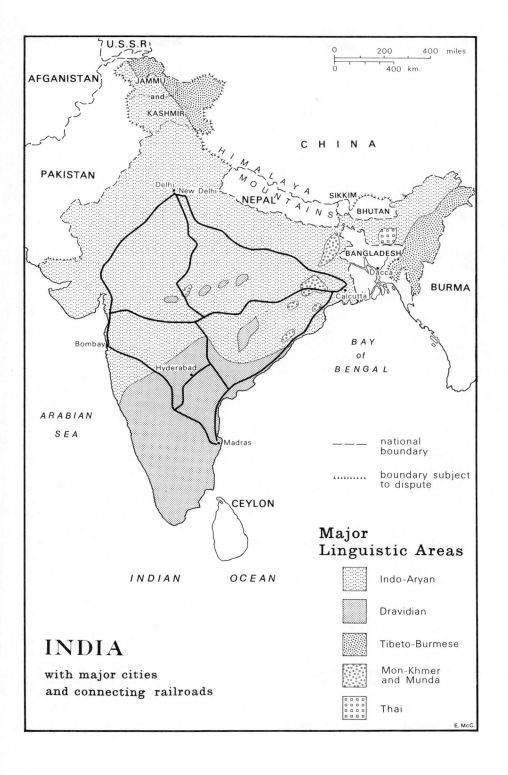

0   200   400 miles
0   400 km.

U.S.S.R.

AFGANISTAN

JAMMU
and
KASHMIR

PAKISTAN

CHINA

Delhi · New Delhi

HIMALAYA MOUNTAINS

NEPAL

SIKKIM

BHUTAN

BANGLADESH

Dacca

Calcutta

BURMA

Bombay

Hyderabad

BAY
of
BENGAL

ARABIAN

SEA

Madras

——— national
boundary

··········· boundary subject
to dispute

CEYLON

INDIAN   OCEAN

**Major
Linguistic Areas**

Indo-Aryan

Dravidian

Tibeto-Burmese

Mon-Khmer
and Munda

Thai

INDIA

with major cities
and connecting railroads

E. McC.

the South—have made India an extremely difficult country to invade (see map, p. 41). Thus, like Great Britain, India has not, for most of her political development, had a need for a standing military. While certain ethnic groups within the country have always regarded themselves as military specialists, Indian military protection has historically been provided by a small professional corps under British leadership. This group, not very visible to the public, was kept out of politics for the entire period of British colonial rule. The practice seems to have continued under India's independent government. It is certainly true that the political importance of the military in India is less than in most other Asian countries.

India has a well-defined sense of political nationality. The nationalist movement dates back into the nineteenth century, and Indians have participated in large numbers in their national political system since the early twentieth century.

Territory and Population

In contrast to Great Britain, India is a nation of continental extent and widely divergent populations (see map, p.41). the country is quite densely populated by many different ethnic and linguistic groups which, as integral participants in the Indian political system, have been legally recognized in the federal structure of the government.

The country is divided into twenty-one states—relatively large units, which retain some political powers under the federal constitution. There also are nine Union Territories, which are administered directly by the federal government in Delhi. Table 2.2 presents the breakdown of population and land area of these units.

While the total land area of India is approximately one-third that of the United States, the population is more than twice the American population. Parts of India are among the most densely populated in the world, and in these areas poverty and malnutrition are most evident. For example, the state of Uttar Pradesh, with over 88 million people, has a greater population than any of the nations of Africa, Latin America, or Western Europe. In territory, it is about the same size as the American state of Arizona (which has only 1.3 million people), and about one-half the size of France and close to the same size as Italy (both these countries have a population of about 50 million, and Italy is considered densely populated by European standards).

The most notable fact about the population of India is its low standard of living. India lacks vigorous economic development and masses of Indians are unemployed, held by custom in the living patterns of traditional villages, weak, ill-fed, and unhealthy. Only 30 percent of the population is literate. These problems have been compounded by a very great increase in the size of population, which grew by 21.6 percent between 1951 and 1961—an increase of over 78 million persons in ten years.

In addition to the problem of poverty, India must deal with problems arising out of a very complex population makeup. The Indian Constitution established the states of India on the basis of the languages spoken in different areas of the

Table 2.2. Population of India

States	Population (in millions)	Land Area (in thousand square kilometers)	Density of Population (per square kilometer)
Andhra Pradesh	43.5	276.8	157
Assam	14.6	78.5	186
Bihar	56.4	173.9	324
Gujerat	26.7	196.0	136
Haryana	10.0	44.2	227
Himachal Pradesh	3.5	55.7	62
Jammu and Kashmir*	4.6	222.2	--
Karnataka	29.3	191.8	153
Kerala	21.3	38.9	549
Madhya Pradesh	41.7	442.8	94
Maharashtra	50.4	307.8	164
Manipur	1.1	22.4	48
Meghalaya	1.0	22.5	45
Nagaland	0.5	16.5	31
Orissa	21.9	155.8	141
Punjab	13.6	50.3	269
Rajasthan	25.8	342.2	75
Tamil Nadu'	41.2	130.1	317
Tripura	1.6	10.5	149
Uttar Pradesh	88.3	294.4	300
West Bengal	44.3	87.9	504
Union Territories			
Andaman and Nicobar Islands	0.1	8.3	14
Arunachal Pradesh	0.5	83.6	6
Chandigarh	0.3	0.1	2,257
Dadra & Nagar Haveli	0.1	0.5	151
Delhi	4.1	1.5	2,738
Goa, Daman & Diu	0.9	3.8	225
Lakshadweep	0.03	0.03	994
Mizoram	0.3	21.1	16
Pondicherry	0.5	0.5	983
Total	548.1	3,2380.5	178**

SOURCE: *India, 1974*, (New Delhi: Publications Division, Ministry of Information and Broadcasting, Government of India, 1974).

* Includes land area claimed by India but now occupied by China and Pakistan.

**Density excluding Jammu and Kashmir.

country. Many of these languages, which for the most part are mutually unintelligible, have well-established, classic written literatures. The official language of the country is Hindi (spoken by about 30 percent of the population), but English has been the working language of the government since independence. The Official Languages Amendment Act of 1967 allows for the continuation of both Hindi and English for official purposes. Government officials are permitted to choose their language of business until they attain a working knowledge of Hindi. Overall there are fifteen recognized, official languages that are used in the several states as the mother tongue. According to the 1961 census, however, there were over 1,600 languages in use, including over 100 non-Indian languages.

Language in India is an issue of grave political importance. The adoption of one language over another implies the dominance of one culture over another; it is an issue that is difficult to resolve and is avoided or compromised wherever possible. For the purposes of political unity, however, some languages have had to be downgraded to the advantage of others—a cause for riot and bloodshed on occasion.

India is religiously a fairly cohesive country. Over 80 percent of the population is Hindu, with small minorities of Sikhs, Buddhists, Jains, Moslems, and Christians. Except for the enduring Hindu-Moslem conflict now mostly directed externally toward Pakistan, the major internal religious difficulties arise from the impact of modernization on the traditional Hindu caste system. This is basically not a religious problem, but one produced by efforts at economic development and consequent social change.

Political Structure

The establishment of India as an independent state in 1947, after much haggling and negotiation over the nature of its future government, occurred in the face of threatened civil war between Moslems and Hindus, which culminated in the dismemberment of British India into two states—India and Pakistan. Partition meant that millions of Moslems who had always lived in India moved to Pakistan, and millions of Hindus from Pakistan moved to India. Intermittent warfare between Moslems and Sikhs resulted in the deaths of one-half million people. Ten million people lost their homes as a result of riots and warfare brought on by partition. The status of certain territories, especially Jammu-Kashmir, is still a cause for continuing distress between the two new states.

The constitution.   In these circumstances, the Indians drafted a highly legalistic constitution that was designed to placate and moderate the conflicts that were expected to arise among different population groups. The structure of the government was intentionally modeled on that of the British government, but some American variations were added. The structure of the Indian government is represented in Chart 2.2, p. 49.

The Indian constitution, unlike the American, is a very long and inclusive document, indeed, the longest constitution in the world, with 395 articles and 8 schedules. It establishes a republican form of government (India decided to stay within the British Commonwealth, but refused to accept the nominal sovereignty of the British Crown), and presents an extremely detailed Bill of Rights. This Bill of Rights includes economic as well as political rights (e. g., the right to earn a living), but the constitution also provides that the national government can suspend the Bill of Rights in times of national emergency. An interesting feature of the Indian constitution is a section entitled "Directive Principles of State Policy," which states the principles and policy goals of the constitution makers. These are republican, egalitarian, and quite socialistic—reflecting the philosophical tendencies of Indian political leaders in the 1940s.

The Indian constitution establishes an extremely complicated federal system, quite in contrast to that of Great Britain, which is a unitary state. In a federal system, states theoretically retain powers upon which the central government cannot infringe. The Indian constitution, however, assigns the most important powers to the central government. Powers are enumerated on lists, and the seventy-seven items on the Union (federal) List include such matters as defense, foreign affairs, and currency. The sixty-six items on the State List include items such as public health, order, and education. There is also a concurrent list of items over which the federal government is supreme, if a conflict should arise with a state. On paper this separation of powers appears similar to that of the American system, but in practice the Indian federal government is relatively more powerful than its American counterpart. The Indian federal government has suspended state governments under the national emergency provision; it has also found it easy, especially in periods when it has had a large majority in Parliament, to amend the constitution. In times of extreme conflict, however, the emergency procedure has been used rather than the amending procedure.

The executive. In India, executive power is vested, on the British model, in a president (comparable in position to the British monarch) and a Council of Ministers (comparable to the British cabinet). The president, who is considered the symbolic head of state, is elected by an electoral college consisting of the elected members of both houses of Parliament and the elected members of the legislative assemblies of the states. He is elected for a five-year term and may be reelected.

The president is supposed to be only a nominal head, acting on the advice of his prime minister and cabinet. Symbolically, like the queen, he has an impressive list of powers, and his signature legitimates all actions of the Indian government. He is not, however, as divorced from politics as the queen, for he is appointed by politicians and is recruited from their ranks.

Today, there is much controversy in India over the precise legal and political status of the Indian presidency. Some constitutional lawyers argue that the constitution clearly provides for presidential authority and for his impeachment if he exceeds his authority. This, they argue, implies that the president should actively protect and preserve the constitution. In legal terms, in fact, the president is not obligated to take the advice of the Council of Ministers, and presidents of India have actively exercised influence with Parliament on the passage of particular bills. During most of India's independent history, presidents have remained symbolic figures not actively challenging the cabinet. Indeed, presidents have been very close to India's political leaders, all of whom have emerged from the dominant Congress party. Presidents have thus been close allies to the cabinet, not competing centers of power.

An example of the type of conflict that could arise in India with respect to the presidency occurred after the death of President Zakir Hussain in 1969. During that year Prime Minister Indira Gandhi confronted a group of conservative Congress party bosses, collectively known as the "Syndicate," with a broad program of bank nationalization. The Syndicate opposed this program and sought to embarrass Mrs. Gandhi by outmaneuvering her in the Congress party nomination for the presidency. They succeeded at the Congress party convention and the official Congress nomination for president went to Sanjiva Reddy, the Syndicate candidate. Mrs. Gandhi responded by ordering nationalization of all banks and ousting a pro-Syndicate cabinet member, Morarji Desai, from her cabinet. She then withheld her support from Reddy and demanded a free, nonparty vote for president in the electoral college. This was, in effect, a show of support for V. V. Giri, the rival presidential candidate nominated by Communists and Communalists. In a very close election Giri defeated Reddy, resulting in an important personal political triumph for Mrs. Gandhi.

The resolution of this crisis upheld the authority of the prime minister vis-a-vis the president since Prime Minister Gandhi's candidate narrowly won. It is instructive to note that Indian politicians placed a great deal of importance on this presidential election, as the same situation could occur again. It is possible for a presidential candidate to secure a base of support in the large electoral college that is quite different than that of the prime minister, the latter being elected by majority vote in the lower house of the national Parliament. However, this situation and, therefore, the true test of the presidency has not yet taken place.

The prime minister and cabinet. Since independence, then, the chief executive decisionmaker in India, has been the cabinet. Based on the British model, the cabinet is dominated by the prime minister, who is recognized as the leading politician in India. This was particularly true under Prime Minister Jawaharlal Nehru, an extremely popular leader who commanded wide support within his party and won astoundingly great victories in national elections. Cabinet ministers must be members of either house of Parliament. The cabinet is collectively responsible to the Lok Sabha, and if it loses on an important measure, motion of censure, or vote of confidence it can theoretically be forced to resign. In practice, however, as in Great Britain, this remains entirely theoretical. Since independence, Indian cabinets have usually had clear majorities in the Parliament and the cabinet has generally had strong leadership. However, the security of the prime minister has declined as the Congress party has lost its position of overwhelming dominance. Indeed the crisis of 1969 over the presidency was the strongest challenge made to any prime minister as yet, and the prime minister's victory was a very narrow one. Since the general election of 1971, Mrs. Gandhi, has enjoyed a much more comfortable margin of support than she had in 1969, but it is by no means certain that she can maintain this support for an indefinite period.

The legislature: composition and structure. The Indian National Parliament consists of two houses. The lower house (Lok Sabha) is the Indian equivalent to the British House of Commons or the United States House of Representatives. It theoretically represents the people, who directly elect 500 members from 500 separate single member constituencies. An additional 25 members are elected to represent the Union Territories. The normal life of the Lok Sabha is five years, but it may be dissolved sooner by the president on the advice of the prime minister. When the Lok Sabha is dissolved, a general election is held for all members of the lower house. If the party in power loses its majority, a new cabinet must, according to the constitution, take over the administration of the country. As in Great Britain, while votes of no confidence and motions of censure are constitutionally possible, the cabinet in India can control the outcome of votes in the Lok Sabha through party discipline. No cabinet in India has ever lost an important vote in the Parliament, and, indeed, the Congress party has never lost its parliamentary majority.

The upper house, the (Rajya Sabha) represents the states in the manner of the United States Senate. It consists of a maximum of 250 members, who are elected by the legislatures of the states (as originally United States senators were) in proportion to the population of each state. One-third of its members retire every two years, and each member serves a six-year term. The upper house also contains twelve members nominated by the president for special achievement in literature, science, art, and social science. The Rajya Sabha is not subject to dissolution by the president and sits even though the lower house may be dissolved.

Relative powers of the two houses. In terms of power, the lower house is somewhat more important than the upper house since the lower house holds the executive accountable and all bills related to taxing and spending must be introduced there. The Rajya Sabha, on the other hand, cannot be dissolved by the president and retains certain powers relating to the states. However, it cannot raise a motion of censure against the government. Any money bill rejected by the upper house need only be repassed by the lower house to become law. In other bills both houses have the same power, and indeed, have generally had the same party composition. In normal legislative matters, the Lok Sabha has usually prevailed but there are some matters with respect to the states in which the Rajya Sabha dominates.

The judiciary. India has a single Supreme Court and centralized judicial system, which exercises the power of judicial review. In other words, the Supreme Court of India has jurisdiction over federal-state disputes, interstate cases, and cases involving questions under the Union Constitution. It is the final appeals court on constitutional matters and questions relating to the Indian federal system.

The Supreme Court consists of a chief justice and thirteen associate justices. Each justice is appointed by the president and serves until the mandatory retirement age of 65. Justices can be removed only on grounds of "proved misbehavior and incapacity."

Judges are appointed to the Supreme Court on the basis of judicial distinction, and not because of their political beliefs or background. They are generally selected from the State High Courts after consultation with the justices of the state court and the justices of the national Supreme Court. There is not the practice, as in the United States, of presidents appointing political supporters without much previous judicial experience.

The Indian Supreme Court has been an effective institution in insuring the political framework within which the system operates. The court does not as actively involve itself in legislative and political battles as does its American counterpart, but it does not shrink from responsibility when called upon. Thus, the Indian court did review the election of President Giri in 1969 and pronounced the election legitimate under the constitution. On the other hand, the court overturned Mrs. Gandhi's bank nationalization program. She eventually resubmitted a nationalization bill amended to conform to Supreme Court objections. These were both highly charged political questions.

State governments. The governments of the states of India are modeled after the Indian federal government. Corresponding to the president are the state governors. These officials are not elected, but appointed by the national president. Governors in India are the symbolic heads of their respective states and exercise the formal executive functions. Thus they sign legislative bills and speak for their states on ceremonial occasions. Governors, however, are also officials of the federal Union. In times of emergency, as when state governments are incapacitated by riot or party turmoil, they can assume emergency powers under "President's Rule," a specific provision in the Indian constitution, governing in place of the elected Legislative Assembly.

Governors can also be very important in times of party instability, a common feature of state politics in India. Since they formally appoint chief ministers, governors have discretionary power when no party has a clear majority in the state Legislative Assembly. Thus governors can and have acted as important political brokers, trying to put coalitions together and finding chief ministers who can run their respective states. When a majority coalition cannot be formed, governors must often assume emergency powers under President's Rule, just to keep the state's government functioning.

The chief minister occupies a position on the state level similar to that of the prime minister on the federal level. He is formally appointed by the state governor, and in practice is responsible to the popularly elected Legislative Assembly. His power is supposed to be great, but in reality depends on his ability to obtain a viable party majority. In terms of the legal structure of state government the chief minister prepares the legislative program and his cabinet oversees its administrative enforcement. The actual makeup of the state-level cabinets varies, as does its party composition. Thus, some chief ministers are much more powerful than others.

Chart 2.2.   India: The Structure of the Federal Government

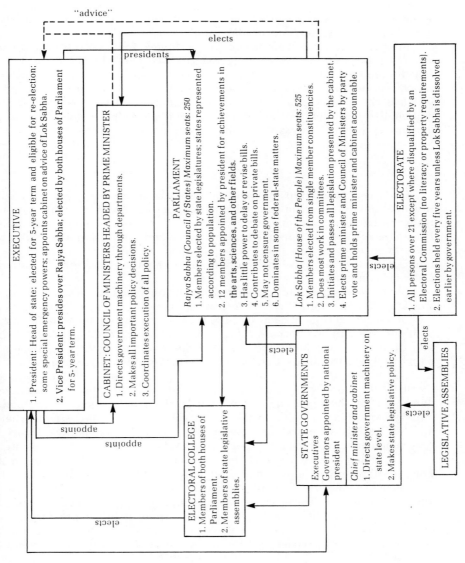

"advice"

elects

presidents

EXECUTIVE

1. President: Head of state; elected for 5-year term and eligible for re-election; some special emergency powers; appoints cabinet on advice of Lok Sabha.

2. Vice President: presides over Rajya Sabha; elected by both houses of Parliament for 5-year term.

CABINET: COUNCIL OF MINISTERS HEADED BY PRIME MINISTER

1. Directs government machinery through departments.

2. Makes all important policy decisions.

3. Coordinates execution of all policy.

PARLIAMENT

Rajya Sabha (Council of States) Maximum seats: 250

1. Members elected by state legislatures; states represented according to population.

2. 12 members appointed by president for achievements in the arts, sciences, and other fields.

3. Has little power to delay or revise bills.

4. Contributes to debate on private bills.

5. May not censure government.

6. Dominates in some federal-state matters.

Lok Sabha (House of the People) Maximum seats: 525

1. Members elected from single member constituencies.

2. Does most work in committees.

3. Initiates and passes all legislation presented by the cabinet.

4. Elects prime minister and Council of Ministers by party vote and holds prime minister and cabinet accountable.

ELECTORATE

1. All persons over 21 except where disqualified by an Electoral Commission (no literacy or property requirements).

2. Elections held every five years unless Lok Sabha is dissolved earlier by government.

elects

ELECTORAL COLLEGE

1. Members of both houses of Parliament.

2. Members of state legislative assemblies.

appoints

appoints

STATE GOVERNMENTS

Executives
Governors appointed by national president

Chief minister and cabinet

1. Directs government machinery on state level.

2. Makes state legislative policy.

elects

elects

elects

LEGISLATIVE ASSEMBLIES

elects

The state legislatures in India also vary in their constitutional makeup. About one-half the states have bicameral legislatures. All are required by the Union constitution to have at least one house that is popularly elected. The size of Legislative Assemblies may vary from 500 to 600 members, and is apportioned according to the size of the population. Their efficiency varies greatly from state to state and often reflects internal party wrangling.

In contrast to federalism in the United States, Indian states do not have separate state judiciaries. Since state governments are established by the Union constitution, conflicts over state law are settled in a single centralized judiciary, which deals with both union and state matters. Thus the Supreme Court of India, which is the final appeals court on both federal and state issues, was intentionally established by the Indian constitution to help promote the unity of the country. (Chart 2.2 presents a structural outline of the government of India.)

CHILE

Chile was conquered by Spain in the sixteenth century. Not possessing precious metals, the colony turned to agriculture and lived in a very poor and rather isolated fashion for most of the Spanish period. The one-half million Indians mixed with the Europeans so that by the end of the colonial period in the early nineteenth century Chile was composed primarily of a Mestizo population, with relatively few Indians or Europeans not integrated into the national Chilean population.

Chile, like other Spanish colonies in Latin America, became Spanish speaking, Roman Catholic, and organized into large landed estates. The independence movement came to Chile at about the same time as to the rest of South America. In 1817 Bernardo O'Higgins and Jose de San Martin led an army into Chile from Argentina and defeated the Spanish royalists. O'Higgins, a native Chilean, became the first leader of the newly independent country.

This was the last time Chile was invaded by an outside army. However, the country did go through a fairly long period of internal instability and turbulence during which she experimented with federalism before she established a unitary, centralized constitutional system of government in 1831. After this early difficulty, Chile managed to develop and maintain competitive forms of government for almost the whole period from 1831 to the present. An "autocratic republic" ruled from 1831 to 1861, dominated by conservative landed interests. This was transformed into a "liberal republic" over the years from 1861 to 1891 by a change in the party structure, which allowed Liberals and Conservatives to alternate in power. These years were characterized by strong presidential leadership. From 1891 to 1918, because of strong political pressures from different economic groups, Chile changed to a basically parliamentary system similar to the British model. In 1918 the system broke down and the political struggle led to the brief military dictatorship of Major Carlos Ibañez del Campo (from 1925 to 1931). A new constitutional system was then established, returning great power to a popularly elected president. This competitive presidential system lasted until 1973, when the military overthrew the elected government of

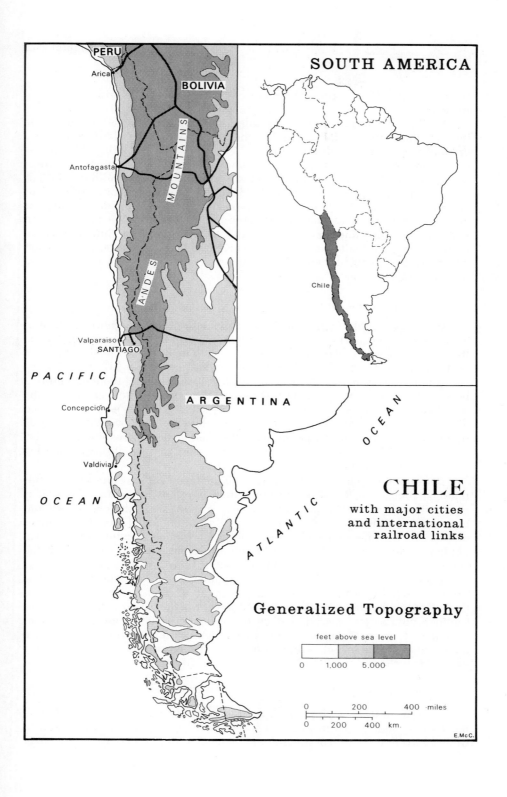

PERU

Arica

BOLIVIA

Antofagasta

M O U N T A I N S

A N D E S

Valparaiso
SANTIAGO

PACIFIC

Concepción

Valdivia

OCEAN

ARGENTINA

SOUTH AMERICA

Chile

OCEAN

ATLANTIC

CHILE

with major cities
and international
railroad links

Generalized Topography

feet above sea level

0   1,000   5,000

0   200   400 miles
0   200   400 km.

E.McC.

Salvador Allende. The general structure of future government in Chile is still unclear.

While Chile has been more turbulent and more prone to the use of the military than either Britain or India, she has, by world standards, enjoyed a gradual evolution in her political process. For over 150 years Chile has been free of foreign warfare. She has generally been able to develop her internal political process without the active intervention of a politically minded military. Rather, the Chilean military has generally followed the lead of the Chilean bureaucracy and political elite. In times of crisis and social dislocation, the military has on occasion stepped in, but not as often or in as thorough a fashion as in many other Latin American, African, and Asian states. The Chilean civilian political system has allowed power to evolve into the hands of new groups and has, therefore, avoided many difficult internal confrontations so damaging to other political systems.

Territory and Population

Chile is a republic on the Pacific coast of South America. A narrow country, averaging only 110 miles in width, but extending over 2,500 miles in length from the southern border of Peru to the Strait of Magellan. it covers a fairly large area (741,000 square kilometers of 292,000 square miles; see map., p. 51.

About 90 percent of Chile's relatively small population (about 9.75 million people according to the 1970 census) lives in the middle of the country, in the area between the cities of Concepción and Santiago. Santiago is the capital and economic center of the country and has a population of over 600,000. In 1970, 55 percent of the Chilean population was classified as urban, despite the importance of agriculture to the Chilean economy. (Table 2.3 presents the population of Chile by provinces.)

Because of its small population, Chile is not faced with the great difficulties that confront India. The Chilean population is relatively homogeneous. It is predominantly white, because of extensive migrations in the eighteenth and nineteenth centuries from Germany, Italy, England, and the Basque provinces of Spain. The integration of these groups of immigrants into the general population has not created great difficulties for the political structure of the country. Most groups have adopted Spanish as their language (in some areas German is spoken, but even among them Spanish is gaining). The population is predominantly Roman Catholic (89.5 percent of the people claim to be Catholic), but the country has a long tradition of religious tolerance. The Roman Catholic church was maintained by the state until 1925 but was then disestablished. Over 80 percent of the population is literate. Most children are educated in public schools, which are not controlled by the church, and today education is compulsory between ages seven and fifteen.

Political Structure

The constitution of 1925 (whose operation has in effect been suspended by the military, but which has not been overturned or replaced) established in Chile a presidential form of government, somewhat similar in structure to that of

Table 2.3. Population of Chile

Provinces	Population (in millions)	Land Area (in thousand square kilometers)	Density of Population (per square kilometer)
Aconcagua	0.16	10.2	15.7
Antofagasta	0.31	123.1	2.5
Arauco	0.11	5.7	19.3
Atacama	0.20	79.8	2.5
Aysén	0.06	88.9	0.7
Bió Bió	0.21	11.2	18.8
Caufin	0.47	17.4	27.0
Chiloe	0.11	23.4	4.7
Colchagua	0.20	8.4	23.8
Concepción	0.74	5.7	129.8
Coquimbo	0.41	39.9	10.2
Curicó	0.13	5.7	22.8
Linares	0.21	9.8	21.4
Llanquihue	0.22	18.4	12.0
Magallanes	0.09	135.4	0.7
Malleco	0.20	14.3	14.0
Maule	0.10	5.6	17.9
Nuble	0.35	14.2	24.6
O'Higgins	0.32	7.1	45.1
Osorno	0.18	9.1	19.8
Santiago	3.40	17.4	195.4
Talca	0.26	9.6	27.1
Tarapaca	0.18	55.3	3.3
Valdiviá	0.32	20.9	15.3
Valparaiso	0.81	4.8	168.8
Total	9.75	741.3	13.2

SOURCE: *Anuario Estadística* (Santiago: Dirección General de Estadística, 1970).

the United States. Chile is a unitary state with all power vested in the central government, the leaders of which are directly elected by the people. The government of Chile is structurally different from the governments of Britain and India, mainly in the legal separation of executive, legislative, and judicial branches.

The executive. Under the constitution of 1925, the chief executive of Chile is the president, who is elected by direct popular election for a term of six years. He may not immediately succeed himself. There is no vice president, but the president may appoint one if he is ill or out of the country. If the president of Chile should die in office, a new election must be called within sixty days. The office is then temporarily held by the Interior Minister, a cabinet officer appointed by the late president.

Unlike the chief executive in a parliamentary structure, the president of Chile is not responsible to the elected legislature and neither is his cabinet. The members of the cabinet are appointed by the president, who may hire and fire them at will. Cabinet ministers may, however, be impeached by Congress under certain procedures. The cabinet oversees the administrative departments, as in parliamentary structures, but the ministers are in the executive branch of government, responsible only to the president. The president and cabinet are not part of the legislature, as in parliamentary systems.

The president of Chile can propose the legislative program and can veto laws passed by Congress; Congress can override his veto by a two-thirds majority of both houses. The president, who is not elected by the Congress as he would be in a parliamentary system, cannot dissolve the legislative body. He must work with the legislature and hope to gain enough votes to get his program through it. This is more likely to occur when the president is of the same political party as the majority in Congress. However, Chile has a multiparty system and presidents must be extremely popular before they can be sure of passage of their legislative programs. Even their own parties will not support them on every measure.

In the past, presidents of Chile have been conservatives or centrists and, normally, have enjoyed at least the temporary support of majorities in the Chilean legislature. The most recently elected president of Chile, Salvador Allende, was the first chief executive in many years to have been elected by a coalition of minority parties. Thus, while he was in command of the executive branch, he confronted a fairly unified opposition in the Congress. Allende was a Socialist, elected with the support of left-wing parties; the legislature was center-right and disagreed with much of the president's legislative program.

The result for Chile was a very stormy period characterized by public demonstrations, mutual threats, widespread strikes, and disorder that threatened to harm the national economy, and a great deal of private manipulation among politicians. Chilean parties are fairly well disciplined, and a president must be very astute to deal with them. President Allende was unable to reach a consensus among the organized groups opposed to his policies and, after much turmoil, was forced to choose between modifying his legislative proposals or resigning. Allende refused to do either; rather, he tried to maneuver and gain support among the contending factions. Allende's problems were made more difficult by grave economic problems facing Chile. Over the last several years, Chile's economy had entered a period of stagnation and low economic growth. The government had contributed to the low growth rate by providing many expensive social services and public employment to the relatively small Chilean middle class. In addition, owing to government policy, some Chilean workers, particularly the miners, had begun receiving higher wages and enjoying a reasonably high standard of living. However, Chilean investment and productivity were not increasing rapidly, and higher living standards could not easily be made available to the rural poor and unskilled, unorganized urban lower classes. Allende was elected by these disadvantaged groups, and his attempts to redistribute Chile's wealth in their direction by promoting inflation meant lowering the living standards of the newly affluent lower middle class. These latter groups were unwilling to give up their newly won achievements. Thus, after a destructive truckers' strike, the opposition parties managed to force President Allende to appoint the heads of the armed forces to civilian posts in his cabinet. Soon afterward the military ousted the Allende government entirely. The president was either killed or committed suicide in the coup and Chilean governmental institutions have since been (at least temporarily) in abeyance, awaiting the next moves of the current military junta.

The legislature. Under the constitution of 1925, the Chilean national Congress has two houses—an upper house, called the Senate, and a lower house, called the Chamber of Deputies. The Senate consists of fifty members, each elected for eight years. Senators represent groups of provinces. By a rather complicated formula, Chile's twenty-five provinces are divided into groups of ten; each group of ten elects five senators. Half the Senate is elected every four years, in a staggered arrangement comparable to the Indian Rajya Sabha. The Senate must consent to presidential appointments and approve of treaties.

Despite the fact that Chile has a Senate that theoretically represents the interests of the provinces, Chile does not have a federal system of government. The president appoints the officials who run the administration of the provinces as well as the chief magistrates in urban areas of over 100,000 inhabitants. These local units have no power, except that which is left to them by the national government. All this is determined by the president, who can change administrative rulings regarding the provinces if he so desires.

The Chamber of Deputies of Chile contains one member for every 30,000 inhabitants or fraction over 15,000. The current Chamber of Deputies has 150 members, but as the population increases, so will the size of the Chamber. Elections for the Chamber of Deputies are held every four years.

The Chamber of Deputies is a deliberative body organized in a way similar to the Senate. Each elects a president and a vice president, who can control the work of their respective chamber by regulating debate, recognizing speakers, and nominating members to standing committees. Both chambers have committee structures that investigate and clear the work for their re bodies. These committees can amend legislation and kill it accord wishes of the parties in each house, no matter the efforts of the pres

As with the United States Congress, the Chilean Congress i technically passes all legislation, that passes the national b taxes, that creates and abolishes public offices, and th administration and holds it responsible. Before the Allende, however, the president held the upper ha initiated most legislation and was able to dominat multifactional arguments. President Allende was vis-a-vis Congress and had to bargain and dea majority opposed to him. The result was gove pass laws, and much mutual mistrust. It e constitutional system by the military, at leas

The Structure of the Government Under the Constitution of 1925

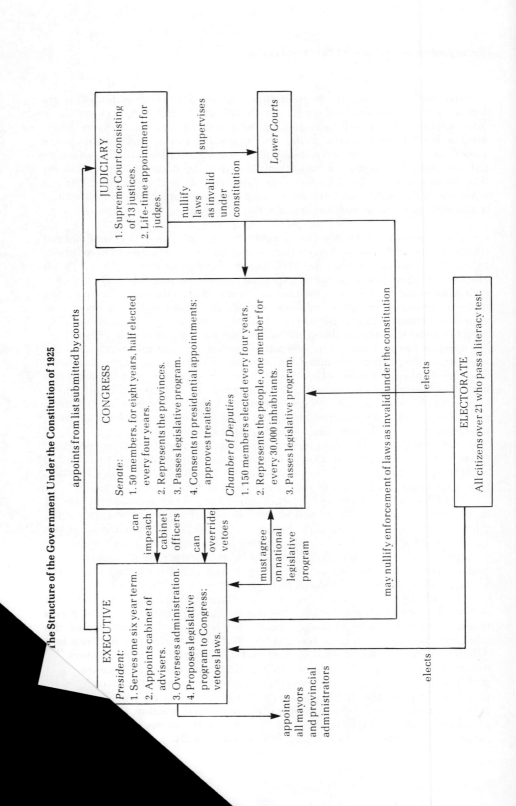

JUDICIARY

1. Supreme Court consisting of 13 justices.
2. Life-time appointment for judges.

supervises

Lower Courts

appoints from list submitted by courts

nullify laws as invalid under constitution

CONGRESS

Senate:

1. 50 members, for eight years, half elected every four years.
2. Represents the provinces.
3. Passes legislative program.
4. Consents to presidential appointments; approves treaties.

Chamber of Deputies

1. 150 members elected every four years.
2. Represents the people, one member for every 30,000 inhabitants.
3. Passes legislative program.

can impeach cabinet officers

can override vetoes

must agree on national legislative program

EXECUTIVE

President:

1. Serves one six year term.
2. Appoints cabinet of advisers.
3. Oversees administration.
4. Proposes legislative program to Congress; vetoes laws.

appoints all mayors and provincial administrators

may nullify enforcement of laws as invalid under the constitution

elects

elects

ELECTORATE

All citizens over 21 who pass a literacy test.

Power is about equally distributed between the two houses, but the powers of the Chilean Congress have generally, until the election of Allende, not been very great vis-à-vis those of the president. Congress supervises and investigates the activities of administrative agencies, but it is severely limited in its ability to initiate legislation. Only the executive branch may introduce bills to amend the budget, to reorganize the local administration of the country, and to create new offices. Congress may refuse to accept these recommendations, but it cannot increase expenditures in any area of administration. It can thus have a veto over the president by reducing his budgets, but it cannot initiate and fund its own programs.

The judiciary. Chile has a long tradition of an independent judiciary. As in India, judges in Chile are appointed by the chief executive from lists prepared by the courts. Courts are, therefore, staffed by the leading judicial authorities in the country. A judgeship is essentially a life-time appointment, except in extraordinary circumstance in which personal behavior is involved.

The Supreme Court of Chile exercises the power of judicial review in a very limited sense. The court may state that the enforcement of a law is invalid under the constitution, but it cannot call the law itself unconstitutional. Thus, if it repeatedly annuls the enforcement of a law, in practice the law has no effect.(Chart 2.3 outlines the organizational structure of the Chilean government.)

The Constitution of 1925 and the Military Coup of 1973

Since the overturn of Allende's government in September of 1973, the four-man Chilean military junta has moved against Allende supporters but has not as yet revoked the constitution. The junta has dissolved the Central Workers Confederation, an 800,000 member labor confederation that had been led by Communists. Most of the socialist measures taken by the Allende government (for example, the nationalization of certain industries) have been revoked by the present regime. Also, seven political parties that had supported Allende have been outlawed and all mayors and city councilmen throughout the country (former Allende appointees) have been replaced by men appointed by the junta. Leftist newspapers are now not permitted to publish; other newspapers enforce strict self-censorship and refrain from criticism of the current government.

Since the overthrow of Allende the military rulers have relied on middle-class organizations such as those representing truckers, shopkeepers, businessmen, and professional employees—all of whom have generally supported the coup. Representatives of these organizations have been meeting with military leaders on a regular basis.

Politicians have generally remained silent since the coup. The Chilean Congress has not met since the day of Allende's overthrow, but it has not been legally outlawed. The cabinet currently running the country is composed almost entirely of military men.

Chilean courts have remained untouched by the military, evidently out of respect for the country's long tradition of an independent judiciary. Because the constitution of 1925 in itself provides for a very powerful chief executive, the military may in fact choose not to promulgate a completely new constitution, but to merely amend the present one. It may in this way attempt to keep the power of left-wing factions reduced by traditional Chilean legal and constitutional means.

It should be noted that the military has established a commission whose function is to study Chile's constitutional problems and to draft a new constitution. This commission, composed entirely of civilian Chilean leaders (including leading politicians of the centrist and traditional conservative parties as well as leading jurists and constitutional lawyers), has been studying the problem and issued a preliminary report in December of 1973. The report called for the establishment of a republican constitution, not very different from the 1925 document, but one in which Congress and the judiciary would have a greater role and the presidency would not be so overwhelmingly powerful. It remains to be seen what the final draft of this constitution will establish.

Comparative Distinctions in Political Structures Among Competitive States

Great Britain, India, and Chile exhibit very broad institutional similarities in their governmental structures: all three states have or have had active legislatures, strong executives, disciplined political parties with strong public support, and independent judiciaries. Within these broad generalizations, certain important distinctions, however, can be drawn.

Great Britain developed her political structure, the parliamentary type, over a very long period of time during which the country was quite insulated from outside influences. The British population in this time developed a strong cultural and political consensus. Changes in British political institutions have thus been slow and gradual, reflecting broad changes in the national political perspective. While India and Chile have, by world standards, also been relatively insulated from outside attack and influence, the latter two countries have been far more turbulent than Britain.

India is the largest, most heterogeneous, and poorest of the three countries. The pressures on government to provide basic services are very great, while basic linguistic and cultural differences do not provide Indian governmental institutions with the stable support common to such institutions in Great Britain. Thus, the Indian central government has, on occasion, taken over the operation of state governments. The Indian Supreme Court has also entered into stormy controversies to settle basic political issues. India, however, like Great Britain, has demonstrated that her institutions—parliament, the prime minister, the courts, the president—are viable political structures, though different in actual operation than similar institutions in Great Britain.

The Indian political structure, while of a parliamentary type, has not concentrated the unitary power of the state in the prime minister and cabinet to the same extent as this power has been concentrated in Great Britain. India has a hybrid system that utilizes the basic parliamentary decisionmaking process. At the same time she retains the traditional checks on abuse of power common to systems that have separation of powers: these are a federal system, an independent judiciary with the power of judicial review, separate elections for president and parliament, separately elected state governments, and a detailed written constitution.

The system of government in Chile, unlike that in the other two states, is based on separation of powers, with a separately elected president and Congress who must agree on the nation's legislative program before it can be passed into law. Chile also has a written constitution and a judiciary with some power of judicial review.

Chile has had a more turbulent political experience than either Great Britain or India and this is reflected in the development of her institutions. Chile has a Spanish cultural heritage, which stresses the importance of a strong chief executive. Thus, the president of Chile has been directly elected and endowed with great powers. The country, however, has been a competitive one with strong political parties and widespread public participation in political matters. Thus, the Congress, which represents public groups and parties, has also been very powerful and elected by a different constituency. Chilean government has remained stable so long as the president and Congress could agree on a legislative program; when they could not the government did not function effectively. The most recent example of the difficulty with divided government in Chile was the overthrow of President Allende by the military. This ended an impasse between president and Congress, but did not (as yet) transform the fundamental values inherent in Chilean society.

No matter what form of institutional structure is eventually reestablished in Chile, it will again have to reflect the political beliefs of the Chilean population. which it seeks to govern. This is, of course, true also of India and Great Britain where political structures are used for representing divergent political interests which permeate their respective societies. In all three countries the structures of government have been strong because they have been accepted in the long run by the general public as legitimate and effective.

POLITICAL STRUCTURES AND INSTITUTIONS IN FRAGMENTED STATES

Patterns of Similarity

Political competition depends on a well-understood system of rules by which political groups can interact, a degree of mutual trust and respect, and an understanding that open competition is a good thing—a value in itself.

Some states, despite the presence of many open political conflicts, have not been able to achieve a stable competitive system. Either sufficient mutual trust is lacking, or it is simply too difficult, given the number and type of politically active groups, to achieve a well-established structure within which competition can safely take place.

Three examples of politically fragmented states are France, Indonesia, and Zaire (formerly called the Congo). These states are very divergent historically, geographically, and economically. All, however, have been unable to moderate complex group conflicts through normal established political institutions. All have, therefore, wavered between periods of free elections, anarchy, and dictatorship—both by the military and political parties. No resolution of group conflict has yet proven stable in these states, for every established structure appears constantly vulnerable to attack from forces within its own community.

Three Case Studies: France, Indonesia, and Zaire

FRANCE

Perhaps the classic model of fragmented politics can be found in France. Indeed, it can be said France has been able to institutionalize her fragmentation in particular political structures, with historic repercussions.

France, in sharp contrast to the three competitive states described above, has experienced an extremely turbulent and chaotic political development. Establishing legitimacy for any form of government has met with great difficulty as each new political system has given rise to sharp ideological conflict and disagreement and a sizeable portion of the French population has always been willing to take up arms against the regime of the day.

This can be seen from a brief description of modern French political history. Before 1789 France was governed by a religiously sanctioned absolute monarchy that had strong traditional backing in all segments of French life. In this period there was no alternative to the power of the monarchy: the king was the personification of the state and the source of all legitimate authority. The monarchy, however, proved to be rigidly inefficient and eventually could no longer militarily defend itself against those who had grievances against it.

The Revolution of 1789 in its early stages was quite moderate. Early revolutionists wished to establish a more modern system of government, one with representative institutions that would work in concert with the monarchy—a sort of constitutional monarchy somewhat similar to the present-day British system. However, the revolution became increasingly radical and after the establishment of the First Republic (from 1792 to 1795) the king was beheaded. The new regime was devoted to destroying all that was traditional in French culture—the aristocracy, the church, the educational system. It was as violent and revolutionary a system as had ever been seen in Europe and, consequently, came under military attack by a coalition of conservative European states.

The revolution in this form was only temporarily supported by the French population. When the revolutionaries turned from attack on the establishment to attacks on each other, the French community found itself divided into two camps—monarchists vs. republicans.

Toward the end of the eighteenth century, Napoleon Bonaparte emerged as the leading military and political figure in France. First as a leader of the Directorate of Five (from 1795 to 1798), and then as first consul in the Consulate of Three (from 1798 to 1801), he restored peace and stability to the country. In 1801 Napoleon had himself crowned emperor, creating the First Empire (from 1801 to 1815).

Napoleon I was an absolute—but not a traditional—leader. He transformed the law codes and the administrative structure of France and turned the state into a modern, efficient political system. He also conquered most of Europe and was regarded as a great hero in France. His accession to power was never opposed within France, and his regime was ended in 1815 only by military defeat at the hands of foreign powers.

With Napoleon's fall France's population became divided into three camps—monarchists, republicans, and Bonapartists (imperialists). Each of these groups was ideologically different from the others; each saw a different basis of legitimacy for the state; each could see no chance of compromise with either of the others. In addition, no single group clearly commanded a dominant position. In these circumstances, France became, as she has remained ever since, a fragmented country. All French regimes have, to this day, been based on manipulations of weak, shifting pluralities vulnerable to every circumstance. The ensuing political history of France demonstrates this occurrence.

In 1815 the monarchy was restored to France. Every reform established since 1789 was done away with; the new king did not accept any legal checks on his power. Popular discontent eventually culminated in the "July Revolution of 1830." This event, far less cruel than its 1789 predecessor, led to the overthrow of the king. A cousin, Louis Philippe, was placed on the throne and a legislature was established with limited suffrage.

The system of 1830 lasted only eighteen years—to the so-called Revolution of 1848. This was also a fairly nonviolent political confrontation, but again the king was overthrown. The main issue in 1848 was universal suffrage, but the entire constitution of 1830 was done away with. The monarchy was ended and the Second Republic established. A presidential system of government was instituted in which the chief executive—the president—was to be popularly elected by universal suffrage and was to share power with an elected legislature. The first elected president under this constitution was Louis Napoleon, a nephew of Napoleon I. He served for one term, but before his term expired he staged a coup and had himself appointed president for life. In 1852, he dissolved the legislature and proclaimed himself emperor, thus creating the Second Empire.

The Second Empire lasted from 1852 to 1870 and like the First Empire was ended by defeat in a military venture, not by internal dissension. Louis Napoleon was a modern dictator, who tried to create popular support for his regime. He used controlled plebiscites, rigged elections, and rigged parliaments. Under his rule France became prosperous. Her system of government seemed to be evolving into a more representative structure, not a totalitarian police state, and most Frenchmen were willing to live with it.

After her defeat by Prussia in the Franco-Prusssian War (1871), France fell into another period of revolutionary violence. Monarchists, republicans, and imperialists continued to confront each other, and new more violent revolutionary groups emerged as well. In 1871, the Paris Commune, the world's first socialist government, was established and then crushed militarily. The legislature left by Louis Napoleon was conservatively inclined but could find no strong leader to serve as a constitutional monarch. The result was the passage of

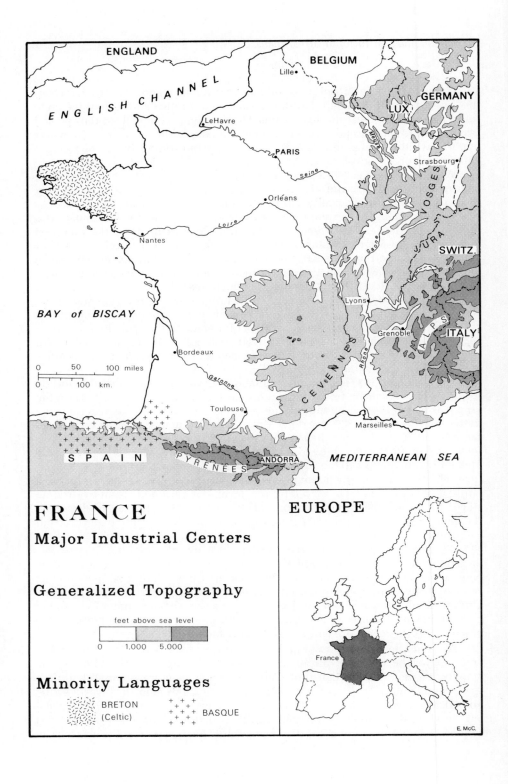

ENGLAND

BELGIUM

Lille•

GERMANY

LUX.

ENGLISH CHANNEL

LeHavre•

Strasbourg•

PARIS

Seine

VOSGES

•Orléans

Loire

JURA

SWITZ.

Nantes•

BAY of BISCAY

Lyons•

ALPS

Grenoble•

ITALY

0   50   100 miles

Bordeaux•

Garonne

CEVENNES

Rhône

0   100 km.

Toulouse•

Marseilles•

S P A I N

PYRENEES

ANDORRA

MEDITERRANEAN SEA

FRANCE
Major Industrial Centers

Generalized Topography

feet above sea level

0   1,000   5,000

Minority Languages

BRETON
(Celtic)

BASQUE

EUROPE

France

E. McC.

several bills that allowed the legislature to govern with a very weak executive. This system became known as the Third Republic. It was the most successful and longest lived (from 1875 to 1940) of all modern French governments. It survived World War I and the Depression and was ended only by the German invasion of France in 1940. The Third Republic institutionalized France's fragmentation in her assembly. All elements in the community fell behind a large number of divergent political parties that compromised their positions in the legislature. The executive power was technically invested in a prime minister (premier) and cabinet, but in France cabinets fell to momentary shifts in voting strength in the National Assembly and the executive remained insecure except when it was given emergency powers to deal with crises (as occurred during World War I).

After the end of World War II France restored a system of government similar to that of the Third Republic. However, during the Fourth Republic (from 1945 to 1958) there were even greater divisions among political parties than the French had previously experienced and the community grew very intolerant of the government's inability to resolve difficult colonial problems. When in 1958 the war in Algeria seemed to be heading France toward civil war, the French legislature invited General Charles de Gaulle to become premier. He accepted on the condition that the constitution be rewritten according to his liking. The new constitution—in use to this day—established the Fifth Republic (1958-), which puts most power in the hands of the executive and has basically reflected the will of France's more conservative elements. This regime has on occasion been vulnerable to attack by other elements within the country and seems to represent only a temporary shift in form, not an end to France's fragmentation.

Territory and Population

France, a modern affluent state, is the largest state in Europe except for Russia and is approximately equal in territory to the American state of Texas. A country with varied geographical features, it stretches across the middle of Western Europe from the Alps to the Atlantic to the Mediterranean. France has high mountains, great river basins, extensive agricultural plains, and long coastal areas (see map, p.62).

France's various regions have produced populations whose views of life and cultural patterns differ widely. Indeed, the country can be theoretically divided into a predominantly industrial Northeast centered in Paris, facing a much more conservative, agricultural South and Southwest. Paris dominates the country in much the same manner London dominates Great Britain. The national leaders in all French fields of endeavor—economic, political, and cultural—are centered in Paris. (Table 2.4 presents a breakdown by area of France's population.)

France had a population of about 50 million by the 1968 census. This represents a very slow, stable growth in population since the eighteenth century, for in 1800 France already had a population of 27.5 million. In contrast, population growth due to foreign immigration has been explosive in the United States. (Table 2.5 compares France's population growth to that of the United States and Great Britain.)

Table 2.4. Population of France

Area	Population (in millions)	Land Area (in thousand square kilometers)	Density of Population (per square kilometer)
Région Parisienne	9.25	12.0	770.8
Champagne-Ardenne	1.28	25.6	50.0
Picardie	1.58	19.4	81.4
Haute-Normandie	1.50	12.3	121.9
Centre	1.99	39.1	4.9
Basse-Normandie	1.26	17.6	71.6
Bourgogne	1.50	31.6	47.5
Nord	3.82	12.4	308.1
Lorraine	2.27	23.5	96.6
Alsace	1.41	8.3	169.9
Franche-Comté	0.99	16.2	61.1
Pays de la Loire	2.58	32.1	80.4
Bretagne	2.47	27.2	90.8
Poitou-Charente	1.48	25.8	57.4
Aquitaine	2.46	41.4	59.4
Midi-Pyrénées	2.18	45.4	48.0
Limousin	0.74	16.9	43.8
Rhône-Alps	4.42	43.7	101.1
Auvergne	1.31	26.0	50.4
Languedoc-Roussillon	1.71	27.5	62.2
Provence-Côte d'Azur	3.30	31.4	105.1
Corse	.27	8.8	30.7
Totals	49.78	544.5	91.4

SOURCE: *Annuaire statistique de la France, 1973* (Paris: Ministere de l'économie et des finances, Institut national de la statistique et des études économiques, 1973), p. 3.

NOTES: Results of last official census, 1968.

France has a fairly high standard of living because her economy has easily been able to adapt to her slow rate of population growth. On the other hand France has appeared to be a nation on the decline, a nation of old and very conservative people. This was particularly true as a result of World War I, when large numbers of young Frenchmen lost their lives. The decreasing marriage and birth rates in the postwar period resulted in a country with a badly shaken morale.

France has a relatively homogeneous population. The French have absorbed many immigrants, especially since the nineteenth century, but these people have adopted the French language and have been integrated into the

Table 2.5. Comparative Rates of Population Growth in France, Great Britain, and the United States (in millions)

Year	France	Great Britain	United States
1800	27.3	11.9*	5.3
1860	37.4	25.6	31.4
1900	38.5	38.2	76.0
1930	41.3	46.0	122.8
1950	42.7	50.2	150.7
1960	46.5	52.7	178.5
1970	49.8*	54.5**	203.2***

SOURCE: *Annuaire statistique de la France, 1973* (Paris: Institut national de la statistique et des etudes économiques, 1973); *Census Report* (London: HMSO, 1961); *Census, 1971 Preliminary Report* (London: HMSO, 1971); U. S. Department of Commerce, *Statistical Abstract of the United States, 1971* (Washington, D. C.: 1971).

*1968 census figure
**1971 census figure
***1970 census figure

general population. All France speaks the same language, though some rural communities retain regional dialects. The country is also homogeneous in terms of religion, being almost entirely Roman Catholic. There are small minorities of Protestants, Jews, and Moslems, but these groups have not proven to be politically cohesive and effective. The major religious controversy in France is between practicing Catholics and secularists, who have raised such questions as the right to state support for church schools. Rural areas tend to have more devout Catholics than the industrial regions, so the conflict takes on regional and class overtones as well.

Despite their history of political fragmentation, the French have a strong sense of nationality. France has had a centralized system of government since the reign of Napoleon I, and a population that views itself in national, not regional, ethnic, or religious terms. (Even those groups that ethnically distinguish themselves from the general population—the Bretons or the German-speaking population of Alsace—seek only greater autonomy within the government, not separation from it.) The French are a skilled and literate people, who read the same language and are aware and alert to the same issues. Fragmentation in France occurs because of the disagreement among groups over the form of authority and political structure of the state; it does not involve disagreement over the extent or existence of the state itself.

Political Structure

The structure of the Fifth Republic is the product of efforts by traditionally minded French conservatives who wished to establish a strong responsible government with a secure executive. Since they did not have a stable party system on which to base such a system and since General de Gaulle was such an exceptional individual, the structure was built around him.

  The executive.   The president is the most important figure in the Fifth Republic. As the chief executive, he heads the government in both political and symbolic terms. He is currently elected by direct popular vote for a seven-year term. However, the first presidential election in 1958 was indirect, utilizing an electoral college in which rural areas were overrepresented. Also, President de Gaulle resigned in 1969 before his term ran out, precipitating a new presidential election.

  The power of the president of France derives from his being elected directly by the populace. To this the constitution has added the power to dissolve the legislature with only the consultation of the premier and the cabinet and to govern by decree during crises. General de Gaulle used this and other emergency powers during the Algerian War. He also enhanced the power of the presidency vis-a-vis that of the legislature because parties friendly to him dominated the legislature during his term of office and supported his initiatives.

  Since 1958 the president of France has also attempted to establish his mandate with the people, over and above the premier and the legislature, by calling national referenda on important policy questions. President de Gaulle won referenda on the Algerian War and on the question of direct election of the president; he was defeated on a question of reorganization of local government and resigned from the presidency soon after. His style of executive leadership was to assume he was directly responsible to the French people, while parties, legislatures, and premiers were intermediaries and not legitimately powerful. President Pompidou continued this tradition when, for example, he submitted the question of British entry into the European Common Market to a referendum. Under Pompidou the president's party was in control of the legislature and the president was dominant on policy matters. He controlled the actions of the premier; indeed he could almost hire and fire him at will. President Valéry Giscard d'Estaing, while not a Gaullist himself, is supported by a coalition similar to that of President Pompidou but may not continue these practices in quite the same way. The assertion of presidential power seems to go against a strong French republican strain, and certainly many Frenchmen oppose it on abstract constitutional grounds.

  The legislature elects a premier and members of the cabinet, but these individuals have, under the Fifth Republic, served and supported the president. They have thus acted more as spokesmen for the president than for the legislature. It is very difficult under the new constitution for the legislature to overturn a cabinet. To defeat a premier, the National Assembly must formally move to censure him and must carry the vote within twenty-four hours with a majority of the assembly's total membership (not just a majority of those voting). If the National Assembly does not vote for the premier's legislation, but fails to censure him, the defeated bill becomes law in France. Thus the structure of France is somewhat parliamentary on paper: a premier selected by the legislature is technically responsible for the legislative program. In practice, however, the system is thoroughly presidential. The president, not the premier, is the most important politician in the majority party in the legislature. He can get his legislative way, even if the premier loses his majority in the National Assembly.

It should be stressed that since 1958 the president of France and the premier elected by the legislature have been members of the same political party and, as such, political allies. As in India, it is quite difficult today to predict how policy in France would be formulated and carried out if the president were elected by one set of parties, while the premier represented his opponents. This situation has not been tested, but the tradition of allegiance to many parties among the French people indicates that one day this problem may have to be resolved.

The legislature. The French legislature consists of two houses—the Senate (upper house) and the National Assembly (lower house). The Senate is indirectly elected and overrepresents the rural areas. The National Assembly is the more important house, in which the fragmentation of the country has been accurately represented. It has been reduced in power, since the Fifth Republic has cut into its traditional strength by constitutional means.

The Senate. The Senate, sometimes nicknamed the "Grand Council of the French Communes" has 283 members elected for a nine-year term, with one-third of its members rotating every three years. This house is indirectly elected by a large electoral college composed of municipal and provincial officials from throughout France. The electoral college overrepresents conservative rural areas at the expense of large cities and industrial regions and the Senate has therefore been dominated by right and center parties.

The Fifth Republic constitution provides that the Senate, like the National Assembly, may sit for a maximum of six months. Compared to the National Assembly, the Senate is somewhat weaker in power but not so weak as it was in the Fourth Republic. The Fifth Republic constitution gives the Senate the power to veto or delay bills passed by the National Assembly.

In the Fifth Republic Gaullists have not been able to elect more than a minority of members to the Senate and other center and right parties have been able to follow a relatively independent party line there on some issues. Senatorial opposition to President de Gaulle's plan for granting greater autonomy to Brittany and Normandy induced him to call a popular referendum on the issue of "the organization of public authorities" in 1969. The president lost this referendum and resigned his office.

The National Assembly. The National Assembly, or lower house, consists of 487 deputies directly elected by universal suffrage for five-year terms. French legislative elections are conducted on two successive Sundays. If a candidate receives a majority of the votes (over 50 percent) on the first Sunday, he wins the seat. If there is no majority winner, the two candidates with the highest number of votes hold a run-off election on the second Sunday, and the winner of that election takes the seat. The two ballot system, as well as the present system of districting, allows parties to bargain among themselves between elections and favors centrist parties at the expense of extremists.

The premier of France is the elected president of the National Assembly and is legally comparable to the prime minister in Great Britain. He is not, however, leader of his party as the British prime minister is, but is designated for his position by the president of France. He is thus dependent on the president, the real leader of his party, though technically elected by the National Assembly. Since 1958, no premier has opposed the will of the president of France.

The National Assembly holds the premier accountable and passes on all legislation. All money bills originate in this house. Both houses must vote on all bills, and the Senate therefore may veto or delay bills passed by the National Assembly. If the bill is repassed by the National Assembly it becomes law. The National Assembly, unlike the United States Congress, may not kill government bills by referring them to committee; all legislation prepared by the government and presented by the premier according to his own time schedule must be discussed and voted by the National Assembly. Also, the Parliament (both houses) may not delay the government budget for more than seventy days; if it does not act on a budget within that time the budget becomes law by government decree. The National Assembly meets only twice a year, once for two months and once for three months. This leaves much discretion to the government, which can rule by administrative decree during the time the legislature is not sitting.

The balance of legislative and executive power in Fifth Republic France. It should be noted here that even with this lopsided executive structure (accompanied by blatant manipulations of voting procedures and districting, designed to reduce the strength of the leftwing parties) the French Fifth Republic has come very close to being defeated in its own legislature. In 1967 the premier had a very narrow majority in the National Assembly and only with the support of small center parties. The president thereupon asked the legislature to dissolve itself for six months under the emergency power provision. A censure motion was moved and defeated in the National Assembly, but only by a vote of 251 to 236, a very insecure margin indeed. Today the Gaullists have a much wider margin, but no one can say how long this will last either. Thus, as with the executive, the development of the French legislature will depend upon the configuration of party strength within it. So long as there is no party in the legislature willing and able to embarrass the president (by denying him a major legislative decision) the possible crisis will be deferred.

The judiciary. France is a country with a tradition of civil law. This approach to the law tends to keep courts outside the political process. In addition the strong republican tradition, which to Frenchmen means leaving policy decisions to elected officials, in France has, over the years, led to a basic unwillingness by French lawyers and judges to be drawn into political controversies. The practice of civil law courts, which handle cases according to written codes that minimize the opportunity for judges to establish legal precedents by their opinions, also serves to reduce the political potential of the courts in France. Thus, as in Great Britain, political questions are left to the

Chart 2.4.   France: The Structure of the Government

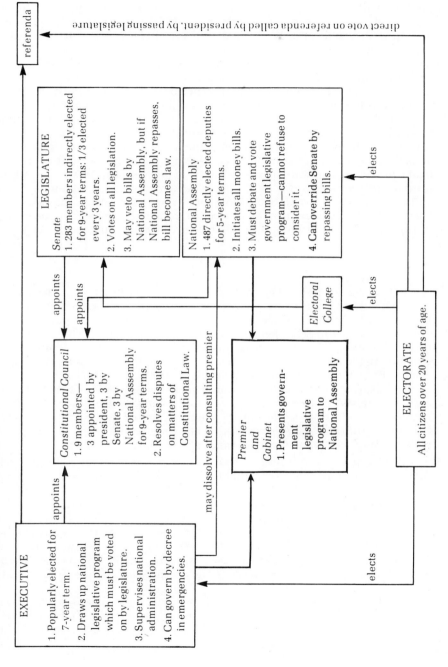

direct vote on referenda called by president, by passing legislature

referenda

EXECUTIVE

1. Popularly elected for 7-year term.
2. Draws up national legislative program which must be voted on by legislature.
3. Supervises national administration.
4. Can govern by decree in emergencies.

appoints

Constitutional Council

1. 9 members—3 appointed by president, 3 by Senate, 3 by National Asssembly for 9-year terms.
2. Resolves disputes on matters of Constitutional Law.

appoints

appoints

LEGISLATURE

Senate

1. 283 members indirectly elected for 9-year terms: 1/3 elected every 3 years.
2. Votes on all legislation.
3. May veto bills by National Assembly, but if National Assembly repasses, bill becomes law.

National Assembly

1. 487 directly elected deputies for 5-year terms.
2. Initiates all money bills.
3. Must debate and vote government legislative program—cannot refuse to consider it.
4. Can override Senate by repassing bills.

may dissolve after consulting premier

Premier and Cabinet

1. Presents government legislative program to National Assembly

Electoral College

elects

ELECTORATE

All citizens over 20 years of age.

elects

elects

elects

political bodies that are more directly elected by the people. French courts, even more than British courts, are outside the political process since judgeships in France are basically nonpolitical appointments. Judges emerge from a specialized educational structure and are recruited into judgeships on the basis of competitive civil service type examinations. Their prestige is not nearly so high as the prestige of judges in Anglo-Saxon countries, where judges are almost always appointed from a political-social elite and where they have considerable opportunity to express their personal views in the writing of opinions.

The Fifth Republic established a courtlike institution, the Constitutional Council, which was supposed to have something like the power of judicial review. This body can legally determine the scope of the president's power vis-a-vis the legislature, for example. It consists of nine men—one-third appointed by the president, one-third by the president of the National Assembly, and one-third by the president of the Senate. They serve nine-year terms and tend to be politicians, not jurists. This council has made some minor decisions but, since it basically runs against traditional French practices, it has not been very influential. (Chart 2.4 summarizes the structure of government in France.)

INDONESIA

Indonesia, an important trading center in Southeast Asia, became an independent state in 1949, before which it was known as the Netherlands East Indies. Unlike India's experience, Indonesian colonial history, particularly in the twentieth century, has been quite turbulent and violent. The Netherlands had in the nineteenth century established a very paternalistic administrative structure in the islands and had made very few efforts at gradually granting the colony the powers of self-government. Early in the twentieth century, a few advisory legislative councils were established, but a rebellion in 1927 (blamed on Communists) caused a violent reaction among Dutch colonial officials. Indonesian nationalist leaders were rounded up and sent to prison, and all fledgling political parties were dissolved. Suppression of political parties persisted until 1940 when Japan invaded and occupied the country.

The Japanese, who enlisted the aid of Indonesian nationalists by promising them eventual independence, established a puppet government that placed nationalist leaders in front of the public eye; nationalists were allowed access to nationwide radio and were able to create national political organizations so long as they did not hamper the Japanese war effort. The Japanese also trained and armed an Indonesian army, so that they might assist in fighting off any attempts by the Dutch to retake the country. When the Japanese were defeated in 1945, the Indonesians were left with a government led by nationalist leaders and a trained armed force. This government declared its independence of the Netherlands in 1945.

The Netherlands attempted to retake her colony, but she had only a weak military force and little world support in this endeavor. Thus, after four years of negotiations and intermittent military skirmishes, the Dutch formally granted Indonesia independence in 1949.

Indonesian politics since 1949 has been extremely stormy and fractionalized. In 1949 a parliamentary system was established with a ceremonial president and a cabinet responsible to an elected House of Representatives. In 1955, 170 political parties contested the national elections and 26 received representation in the house. This situation, which led to great cabinet instability, was ended in 1957 by President Sukarno who declared martial law and instituted his own program of Guided Democracy.

"Guided Democracy" was a system of government that banned the traditionally democratic parties and institutionalized competition among three groups—the nationalists, the Indonesian Communist Party (PKI), and the military. Indonesia never adopted a permanent written constitution, but Sukarno established mass organizations with hand-picked members from among the three groups and attempted to play the role of political broker among them. Great uncertainty and immobility resulted because the actual political positions of Indonesian leaders was unclear. This situation lasted until 1965 when open warfare broke out between the PKI and the military.

In 1965, one of Sukarno's own regiments tried to seize the government by force and in the process murdered six generals. The army blamed the coup on the PKI and proceeded to destroy the entire Communist apparatus, killing an estimated 300,000 persons in this effort. The army, which always represented the interests of the Outer Islands more sincerely than either the nationalists or the Communists, then restaffed the legislature with its own men. Lieutenant General Suharto was appointed acting president in 1967 and then president in 1968.

General Suharto has used the military to restore civilian life to a state of normalcy. He has also appointed some new councils and a new political party of his own. In 1971, the first parliamentary elections since 1955 were held—an event which may augur some new changes in the structure of power within the Indonesian system. The basic ethnic and regional divisions persist, however, and much has to be accomplished to reverse the pattern of administrative and economic deterioration. In the long run, these are the keys to the unity of Indonesia and states like her.

Territory and Population

The Republic of Indonesia, the largest state in Southeast Asia, covers an area more than twice the size of France. An archipelago stretching over 3,000 miles, it lies across the equator in the Indian and Pacific oceans between Malaysia and New Guinea. The nation occupies an extremely important strategic position between East and South Asia and historically has been an important center of trade. (see map, p. 72).

With a population estimated at over 118 million according to the 1971 census, Indonesia is the most populous state of Southeast Asia. The population is quite unevenly distributed among the islands. Almost two-thirds of the people live on Java and Madura, which comprise only about 6 percent of the land area. Other areas, such as Sumatra, are underpopulated but are very rich in natural resources.

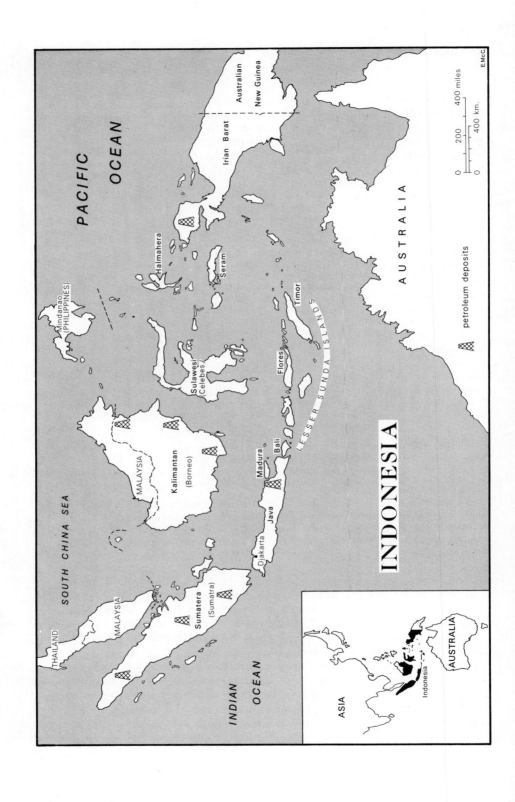

The Indonesian population is extremely complex, consisting of hundreds of tribal and ethnic groups. Seventeen language groups are recognized by the government, and different languages are spoken on different islands. Over 2 million Chinese in Indonesia maintain a separate cultural identity and are resented because of their dominant economic position. (A breakdown of population and land area appears in Table 2.6)

Indonesia is an underdeveloped country, but one very rich in natural resources. Only about 50 percent of the population is literate—a relatively low figure by Western standards. Almost 85 percent of the population is engaged in subsistence agriculture and is very poor. Since independence production in most fields had declined. Economic difficulties have added to the fragmentation of the country.

However, regionalism is the major source of Indonesia's fragmentation. Java, the seat of political power, has the bulk of the population. Leading nationalist and Communist groups have been based on Java (especially, on West Java), where the people are most overcrowded and impoverished. The Indonesian structure of government since 1950 has been a centralized one; a federal structure originally adopted in 1949 was tainted by Dutch affiliation and abandoned. In the centralized system, regions rich in resources are taxed and the revenue is spent in the areas where most of the people live. At various times, several Outer Islands have claimed their rights were being infringed upon and their resources were being exploited. There have been continual military clashes between the regions and Java over this issue. Communications among the islands are very difficult and national unity depends on a united military force.

Regional problems are compounded by other factors. Indonesia is primarily a Moslem country, but the practice of Islam on Java is quite different than that on

Table 2.6. Population of Indonesia

Area	Population (in millions)	Land Area (in thousands of square kilometers)	Density of Population (per square kilometer)
Java and Madura	76.1	122.0	623.7
Sumatra	20.8	457.0	45.5
Sulawesi (Celebes)	8.5	182.2	46.6
Nusa Tenggara (Outer Islands)	6.6	359.5	18.3
Kalimantan (Borneo)	5.2	717.2	7.2
West Irian	0.9	479.2	1.8
Total	118.1	2,317.1	50.9*

SOURCE: *Statistik Indonesia, 1970-71* (Djakarta: Central Bureau of Statistics, August 1972), pp. 22-3.

*Total includes Outer Islands and West Irian.

the Outer Islands. Javanese Islam has many Hindu elements and tends to be quite secular and tolerant; on the Outer Islands the population is much more devout and maintains Islam in a purer form. Thus many Javanese could be pro-Communist and Moslem at the same time; there are virtually no Communists in the Outer Islands. Thus there are some great difficulties in mutual understanding among the islands.

Indonesia's fragmentation has not challenged the nature of the state itself. Regional groupings, which have been quite nationalistic, have not favored secession or civil war. They accept Indonesia as their nation but would like special privileges within the system. Thus, there is continual pressure over the form of the state and the manner in which authority may be exercised.

Political Structure

The current political structure of Indonesia is a transformed version of Indonesia's political processes under Guided Democracy. By that system, executive powers were vested in a president, personified by Sukarno, the great nationalist leader.

Sukarno had never run for popular election in Indonesia. In 1949 he was appointed president, and in 1963, under Guided Democracy, president for life, by virtue of his special role as preeminent leader of the Indonesian revolution. He ran the country through a large legislature, the Provisional People's Consultative Congress (PPCC), to which he was able to appoint members. It is unclear how much power Sukarno actually exercised under the structure of Guided Democracy; it is clear he depended on the Communist party organization, which he tried to balance off against the military. When these two factions faced each other in 1965, the military crushed the Communists and arrested Sukarno, ending his political career. Sukarno was kept under house arrest until his death in 1970.

The executive today.   Today's Indonesian government vests total executive power in the hands of President Suharto. In 1966, immediately following the military takeover of the government, General Suharto took the position of acting president, while leaving Sukarno in the ceremonial role of head of state. In 1967 Suharto also assumed the position of prime minister and reorganized the cabinet, taking the position of defense minister in it. In 1968 he finally assumed the position of president and head of state.

Using his executive powers, Suharto, in 1968, dismissed 123 members of the PPCC and replaced them with his own nominees. He also increased the size of the legislature by sixty-seven seats, filling them with his own supporters.

In July of 1971 Indonesia held a general election to the legislature, the first such election since 1955. Politicians pledged to support Suharto won 73 percent of the seats, though many of the old political groups were permitted to compete to a certain extent. Suharto's supporters, through their tacit control of the military and the government administration, had a distinct advantage over their opponents and the result of the election was never in doubt. Suharto remains president, prime minister, and defense minister.

Chart 2.5.   Indonesia: The Structure of the Government

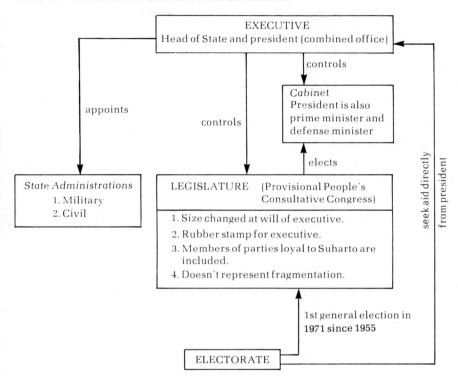

Today political decisions in Indonesia are made by President Suharto who, while personally in command, relies on advice from supporters in the military and the pre-Guided Democracy political parties. The president governs the country directly: most Indonesian provinces are governed by military administrators and legislative assemblies appointed by Suharto. The legislature can be changed in size and makeup by the president at his discretion, and the president himself has never stood for popular election, nor does he plan to do so in the near future. Indonesia's constitution is vague and Suharto draws his overriding power from his role as leader of the Indonesian military.

The legislature.   Under Guided Democracy, competitive political parties were outlawed. The previous national legislature, elected in 1955, was replaced by a rubber-stamp body consisting of representatives of functional and regional groups who were all handpicked by Sukarno. The supreme legislative body was the PPCC, and no parliamentary election was held while Sukarno was leader.

Policymaking in the country deteriorated rapidly under Guided Democracy into a situation in which decisions were avoided rather than made. There was no established system of ministerial responsibility, and the government took little action on important problems. Sukarno had relied on Communist organization to carry out his pet projects.

Under Suharto, many of the political parties that had existed before Guided Democracy were revived, while the Communist party has now been outlawed. The legislature is now popularly elected rather than appointed, and there has been some restoration of the rights of free speech and press.

On balance, however, the Indonesian legislature remains subservient to the president. Over the years precedents have been established that allow presidents to interfere in an open-handed way with the legislature's operations. Politics in Indonesia consists of persons seeking the favor of the president, rather than representing constituency interests. Thus while Indonesian society remains as complex as ever, this complexity is not recognized in or dealt with by the legislature, and solutions to all problems depend on presidential guidance and initiative.

The judiciary.   Indonesia's judiciary is patterned after the Dutch judiciary and is in some respects similar to that of the French. The law is codified but includes some customary practices that apply differently to different groups within Indonesian society. Indonesian villages are thus governed by customary law, while major national cases are heard in the national court system.

The Indonesian judiciary is not very prestigious and has almost no impact on politics. Indeed the entire modern judicial structure is very weak and few important controversies are brought before it. Its main role seems to be in handling the normal, routine matters in commercial and criminal areas, while important political conflicts are handled administratively or militarily. (The Indonesian government structure is outlined in Chart 2.5).

ZAIRE

Zaire, formerly called the Democratic Republic of the Congo, and before that the Belgian Congo, is one of the largest and wealthiest of African states. It is a relatively important state by virtue of an extraordinary wealth of natural resources, though it is relatively sparsely populated by world standards. It is an inland state and is central to a very large number of African tribal groupings.

Like Indonesia, Zaire has had an extremely stormy transition from colony to independence. Under Belgian rule, the Congo was developed economically and its population cared for with every kind of social service. Health care was probably better in the Congo than in any other area of the colonial world. The native population, trained by the Belgians in technical skills, had a very high literacy rate, although generally only to a sixth-grade level. Administration of the colony was carried out in a rather paternalistic manner by Belgian officials.

Belgian colonial policy was aimed at insulating the Congolese from the Belgian way of life and, thus, Belgian administrators communicated with natives in Congolese languages, rather than teaching the Congolese French. In this way different groups in the Congo continued to speak their own languages for official purposes, even under Belgian rule. Also, Belgian administration did not lead to the establishment of a permanent white upper class as often occurred in other African colonies. It was Belgian policy to allow European technicians and administrators to go to the Congo, but only on a temporary basis. The Belgians sought to leave the natural tribal and social structure virtually intact, wishing to work alongside it rather than reorganizing it.

Using this reasoning, Belgium was very slow to introduce to the Congo institutions of self-government, which were regarded by the Belgian government as Western and of little particular use in the Congolese situation. However, in the 1950s, as Great Britain and France began to grant independence to their African colonies, these new states entered world bodies such as the United Nations. Pressure was brought to bear, and Belgium, a relatively small country vulnerable to world opinion, established legislative councils and permitted the formation of political parties in the Congo in the late 1950s. Very soon after that and after much internal rioting in the Congo, Belgium agreed to grant the colony independence; a provisional constitution was signed in 1960.

The granting of independence, followed by the departure of Belgium's administrators and technicians, left very few persons in Zaire capable of keeping the administration together. Though an election was held and a president and prime minister were legally chosen under a new parliamentary style constitution, the new regime had little legitimacy and quickly collapsed. Leaders of provincial regions seceded from the central state; tribal warfare broke out everywhere; and various outside powers tried to take advantage of the chaos. Only after much killing and the use of the United Nations military forces was anything like unity restored to the country. The result was a political structure that centered authority in the hands of General Joseph Mobutu (now called Mobutu Sese Seko), leader of the armed forces. General Mobutu had intervened in the political process on several occasions. Finally in 1965 he dismissed the government and proclaimed himself president.

Territory and Population

Zaire is located in equatorial Africa, entirely inland except for a twenty-five mile strip of land on the Atlantic Ocean near the mouth of the Zaire River. It is a very large country, occupying a land area four times the size of France and larger than the states of Texas and Alaska combined. The Zaire River, one of the world's longest, flows more than 2,700 miles through this large and varied country (see map, p.78). Zaire has highlands, lowlands, and jungle areas and is well endowed with the abundant wildlife for which Africa is famous —elephants, gorillas, lions, and hippopotamus among others.

Zaire is extremely rich in mineral and agricultural resources. The country produces 6 percent of the world's copper and 45 percent of the world's cobalt and industrial diamonds. The country also has deposits of gold, uranium, zinc, and iron. Zaire also produces and exports timber, coffee, cotton, rubber, tea, and cocoa.

Estimated in 1971 at 20.5 million, the population of Zaire, though relatively small, is extremely diverse. Zaire contains people from well over 200 tribes that

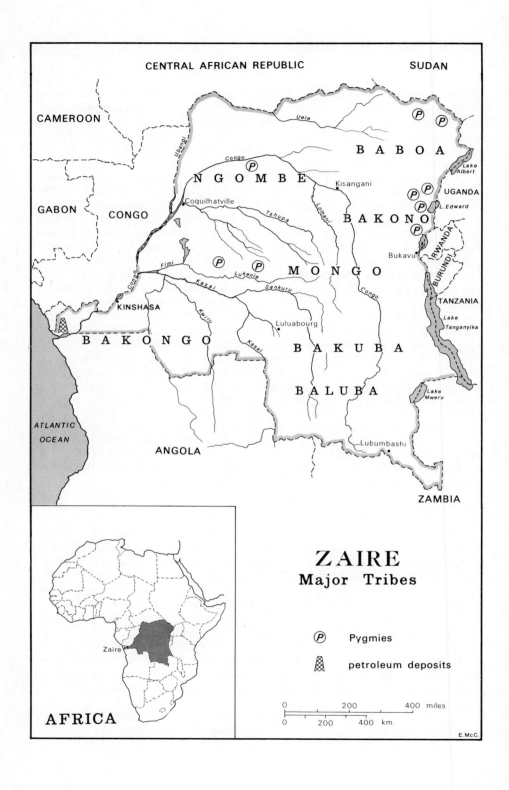

CENTRAL AFRICAN REPUBLIC

SUDAN

CAMEROON

GABON

CONGO

Uele

B A B O A

N G O M B E

Congo

Kisangani

Coquilhatville

Tshupa

Lomani

B A K O N O

Lake Albert

UGANDA

L. Edward

RWANDA

BURUNDI

Bukavu

Congo

M O N G O

Fimi

Lukenie

Kasai

Sankuru

KINSHASA

Kwilu

Luluabourg

B A K O N G O

Kasai

B A K U B A

B A L U B A

TANZANIA

Lake Tanganyika

Lake Mweru

ATLANTIC OCEAN

ANGOLA

Lubumbashi

ZAMBIA

ZAIRE
Major Tribes

AFRICA

Zaire

Ⓟ   Pygmies

⬚   petroleum deposits

0   200   400 miles

0   200   400 km.

E. McC.

fall within three major ethnic subdivisions—Negroes (Bantu, Sudanese, and Nilotic); Pygmies; and Hamites. These large groups are culturally and linguistically quite different from one another and have maintained historic rivalries. Indeed, over 700 different spoken dialects are used in Zaire. (Table 2.7 presents a regional breakdown of Zaire's population.)

Many tribal groupings are generally traditional in outlook and tend to be fairly isolated from one another and from the central government. The social systems of these groups are structured by custom and receive little information or influence from the outside. Because there is so little communication among conflicting tribes, tribal warfare can become quite uncompromising and exaggerated. Zaire has suffered from a series of such confrontations, resulting in much bloodshed during the first years of independence. The aftermath of this warfare has been a continuation of tribal and ethnic hostility, which occasionally still erupts into open fighting.

Zaire, while rich in resources and important in certain industries, such as mining, is basically not an industrialized country. Only a small portion of its people work in modern occupations and have some contact with modern thought. Thus, about one-third of the population, evidently trained in mission schools, professes Western religion (5 million Catholics, 1 million Protestants). These persons tend to live in the towns. The tribal groups (two-thirds of the population) still live a basically subsistence way of life, depending on hunting and gathering for their food supply. While there is some modern agriculture (a major source of exports), this does not really touch the tribal populations very much. They generally remain in their small cultural units, though today there seems to be some gradual movement of people from villages to the larger towns.

Table 2.7. Population of Zaire

Area	Population (in millions)	Land Area (in thousands of square kilometers)	Density of Population (per square kilometer)
Kinshasa	1.4	2.0	700.0
Bandundu	3.1	299.9	10.3
Haut Zaire	3.0	503.2	5.9
Kasai Orientale	1.8	61.8	29.1
Kasai Occidentale	1.7	261.3	6.5
Kivu	3.4	259.1	13.1
Bas-Zaire	1.6	59.1	27.0
Shaba (previously Katanga)	2.1	497.0	4.2
Equateur	2.4	402.1	5.9
Total	20.5*	2,345.5	8.7

SOURCE: United Nations, *Monthly Bulletin of Statistics* (New York, 1972).

*Data is based on estimates for 1971.

Political fragmentation is basic and fundamental to Zaire. While Indonesia is also a basically fragmented society, its problems in this regard are not quite as severe as Zaire's. The major political groups within Indonesia, as in France, agree on the size of the state and the population within it. In contrast, a large portion of the population in Zaire is simply unaware of or disagrees with the established boundaries of the state. Many tribes spread across African frontiers, a geographic situation not possible in an island country like Indonesia, where frontiers are insulated from one another by oceans. While national consciousness is much stronger on Java than on the Outer Islands, regional rebellions in Indonesia have generally aimed at reforming the national government, not at seceding from it. In Zaire, the heartlands of many tribes are found not within the country, but across the border. Thus, political rebellions have generally aimed at secession, not takeover or transformation of the national state. For example, Katanga, one of Zaire's richest provinces, has resorted to military rebellion several times in attempts to establish itself as an independent state.

There is little cultural unity among the people of Zaire: they have not fought a revolutionary war together; they have never been governed in a uniform manner; they have had little opportunity to develop national institutions within which they could communicate with one another; they do not share a single religious tradition. Zaire thus achieved the legal status of nation well before her people had a strong organized national consciousness. This situation is compounded by tribal complexities that are found throughout Africa: many tribes, whose economies lead them to migrate seasonally (i. e., hunting or grazing cattle), never develop loyalty to any territory. Rather, they express their loyalties to tribal or familial groups. Thus many people in Zaire feel closer to tribal brothers in Angola than they do to their fellow countrymen.

This situation raises some complex theoretical problems referred to in Chapter 1. The issue of whether a wandering tribe with little permanent connection to the land can be regarded as a nation, as defined in international law, is difficult to resolve. Despite the actual loyalties of persons to family and tribal groups, African political leaders generally profess a very Western concept of nationality. They are concerned about their borders even though much of their population may not be. Yet when so little fundamental loyalty links the people to the government, many African states, like Zaire, are understandably weak.

Political Structure

The constitution of 1960 established a parliamentary structure of government with a president serving as symbolic head of state (with some powers) and a prime minister responsible to a House of Representatives. The first president of Zaire was Joseph Kasavubu and the first prime minister was Patrice Lumumba. Lumumba was leader of the largest party, the Mouvement National Congolais (MNC), which held 74 of 137 seats in the Chamber of Deputies. Kasavubu was head of a rival party, the Abako.

Upon independence, there was a mutiny in the army and Moise Tshombe, leader of Katanga, declared his province independent. Prime Minister Lumumba requested military assistance from the United Nations and Secretary General Dag Hammarskjold dispatched United Nations forces to Zaire, but only on condition that they not interfere in internal political rivalries. The troops could therefore not be used by Lumumba against Tshombe. Colonel Mobutu of the army seized power and dismissed both prime ministers—Tshombe and Lumumba—and the president. Lumumba was arrested and mysteriously killed. Zaire thereupon disintegrated into four rival regions, each with its own leader—Kasavubu and Mobutu in Leopoldville, Antoine Gizenga (Lumumba's successor) in Stanleyville, Moise Tshombe in Katanga, and Albert Kalonji in Kasai.

After four years of intermittent tribal warfare and clashes with United Nations troops and much interference from outside powers, Zaire succeeded in reestablishing a degree of unity. The war had brought much turmoil, including the use of hired white mercenaries, open rivalry between the United States and the Soviet Union in terms of supplying equipment to different sides, the death of Secretary General Hammarskjold in a plane crash, and the exile of Tshombe (who eventually was kidnapped and murdered in 1969). In 1965 Mobutu declared himself president for the second time. He was able to establish his authority by relying on the military and by having several ministers executed on the grounds they had conspired to overthrow him. Mobutu then proceeded to establish a structure of government in Zaire that he thought would center all authority in his hands.

The executive. The current structure of government, established in a new constitution adopted by a referendum in 1967 and approved by 90 percent of the voters, centers all power in the president—Mobutu Sese Seko—who is also chief executive, defense minister, and commander in chief of the armed forces. The president is elected for a seven-year term by universal suffrage.

He makes all executive and legislative decisions. President Mobutu has suspended the operation of all political parties; the only political organization in Zaire today is the Popular Revolution Movement (MPR), a mass organization sponsored by the president and pledged to his support. Mobutu is assisted in his decisionmaking by advisors, the eight-member National Security Council. The president is personally in command of the army and the police, the major source of his political power.

The legislature. The constitution of Zaire establishes a unicameral legislature, the National Assembly, to be elected every five years. The constitution stipulates that only two parties may exist, but only the MPR has been permitted to organize. The president also has a cabinet, the National Security Council, to assist him in administration. These ministers are responsible to Mobutu and not the legislature; the latter acts as a mere rubber stamp. Many administrative tasks are still carried out by the military, the group most loyal to Mobutu.

The judiciary. In Zaire judges are presidential appointees. There seems to be some precedent for judicial participation in politics since the 1965 elections were overturned by the Appeals Court on the ground of electoral irregularities.

Chart 2.6. Zaire: The Structure of the Government

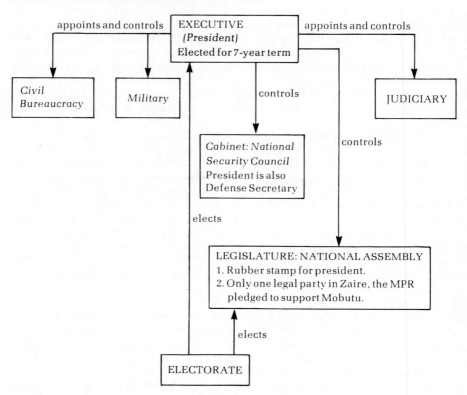

Thus, in the past, political questions have been brought before the courts in Zaire. Today, however, the judiciary, as much as other governmental institutions, is subservient to the will of the president, who makes all appointments and controls all decisions. (The structure of the government of Zaire is summarized in Chart 2.6.)

Comparative Distinctions in Political Structures Among Fragmented States

France, Indonesia, and Zaire have some basic similarities in governmental structure, reflecting the inherent political disunity of each state. All three states have large numbers of unreconciled political groups that have not been able to develop political institutions—like parties and legislatures—that can for very long peacefully represent the social divisions of the community in the national political structure. All three countries have had turbulent and recurring political crises (in some cases, spilling over into civil war) and have reacted to them by placing the preponderance of power in the hands of an executive who rules not through a legislature or political parties, but through the military and bureaucracy. This executive, in turn, has not developed overwhelming legitimacy, and group dissatisfaction on a broad scale persists in all three states.

Beyond these broad similarities certain distinctions should be drawn, however, among the three states. France, unlike Indonesia and Zaire, is a modern, highly developed country with a well-fed, literate populace and a tradition of civilian representative government. While structurally the president of France rules the country with little difficulty from the legislature and the political parties, French government does indeed depend on public support. France has free elections and a free press. The French vote for their favorite politicians; French popular opposition to the president may still one day change the nature of the regime—a fairly common occurrence in the history of France.

French history though superficially similar to Chilean history is in some important respects different: in Chile the Congress and the political parties have for a long time been powerful institutions capable of developing popular backing and normally have shared power with the president. When this sharing broke down, the Congress and opposition parties were able to force the president to take military advisers and opened the way for the military overthrow of the president. France, in contrast, has not historically been able to develop a sharing of power between executive and legislature. In legislative periods, the French executive has been at the mercy of the legislature; in executive periods, the situation has been reversed. France remains, however, a country with a civilian government generally responsible to civilian groups.

In comparison to France both Indonesia and Zaire, which have had briefer experience with representative institutions, have concentrated far more power and legitimacy in the persons of their respective presidents. Both countries have regimes in which the president rules primarily through the military rather than the civilian administration. In both these countries legislative institutions and political parties that exist do so with the permission and sponsorship of the president rather than because of widespread public support. The generally low level of economic development of these two countries has meant that their respective populations have a low level of national political awareness and little basic economic or cultural unity on the national level. Thus, under the superficial facade of presidential dictatorships the Indonesian and Congolese communities remain divided and fragmented into many competing groups that retain their regional and tribal loyalties.

POLITICAL STRUCTURES AND INSTITUTIONS IN NONCOMPETITIVE STATES

Patterns of Similarity

Where some states have established rules for governing politics through orderly competition, and others have been so socially fragmented that no system seems very secure, a third group of states has evolved political frameworks that do not genuinely respect the value of open competition.

In these states authority tends to be viewed as legitimate only when it is monolithic and uncontested. The underlying social structure must also be rather monolithic, and general attitudes among the population tend to regard open criticism of political authority as not only of little value, but basically immoral. Thus the institutions and structures within which open competition occurs in competitive states are not regarded from the same ideological viewpoint in noncompetitive states. Political parties, if they are permitted to exist, must be severely restricted in their rights to free and open speech. Elections, if they are conducted, must present a monolithic seal of approval for the regime of the day. Legislatures must also speak with unanimity on public issues.

A noncompetitive political structure must rest on a social structure that supports this view of authority. Three examples of noncompetitive states are the Union of Soviet Socialist Republics (USSR), Egypt, and the People's Republic of China (PRC). These states, quite divergent in their levels of economic development and in their traditional cultures, are similar, however, in that they have developed political structures that are, on the surface, entirely monolithic, concentrating all decisionmaking power in a small self-acknowledged elite. They are also similar in that the wider society in each system seems to accept this organization of politics as moral and ideologically correct. Groups and individuals in these states do not generally believe in openly challenging political leaders or in publically stating their grievances. These activities are most often left for informal bargaining and maneuvering behind closed doors.

Noncompetitive states are emphatically different from fragmented states, in which authoritarian factions can occasionally seize power. In such states the power structure is always transforming itself to allow the various fragments of society to become part of the system. In noncompetitive states, society is unified and not fragmented; the majority of the people support the state and value the monolithic structure of politics as a moral and ideological virtue.

Three Case Studies: The USSR, Egypt, and the PRC

UNION OF SOVIET SOCIALIST REPUBLICS

The Soviet Union, before 1917 known as the Russian Empire, is today the largest country on earth territorially and one of the most powerful militarily. It is also an authoritarian state, which historically has never valued open political competition.

Russia, the last country in Europe to free its serfs (1861), continued its basically feudal social and class structure into the twentieth century. The absolute monarchy lasted until the 1860s. In the latter part of the nineteenth century, however, the monarchy began to encourage industrial expansion and this led to the emergence of a small Russian middle class. Political discontent with the absolute power of the tsar began to build and culminated in the revolution.

The Revolution of 1905 was an abortive attempt to force the tsar to restrict his own power. Its major success was in forcing the tsar to appoint a legislative council, the Duma. This was Russia's first nominally representative institution in modern times. The Duma, however, had little power. By 1905 the population of the British colony of India had greater powers of self-government and representation than did the people of imperial Russia.

During World War I Russia lost a great deal in men and material, and its ancient political structure was considerably weakened. In 1917 a successful revolution was staged by republican moderates, who overthrew the tsar. This "March Revolution" was quickly succeeded by the Bolshevik "October Revolution," which was far more radical. The tsar and his family were killed, and the traditional structures of authority and legitimacy came under attack. Over the next twenty years religion, education, and all voluntary associations came under direct government supervision. All political officials throughout the country, at every level, were replaced by ideologically trained members of the new Communist party of the Soviet Union (CPSU). Merely expressing loyalty or support for the new regime was not enough: the new state was as monolithic and authoritarian as the old; it demanded skilled and active support, not mere passive obedience.

The Bolshevik Revolution has, since 1917, gone through various stages, and the structure of the state has changed to reflect these stages. Immediately following the Revolution of 1917, the USSR, under the leadership of V. I. Lenin, experimented with many political and social reforms. This open, euphoric period in Russian history lasted only briefly. Lenin died in 1924 and the fight among prospective candidates to succeed him as leader of the CPSU became violent and cruel. By 1928 Joseph Stalin emerged as the dominant personality within the system and he proceeded to entrench his position by "purging" his opponents. The main instrument in this purge was the secret police, an organization established in 1918 under Lenin's regime. Stalin's main rival, Leon Trotsky, was banished and later murdered in Mexico. Over the years, many of Stalin's lesser opponents were tried and executed for trumped-up charges, while many others were exiled.

Stalin's regime was authoritarian and utilized terrorist techniques. The country was forcibly industrialized, suffering the deaths of millions in the collectivization of agriculture. A secret police apparatus was established (a familiar political mechanism under the tsars) and complete control was exercised over all voluntary associations and all media of communication. Stalin was as absolute a ruler as any tsar.

Since Stalin's death in 1953 there has been a gradual shift away from the use of terror in the USSR. Authority is still concentrated in a very small number of hands, and there is no open political competition in any meaningful sense. The leaders of the Soviet Communist party attain their position by working up the party hierarchy; decisions are made and leaders selected informally within this hierarchy. Political infighting can still be cruel, but murder and the use of the police are no longer considered normal in any given power struggle. Antigovernment protest appears small in scale and limited to members of the intelligentsia—artists, writers, historians, and scientists among others—and to members of the disaffected nationalities—Jews, Crimeans, and Tatars. The broad mass of the Soviet people evidently support their regime.

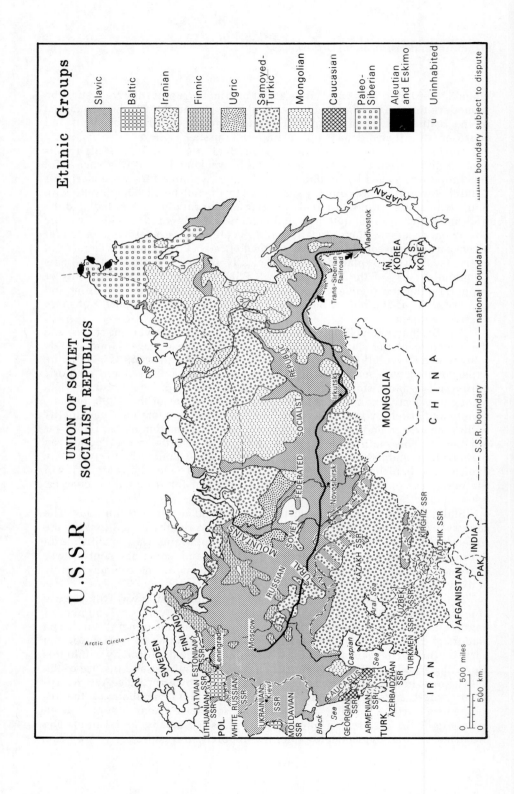

U.S.S.R

UNION OF SOVIET
SOCIALIST REPUBLICS

Ethnic Groups

Slavic

Baltic

Iranian

Finnic

Ugric

Samoyed-
Turkic

Mongolian

Caucasian

Paleo-
Siberian

Aleutian
and Eskimo

u Uninhabited

.... boundary subject to dispute

──── national boundary

──── S.S.R. boundary

Arctic Circle

SWEDEN

FINLAND

LATVIAN SSR
LITHUANIAN SSR
ESTONIAN SSR
POL.
WHITE RUSSIAN
SSR
Leningrad
Moscow
UKRAINIAN
SSR
Kiev
MOLDAVIAN
SSR
Black Sea
CAUCASUS
GEORGIAN SSR
ARMENIAN SSR
AZERBAIDZHAN
SSR
TURK.
Caspian Sea

RUSSIAN

URAL MOUNTAINS

SOVIET

FEDERATED

SOCIALIST

REPUBLIC

Novosibirsk

Irkutsk

Trans-Siberian
Railroad

Vladivostok

N. KOREA
S. KOREA

JAPAN

MONGOLIA

CHINA

Aral Sea
KAZAKH SSR
UZBEK SSR
TURKMEN SSR
KIRGHIZ SSR
TADZHIK SSR
IRAN
AFGANISTAN
PAK. INDIA
TURK.

0   500 miles
0   500 km.

Territory and Population

The USSR, by far the world's largest country, covers one-seventh of the Earth's surface (see map, p.86). It ranks third, behind China and India, in population, which in 1970, was estimated to be 241.9 million.

Much of the USSR, in comparison to European Russia, is relatively underpopulated: the Arctic region, because of its severe climate; and Soviet Asia and Central Asia, because of their meager resources and poor communications. Table 2.8 presents a regional breakdown of population in the USSR.

In terms of population the USSR is a complex state, containing over 100 separate ethnic groups. These include major racial and linguistic groups—Indo-European, Altaic, Caucasian, Uralian, and other smaller Asian groups. There are large Turkic and Mongol minorities, especially in Central Asia, where they constitute majorities in their respective provinces. These peoples have different, not mutually intelligible languages and great cultural diversity. There are also many religious groups in the USSR, though the government sometimes regards these as "nationalities" (e. g., the Jews). Religion appears to be of little importance in the USSR, except when it takes on the aura of a nationality question.

In terms of population and culture, the country is dominated by the so-called Great Russians of European Russia. These people, who comprise about 50

Table 2.8. Population of the Soviet Union

Constituent Republics	Population (in millions)	Land Area (in thousands of square kilometers)	Density of Population (per square kilometer)
RSFSR*	130.1	17,075	7.6
Ukraine	47.1	601	78.3
Kazakhstan	12.9	2,756	4.6
Uzbekistan	12.0	409	29.3
Belorussia	9.0	208	43.2
Georgia	4.7	70	67.1
Azerbaijan	5.1	87	58.6
Moldavia	3.6	34	105.8
Lithuania	3.1	64	48.4
Kirgizia	2.9	198	14.6
Tadzhikistan	2.9	143	20.2
Latvia	2.4	64	37.5
Armenia	2.5	30	83.3
Turkmenistan	2.2	468	4.7
Estonia	1.4	45	31.1
Total	241.9	22,232	10.8

SOURCE: *National Economy of the USSR, Statistical Summary* (Moscow, 1970).

*Russian Soviet Federal Socialist Republic.

percent of the total population, are also the best educated and highly trained people in the country. The Great Russians, taken together with the other Indo-European groups (Ukrainians, Byelorussions, Poles, and Slovaks among others) comprise two-thirds of the country's population.

The Soviet Union is a Western country, mainly because the Great Russians, the most Westernized group within it, have been able gradually to assume dominance in the country vis-a-vis the Mongolian groups. Westernization can be seen in the development of modern architecture and the arts, massive industrialization, and a modern urban style of living especially in Moscow and Leningrad (formerly St. Petersburg). The USSR today is much more like its capitalist rivals in Western Europe in terms of living patterns than it is like its Asian counterpart, the People's Republic of China.

The USSR is thus a highly developed, highly literate country. With its great investment in military and capital goods, it is one of the major military powers of the world, along with the United States. Because of its correspondingly lower investment in light industry and consumer goods, it is a much less affluent society, however, and its people work longer hours for fewer material rewards than do most peoples of Western Europe and North America.

Political Structure

In terms of its constitution of 1936 currently in effect, the USSR has a federal system and a parliamentary form of government. The structures of government at all levels are elaborately maintained, but they do not perform the same functions as similar structures in competitive states.

The country is formally designated a federal state, composed of fifteen legally equal Soviet Socialist (Union) Republics. Each of these retain some formal powers according to the constitution and are governed internally by their own legislative and executive institutions. As on the national level, each republic has an elected Supreme Soviet (legislature), a Presidium (steering committee), and a Council of Ministers. The USSR also has twenty Autonomous Regions—smaller units than the Union Republics—which also have an internally elected government structure. There are also ten National Regions, which are administered by the central government, but are located within the Russian Soviet Federal Socialist Republic (RSFSR).

The legislature.   The legislature of the USSR, the Supreme Soviet, consists of two chambers—the Soviet of the Union and the Soviet of Nationalities. The Soviet of the Union (the lower house) is elected on the basis of one deputy for every 300,000 citizens.

The Soviet of Nationalities (the upper house) formally represents the complex of political units established in the Soviet federal system. Thus the largest units, the Union Republics, elect twenty-five deputies each to the Soviet; Autonomous Republics elect eleven deputies each; Autonomous Regions elect five deputies each; and National Regions elect one deputy each.

The Supreme Soviet is elected for a four-year term and technically passes all the bills that become the country's legislation. It also may amend the constitution by a two-thirds majority in both chambers. Both houses are formally equal in power. In 1962 there were 791 members of the Soviet of the Union, 652 in the Soviet of Nationalities.

The executive.   The Supreme Soviet elects a Presidium, a group of men which is headed by a chairman, the nominal chief of state of the USSR. In formal terms, the Presidium is a steering committee for the Supreme Soviet. The Presidium, which in 1971 consisted of thirty-seven members, is a much more manageable body than either of the massive chambers of the Supreme Soviet. Thus the Presidium convenes the Supreme Soviet, issues decrees, dissolves the Supreme Soviet and orders new elections, conducts national referendums, awards honors and titles, orders general or partial mobilization, ratifies treaties, appoints and receives diplomatic representatives, and can proclaim martial law. The Presidium, therefore, even on paper, retains most of the formal executive powers vis-a-vis the total Supreme Soviet.

The USSR also has a Council of Ministers, defined by the constitution as the chief executive organ in the country. It is accountable to either the Supreme Soviet or the Politburo, when the Supreme Soviet is not in session. The members of the Council of Ministers formally head the administrative departments of the USSR. In practice, however, the ministries are constantly being revised by the Politburo. In formal terms, the Council of Ministers carries on the departments, executes the economic plans, and sets guidelines for the enforcement of major measures in the USSR.

The Council of Ministers is formally equivalent to the cabinet in a parliamentary system. Its members form an interlocking directorate with leaders of the Presidium, and usually the same men have the highest posts in both bodies. Thus the same men who direct party policy also directly control the state administrative apparatus.

The judiciary.   The USSR is a country with only limited traditions of the rule of law. Judges can be said to be trained and recruited as members of a bureaucracy, but the Soviet bureaucracy is permeated by political factions and party considerations. There is no tradition of judicial participation in political decisions while there are strong traditions of political interference with judicial proceedings. The Soviet court structure, as do other formal structures, serves the interests of the Soviet Communist party and, even though the use of terror has lessened, party leaders stand above the judiciary and judicial proceedings.

Sources of Legitimacy

Ideologically, the USSR professes to be a Marxist-Leninist state, and this theory holds that formal government is an instrument of oppression by one class over another. According to the theory, the state will "wither away" (i. e., the government will disappear once the working class is in power). On the basis of this line of reasoning, the Soviet apparatus has never invested formal in-stitutions of government with great legitimate power. Decisionmaking authority has not been vested in formal government institutions, but in the single political party in the country, the Communist Party of the Soviet Union (CPSU). (The structure of this organization is discussed at length in Chap. 5.)

Chart 2.7.   The Soviet Union: The Structure of the Government

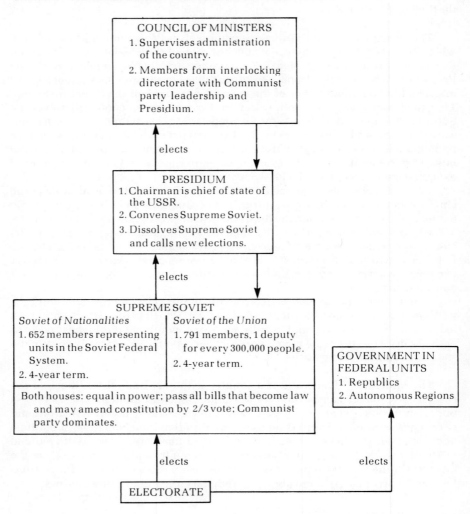

COUNCIL OF MINISTERS
1. Supervises administration of the country.
2. Members form interlocking directorate with Communist party leadership and Presidium.

elects

PRESIDIUM
1. Chairman is chief of state of the USSR.
2. Convenes Supreme Soviet.
3. Dissolves Supreme Soviet and calls new elections.

elects

SUPREME SOVIET

Soviet of Nationalities
1. 652 members representing units in the Soviet Federal System.
2. 4-year term.

Soviet of the Union
1. 791 members, 1 deputy for every 300,000 people.
2. 4-year term.

Both houses: equal in power; pass all bills that become law and may amend constitution by 2/3 vote; Communist party dominates.

GOVERNMENT IN FEDERAL UNITS
1. Republics
2. Autonomous Regions

elects   elects

ELECTORATE

The Soviet system, despite its elaborate formal structure, is thus not based on the same concept as are competitive states, which have superficially similar structures. In the USSR, where there are formal elections and the establishment of massive legislative bodies, there is no great respect for public opinion and no desire to represent that opinion. The CPSU is an elite group or "vanguard," not just a political party trying to sell itself to the general community on the same basis as similar parties. The CPSU does not regard itself as legitimately in power because the people elected it (as would be the case in a competitive system).

Rather, it regards itself as the unique bearer of a historic mission, which it alone understands. It pursues this mission single-mindedly, while trying to educate the population to its purpose. Thus the system of responsibility is reversed; the people are held responsible for following the dictates of a wise and all-knowing party. The Soviet concept of democracy thus achieves its legitimacy not through the majoritarian support of the people demonstrated in an election; legitimacy is derived from the commitment of party leaders to pursue actions that anticipate the expressed or deduced needs of the people. The party may not be unseated by the people through any formal institution. Also, no other parties are permitted because ideologically only the CPSU is considered virtuous and true. Ideological changes can occur only within the CPSU, where interpretations are discussed by the most "enlightened" men; it is not considered legitimate for non-Communists to interfere in the interpretation of Communist doctrine.

Elections in the USSR, while institutionalized and respected, thus, do not serve the purpose of registering public opinion in an arena where conflicting parties and candidates confront each other. The CPSU is considered the only legitimate spokesman because it is the only ideologically pure institution in the state. Thus it is not quite moral or legitimate for the CPSU to face some other party on an equal basis. Elections, therefore, do not present choice in policy. Generally every district will have only one official candidate running for office, and voters may vote only for or against the official candidate. Negative votes have never amounted to more than 1 percent of the ballots cast in any Soviet national election. In any event, the elected institutions themselves have little power since all important policy decisions are made by the party, not by the elected government structures.

The Soviet constitutional structure thus appears to be a facade behind which a relatively monolithic elite (the CPSU) can control the state. The basic functions of the elected structures are educational, not political. By having national elections, the CPSU can present its views to the people and engage their active support. Also, elections symbolically reaffirm the legitimacy of the regime, and the contact with party leaders that elections promote tends to revitalize public spirit and enthusiasm. By having large formal executive and legislative institutions, and a federal system, the USSR can reward groups and individuals with symbolic posts and symbolic representation. The top leaders of the government are the top men in the CPSU, and there never can be any real independence of government policy within the party structure. In the USSR there is one legitimate source of authority—communist doctrine as expounded by the Soviet Communist party. (The structure of the government of the USSR is presented in Chart 2.7.)

EGYPT

Egypt is a nation with an ancient culture and history. In modern times, however, she has been subjugated by a variety of foreign powers. From the early nineteenth century until World War I, Egypt was governed by an absolute monarchy as part of the Ottoman (Turkish) Empire, which itself was a

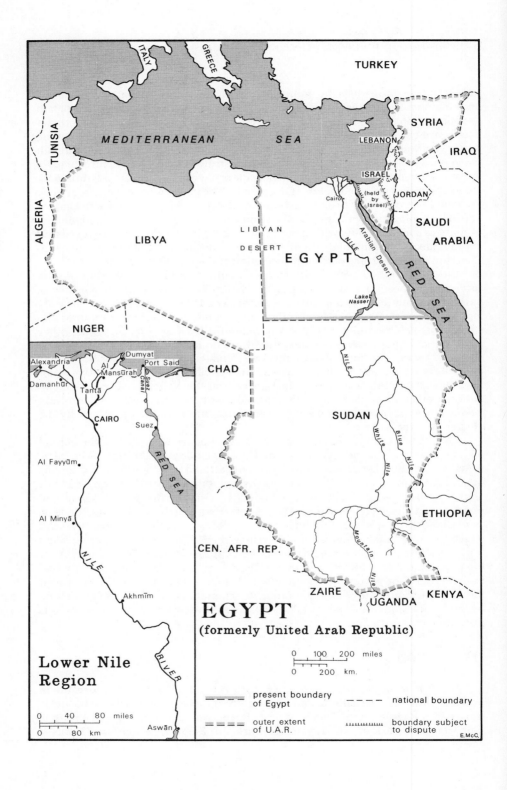

TURKEY

GREECE

ITALY

SYRIA

LEBANON

IRAQ

MEDITERRANEAN   SEA

ISRAEL

Cairo

(held
by
Israel)

JORDAN

ALGERIA

TUNISIA

SAUDI

ARABIA

LIBYAN

DESERT

EGYPT

NILE

Arabian Desert

RED SEA

LIBYA

Lake
Nasser

NIGER

NILE

CHAD

SUDAN

White Nile

Blue Nile

CEN. AFR. REP.

ETHIOPIA

Mountain Nile

ZAIRE

UGANDA

KENYA

EGYPT
(formerly United Arab Republic)

0   100   200 miles

0   200 km.

present boundary
of Egypt

national boundary

outer extent
of U.A.R.

boundary subject
to dispute

E.McC.

Lower Nile Region

Alexandria

Dumyat

Port Said

Al
Mansūrah

Damanhūr

Tanta

Suez Canal

CAIRO

Suez

RED SEA

Al Fayyūm

Al Minyā

NILE

Akhmīm

0   40   80 miles

0   80 km

RIVER

Aswān

protectorate of Great Britain. Egypt while internally self-governing, had little control over its foreign affairs. The British were able to extract major concessions from Egypt's kings (such as control over the Suez Canal) by lending them relatively small sums of money. The British also maintained troops in the country as well as a British High Commission. The country had few popular institutions, and the nationalist movement had to operate more as an underground conspiracy than as an open political party. In legal terms, Egypt was a British protectorate.

After World War I, the Ottoman Empire collapsed and was formally and legally dismembered under provisions of the Treaty of Versailles. Egypt became an independent monarchy but still remained under British influence. The new constitution of Egypt (1923) established a parliamentary style government. Two-fifths of the upper house (Senate) was appointed by the king; the lower house (Assembly) was indirectly elected by universal male suffrage. This system saw the nationalists, now organized in the Wafd party, come to prominence. Parliamentary government, however, lasted only from 1923 to 1928, when King Fuad dissolved the Parliament and carried on government by royal decree. He was succeeded by his son, Faruk I, in 1936. Faruk, a notably corrupt and ineffectual ruler, remained in nominal power with British support until 1952, when he was overthrown by the military. The government of 1952, first headed by General Mohammed Naguib, and in 1954, by General Gamal Abd al-Nasser, established the political system Egypt retains today.

Territory and Population

Egypt occupies the northeast corner of Africa and the Sinai Peninsula (Sinai has been occupied by Israel since the 1967 War). The country straddles the Suez Canal and in peacetime should guard the crossroads from the Indian Ocean to the Mediterranean Sea. Thus, at a major junction for world trade, Egypt is seen as strategic by all world powers from a military point of view (see map, p.92).

The population of Egypt today is estimated as approximately 32 million. Since 96 percent of Egypt's land area is uninhabitable desert, almost all of Egypt's people live along the 750-mile stretch of the Nile River. Parts of the Nile Valley can be as wide as 14 miles, but other areas are narrow gorges. The Nile Delta, which widens to form a triangular area of 155 miles from East to West and 100 miles from North to South, contains over 20 million people. With the population of the canal zone area, this yields a population density of over 732 people per square kilometer, one of the most densely populated areas in the world—comparable only to parts of China, India, and West Java. (Table 2.9 presents a breakdown by area of Egypt's population.)

The population of Egypt is fairly homogeneous. The vast majority of the people are Moslem and speak Arabic. Although there are many dialects, they are generally mutually intelligible. About 8 percent of Egypt's population are Coptic Christians. These people are mostly concentrated in Middle Egypt. In the towns, they tend to be better trained than the average Egyptian, usually being found in clerical positions and having a reputation for manual skills; in the country they live with and mix well with the rest of the population.

Table 2.9. Population of Egypt

Governates	Population (in millions)	Land Area (in thousands of square kilometers)	Density of Population (per square kilometer)
Cairo	4.22	0.21	19,701.2
Alexandria	1.80	0.28	6,217.6
Port Said	0.28	0.30	912.3
Suez	0.26	0.83	313.7
Ismailia	0.34	0.39	855.5
Damietta	0.43	0.60	717.6
Behera	1.97	4.59	428.9
Gharbiga	1.90	1.99	952.6
Daqahliya	2.28	3.46	658.5
Sharqiya	2.11	4.70	448.7
Munhtiya	1.46	1.51	964.2
Qalyubiya	1.22	0.94	1,292.9
Kafr el Shiek	1.12	3.49	320.6
Giza	1.65	1.08	1,529.9
Beni Suef	0.93	1.31	708.4
Faiyam	0.94	1.79	524.5
Menya	1.71	2.27	752.0
Asyut	1.42	1.55	914.3
Syhag	1.69	1.54	1,097.2
Qena	1.47	1.81	811.8
Aswan	0.52	0.88	589.4
Red Sea	0.03	--	--
New Valley	0.06	--	--
Matruh	0.12	--	--
Sinai	0.13	--	--
Total	30.06	35.794.40*	839.7**

SOURCE: *Statistical Abstract of Arab Repubic of Egypt 1951-52—1970-71* (Cairo: Central Agency for public Mobilization and Statistics, June 1972).

*Area shown is only cultivated regions of Egypt. Total land area, including non-cultivated areas, is approximately 1 million square kilmeters.

**Density for cultivated land area. Density for total land area is 30 persons per square kilometer.

Egypt is a poor country with severe problems of economic development. The country lacks the agricultural resources to support her growing population; she also lacks the industrial resources necessary to produce goods that can be used for foreign exchange. The population is basically unskilled: less than 50 percent of the people are literate and over 60 percent of the people still live on agricultural production, earning only the barest subsistence. Egypt has faced great obstacles in furthering her efforts at modernization. The people tend to be devout and traditional, clinging to the old ways of doing things.

In addition, Egypt's continuing dispute with Israel has cost her dearly in economic terms. In addition to the diversion of much revenue from the domestic sphere to purchase of military equipment from the Soviet Union, Egypt had lost much of this equipment in the 1967 War along with the Sinai Desert and its oil resources. The closing of the Suez Canal, a result of the 1967 War, has cost the country much in canal revenues. Since the end of the October 1974 War (another costly venture in terms of the loss of military equipment), work has begun on clearing the canal, but agreement has yet to be reached on the final disposition of Israeli-occupied territory. While oil-rich Arab states have supported Egypt in her negotiations with Israel, a long-term Arab or United States commitment to the overall economic development of Egypt has not yet been established.

Political Structure

When King Faruk abdicated in 1952, Egypt's monarchy came to an end. A republican form of government was proclaimed in 1953, and General Naguib proclaimed himself president and prime minister. At the time there were no popular elections, no legislative body, and no political parties. Naguib enforced his rule entirely through the military; in 1954 he was deposed by a group of rival military officers, led by General Nasser. Nasser led the government, again through the military apparatus and a military command council, until 1957. To this date Egypt had no civilian executive or legislative institutions. All decisions were made by the military and executed by them. In 1958 when Egypt united with Syria, a rubber-stamp legislature representing both Egyptians and Syrians was established with half its members appointed by Nasser, the other half indirectly elected.

In 1957 the National Union, now known as the Arab Socialist Union (ASU), was formed. This was to be the only political party in the country and was to act as an administrative organization, linking the central government to the village governments. (The structure of the ASU is discussed in Chap. 5) Nasser was the leader at the national level, supervising provincial governors, who in turn supervised village councils. There was no popular election in Egypt until the formation of the UAR, when Nasser received almost all the votes on the referendum approving the merger. The merged government of Egypt and Syria lasted only until 1961, when the Syrian government was overthrown by a military coup.

Present Political Structure: Executive, Legislative, and Judicial Institutions

In 1962 the Egyptian government was reorganized into an executive council of 25 members and a defense council of 20 members. There still is a rubber-stamp legislature, the National Assembly, to which in 1969 the Arab Socialist Union elected 319 of 350 members, the rest being independents. The country is divided into 25 governates, each headed by a governor appointed by the president on the advice of the minister of local government. Governors are responsible for the normal administrative functions of their areas and have their own budgets and development programs. The police are centrally con-

Chart 2.8.   Egypt: The Structure of the Government

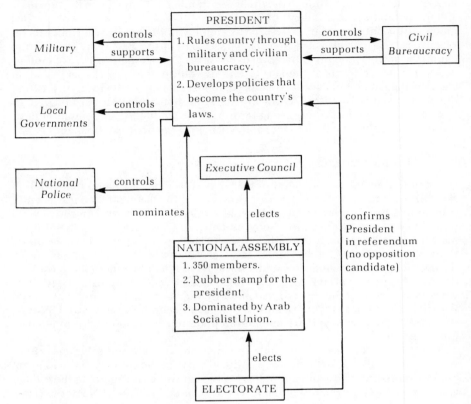

trolled, and there are no open national elections as there are in competitive states. Some municipalities elect town councils, but these are nonpartisan elections.

Egypt is a secular state, bent on establishing a modern, efficient system of government. The traditional Islamic courts have been replaced by secular ones, and there currently is a strictly secular legal code. While traditional religious leaders may at times be consulted because of their influence with the people, the government remains quite absolute and authoritarian.

Political competition, once a popular notion with Egyptian nationalists, never was a concept that drew a wide following throughout the community. Now the nationalist image has been usurped by an absolutist military regime, not by a political party as in the new states. The state was established by the military, which proclaimed nationalist and socialist goals; the state is carried on by the military and civilian politicians friendly to the Arab Socialist Union.

Sources of Legitimacy

Egypt offers a great contrast to India, Indonesia, and the Soviet Union. Unlike the first two nations, Egypt has never enjoyed a long period of stable internal self-government or any period of flowering for a civilian, nationalist political party. The country has been repeatedly under attack—from the invasion of Napoleon in 1801, through the British onslaughts to World War I, and again in the North African campaigns of World War II. Through this turbulence no system of popular self-government was ever established, save for a brief Wafdist experiment of the 1920s. Thus, Egypt has generally had a system that concentrated legitimate power in the hands of a single man—first a monarch, later a military dictator. By custom, Egyptians have not been a divided, fragmented people constantly bringing their grievances to the capital or organizing divisive political organizations. Rather, they have respected centralized authoritarian government, regarding the system as appropriate and moral. Egypt has much fewer elaborate mechanisms than the USSR for measuring and reinforcing the underlying popular acceptance of her current regime. The Egyptian population has not been, and is not now, as highly mobilized as the Soviet population. Egyptians are not as aware of government policy and are not as exposed to ubiquitous governmental institutions as are Russians. On the village level, the central government in Egypt has generally fit into the traditional pattern of local government rather than transforming it. Although there remains a great gap in goals between the modernist leadership and the tradition-oriented population, Egypt remains a noncompetitive state in which the people appear to support their political leaders.

The difference between the USSR and Egypt in terms of basic structure also lies in the ideological source of legitimacy of each state: in the USSR, institutions are entirely civilian, governed by the Soviet Communist party, and Marxist-Leninist ideology is the chief justification of all political action; in Egypt, the military—and in the case of Nasser, the personality of the president—has been the legitimate sources of authority. Civilian institutions, such as the Arab Socialist Union, and civilian leaders such as President Anwar Sadat, must find military support for their actions. (The structure of the Egyptian government is summarized in Chart 2.8.)

PEOPLE'S REPUBLIC OF CHINA

The People's Republic of China, located on the Chinese mainland with its capital at Peking, was inaugurated in 1949; its formal structure was based on the principles of Marx, Lenin, and Stalin, with contributions by Chairman Mao Tse-tung.

The PRC, like India and Egypt, is the seat of an ancient culture. Like these two states, China was dominated by Western powers in the modern period, though she never became an outright colony. Historically, China has always been an authoritarian state, governed by an established bureaucracy and an emperor. Chinese culture has never valued open political conflict as a virtue.

In the nineteenth century the governing Manchu Dynasty in China was in decline. The regime produced a series of weak and ineffectual emperors. Rebellions were frequent and the central government's control over the various provincial areas was weak and, in some cases, only nominal. In these circumstances European powers, seeking markets in China, were able to extract treaties giving them special privileges from the Chinese. China was defeated in two wars (the Opium Wars of 1839 to 1844 and 1856 to 1860), which resulted in the opening of the opium trade in China for the benefit of European merchants, over the objections of the Chinese government. Later treaties divided China into "spheres of influence" (i. e., different European powers established monopolies over trade in specific areas of China); granted Europeans the right of "extraterritoriality" (i. e., they were not subject to Chinese civil and criminal jurisdiction but were tried in their own courts); and guaranteed the rights and safety of Christian missionaries. These treaties were enforced by European military power. With its legitimacy threatened throughout the century and its inability to defend itself against foreigners, the Chinese political system continually lost popular support. China was already a very populous nation and Europeans never were more than a small minority in China; this fact made the Manchus appear even more ineffective in the public mind.

The late nineteenth century saw the rise of Chinese nationalism. There were many popular revolts against the emperor, including the great T'ai P'ing Rebellion of 1851 to 1864, which very nearly overthrew the imperial structure. Chinese life was largely undisturbed by the presence of Westerners; the rebellions were a reflection of Chinese discontent with their own leadership. Western pressure, however, began to be felt at the fringes of Chinese society with the introduction of diplomatic relations and China's attempt to reorganize its military along Western lines. Pressure for change became insurmountable when China was defeated by Japan in the Sino-Japanese War of 1894 to 1895. The country was forced to cede the traditionally Chinese territories of Taiwan (Formosa), the Pescadores Islands, and the Liaotung Peninsula to Japan as outright colonial areas. China was also forced to grant independence to Korea. The war was a signal to the European powers that they could scramble for further privileges as well. China seemed to be disintegrating and the government that at first, following the Sino-Japanese War, promised reforms, settled back into a conservative reaction. The Boxer Rebellion of 1900, an anti-Western uprising, was put down only with the assistance of European troops. By 1911 the Manchus were finally overthrown and the Republic of China was proclaimed in 1912.

The Republic of China, which lasted from 1912 to 1949, saw nothing but uninterrupted turbulence, instability, and warfare. It opened with a period of intense conflict among Chinese warlords, from which Yuan Shih-kai finally emerged as military dictator. There was constant economic and military interference from foreigners. During World War I Japan attempted to widen her military presence in China, and her gains were confirmed by the Treaty of Versailles. Yuan Shih-kai was overthrown and a constitutional government based on republican principles under Sun Yat-sen was inaugurated, but only after much factional fighting. The 1920s proved to be a period of continuous strife among the warlords until General Chiang Kai-shek, with advice and support from the USSR, was able to defeat his rivals. Nationalist party (Kuomintang) rule was not firmly established until 1928 and, even then, had much to fear from a growing, militaristically inclined native Communist movement. In 1932 Japan invaded China again, ending all chance of stability. By 1945 the strength of the Nationalists had been depleted by internal corruption and war weariness. The Chinese Communists drove the Nationalists from the country with Russian military assistance, and by 1949 mainland China was under native Communist control, with only the island of Formosa in the hands of the Nationalists—a situation that persists to the present day.

Territory and Population

In territory and resources, the People's Republic of China is a large, well-endowed nation, but not taken in proportion to the size of her population. The country has great river systems, high mountains, broad plateaus, and long coastal areas. Her territory is about equal to that of the United States and has similar climatic variations. (see map, p. 100) However, her population is the world's largest. The PRC must develop this territory and population to become a great power, a goal of the present government, but she does not have either efficient agriculture or massive industry. As in India, the pressure of great populations, living traditionally on the land, on scarce resources, slows efforts at rapid industrialization.

The population of the PRC, over 700 million people, consists of many ethnic groups. Most of the population is concentrated in Manchuria in the North and along the great river systems in the South. (Table 2.10 shows the distribution by area of this population.)

As in India, language in the PRC is the major basis of distinction among these groups, though cultural differences exist as well. The major Chinese language group is Tibeto-Chinese. While the Chinese language has a single written form in which characters (ideographs) express universally understood concepts, the oral forms of the language differ from region to region and are not mutually intelligible. Mandarin Chinese is spoken by a majority of the population, but very large numbers of people speak other dialects. In addition large numbers of people speak the Tibeto-Burman languages, as well as the Altaic (Mongolian and Turkic) tongues.

The Chinese written language is extremely complex, and so long as oral Chinese is so different in various regions of the country a phonetic alphabet will be difficult to achieve. The Chinese have attempted to simplify the language, but of the 2,000 most common characters only 28 percent have fewer than eight strokes; the rest contain from nine to twenty-seven strokes. With this form of written language literacy and consequent modernization is a difficult and costly task. Part-time educational programs for peasants and workers have been a feature of government policy, but no literacy statistics have ever been published.

Despite their linguistic complexity, the Chinese people have a greater level of homogeneity in culture than do the Indian people: in the PRC, there is a

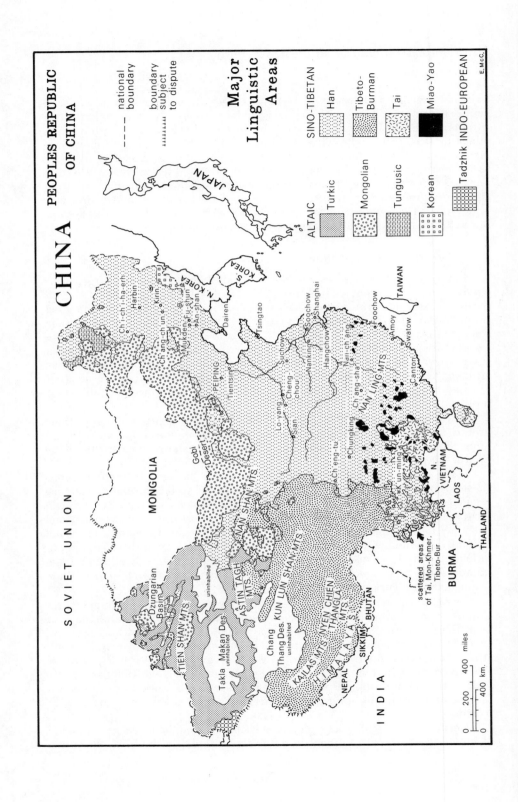

CHINA

PEOPLES REPUBLIC OF CHINA

national boundary

boundary subject to dispute

Major Linguistic Areas

SINO-TIBETAN

Han

Tibeto-Burman

Tai

Miao-Yao

ALTAIC

Turkic

Mongolian

Tungusic

Korean

Tadzhik INDO-EUROPEAN

E. McC.

SOVIET UNION

MONGOLIA

JAPAN

N. KOREA

S. KOREA

Chi-ch'i-ha-erh

Harbin

Kirin

Mukden

Fu-shun

An-shan

Dairen

Ch'ang-ch'un

PEIPING

Tientsin

Tsingtao

Lo-yang

Sian

Cheng-chou

Suchow

Nanking

Hangchow

Shanghai

Soochow

Nan-ch'ang

Foochow

TAIWAN

Amoy

Swatow

Canton

NAN LING MTS.

Ch'ang-sha

Chungking

Ch'eng-tu

Kweiyang

Kunming

Gobi Desert

Dzungarian Basin uninhabited

TIEN SHAN MTS.

Takla Makan Des. uninhabited

ASTIN TAGH MTS.

NAN SHAN MTS.

KUN LUN SHAN MTS.

Chang Thang Des. uninhabited

KAILAS MTS

NYEN CHIEN THANGLA MTS.

HIMALAYAS

NEPAL

SIKKIM

BHUTAN

INDIA

BURMA

N. VIETNAM

LAOS

THAILAND

scattered areas of Tai, Mon-Khmer, Tibeto-Bur.

0   200   400 miles

0   400 km.

Table 2.10. Population of the People's Republic of China

Administrative Divisions	Population (in millions)	Land Area (in thousands of square kilometers)	Density of Population (per square kilometer)
Peking Municipality	7.8	7.1	1,098.5
Tientsin Municipality	4.0	--	--
Hopeh	43.0	202.7	212.1
Shansi	20.0	157.1	127.3
Inner Mongolian Autonomous Region	13.6	--	--
Liaoning	28.6	150.0	190.6
Kirin	20.0	187.0	106.9
Heilungkiang	25.0	463.6	53.9
Shensi	21.0	--	--
Kansu	13.0	--	--
Tsinghai	2.0	--	--
Ninghsia Hui Autonomous Region	2.6	--	--
Sinkiang Uighur Autonomous Region	8.0	--	--
Shanghai Municipality	10.0	--	--
Shantung	57.0	153.3	371.8
Kiangsu	47.0	102.2	459.8
Anhwei	35.0	139.9	250.1
Chekiang	31.0	101.8	304.5
Kiangsi	25.0	164.8	151.6
Fukien	18.0	123.1	146.2
Honan	50.0	167.0	299.4
Hupeh	32.0	187.5	170.6
Hunan	38.0	210.5	18.5
Kwangtung	42.0	231.4	181.5
Kwangsi Chuang Autonomous Region	24.0	220.4	108.8
Szechwan	70.0	569.0	123.0
Kweichow	20.0	174.0	114.9
Yunnan	23.0	436.2	52.7
Tibetan Autonomous Region	1.3	1,221.9	10.6
Total	731.9	6,552.9*	111.6**

SOURCE: Estimate for 1967 to 1972 in D.P. Whitaker and R. Shinn, *Area Handbook* for the *People's Republic of China* (Washington, D.C.: Government Printing Office, 1972).

*The figures not available are generally for underpopulated areas in the Northwest. Total Chinese land area, including these regions, is estimated 9,597,000 square kilometers.

**Population density for total Chinese land area, including underpopulated regions, is 76.2 persons per square kilometer.

majority dialect and a majority written language; there is a basic acceptance of Han Chinese cultural attitudes with respect to ethics and family organization; and religion is not a divisive element as it is in India, Chinese religions have no caste structure and tend to be more like philosophic or ethical schools than rigid orthodoxies. Many Chinese have adhered to a form of ancestor worship and a collection of beliefs drawn from a variety of religions, but even before the Communist Revolution traditional religion was considerably weakened in China. The current government has moved against Buddhism in Tibet, primarily because the religion there has supported a political movement, Tibetan subnationalism. The government also has moved against Christians (less than 1 percent of the population) because of the close connection of Christian missionary activity with Western imperialism. Overall, however, religion is not an important divisive force in China. The ethnic differences of Mongols and Turks in Central Asia, Burmese, Tibetans and Thai in the South and the rest of the country, are much more notable.

The PRC is still primarily an agricultural country. About 75 to 80 percent of the population work as peasants, and 75 percent of the land in China is farmed the traditional way. The present regime has made great efforts at industrialization but the PRC remains with a densely populated countryside in which much of the food produced is used to support the peasant and his family. Unless the government can move much of its agricultural population off the land into industry or bring industry to the agricultural communes efforts at industrial modernization will be made very difficult. In order to accomplish this, sources of food supply to support the industrial sector must be found. Despite the fact so many of her people are in agriculture, the PRC must import agricultural goods to keep them alive.

Political Structure

The People's Republic of China, after a period of interim government following the revolution, adopted a formal constitution in 1954. The purpose of the document, like that of the Soviet constitution, was to establish a people's democracy of workers and peasants according to Marxist precepts. As in the USSR, the constitution in the PRC established a broad formal structure of state, behind which at each level stands a single ubiquitous and monolithic organization, the Chinese Communist party (CCP). (The structure of the CCP is discussed in Chap.5.)

Under the 1954 constitution, the PRC is established as a unitary state. The country is divided into twenty-one provinces, five autonomous regions, and two municipalities. Since provincial separatism is one of the great problems that was never resolved under the Manchus and the Nationalists, the current regime has taken many special measures to destroy it. Thus the national legislature, the National People's Congress, is unicameral and theoretically represents the people directly; there is no specific representation of provinces as would occur in a senate or other upper house. The central government controls the provinces and regions directly through the central administrative apparatus and the CCP; the regions and provinces have been established to guarantee some independence in cultural matters, but have no independent political power.

The legislature.   The National People's Congress is indirectly elected by universal suffrage. The people elect members of local congresses, and provincial congresses elect members of the national body. All elections are based on single slates of candidates proposed by the appropriate level of the CCP. As in the USSR, elections in the PRC serve the purpose of confirming decisions already made within the party. Unlike the USSR, parties in the PRC other than the CCP are permitted to nominate candidates. However, these parties, which only symbolically represent minority groups, must support the regime and the leadership of the CCP. No election is truly competitive.

In structural terms the elected National People's Congress, with about 1,200 members, has formal authority over all matters. In times when it is not in session, its standing committee (elected by the National Congress) runs the government. The National People's Congress also elects the chairman of the PRC who is chief executive and head of state. He is equivalent to a king or president in formal terms and is constitutionally more important than the chairman of the standing committee. In addition the National People's Congress elects two vice chairmen.

The executive.   The executive branch of government in China consists of the State Council, similar in formal terms to a cabinet in the parliamentary system. On the recommendation of the chairman, the National People's Congress elects the members of the State Council and its leading official, the premier. The State Council and the premier lead the administrative departments and oversee the enforcement of all laws in the country.

The judiciary.   As in the USSR, the courts in the PRC do not engage in political controversy. The courts are accountable to the National People's Congress and are dominated by members of the CCP.

Sources of Legitimacy

The function of this structure, then, as in the USSR and to a lesser extent in Egypt, is to mobilize the population behind the regime. The PRC is governed by a fairly closed bureaucracy, which would like to modernize the country. To accomplish this, the active support of the people must be enlisted. Elections are conducted so the people can be "educated" to the purposes of the state; congresses are held so the people may feel represented within their own government; the party has local roots so it may recruit talented young leaders for the future. Discussion of issues occurs within the party, but decisions made at the top are carried out by the total organization. As with the Soviet Communist party, the CCP is considered the only virtuous group that is progressive and understands the Marxist-Leninist-Maoist march of history. To disagree with the party is to hinder progress. Thus competition is not only ideologically immoral, but in a developing state like the PRC, it is positively destructive.

All politics in the PRC is, therefore, Communist politics. Youth groups, the army, and provincial groups all are a part of Chinese politics (as they would be in the USSR), but they exist only within the party. Political conflict occurs, but in the guise of internal party factionalism. The Great Proletarian Cultural Revolu-

Chart 2.9.   The People's Republic of China: The Structure of the Government

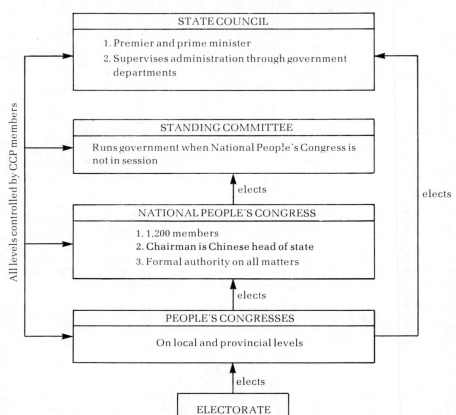

tion, in essence a major attempt to revitalize the party's ideological dynamism and, as such, a major political confrontation within the CCP, was such a crisis. Actions of youth and student groups (the Red Guards) at this time were directed at many targets—politicians, universities, cultural institutions, and the like—and the effect of the entire affair was to replace one group of CCP leaders with another. This reaffirmed the authority of Chairman Mao and undermined groups of bureaucrats opposed to him. The Cultural Revolution demonstrates that Chinese politics is, to an extent, issue-oriented and is not entirely the result of mere personal factionalism. However, there is today no open competition in the PRC, despite some regionalism and party factionalism, and the chief source of legitimacy remains the CCP. (The structure of the government of the PRC is summarized in Chart 2.9.)

Comparative Distinctions in Political Structures Among Noncompetitive States

The USSR, Egypt, and the PRC all possess political structures that are superficially similar to institutions in competitive and fragmented states. However, the operation of these structures and the political support they represent are very different from those in either competitive or fragmented states.

In competitive states, formal political structures reflect the divisions within society and political decisions are the result of competition among groups that are legitimately represented in these institutions. In fragmented states, formal political structures do not effectively represent all the divisions of society and are, compared to similar structures in competitive states, relatively weak and of short duration. In contrast, formal political structures in noncompetitive states tend to be of long duration, but they are not representative of divisions in society—primarily because societies in noncompetitive states have relatively few important political divisions. Thus, the primary function of political structures in competitive and fragmented states, the resolution of conflict among legitimate political groups, is lacking in noncompetitive states. In the latter, structures are a facade behind which the primary wielder of authority—whether it be military, civilian, or bureaucratic—exercises predominant power.

Beyond these broad similarities, the USSR, Egypt, and the PRC are different from each other to a certain extent because they utilize different approaches to politics. The USSR and the PRC, both vast countries with large populations and a history of regional differences, constitutionally and formally recognize the cultural rights of minorities. Also, both these states have maintained elaborate representative bodies of a legislative type. Both countries hold elections to enlist public support behind the ruling political party, and in both the Marxist-Leninist party—the CPSU and CCP—is the preeminent political institution. In the USSR and the PRC all political institutions are governed by an elite that is considered qualified to lead the country by virtue of its leadership position within the ruling political party. All other governmental institutions—the provinces and regions, the executive, legislative, and judicial agencies—serve the interests of the party and are legitimized by reference to Marxist ideological principles.

Egypt differs from the USSR and the PRC in a number of important respects, but the major structural distinction lies in the fact that Egypt does not vest the preeminent authority of the state in a political party. Rather, power is exercised in Egypt by a president, buttressed by the military, the bureaucracy, the party (ASU), and the local power structure. Egypt is socially a much more homogeneous country than either the USSR or the PRC; also the regime in Egypt has not been as committed to total mobilization of the population as have the regimes in Marxist states. Thus the myriad of state agencies that characterizes Soviet and Chinese government do not exist in Egypt.

Of the three states, the Soviet Union is by far the most highly developed economically and has had a commitment to total political mobilization longest. The PRC, because of her comparative state of underdevelopment, low literacy, and greater survival of traditional forms of organization, does not equal the Soviet Union's capacity for dictatorial power in her govenmental structure and still on occasion experiences great factional and regional upheavals. Egypt, not so committed to totalitarianism, reflects the loyalty of a tradition-oriented population; here the regime, though interested in economic development, has sought to accommodate this interest to the aims of the population rather than to confront and transform it. Egypt has, thus, not required major formal institutions of state to pursue this policy.

POLITICAL STRUCTURES AND INSTITUTIONS: COMPARING COMPETITIVE, FRAGMENTED, AND NONCOMPETITIVE STATES

Of the three types of states here considered competitive states have developed their different political structures to their highest levels of general usefulness. In them strong executives are checked by strong legislatures. Executives have authority over bureaucracies and the military, while regional, economic, and social interests receive separate representation in the political parties and legislatures. Individual and group conflict are resolved mostly through the sharing of power among the established political groups in the executive and legislative branches and also through the courts and other lesser structures. The major structural characteristics of these states then are due to the general tendency of the population to utilize them for the resolution of disputes as well as for the development and application of policy on all levels.

In contrast, structures in fragmented states are generally weak. Legislatures tend to be too divided to reach policy decisions and too aggressive of their prerogatives to permit the emergence of a strong executive. Similarly, executives tend to be too weak to enforce policy except for short periods when they can overcome the authority of the other structures—usually by a coup. In fragmented states, however, such coups also tend to be short-lived, reflecting the tendency of these societies not to accept any structures of government as legitimate for very long.

Noncompetitive states usually have many structures, but usually only one is the source of authority and all the others are facades or symbols. This reflects the relative lack of social differentiation in these societies. Thus the USSR and the PRC have all-powerful political parties; Egypt has an all-powerful coalition of the military and the bureaucracy. Although all three states have legislatures, executives, judiciaries, and elections these and other institutions of government are reflections of and not checks on the primary structure (the party or military bureaucracy) in power.

Chapter 3

Political Culture and Socialization

POLITICAL CULTURE AND SOCIALIZATION: A FRAMEWORK FOR COMPARISON

Every political system consists of the interrelationships and behavior patterns of persons seeking and dispensing political favors and decisions. In the broad sense these relationships involve every member of the given society. Persons develop attitudes toward politics and political leaders. People may be demanding of personal attention and willing openly to participate in political activity, or, on the other hand, be submissive, silent, and difficult to reach.

Every given society develops a common norm for political behavior through its general cultural processes. People adapt their own personalities to those of persons around them—to friends and, especially, to family. The institutions that dispense general social values—the family, the schools, the church, as well as the media of communication—also instruct in political attitudes.

The whole complex of behavioral norms, attitudes, and beliefs that relate to politics in a given society is sometimes referred to as a "political culture." Political culture is a segment of the total culture of a society and is derived from the same sources. People are inculcated into their general political beliefs in a manner similar to their other cultural values, i. e., they become politically "socialized." Socialization, while it may include the formal processes of education, is a far broader concept. Schools in every nation will instruct their students to be patriotic and loyal to the prevailing government. However, political attitudes taught in school must be reinforced by both general social behavior and the sharing of a consensus on a wide range of issues among the most influential segments of the population.

POLITICAL CULTURE AND SOCIALIZATION IN COMPETITIVE STATES

Patterns of Similarity

In competitive states, such as Great Britain, India, and Chile, people must be accustomed to support the values of competitive politics. They must believe that discussion and mutual criticism are constructive, that people are rational and virtuous so that elections based on popular opinion are moral and legitimate. They must also abide by specific restraints: persons who win electoral victories do not stamp out the opposition; persons who lose elections do not immediately stage military insurrections. In competitive states these beliefs must be present, but in practice of course this occurs in varying degrees in different places.

Three Case Studies: Great Britain, India, and Chile

GREAT BRITAIN

Great Britain includes the populations of England, Scotland, Wales, and Northern Ireland. Of about 54.5 million people, almost 44 million are English and this single cultural group heavily dominates the country. This dominance is compounded by the fact that the whole country is controlled from London, which, with 8 million residents, contains 20 percent of the total population of the country, including the British elite in all spheres of national activity.

The minority populations of Scotland, Wales, and Northern Ireland have retained an ethnic awareness and, because of this, have been granted some special safeguards. Northern Ireland with her deep religious divisions, is now governed directly from London, but this is only a temporary expedient. The British recognize that some actions will have to be taken to allow self-government to the Irish, as well as to Scotland and Wales. Some domestic matters are now administered differently in Scotland and Wales than in the rest of the country, and the present government is considering allowing Scotland and Wales separate subordinate parliaments to deal with the internal affairs of these two areas. However, Great Britain is not a federal system, and all arrangements affecting minority populations or regions are now and will ultimately be subject to the will of the national Parliament at Westminister, London.

Cultural Values and Historic Approaches to Politics in Great Britain

British political culture is often described as "elitist" or "class-oriented." In Great Britain people have traditionally viewed themselves in terms of social rankings, which have, in turn, been based on such factors as income, family, name and position, education, style of life, speech, occupation, place of residence, and the like. The British, in the past at least, have accorded high regard to "gentlemen," persons who by personal achievement as well as breeding are regarded as superior to others.

The British upper classes are distinctly a minority in the country, but they have monopolized control over the government. Both upper and lower classes have thus accepted the proposition that the ruling class (the upper class) should do the ruling. This phenomenon is often described as the "deferential" aspect of British society. While two-thirds of the population calls itself "working class," many of these people will support aristocratic leaders and vote for the Conservative party, an institution that throughout most of its history has been dedicated to upper-class rule.

Class is somewhat more obvious in Great Britain than in the United States, but is gradually becoming less prominent. The British aristocracy has its own style of speech and life; the country does not have a massive middle economic group into which class distinctions seem to disappear. However, in recent years people have begun to move more rapidly up and down the social ladder. Many old aristocratic families have become impoverished, while sons and daughters of the working class have more educational and occupational opportunity than ever before. Thus, class lines have tended to become hazy. Persons have become more socially mobile because they are occupationally mobile. The advent of the automobile and modern highways have accelerated this process even more.

While class is sometimes considered the major variable in British political culture, its importance has at times been overestimated. Great Britain is a modern complex country, and while it has a culturally homogeneous population compared to many other nations, other factors besides class have been important in the political structure. Religion, for example, seems relatively unimportant today, but in the past religious bigotry, especially between Protestants and Catholics, provided a basis for much political hostility. A residue of this old conflict can still be found in Northern Ireland, where Protestants (in the majority) are pitted against Catholics in a struggle that appears to be almost insoluble in the face of the uncompromising positions taken by militants on both sides. The religious conflict in Northern Ireland is unique to that region and, definitely, does not characterize the norm of British political life. In England, Scotland, and Wales religions today tend to be tolerant and politics does not generally revolve about religious issues.

Similarly, race has not been a very important issue in British politics, mainly because there are only very small nonwhite racial groups in the country and only a minority of the British population has contact with these people. However, the influx of immigrants from Africa, India, Pakistan, and the West Indies during the 1960s stirred up enough racial animosity in Great Britain that racist speeches and politicians became visible for the first time in many years. We must not overestimate racism as an important aspect of British political culture, however. While it can be argued race had an impact on British politics in the 1960s, this impact was restricted to certain localities only.

The patterns of political behavior in Great Britain have evolved over a very long period of time. The traditions of a limited government, respect for the rights of individuals, and the desire to maintain a continuity with the past are deeply engrained values in British political culture. Though in constitutional form the country is still a monarchy, the powers of the British royal family were restricted in the seventeenth and eighteenth centuries first by a mercantile and then an industrial class. The new power groups chose even then to exert their influence through old institutions, such as the Parliament and the cabinet. In Great Britain these structures have been adapted to new purposes, without the experience of a bloody revolution that France endured.

Similarly the deep respect the British have for freedom of thought and expression has seen the coming and going of many different kinds of political groups. Early political factions bent on narrow political gains have given way to modern mass political parties with strong grassroots organizations. The philosophies of the nineteenth-century liberals and conservatives have been adapted and changed by twentieth-century socialists and conservatives. Politicians still operate within the same structural framework, however, and voice nominal loyalties to the same symbols—to the queen, to Parliament, and to British constitutional traditions.

Processes of Socialization in Great Britain

The British family is the child's first agent of socialization into the nation's political culture. In Great Britain, the stability of political institutions over long periods of time allows parents to communicate attitudes toward special political groups to their children. It has been borne out in many surveys, for example, that British children have a very pronounced tendency to vote in a way similar to their parents.[1] Since the British have tended to perceive themselves as members of socioeconomic classes, this also indicates a persistence of class orientation toward politics and the choice of political parties over time. In other words children of working-class parents tend to see themselves as working class and have tended to accept their parents' view that the Labour party favors working-class interests. Comparably, parents who support the Conservative party have communicated their middle- and upper-class views as well as their voting habits to their children.

In the family certain important political traits emerge. British women, for example, are more conservative, both in attitudes and party preferences, than men. Few women become political candidates in Great Britain, and women do not vote as frequently as men. These patterns of behavior seem quite fundamental, though it should be noted there are variations in these matters among the social classes. The Labour party, for example, has had notable women among its members, dating from Beatrice Webb in the early twentieth century to Barbara Castle, a cabinet minister in the 1960s. Statistically, however, very few women participate in politics in either major party.

The British educational system is the major formal socializing agent in the country. Compulsory education to age eleven became national policy in 1870, but free secondary education was not introduced until 1944. The vast majority of the British population has been trained to read and write, but many persons have not received much further formal training than that. Since 1918 children in Great Britain have stayed in school until the age of eleven, when they were required to take an examination that determined whether they would be permitted to continue their education beyond age fourteen. However, most children left school at age fourteen. In 1947 compulsory education was extended to age fifteen, but as recently as 1962 two-thirds of the country's youths ended their formal education at that age. In 1972 the legal age for leaving school was raised again to sixteen. A very small proportion of the British school age population today enters universities and college graduates still constitute a true intellectual and social elite in the country.

The 1960s saw the establishment of new institutions—comprehensive high schools and "red brick" universities—that have challenged the old educational assumptions to a certain extent. The goal of the 1965 educational program—a high school education for all—has yet to be achieved, though schools now offer programs to students from the ages of eleven to sixteen. Similarly the new universities have not filled the needs of the nation and will probably have to be expanded into the 1970s and 1980s. The new institutions have, however, already challenged entrenched prejudices against the establishment of nonelitist educational institutions in Great Britain.

Most British people continue to be socialized into their political system by the work they do. Most Britons are working by the age of fifteen and their colleagues are a major influence in the formation of political attitudes. Within the sphere of work the grassroots organizations of the political parties can be felt. The Labour party recruits much of its support from trade union members; the Conservative party works on a regional basis and is strong among white-collar workers and professionals. Through campaigns and organization the parties are themselves major instruments of socialization. The press reinforces these party preferences as Labour, Liberal, and Conservative voters are able to read newspapers that support their respective viewpoints. The church and the electronic media, in contrast, are scrupulously neutral in politics in Great Britain.

INDIA

Cultural Values and Historic Approaches to Politics in India

Unlike Great Britain, India has never been a homogeneous society dominated by any single ethnic or cultural group. An ancient civilization, India has many patterns of thought and behavior that can be viewed as traditional, but these traditions emanate more from the mutual recognition of symbols and spiritual values by Indians than from the actual power of any political center. A main feature of Indian culture is the interplay of religion and political concepts and values, two spheres of thought Indians have long viewed as complementary and not contradictory.

In India, even more than in Great Britain, social status has in the past affected the nature of the political process. Indian society has been described as a "caste" society based on the very rigid tenets of orthodox Hinduism. At birth, Indians inherit their social status from their parents, which, according to their religion, is unchangeable. Thus, Indian society has traditionally been stratified into five theoretically distinct categories. The highest caste, the Brahmins, are the priestly group of Hindu leaders, who historically have been political leaders as well. Below them, the Kshatriyas are conceived of as a military or warrior caste. The third group, the Vaisyas, consist of a traditional middle- or upper-middle-class group—tradesmen, retailers, and landowners. The mass of the population, probably as high as 80 percent of the total, are Sudras (serfs), who devote their lives to working on the land. In addition to these groups are the Pariahs or Outcastes, who numbered about 50 million at independence in 1947. These are descendants of slaves or criminals, who for one reason or another lost their religious caste status. Outcastes are by religious dictum restricted to the most despised and menial occupations. Often called "untouchables," they have traditionally been considered to be so despicable that for a Hindu to be touched or to stand in the shadow of a Pariah is to be defiled.

The Hindu caste system has in a sense united the nation. While different groups within the population speak different languages, Hinduism, practiced by 85 percent of the people, is the dominant religion. Although there are some ethnic overtones to the caste system—Brahmins tend to be relatively light-skinned northerners and Outcastes tend to be dark-skinned southerners—the structure has been mutually understood and accepted by most Indians.

Since independence, India's modernizing elite has attempted to transform some of the basic tenets of the traditional caste system. Traditional India produced few workers for modern enterprises and assigned them low status. For development plans to have any chance of success people have to be taught to conceive of modern economic and industrial activities as worthwhile and productive. They have to leave traditional occupations sanctified by religion for new ones. Since 1947, then, India's political elite has waged a serious campaign against rigid interpretations of Hinduism. Untouchability is forbidden in the Indian constitution; development plans include efforts to reeducate people away from the more rigid aspects of caste structure.

The current attempt at changing the Indian social system is not the first attempt at restructuring Hinduism in India. Before independence India saw many attempts, drawn from many sources, at transforming her religious structure. Generally, with the leading castes in the forefront of such reforms, change was accepted as normal and viewed as attempts at improvement within the traditional system. The very complexity of Indian society has always made for a constant interplay of competing groups, and India has developed a tradition of change that now serves as a backdrop for the efforts of modernizing leaders.

Thus, some important transformations have gradually taken place in Indian cultural patterns. Previously restrictive caste groups have transformed themselves into associations and federations. Rather than resigning themselves to the religious order they have become political pressure groups, though they have made relatively few demands on political authority. India's governmental bureaucracy has been so unresponsive in the past that few Indians expect much from their national government. They rather form groups to satisfy their own needs for personal identification. Political pressure groups in India neither state demands clearly nor hotly pursue them. People think rather ambiguously, and Indian cultural patterns provide a high tolerance for ambiguous actions on the part of political leaders. Indians are also used to viewing authority as having many sources and decisionmaking as a many-sided negotiation. With this cultural view, new patterns of political behavior, evident in the emergence of pressure groups, have not resulted in policies sharply divergent from traditional Indian practices.

Processes of Socialization in India

As in every society, the first agent of political socialization in India is the family. The Indian family has a generally diffused pattern of authority with little differentiation by age group. Indian children tend to be indulged by their parents to an extreme extent and are permitted considerable freedom within the family but are treated unequally according to status and rankings derived from traditional beliefs. Children consequently often develop early a tendency to satisfy their needs by themselves, rather than looking to authority figures. The Indian personality has thus been described as generally basically self-directed and introspective. Children carry these attitudes—a feeling of self-reliance with few demands and expectations from external authority—into adult life.

The traditional sector of the Indian social order, which today still comprises fully 80 percent of the Indian people, is quite hierarchical. Indians, who expect and demand little from external authority, seem to find security in relationships that are formally structured, as their relationships within the family (despite the general indulgence of children by parents) are also generally based on status and rankings. Equality is thus not a well understood or respected doctrine in India. Leaders or persons occupying high positions in the social order are accorded great respect, and national figures, such as leaders of religious sects and some political leaders, have often been conceived of as charismatic or endowed with special magical qualities.

Indians have thus developed a high tolerance of ambiguity, deriving from traditional Indian philosophical conceptions and the traditional family structure, in all spheres of life. Indians do not see life as a progression of forces in conflict, as a struggle between good and evil or right and wrong. Indian philosophy rather conceives of life as a mixture of contradictions in which rights and wrongs coexist together and in which the highest goal is the achievement of natural harmony. Out of this view of life, Indians can derive a tolerance and acceptance of many different kinds of leadership and authority.

It is interesting to note that socialization patterns in the West that have assigned different statuses to people on the basis of sex and education are not nearly as characteristic of India. Educational institutions in India are not as important as in Western countries in bringing about broad national attitude changes since only a small minority of Indians receive formal training. The country is only about 30 percent literate. India's educated elite views politics and modernization in a vastly different perspective than Indian peasants do, and changes in national opinion will depend upon the extent to which peasants are willing to accept and follow the leadership of this elite.

On balance, new institutions in India, introduced since independence, have become more infused with traditional views than they have modernized the traditional sphere. The introduction of elections has shifted power away from the nationalist modernizers to state and district organizations as well as to rural and caste associations. These tradition-based organizations, which must be utilized by the major national political parties, have infused the political process in India with a traditional flavor and outlook.

India thus remains a traditional country, led by an elite that still seeks to bring its people into a more modern world. There remains a great cultural gap separating the elite from the people, and the new organizations and political party branches are structures that are attempting to forge links between these two groups. At present, the modernizing elements seem to have become more traditional, and efforts at modernization of Indian social attitudes have achieved only mixed success.

CHILE

Cultural Values and Historic Approaches to Politics in Chile

More like Great Britain than India, Chile can be described as a class-conscious society in which political power has, until very recently, been largely monopolized by landholders in coalition with an urban-based propertied class. This coalition has recently been challenged by the emergence of new dynamic groups centered in the Chilean countryside, resulting in a basic change in the style of Chilean politics. In the past Chilean politics could be described as a bargaining process in which parliamentary activity and group manipulations have dominated. Under President Allende the system could be described as a mobilizing process, in which a previously apolitical mass constituency had been drawn, through new political groups and parties, into the focus of political conflict. Allende's new system, which seemed at once more dynamic and more unstable than the old system, has now been overthrown by military coup. However, the forces that led to the emergence of the Allende regime still exist in Chilean society.

The political system of Chile for most of the nineteenth and much of the twentieth centuries has been dominated by a generally right-wing elite, which has depended on large landholders, who control most of Chile's land and the peasants who work on it, and on the institutions of law enforcement (including the military). This elite exercised direct control over the government through rightist political parties and, for a long time, maintained stringent requirements for voting, thus effectively keeping Chilean peasants out of politics. For most of its period of ascendance it was closely allied to a conservative Catholic church.

Chile has thus had a long tradition of bargaining and coalition-formation among rival political groups, but only within the confines of a closely defined mutual consensus set by its ruling elite. Chilean political groups played the manipulative parliamentary game, forming popular fronts, dissolving them, and forming new fronts. However, all parties, Left and Right, until the emergence of the Allende constituency, participated in this game with a conscious intent to avoid the pressures of mass politics. Chilean parties sought and represented middle-class constituencies and sought to avoid massive social reform and upheaval.

Until the Frei government in the 1960s the mass of impoverished Chileans in the past generally accepted the working of their constitutional order with restraint, content with waiting for reform and change through established constitutional processes. However, in the 1960s the activities and aims of Chileans became channeled into diverse organizations that were not regarded as legitimate on a national scale. These organizations mobilized popular discontent with the slow pace of reform and contributed to the emergence of the Allende regime, which has now been overthrown. Unlike Great Britain, therefore, Chile, before the coup, did not have a disciplined moderate party system with mass national support. Unlike India, Chile did have a strong group politics based on group demands rather than on the charismatic appeal of individuals or the psychic needs of individual citizens.

Since the emergence of mobilization politics in Chile immediately preceding and during the Allende regime (from 1970 to 1973), Chilean politics has largely consisted of three distinct, politically aware constituencies. These are the traditional upper landowning and industrial classes, the urban middle classes who are now (since the military coup) in coalition with the upper groups, and the newly mobilized lower status urban and rural groups. Each of these three major groupings demonstrate a somewhat different attitude toward politics.

These three constituencies can best be understood when we realize Chile is basically a moderately developed industrial country. In 1960 only 39 percent of the population was engaged in agriculture. There has been a steady migration of population from the countryside to the cities during this century, though there has not been a corresponding increase in industrial productivity. Thus, Chile has experienced substantial economic growth, but in an extremely unbalanced manner. More products are manufactured in Chile than ever before, but purchasing power still remains largely confined to the middle and upper classes. Chilean professionals are paid very poorly and must work at several jobs to support a family. Chile, in fact, exports skilled manpower. A level of industrial maturity that would enable the large mass of Chilean workers as well as the marginal urban and rural populations to afford a higher standard of living has not been achieved. Such a situation has been described as one of "industrial stagnation."[2] The economic aspirations of the lower economic groups has given strength to new leftist political groupings and has challenged the political dominance of traditional rightist parties, culminating in the election of Allende and eventually contributing to his inability to govern.

Because of the relative inability of Chile's industrial sector to provide great quantities of better paying jobs, social mobility in the country has not been dynamic. Certainly Great Britain is a more mobile society, while India is far less mobile. Most Chilean managers, who comprise much of the comfortable Chilean middle class, are sons of businessmen or professionals. Very few sons of blue-collar workers become white-collar workers, the first step to higher social status. The managerial group, which in the past has acted as a unified elite with the landowners, has dominated all institutions of power and authority in the country. They have, however, been relatively unable to assimilate the lower groups to their own values and perceptions of politics.

The result of all this is a somewhat fractionalized political culture. The Chilean upper class is extremely traditional in its outlook. It is devoted to authoritarian leadership by property owners and frowns on political participation by the masses. The main thrust of the right wing is to defend the moral mainstays of the old order, exemplified in the conservative teachings of the Roman Catholic church. The upper class is archly anti-Communist and antireformist. It is a strictly status-quo-oriented group, resisting all pressures for moderate or radical change.

The Chilean middle classes generally recognize the lack of equal opportunity in Chile. They do, however, constitute a fairly conservative group on questions of economic reform and the needs of the state. This group finds itself caught between the conflicting demands of entrepreneurs, who wish to expand their businesses by keeping wages down, and workers, who are interested in

higher wages and social reform. Middle-class professionals, lower-level managers, self-employed businessmen and some well-paid workers for example in
mining, recognize the problems facing Chile but have been unwilling to support
radical proposals to deal with these problems. They oppose schemes that would
radically redistribute the country's wealth, fearing it would mean a lowering of
their own standard of living. Thus, the Chilean middle class is quite intolerant of
the Communist party; most middle-class persons support the prevailing system
of land tenure, and they generally oppose workers participating in industrial
decisionmaking.[3] The overall result is a fairly conservative outlook, not very
conducive to rapid development.

The poorer segments of the Chilean working class, newly enfranchized and
mobilized behind a socialist coalition of parties, until these parties were
outlawed by the military junta in 1973, is the main new dynamic force in Chilean
political life. It would be a gross oversimplification to view this group as a
monolithic unit. As is the case throughout Chilean society Chile's working
classes are organized into a variety of organizations. As with other Chilean
political associations, these groups have spawned an elite of their own whose
concern has been to maneuver itself into parliamentary power by the usual
strategy and tactics employed by parliamentary politicians. More than other
groupings, the leftist coalition has been fragmented into component organizations. Under President Allende, the new grouping took to mobilizing mass
demonstrations and attacking available scapegoats in an effort as much to keep
its own adherents together as to keep its opposition off balance. This was the
most ideological coalition in Chilean politics and the most given to techniques of
political mobilization. The overriding rhetoric of Marxist equalitarianism thus
served as an umbrella that covered over, but did not end, the separate interests
of diverse working-class groups. Indeed, many peasants, the direct target of the
socialist leadership, still gave their support to the Christian Democrats, a
moderate center-left party. The leftist grouping has now been overthrown, along
with President Allende, but the Chilean political culture still prevails; the elite
(which in recent times has been widened to include more parties) has divided
up the political spoils through parliamentary (and now military) tactics, while
the mass of the people have been promised much but are expected to await true
political and economic reform.

Processes of Socialization in Chile

Chile's population shows the same disparity in patterns of socialization as it
does with respect to its general economic and political structure. While not so
complex or diversified as India, Chile lacks the all-encompassing patterns of
traditional thinking that unifies the Indian population. Chile has a diverse
population drawn from many Western sources. However, the country is small
and has, for a long time, been dominated by an integrated elite.

Although about 90 percent of the country counts itself as Catholic in religion,
this group is quite diverse when it is subdivided by place of national origin.
Spanish Catholics have been a more conservative group than German Catholics,
the latter being quite numerous in Chile. However, the overwhelming domi-

nance of the church and the relevance of religion in Chilean politics serves as a socializing link among different segments of the Chilean population. The church itself does not directly promote its political views, but political and social groups devoted to religious ideals foster particular political attitudes that originate in church thinking.

The role of the Catholic church in Chile has been undergoing important changes, especially since the election of Eduardo Frei as president in the 1960s. The church has always had both conservative and progressive elements, but since the 1960s groups of Catholic intellectuals, many of which are less conservative politically than religious groups had been in the past, have become extremely active in the work of several political parties. Thus many Catholic organizations have supported the Christian Democrats (a left-center party), while other even more radical groups have worked within the Socialist-Communist Popular Front. Even within the church's hierarchy, the progressive wing, until recently, seemed to be growing more rapidly than the conservative elements.

The educational system in Chile, like that in Great Britain, is highly centralized and therefore acts as a unifying social force just as the church does. Most of the population (over 80 percent) attends school and is literate, but very few Chileans receive a secondary or university education. While education in Chile is for the most part secular, Chile's elite is able to support private institutions under the auspices of Catholic religious orders, and the country has several Catholic universities. Chilean public universities have been dominated by leftist students and faculty and supported President Allende actively. The leftist bent of Chilean public universities has been a political issue, being the main critical point emphasized by anticlerical parties, and, indeed, the military junta has instituted stern measures to root out its opponents in them.

Chile, like Great Britain, is a generally class-based society and different segments of the Chilean community experience different patterns of political socialization. The Chilean upper class, consisting of the old landed aristocracy and new moneyed classes, is in itself not a unified group. The older landed elite tends to be conservative and supports the church; this group promotes church thinking and sends its children to Catholic schools. The newer moneyed classes tend not to be tied to the church and support public education and a more open approach to politics. This latter group is untraditional in outlook, and family and school unite to instill the same values in the children of this group.

National origin seems to affect the attitudes and relative social position of some groups in Chile. Germans and those of German descent, who have on the whole been a skilled and industrious segment of Chilean society, have risen more rapidly in social status than other Chilean groups such as Indians or Mestizos. German Catholics are in the forefront of the major new political parties, and German Protestants tend to be among the leading anticlerical Chilean groups. Other European immigrants have done equally well in the Chilean social structure, reflecting a degree of European cultural bias in Chile. These groups, which also socialize their young through the family and the public schools, have stressed the importance of hard work, education, and the desirability of improving their social position. The children of these immigrants have carried forward the beliefs of their parents and have notably succeeded in entering the Chilean middle class.

Membership in the lower classes, consisting of an urban and rural proletariat, tends to be at least partially racially determined. A large proportion of people in the lower Chilean groups are Mestizos and dark-skinned Indians. These people tend to be less well-educated and have relatively little opportunity for social mobility. This is especially true in the rural areas where the availability of public schools is limited. Among the rural lower classes (mostly sharecroppers) traditional concepts of society persist. Children take the occupations of their fathers, and people look to the upper classes for authority and leadership. This social situation is now breaking down to a certain extent in the urban areas for Chilean industrial workers who are less tradition-oriented. However, the left-wing parties, though they made great efforts, never were able to mobilize all of the lower classes and had only limited success with rural groups. The persistence of traditional socialization patterns seems to have led to a situation in which lower class groups in Chile, in a manner similar to that in Great Britain, look for leadership to the middle and upper classes rather than to parties with a distinct left-wing, working-class character.

On the whole, then, Chile is a moderately developed country that has experienced great difficulty in achieving social and economic modernization on a par with the world's more highly developed countries. This has resulted in great social and political pressures on Chile's political system. In spite of a history of a strong respect for constitutionalism and a fairly homogeneous population, Chile has experienced much political turbulence. This turbulence has been the result of broad popular demands on the system and the response of a broad-based elite; it is not the result of elite conspiratorial bargaining. Chile's competitive political system was devised for the use of Chile's moderate middle classes. When Chile's lower classes sought entry into the system, the framework of Chilean politics collapsed. It remains to be seen what sort of system, of a permanent type, will again reemerge from the military coup.

Comparative Distinctions in Political Culture and Socialization Among Competitive States

While it can be said that Great Britain, India, and Chile all have or have had political cultures and socialization processes that support political competition, i. e., all three countries have developed widespread respect for constitutional norms and political sharing among their elites and masses, there are some very important distinctions among the three.

Great Britain is a homogeneous country with a national political culture supported by traditional family beliefs, modern national educational structures, national political parties, and a modern economic structure on a national scale. Tribal, religious, and regional differences are minor, having been generally overwhelmed over the years by a national political consciousness. Thus, what British children learn within the family tends to be generally reinforced by schools, by their later experiences on the job, and by what they learn from their peers. While class differences persist to a certain extent, there has been enough social mobility in the country to allow the general blurring of class lines as a new middle class has emerged. In Great Britain, there has been substantial opportunity for persons of the lower class to move or see their children move up into the middle class. Also, the great dominance of London as the country's cultural, political, and economic center has contributed to the intermingling of the nation's elite and the nationalization of its values and goals.

In contrast, both India and Chile are more diverse countries with more fractionated processes of socialization and a less integrated national elite. In India linguistic and regional differences are very great, and there is no single cultural capital or source of cultural values for the entire population. The elite is committed to modernization and schools tend to stress modern Western concepts, which often are at variance with traditional Hindu thought. While the family and the Hindu religion are major sources of culture, they are not reinforced directly by formal structures of socialization like schools and political parties. Because only a small minority of the people come into contact with modern social structures, traditional cultural patterns remain extremely important. However, as more people are drawn into a national economy and find themselves no longer part of the traditional Hindu community, the basic conflict between modern and traditional political thought will become a greater disruptive element in Indian society.

Such disruption has indeed plagued Chile, a country in transition between traditional and modern values. Traditional cultural patterns, which in the past permitted the peaceful evolution of political life in Chile in the hands of a unified elite, have broken down, while basic disunity in the modern sectors exists because national development has not been able to bring many workers and peasants up the economic ladder. The country is thus divided into three basic groups—lower, middle, and upper classes—each with different perspectives. The socialization processes also are fractionated (cities, for example, have different coalitions and organizations than rural areas) tending to reinforce divisions between the elite and the lower groups and making social mobility up from the lower classes difficult. In terms of her political culture, then, Chile is in a critical transitory period, and it is difficult to predict how the disruptions of her social and political structures will be resolved.

POLITICAL CULTURE AND SOCIALIZATION IN FRAGMENTED STATES

Patterns of Similarity

In fragmented states, national behavior patterns are tenuous when compared to subgroup loyalties and subgroup perceptions. In these states communities are only weakly united coalitions, and different groups can vary considerably in their basic political outlooks. Those variations are deeper than the factional differences found in places such as Great Britain, India, and Chile. Groups in fragmented states tend to disagree not merely on particular policy goals of the established system; they differ on the nature of the system itself. They challenge constitutional forms and the basic rules upon which the structure rests. Some groups may even challenge the idea that there need be any political structure at all.

Three Case Studies: France, Indonesia, and Zaire

FRANCE

It is often noted that French political culture is inherently self-contradictory. On the one hand, France can be conceived of as the pinnacle of individuality in which every citizen is free and influential. On the other hand, the state in France, with a history of strong, centralized, bureaucratic rule, is also viewed as the embodiment of supreme authority. The conflict between governmental authority and the rights of individuals has cruelly plagued French politics since the Revolution of 1789.

Cultural Values and Historic Approaches to Politics in France

France has never developed a tradition of compromise and respect for moderation in political affairs. Groups and individuals representing different interests and points of view tend to confront one another and the government establishment itself as implacable enemies. Voluntary associations or political parties, which in competitive states would serve to stand between the individual and the state and to compromise different points of view, are very weak in France.

France can be called a Roman Catholic nation since over 90 percent of all Frenchmen have been baptized into the Catholic faith. On the other hand, the church has long considered the country to be "de-Christianized" and the enduring conflict between believers and nonbelievers has divided French society at all levels. Indeed, it has been estimated that only 62 percent of Frenchmen consider themselves practicing Catholics. Many more men than women have severed their connections with the church, and religion seems to have affected the general political orientations of different social groups.

Minority religious groupings—among them Jews and Protestants—also seem to have developed approaches to politics that support the interests of their respective religions. It is widely believed, for example that the majority of the French Jewish community, regardless of socioeconomic status, voted against General de Gaulle (after he had taken a number of positions supporting the Arabs against Israel) in the referendum of April of 1969 that forced his resignation. Similarly, Protestants who, on the average, are wealthier and better educated than most Frenchmen, lead a rather clannish existence and vote more for leftist parties than their socioeconomic positions would normally indicate.

France has been and remains primarily a nation of small inbred communities in which such matters as differences over politics or religion tend to reinforce each other. The basic French political concepts of "Left" and "Right" refer to generalized theories of political culture that distinguish one set of political communities from another. Thus, in the past the term "Left" indicated a preference for republican government, opposition to monarchy, a secular state with no clerical interference, equality of citizens as opposed to a hierarchical class structure, and a commitment to general welfare over the rights of property. In contrast, the term "Right" was associated with monarchism, clericalism, and a privileged position for the propertied and aristocratic classes.[4]

These terms have lost their precise meaning since France is now firmly established as a secular republic committed to an equalitarian social structure. There is no realistic movement devoted to monarchy, aristocracy, and the church. However, the general cultural biases derived from previous periods still serve to distinguish groups of Frenchmen from each other. Today French politics remains doctrinaire and complex, reflecting the difficult inheritance of the past and the pressures of contemporary politics.

One of the basic features of French political culture, which in the past served to fragment the state into competing political communities, has been a basic dichotomy in the French approach to authority. For much of French history republicans, reflecting the values of the French Left, have been opposed to the free exercise of executive authority. Possibly their opposition derived from the original French revolutionary dogmas that criticized the prerogatives of the monarchy. In any event, the concept grew that the state as personified by the executive (i. e., the president) should be kept limited and weak, while political parties conceived of as representative of the people should be all-powerful. Opposing this point of view has been the French Right, which supports the Napoleonic tradition. According to this conception the chief executive is viewed as the embodiment of the public will and as the supreme symbol of all that is good in the state. Parties are viewed as selfish factions artifically dividing the community. The two views are utterly opposed to each other, serving as the fundamental constitutional bases for entirely different kinds of states. For this reason there could be no real compromise among French political groups. Some played a republican brand of politics, denying all legitimacy to the opposite viewpoint. Others played a Napoleonic form of politics, asserting that parties of the Left were neither qualified to rule nor morally justified in any aspect of their approach to public affairs. The result, until the advent of President de Gaulle, was a politics of direct confrontation with neither view really reflecting a majority position within the French national community.

Since the establishment of the Fifth Republic in 1958, a republican regime in theory but an executive regime in practice, this enduring French conflict has become vague and confused. With the president now directly elected by the people, the argument that only legislative parties elected to the National Assembly can serve republican causes has lost some weight. All French parties today, except the Communists, are now committed to accepting some form of presidentialism.

Gaullism, as a strain of French political culture, has served to confuse other dichotomies in classic French political thinking. The advent of a relatively right-wing executive regime has induced elements of traditionally opposed groups to work together in a manner previously considered impossible. Today, the gap between practicing and nonbelieving Catholics can be bridged by a common urge to restrict executive powers. Today, Catholic Republicans can work with Communists and Socialists for mutual benefits. However, as before they do this out of a politics of confrontation and not a spirit of compromise: they join together against a common enemy, whom they wish to thwart or overturn; they do not band together for moderate goals expecting to attain them within the present system.

In summary, it can be said that France has a revolutionary political culture in the midst of a strong strain of political conservatism. Groups in France of all political persuasions have always been willing to resort to violence or other extraconstitutional devices to frustrate or overthrow their competitors. However, every ensuing French regime has retained many of the characteristics of its predecessors. All French regimes are governed by Frenchmen and since there still are few strong instruments in France for developing compromise and mutual cooperation among conflicting groups, every French regime can be said to contain the elements of its own revolutionary destruction.

Processes of Socialization in France

France is a country with sharp social dichotomies between its urban and rural populations. Each major population group has its own social structure and socialization process. Children growing up in French rural areas appear to come from more cohesive family units than urban children. However, this may be merely a superficial fact since rural families tend to live a comparatively isolated existence.

In France the least politically oriented persons are in the rural areas. In contrast, children of working-class families are drawn early into the great network of urban political and social organizations and gain the political consciousness that accompanies these organizations.

Most people in rural areas live in small villages and tend to retain an extremely conservative outlook compared to those living in urban areas. In the countryside the church is normally more influential than in the cities and traditional political viewpoints predominate. The closeness of the family and the village communities reinforce traditional attitudes on public matters—the belief in the value of republican government, small business, and small communities.

France's urban-rural dichotomy is made more complex by the inherent class structure in each sector, which is perpetuated rather than bridged by the educational system. France retains a very traditional educational system, based on an authoritarian school establishment. It has unquestionably been the case that the propertied classes have managed to educate their children and get them greater occupational opportunities than have the poor. A French child goes to school from age six to age fifteen. At age fifteen he is tested to determine whether he will go on to an academic high school (leading to a university), a technical school (leading to a trade), or to work. Over 80 percent of the children of industrial workers and 90 percent of the children of agricultural workers go directly to work at this age.[5]

The French school system is based on the concept that some persons learn better than others and that, therefore, those persons who get into higher education are better than those who do not. The French do not make great efforts to achieve equal educational opportunity at the lower levels, and the children of the wealthy, who are earlier exposed to cultural matters than the children of the poor, have a great natural advantage. This concept thus perpetuates the class divisions of French society, inducing the wealthy to retain the same kind of sense of superiority to their working-class contemporaries as their parents did. Also, children of the working class are taught to see the lower levels of society as their rightful place. They thus perpetuate their own positions within the social scheme, retaining the economic and corresponding political attitudes of their parents.

Political preferences and attitudes, like general social attitudes, are perpetuated in this educational environment. Social groups are organized about particular school districts and particular political organizations. The family is influenced in its values by its social environment and, in turn, passes these values on to its children. Thus, practicing Catholics send their children to Catholic schools, while nonpracticing Catholics do not. The French educational structure thus perpetuates these basic divisions. There is no great public leveler, no single socializing force, no unifying thread of religious tolerance that brings Frenchmen to view themselves as part of an overriding national whole. They continue to see themselves as Frenchmen but their individual traits and their separate groups are of overriding importance.

INDONESIA

Cultural Values and Historic Approaches to Politics in Indonesia

The feudal period. Indonesia has, in the past, been the seat of several successive trading empires, each reflecting a different cultural heritage that the islands have, to some extent, absorbed: first were the Hindu empires of Sri-Vijaya (from 732 A.D. to 880? A.D.) and Majapahit (from 1293 to c.1520), later superseded by the Islamic empire of Mataram (1520? to the seventeenth century). Finally the Dutch, representing the European Christian tradition, took control of the islands in the seventeenth century.

Preceding the empire of Sri-Vijaya, Java had also seen the existence of rice-based inland states, similar to the Indianized states of the Asian mainland. In these early states, the typical Hindu-Buddist political concepts prevailed: there was a theoretically absolute king, symbol of the highest status in the religious pantheon, whose existence held the state together. The king was seen by the general population in terms of his religious significance, not in terms of any services he provided.

For the general population the basic social unit was the village, while the king and the ruling class lived in the fairly inaccessible capital city. The villages dealt with the central government through their own headmen and the people were not generally called upon to do much more than certain services necessary for the maintenance of the central administration. Life in the villages was fairly static, based on subsistence agriculture.

Among the ruling classes, in contrast, political life was insecure and unstable. There were frequent changes of king and dynasty, even though every king sought to legitimize his rule by presenting himself as the defender of the existing order, which he would do either by inventing a mythological genealogy for himself, or by claiming to be a reincarnation of some important religious figure in the Hindu or Buddhist pantheon. Obviously, this method of legitimizing one's rule was open to every usurper. In this governmental system, concepts of representation and of the "rights of the people" really did not exist.

Precolonial Javanese kingdoms (the Majapahit kingdom in particular, but also the Mataram kingdom in most important respects) generally were fairly loosely administered because of the lack of good transportation and communication. In theory, the king was an absolute ruler with the power of life and death over his subjects, but he was actually restrained by acknowledged customary law. This meant that royal regulations, in the Majapahit kingdom especially, bound only certain groups, and representatives of these groups had to be consulted before the king could give an order.

The colonial period. When the Dutch took control of Java in the seventeenth century their main purpose was to engage in a profitable trade, if that were possible. The Dutch, at that time, were not interested in spreading Western cultural ideas or in transforming native political institutions. Rather, they tried to work through the existing political framework and, in so doing, came to occupy a position in Java comparable to the old feudal states of the Majapahit and Mataram kingdoms. The Dutch system of administration developed from this period into one of indirect rule and was confined pretty much to Java: the Dutch, like the feudal rulers before them, were for a long period (up to the nineteenth century, in fact) content to exact tribute from the local Javanese rulers and little more and did not introduce new institutions or concepts of government into native society.

For the most part, in the colonial period the complex and varied activities of government were carried on by the Dutch for the native Indonesians. Very few natives were educated, and those who were educated could find no employment better than a subordinate position in a government or commercial office and had no chance to play an independent part in the country's economic production. Politically, all the decisions on public policy were made by the Dutch central government in the Netherlands, even though some attempts were made to introduce local government and representative councils. Local government, in the manner practiced in the Netherlands itself, was impossible to attain, however, because the whole concept of local community responsibility had never existed in Java. During the Dutch colonial period, Javanese villages continued to be governed by a traditional leadership under the customary law.

The cultural separation between Dutch and Indonesians began to break down, to a certain extent, in the twentieth century. Under nineteenth- and early twentieth-century colonial policies designed to increase productivity and the standard of living, the Dutch extended services to the people by developing communications and transportation, and by introducing some political innovations. The growth of the colonial administration required the education and training of many native Indonesians in Western ideas and skills, both technical and bureaucratic. Eventually (beginning in the 1920s) these factors led to the emergence of political consciousness and nationalist feeling among this new Dutch-created, middle-class native elite. The Dutch, however, would not entertain any demands for native self-rule and Indonesians had no experience in high administrative posts until the Japanese occupation of 1940 to 1945.

Indonesia today. Today, the existence of two coordinate political cultures— one urban-elite and one rural-traditional—continues in Indonesia. This dual system can be traced to feudal times, having been reinforced by Indonesia's colonial experience. Today's Indonesian elite consists of men who, for the most part, have been educated in the Netherlands or in Dutch-established schools in Indonesia. These leaders share many Western ideals and concepts that the general population does not appreciate.

The preservation of local institutions and loyalties, which was fundamental to Dutch colonial policy, has helped to prevent the development of a concept of allegiance to the national state in Indonesia. Loyalties among the Indonesian elite are to personalities and not programs, and the ability to develop mass support really depends on pulling strings with village headmen and religious teachers. The elite has been more concerned with individual power positions than with carrying out policy; they have had only indirect contact with the masses whom they view paternalistically and look to government for their private affairs—much as in the feudal and colonial periods.

The basic unit of social organization in Indonesia is still the village, a territorial group of people with strong ties of kinship. The village chief or leader is elected by the heads of households and decisions affecting the interests of the village are made by a council of elders. (The details of village organization do, of course, vary from tribe to tribe.) Decisions are arrived at after polite discussion in the spirit of mutual aid (*gotong rojong*) and, in theory at least, are supposed to represent a distillate of opinion (*musjawarah*), an implied consensus rather than a course of action to which some members of the group would vocally maintain their own disagreement.

The Indonesian village is a fairly closed society, traditionally self-sufficient and living under its own customary law. It frowns upon individual initiative as a social value and champions the collective spirit of the community. Changes in law and customary practice are generally the product of spontaneous evolution within the community as a whole and not the result of the work of individuals.

Such traditional concepts as *musjawarah* and *gotong rojong*, while derived from the intimate operations of a tight village community, were elevated to a national level by President Sukarno in his concept of Guided Democracy. Ostensibly an attempt to fuse Indonesia's modern and traditional spheres of thought, Guided Democracy was in practice an attempt to overcome governmental weakness and immobility that had resulted from the divisive parliamentary system that had emerged after independence. Largely aimed at the subversion of party strength by the introduction of the principle of functional representation, Sukarno's government under Guided Democracy was justified on the grounds that it had abandoned the worst features of what was labeled "Western-style parliamentary government." The new system was theoretically and culturally supposed to be more in harmony with Indonesia's village traditions, and the new institutions created were supposed to be based on traditional Indonesian methods of reaching agreement rather than on majority rule.

The methods of Guided Democracy have nominally been retained by President Suharto, who overthrew Sukarno in 1965. In operation, these procedures have meant that new assemblies would have to be made up of people appointed by the president who would then be guided by *his*, not *their*, decisions. The president is thus viewed as a village chief on a national scale. Although selected on the basis of particular groups in society (trade unions, youth movements, peasants, journalists, artists, women's groups, and the like) the new functionally based committees and cabinet were to reach unanimous decisions, as councils of elders do in the traditional village. Those who could not agree could not continue to be seated on the councils.

Since 1965, political power in Indonesia has been in the hands of General Suharto and his allies. However, very much in keeping with Indonesian traditions, the new leadership has attempted to preserve the appearance of continuity with tradition. Sukarno was maintained as president, though he was stripped of his title of "President for Life" and kept under house arrest until his death. The same councils and congresses that existed under Sukarno have been maintained, but their membership has been altered.

The conflict of values engendered by the two different sources of Indonesian thought—the Indonesian village and the West—have, thus, plagued the new Indonesian state since independence. Under Guided Democracy the leadership wanted more "business-mindedness" on the part of the people but maintained its own romantic desires to hold on to the familistic concepts of *gotong rojong*. It would like to develop a blend of the traditional village life and the modern world of commerce and advanced technology. However, the autonomous development of localized political units, a long-respected value in Indonesia, has, from the inception of independence, impeded the development of a unified national culture.

Processes of Socialization in Indonesia

As Indonesian culture is fragmented into modern and traditional schools of thought, so Indonesian processes of socialization are complex and vary considerably throughout the country.

Because Dutch investment was heaviest on Java, this island has seen the greatest breakdown of the traditional rural social values. Many Indonesians on Java had been forced off their own small plots of land and driven to work on large plantations. Direct contacts with the Dutch led to both a higher understanding and appreciation of Western concepts as well as, in reaction, the first awakening of Indonesian national consciousness.

On Java the Dutch provided Western technology to improve the efficiency of their enterprises. They also established a small number of technical schools for training Indonesians for lower- and middle-level jobs in Dutch-owned industries. In the twentieth century these institutions produced a small Indonesian middle class, a group of people who had emerged from fairly traditional families, but who now were semitrained in modern Western skills. Compared to most Indonesians this group constituted an elite, though they continued to rank much below the Dutch in social status. These people were to become the major source of support for Indonesian nationalism.

In addition to this transitional group, Indonesian society also produced another elite drawn from the old Indonesian aristocracy. This group was not so heavily concentrated on Java and tended to be more devoutly Islamic. The sons of native *rajahs*, many of these people were sent to Europe for their education. Often extremely sophisticated and well trained, they developed deep resentments against the colonial power that denied them authority in their own country. This group tended to go into the lower levels of the governmental administration and was afforded great opportunities for advancement by the Japanese during the occupation.

The brief Japanese occupation of Indonesia during World War II saw rapid development in the Indonesian socialization process, this time national in scope. Again the influence of the new developments was greatest in Java, but major communications links were established among Java and the Outer Islands at this time. Nationalist organizations throughout the country were able to organize and recruit members and to establish long-term relationships with one another. A radio network reaching the Outer Islands was established that carried speeches by Indonesian nationalist leaders, giving the population personalities with whom they could identify in national terms. An army was also established, allowing Indonesians of all classes and areas to enter and be trained in technological skills.

Today's Indonesian national elite, the army, the politicians, and even the late PKI, could not have achieved their positions of support and recognition among the people without the experience of the Japanese occupation and the process of socialization developed during World War II and the intermittent revolutionary war of 1945 to 1949. It is true that Indonesia never achieved a unity or consensus comparable to the Indian National Congress—indeed, a unified Indonesian national movement in the organizational sense never was established—but a sense of an Indonesian national society did begin to permeate most of the Indonesian population.

Today, rural Indonesia remains much more traditional and Islamic than West Java, which is urban and overpopulated. Rural areas retain customary law and traditional political organizations. To the villager the capital, which provides few services, is, as in ancient days, remote to his experience. Rural communities are poorly developed economically and have little opportunity for Western style educations for their youth. However, some national networks (particularly the army) recruit in all areas and serve as a unifying socializer.

In Indonesia a Chinese community of some 2 million persons maintains a completely separate cultural identity from the rest of the population. The

Chinese speak their own language and maintain their own educational and cultural institutions. Before 1955 the Chinese also monopolized the economic life of rural sections of Java, but their shops have since been nationalized. The Chinese in Indonesia have been supporters of the government of the People's Republic of China and retain close ties with relatives on the mainland. Indonesian leaders have viewed them with suspicion, and the feeling has certainly been mutual. National integration has, as yet, not touched the Chinese and has only weakly begun for much of Indonesia's rural population. Indonesia's fragmentation is thus still pervasive despite some major socializing institutions.

ZAIRE

Cultural Values and Historic Approaches to Politics in Zaire

Zaire, like Indonesia, was a major colony of another small European power, Belgium. Belgium was interested in making a profit and keeping stability in its African territory, much the same as the Dutch were in Indonesia. The Belgians developed an extremely effective, though highly paternalistic, governmental structure that provided a very high level of social services to the Congolese population. However, like the Dutch in Indonesia and unlike the British in India, the Belgians did not provide the Congolese with an opportunity to build national consciousness through their own organizations, nor did they overcome the basic tribal and linguistic fragmentation of the colony. Unlike Indonesia, Zaire never had the unifying experience of an anticolonial foreign occupation and a revolutionary war.

As a colony, the Belgian Congo achieved a widely respected record for efficiency and enlightened administration by African standards. Belgium maintained a large number of civil servants—over 10,000—in both rural and urban areas. These government officials learned the native languages and governed directly. Every Congolese must have been aware of the colonial establishment because of the direct interest the government took in agricultural production (especially cotton) and also because of the services the government provided to make greater production possible. Belgium provided the Congo with a dense network of roads and with extensive health and sanitation programs.

Belgian colonial policy was carried out by a triumvirate, consisting of the Belgian government, the Christian missionaries (80 percent of whom were Roman Catholic), and private corporations. All maintained extensive operations and counted themselves as quite successful: the government had an efficiently administered territory; the missionaries made many converts; and the corporations made high profits. However, the interests of the three groups occasionally conflicted. The philosophy of Belgian colonialism was based on preventing exploitation of native peoples as much as possible, while the companies were more interested in making money. The triumvirate, however, generally worked together quite well. The Belgian bureaucracy was all-powerful, not accountable in any effective manner to any group. The Belgian parliament did not exercise close control over local Congolese matters, and the Congolese did not participate, even to a limited extent, in colonial rule. Indeed, native opinion was unheard until 1956, just four years before the colony became independent.

The area of the Congo has always been naturally subdivided by many different tribal groups who speak different languages and follow different customs. Unlike India or Indonesia with their unifying religious cultures, the Congo has had little except the Belgian colonial experience, its pervasive economic structure based on transportation, and a common administration to provide social and political homogeneity. However, the structure introduced by Belgium was run *for* the Congolese, not *by* the Congolese. It is difficult today, therefore, to isolate and discuss a truly native political culture in Zaire.

Processes of Socialization in Zaire

In the Congo, Belgian administrators learned the native languages, but the Congolese were not taught French. The Congolese were taught specific economic tasks but did not receive more than a sixth-grade education and that in their own native tongue. Indeed, the first university for native Congolese was not opened until 1954, sixty-nine years after Belgium had taken over the Congo. Thus, even though Belgian colonialism had the potential to be a unifying force, Belgian policy was conducted in such a way as to divide, not unify, the area. Political socialization in the Congo was intentionally hindered by the colonial power. With populations confined to their own cultural areas and with no educated native elite, the Congolese were unable to develop a strong spirit of nationalism. Few Congolese, including the leading groups, viewed themselves as part of a national community. The traditional tribal structure, promoted and protected by the Belgians, remained far more important.

Belgian colonial policy was based on the assumption that if the Congolese were provided with basic education and a high level of economic well-being they would not demand political rights. However, disputes within Belgium over language and Congolese educational policy spilled over into the Congo. Also, pressure for independence built up from the international community, when in the late 1950s it became evident that all former British and French Africa would soon be self-governing.

Belgium, unlike some of the other European colonial powers, was not an assimilationist country bent on some sort of civilizing mission. The Belgians tended to segregate themselves from the natives, and the Belgian population in the Congo tended to be transient. Belgians did not establish large white separatist communities but would only stay in the Congo a few years and then return home. At independence there were only 100,000 Belgians among a population of 14 million Congolese.

While important Belgian economic interests, especially the mining group organized behind the Union Minière du Haut Congo, wished to hold on to the Congo at great cost, the Belgian government did not long resist pressure to grant the colony independence. In 1957 the first Congolese political parties were permitted to operate and in 1960 independence was granted. Belgium withdrew its administrators and all the responsibilities for holding the country together fell to a small native elite who viewed one another with suspicion and mistrust.

The country promptly disintegrated into tribal warfare, only to be tenuously united by military force by 1965.

Zaire today is still characterized, outside the major cities, by tribal, rather than modern governmental political organization. Belgian colonial administration had segregated native populations from each other by keeping indigenous populations in quarters surrounding European cities. There were six colonial regions. The Belgians encouraged tribal associations and political parties tended to organize along tribal lines. Patrice Lumumba tried to organize a nontribal nationalist movement, and while it did not achieve the dominance of a majority it was clearly the most important group in the country. Lumumba's movement was quite short-lived and politics after his death took on the character of tribal and regional armed conflict. Provinces were divided and subdivided into new tribal entities; from the six original Belgian areas of 1960, twenty-one were established by 1962. Few civilian links remained to hold the country together. Only the military, through force of arms, could attempt to restore the original structure, and that very tenuously. The people of Zaire are thus only now establishing a set of national political norms. As a nation they have no common political culture; they have a legal state with the trappings of a central government, but only the beginnings of truly national organizations. The economic and, therefore, social subdivisions of Congolese society continue, and only great efforts can serve to make these people view themselves as a nation.

Comparative Distinctions in Political Culture and Socialization Among Fragmented States

Compared to competitive states, fragmented states have not developed a strong national political culture that compels the population to maintain undivided loyalty to national leaders and a national government. However, in this respect certain distinctions can be drawn among France, Indonesia, and Zaire.

France is a highly developed country with a national language and cultural heritage and a national economy. Frenchmen have a long common national history and do not argue about the identity of their nation; indeed, France is unquestionably one of the more nationalistic states of Western Europe. However, Frenchmen differ profoundly over how the state ought to be governed and retain deep loyalties to narrow-based groups that do not have a national perspective. Thus, Frenchmen regard their local communities and their political party identifications as perhaps more essential than their national loyalties. No overriding national consensus (as exists in Great Britain, India, and to a lesser extent in Chile) serves to overpower these narrower loyalties in France. France is thus almost always potentially on the verge of breaking down into intense partisan conflict.

In Indonesia and Zaire national consciousness is considerably weaker than in France. In both these states populations are largely poor and uneducated and retain traditional regional and tribal loyalties. Indonesia has gone through many radical political transformations to accommodate different regional and group perspectives. In Zaire so many persons regard their loyalty to the tribe as of primary importance that the whole provincial organization of the country has been altered. Both these countries have been unable to retain civilian political structures in the face of group conflict. Both are now military dictatorships that seek to compromise group conflict through various representative devices, but that rely on the military in the face of incipient secession and revolution. In both countries processes of socialization—education, communications, and political organization—tend to be weak and not national in scope.

POLITICAL CULTURE AND SOCIALIZATION IN NONCOMPETITIVE STATES

Patterns of Similarity

Political systems that are characterized by extensive concentration of authority and little tolerance of opposition must rest on deeply engrained behavior patterns and cultural attitudes widespread throughout the population. People must be willing to accept undivided authority and must view open criticism as being not quite moral or at least unseemly or inappropriate. People must view themselves as part of a hierarchy; they must see that hierarchy as a normal, justifiable social structure. In other words, the lack of competition in noncompetitive states is as deeply understood and appreciated by their populations as is competition in competitive states. Although fear of force may be present, people do not have to be constantly beaten into submission by the given authorities, nor do their normal day-to-day attitudes reflect simple reactions to fear and pressure. Authority in these states takes on certain traditional aspects that receive widespread support and understanding. If this were not so, these states would be fragmented rather than noncompetitive. Three examples of noncompetitive states are the Soviet Union, Egypt, and the People's Republic of China.

Three Case Studies: The USSR, Egypt, and the PRC

UNION OF SOVIET SOCIALIST REPUBLICS

Cultural Values and Historic Approaches to Politics in the USSR

The Soviet Union is at once a revolutionary state, deriving many of its official beliefs from Bolshevik ideology, and a traditional state, building upon the values and social structure of the Russian past. As in other complex cultures, there exist some important tensions and contradictions in the Soviet view of life and politics, but in the USSR more than most countries, there is a conscious attempt to establish cultural homogeneity and unity, utilizing all the resources of the state.

Soviet political culture reflects values of the Russian political past, though it claims to have done away with these. Before the Bolshevik Revolution, Russia was governed as the last absolute monarchy in Europe. Under this regime all groups that resisted tsarist domination had systematically been eliminated. The church had been subordinated to the state by Peter the Great in the seventeenth century.

Up to the middle of the nineteenth century most of the Russian population (about 80 percent) were serfs bound to a subservient position in a rigid, almost feudal, social structure. Under this system most of the population was not permitted to leave the land to which they were legally tied. They were guaranteed a minimum living standard but had no political rights, and remained entirely outside the political system. In legal terms, they were owned either directly by the monarchy or by the nobility. The nobility, because of the institution of serfdom, was totally dependent on the tsar, since he was the pinnacle of the legal structure from which they drew all their privileges.

The Russian nobility was thus eclipsed by strong Russian tsars, so that all symbolic leadership of the community came to rest with the imperial family. Unlike Western Europe, Russia had experienced few activities that could have led to the development of an independent-minded middle class and a parliamentary tradition. Russia had no free cities and no independent class of burghers and craftsmen surviving from the middle ages. The Russian tsars ruled a well-entrenched traditional political system that tolerated little criticism and no official opposition. Nineteenth-century Russian politics was characterized by government censorship, by the use of secret police for political purposes, and by absolute executive rule.

The nineteenth century proved to be a time of rapid change for Russia. The serfs were freed by Tsar Alexander II, though the aristocracy retained ownership of most of the land. Conscious efforts were also made on the part of Alexander II to develop the country economically. There was much investment in transportation and heavy industry, and many Russians moved into new occupations and new spheres of activity. The formerly rigid class structure gave way as a new politically consious middle class emerged.

In the twentieth century Russian tsarism was shaken by the impact of international warfare and political ideas from Europe. Within the country most people still viewed the tsar as the pinnacle of the political and social order, supported by his sanctified position as leader of the Russian Orthodox church. The Russian peasant could not conceive of criticizing the tsar, for this would mean expressing opposition to all legitimate traditional institutions in the country. However, the new middle groups, aware of political currents outside Russia, wished to limit the monarchy and to introduce a more egalitarian social order. In 1905, these groups forced Tsar Nicholas II to establish the Duma, and in 1917 they supported the revolutions that finally overthrew the monarchy. There were, however, no strong precedents for the Duma of 1905 or the Constituent Assembly of 1917, and Russian politicians had no grassroots support and little concept of political organization.

Russian political life had thus been warped by the tsarist regime's tendency to respond to pressure with techniques of repression. Unlike the states of Western Europe, Russia had no established respected body of law to protect challenging groups from the arbitrary and total power of the tsar. The use of censorship, secret police, the repression of intellectuals were all devices used by the tsars in the nineteenth century and were not the original inventions of the CPSU once it came to power.

There was only a weak tradition and record of failure of legislative groups in pre-twentieth-century Russia. Legislation had traditionally been the will of the tsar, and Russian reforms historically had been imposed from above rather than reflecting the organized interests of groups within the community. The Russian class structure was so rigid spontaneous pressure from below was weak and dispirited. Neither the peasants, nor the provincial nobility, nor the Europeanized society of Moscow and St. Petersburg had the political experience to launch a system of open competitive participatory democracy.

The Bolsheviks, who finally took over control of the country in late 1917, thus found themselves in a country that had gone through some important but not very widespread recent social changes. Capitalism, as a way of life and thought, had not deeply penetrated into Russia; the small Russian bourgeoisie was weak and had not been able to transform the values of the mass of the people, the peasants, in any important way. This latter group remained traditional and passive about politics, expecting to be governed as they always had—by the absolute authority of the chief executive.

The new Bolshevik government was Marxist and anticapitalist. It was therefore concerned about the national political culture and wished consciously to create and control it. The leadership in 1917 had thoroughly utopian aims for the future, which they insisted belonged to all the people. They also believed that their goals and values could only be achieved if the people could be moved from the capitalist or precapitalist pattern of behavior to the socialist pattern of behavior perceived by Marx.

All elements of thought—art, music, literature, all communication—came under the purview of the party, whose major function according to Marxism-Leninism was to transform Russian Man into Soviet Man. As Marx believed human behavior to be a product of its socioeconomic environment, the Bolsheviks sought to manipulate this environment. Lenin created the concept of the "cadre" party, which served the state in practical terms as an elite, but in philosophic terms as specialists in the understanding of the processes of history. The Bolsheviks never conceived of themselves as responsible to the people whom they sought to manipulate. Rather they viewed themselves as a "vanguard", or leadership group. They believed they understood the processes of history as explained by Marx better than the rest of the people. Also, the leaders of the CPSU were considered to be better "qualified "' than their followers, and because of their expertise they were given positions of great respect and authority within the party. The result was a political structure that, while dedicated to modernization and bettering the living standards of the people, was extremely centralized and authoritarian. This was a regime much more efficient and much more dedicated to mass activity than the tsarist regime, but it incorporated many of the values of the earlier regime and received support on a similar cultural basis. Now the CPSU was the sole legitimate pinnacle of all political, economic, and social systems in the state and at the same time the arbiter of all social values.

Processes of Socialization in the USSR

Unlike the tsarist regime, which had been content to arrest its enemies and censor its critics, the CPSU sought to create an entirely new cultural life for the USSR. No institution was to be left untouched, including the family.

All communications—in art, music, literature, scholarly fields, and the daily newspaper—were to satisfy the demands established by official committees of the state. For a time all art had to be "socialist art" and all music had to be "socialist music." This went much further than mere censorship, the deletion of elements found undesirable by officials. Rather Soviet culture became sponsored by the state. The only art was art requested by the government; the only books were books in praise of the government. Artists deviating from official norms could be arrested on charges of subverting the values of the state. Punishment went much further than merely forbidding the publication and dissemination of undesirable works.

Soviet policy in this area has fluctuated greatly since 1917. In the extremely authoritarian Stalinist era, all artists served the state for fear of police reprisals. Since that time there has been some loosening of official policy, but even in the most lenient times writers have had to fear going to prison or work camps for anti-Soviet activity if they were not extremely careful about their work.

Soviet socialization processes are all-encompassing and do not stop at the arts. In the USSR almost the whole population is mobilized into the economy and state activities. The Soviet Union today is a highly developed country with a literate populace and, therefore, has many organizations established for specific purposes. The CPSU penetrates all these groups, which are major instruments of socialization. They include trade unions, voluntary organizations, recreational groups, and professional groups. All represent the aims of their members in one sense, but more importantly they promise the values of the regime to their members through meetings and propaganda.

The primary socializing instrument used by the CPSU is the educational system. A very large percentage of Soviet women work, and Soviet children are generally left in state-run day-care centers from the time of early infancy. This is the first level of a tightly interlocking national system of education that is under the direct supervision of the CPSU. The Soviet school structure is accompanied by party youth organizations at every level. Children are not instructed only in subject matter, but in moral virtue, patriotism, and loyalty to the party. The best students are rewarded with positions in the party youth apparatus, regarded as a great privilege in the USSR. The total educational system is thus used to recruit the best qualified new leaders into the CPSU. Also, the leaders of all segments of Soviet society, because of the interlocking of educational and party activities, are in most cases CPSU members. Thus Communists trained in official ideology create the culture and distribute it to the rest of the country.

The major socialization agent in the USSR then is the CPSU itself, a mass organization devoted to cultural change at all levels of Soviet life. The CPSU runs all local political activities as well as the economic life of local Soviet communities. Immediately following the revolution of 1917 it instituted massive adult education programs, and economically it has transformed the country. Today there seem to be no monarchists in the USSR and only the very old seem to show any real interest in religion. The cultural pinnacles of the tsarist state seem to have been destroyed, replaced by the ideological pillars of the new Marxist CPSU regime.

EGYPT

Cultural Values and Historic Approaches to Politics in Egypt

Egypt has, like the USSR, experienced an important twentieth-century revolution that overturned many traditional ruling groups. Also like the USSR, Egypt has inherited powerful cultural attitudes and values that, when combined with the desires of her revolutionary elite, result in some complex inner contradictions. The country is a nationalist state with an Islamic past. While today's leaders claim to be nationalist modernizers, they behave and play their roles in a context that is profoundly Moslem.

From a traditional Islamic viewpoint there is no separation between politics and religion. The same cultural and moral attitudes that affect economic and social life are viewed as affecting political life as well. In traditional Egypt the law of the country was Islamic law, detailed in the Koran and the Shari'a, the two major religious texts of the Moslem religion. This code covered all aspects of human life and in its final meaning was interpreted by a group of religious scholars known as the *ulema*. These men were the pillars of the traditional Islamic community, giving the Arab world a cultural unity and a common political basis. Historically their political predisposition has been always to support the state and the secular authority.

In the nineteenth century Egypt came under the influence of European powers, particularly Great Britain. Modern economic enterprises were introduced and with the construction of the Suez Canal, Egypt became an important trading center. The country gradually began to modernize; new urban centers developed and a new middle class emerged. In the agricultural villages, where most of the people lived, life went on very much as before, in the Islamic tradition under Islamic leaders. The people offered symbolic loyalty to their monarch, a military figure, but their own way of life remained peaceful, traditional, and centered around Islam.

The emergence of the nationalist movement in Egypt in the twentieth century is quite complex, but it follows a pattern established in many other newly emergent nations. After some thirty years of agitation against foreign powers and the domestic supporters of these powers, the new nationalists made their move. In 1952 King Faruk, a corrupt and ineffectual leader, was overthrown by the military and the monarchy was abolished. Faruk was succeeded by General Naguib, who, in turn, was succeeded by Colonel Gamal Abd-al-Nasser in 1954. The new leadership was drawn entirely from the military and from the new modernizing middle class. In a sense they were appropriate leaders from an Islamic cultural viewpoint: they were military men demonstrating authority by traditional methods. However, modernization and industrialization held an implicit threat for Islamic tradition and the agricultural way of life of most Egyptians. They also implied a challenge to the power of the *ulema* and the old law codes, for the new elite in Egypt, as in the USSR, wished to transform old patterns of behavior to suit the needs of their goals of modernization.

Egyptian political culture has always consisted of a pattern of loyalties to small groups—to the family, or to a religious group. The nationalist movement has affected these smaller groups differently. In the urban areas where there is a small middle class there has been a dramatic introduction of modern attitudes. Here persons have received modern education and have developed modern techniques and skills. Even women in the urban areas have, to a certain extent, been permitted to acquire modern education and also to compete for jobs. In contrast, the agricultural areas have seen fewer fruits of modernization and in them social change has been comparatively limited.

In traditional Egypt the political culture was basically passive and conservative. Islam, though a complex religion with many sects, has generally emphasized the dominant importance of the collective group over the individual. It also has in general supported established authority and promoted social unity as the highest political good. Islamic leaders have conceived of the state as the agency that can uphold the faith and safeguard the unity of the faithful; they have not acted as a political interest group making demands upon government. In traditional areas of Egypt, then, most people still view the state as above them and the product of the will of God. Rebellion against this kind of state is either considered inconceivable or immoral. Even though Egyptian political leaders have seized power by force of arms, they have been able—and, indeed, have found it necessary—to draw legitimacy for their coup from Islamic texts and teachings. In traditional areas, the modernizing elite is viewed as the successor to the old monarchy and is supported on the same basis.

Processes of Socialization in Egypt

As Egyptian culture is subdivided into a modern and a traditional sphere, so are Egyptian socialization processes. In the urban centers, the people learn by modern methods and by experience through modern techniques. Here, extensive secular school systems and adult education programs have been established. Here, also, people are employed by modern enterprises and learn up-to-date methods of doing things. Modern communications, which recruit people into the political system, exist. People learn to recognize political leaders and directly experience the impact of government policy. In contrast, those in the rural areas remain largely uneducated and generally untouched by modern thinking and politics. They fulfill their normal agricultural tasks utilizing traditional methods. They still look to family and religion as their basic sources of identity and still view the state as an elevated institution to be submissively supported as an extension of their religious faith.

In Egypt, as in the USSR, all media of communication, all voluntary organizations, and all institutions of socialization serve the purposes of the state. Under President Nasser, a charismatic figure loved throughout rural and urban Egypt, the army itself served as an important socializing agent by recruiting soldiers from all over the country and instructing them in national values. The Egyptian revolution, however, has been less highly organized and less hierarchically controlled than that in the USSR. While news is managed and censored in Egypt, there has not been a broad-based political-education effort to root out old behavior patterns and substitute new ones. While the regime proclaims socialism as an aim, this is more a set of humanistic aims than a rigorous ideology promoted by the state against the traditional habits of the people. In Egypt the regime recognizes it is supported by popular traditions.

PEOPLE'S REPUBLIC OF CHINA

Cultural Values and Historic Approaches to Politics in the PRC

The People's Republic of China, like the USSR and Egypt, has experienced a major twentieth-century revolution. Following the writings of Marx and Lenin, the leaders of the PRC have since 1949 attempted to establish an entirely new social order. As in the USSR, there has been a conscious attempt to replace old behavior patterns and cultural values with new ones through manipulation and control of all instruments of socialization and communication. As in the USSR, local leaders have been replaced by political functionaries loyal to the central Communist government. The Chinese regime has attempted to mobilize the entire population behind the goals of modernization. However, as in the USSR and Egypt, there exist strong traditional tendencies that both conflict with and support the new system.

The People's Republic of China is the seat of an ancient culture and the home of the largest population in the world. The Chinese people, while they occupy a large territory and are not broadly integrated in the modern socioeconomic sense, have still long been united in cultural matters. Although Chinese dialects are not all mutually intelligible when spoken, the complicated Chinese writing system has long been uniform throughout the country and was used as the basis for the old imperial bureaucracy. The former Chinese elite was unified in terms of education and philosophy. All over the country the respected classes read the same literature and mastered the same philosophic schools of thought. The concepts embodied in this ancient past form the backdrop for the Chinese political culture today.

Traditional China was a culturally authoritarian state that emphasized the importance of the family above all else. The entire state was perceived as a hierarchy at the head of which was the emperor. The state was supported by deeply engrained habits that stressed duty to one's social superiors, self-discipline, and an extremely puritanical strain of morality. The average Chinese family itself reflected this hierarchical organization. Every member was ranked in importance and owed reciprocal duties and responsibilities to other members. Thus younger brothers owed obligations to older brothers and older brothers to fathers. In turn fathers were responsible in the economic and cultural sense for the well-being of the children. They were required to provide their children with education and an understanding of the cultural patterns of the greater society. The family was conceived of as a link between the past and the future and this aspect made for an extremely conservative outlook. Respect for the elderly and traditional ways of doing things was a necessary part of the social system, and reverence for the past was the basis of a deeply rooted sense of morality toward all human relationships.

The political system was viewed as the highest level in the hierarchical social order. A vast majority of the Chinese people lived in small agricultural villages and their only link with the central Chinese government was through the central bureaucracy, which collected taxes and performed a limited number of services for the community. The public viewed itself as being bound to the emperor through a system of duty and responsibility, much as younger children felt duty bound to their elders. The emperor was conceived of in traditional terms as an absolute monarch within the pervasive system of moral obligations. Thus a corrupt or weak or inefficient emperor could be opposed legitimately on the grounds that he was not performing his duties according to his responsibilities. In this circumstance the emperor was viewed of as having lost the 'mandate of heaven." In times of crises such as flood, drought, or warfare the imperial system was periodically challenged and emperors were replaced using this age-old rationale.

Traditional China was thus a relatively rigid class system governed by an elite that was educated to rule. This elite, centered in the imperial bureaucracy, derived from the wealthy merchant and landowning groups. The difficulty of the Chinese written language combined with the fact persons could be admitted to bureaucratic posts only after passing difficult written examinations in the Chinese classics meant very few persons outside the leisured classes could get into an important position in the political hierarchy. However, there were cases in which the brilliant sons of peasant families were able to achieve sufficient learning to pass the exams, and it was widely believed in China the system was responsibly and fairly administered. The basic values of the system were an appreciation for order and morality, supported by the widely respected Chinese ethical systems of Confucianism and Taoism.

The People's Republic of China has thus inherited an appreciation for a hierarchical social order, a reverence for legitimate authority, and a widely accepted sense of duty by the population toward the state. However, where the old system perpetrated a desire to save and preserve old knowledge and old methods, the new regime wishes to transform China into a modern industrial state. This means transferring loyalties from small families to large collective political groups. It also means an attack on the old agricultural class structure.

The concepts utilized by the contemporary regime are found in Marxist writings as interpreted for use in China by Mao-Tse-tung. These include especially an attack on the old class structure and a new emphasis on equalitarianism, modern education, and massive political reeducation. As in the USSR, the regime in the PRC believes that no aspect of culture can be left to chance. The new China is to be created purposefully by the elite or vanguard of the state—the Chinese Communist party—who understands the processes of history. The mass of the people, through the use of extensive bureaucratic organization, are to be mobilized behind the regime. They are to become active supporters and workers in massive enterprises and projects while traditional village loyalties and archaic behavior patterns are to be forgotten. The new culture stresses mutual obligations and morality but aims for a progressive and utopian future rather than stressing the values of filial piety and nostalgia.

Processes of Socialization in the PRC

Since 1949 the PRC has experimented with her policy on cultural matters. In the 1950s an attempt to permit some freedom of thought, the "Hundred Flowers Bloom" period, resulted in open criticism of the regime. The government cracked down on critics and instituted a conscious policy of instilling new values in the Chinese people. The contemporary processes of socialization in the PRC constitute a radical attack on the Chinese past, though they rest on the moral support of the people who still feel an obligation and duty to the state and to each other based on tenets of this past. Today Chinese Communist party (CCP) functionaries have replaced the imperial bureaucracy; where in the past central government projects were limited in scope, today they are extensive. They can take the form of restructuring entire regions into large communes or introducing new industries.

The new values of collectivization and modernization are taught through a massive political education program. As in the USSR all levels of education are linked to the CCP apparatus. The best students are recruited into party youth groups so that by the end of the educational process the top representatives of all professions are loyal party members. In addition to this the Chinese organize adult political education programs in all parts of the country.

As in the USSR, the Communist party in the PRC has established organizations to educate and socialize the population in all regions, at all age levels, and in all occupations. Not only in schools, but in agricultural collectives, in factories, and in army units people are taught the teachings of Chairman Mao and the virtues of his regime. Pamphlets espousing the aims of Chinese leaders are published in great number and read widely; in areas in which people are largely illiterate, group discussions of the texts are led by party workers to develop active popular support and understanding.

All Chinese media of thought and communication are also manipulated to build the new society. Patriotic poems, new operas, and theatrical productions all reinforce the values the party wishes to instill in the people. In the PRC, more than in the USSR, great works of the classical past have been deleted from current libraries and theater repertories. The conscious effort to create new cultural values goes down to the nursery school level, where children from their earliest years are taught the values of patriotism and hard work through songs, plays, and stories.

The massive cultural campaign includes a great investment in formal schooling, interrupted during the Cultural Revolution, but now evidently being reestablished. While the Soviet Union is a literate society with many trained technicians, China lacks educated professionals and managers. Since the Cultural Revolution many school programs combine both work and academic education. Students spend portions of their time in a factory or on a farm. Many Chinese workers are formally enrolled in such education programs, but these people constitute a small minority of the population. Formal education is still not widespread in China.

The new cultural attitudes have undoubtedly penetrated the Chinese urban population much more deeply than the peasant groups in the countryside. Despite efforts at mass collectivization, China remains largely a country of peasant villages that retain much of the old Chinese cultural patterns. As in Egypt, the respect for authority natural in these areas in the PRC has served as a support for the current regime, but the PRC more than Egypt claims to be a revolutionary state wishing to uproot the old social patterns. In this lies the great conflict and contradiction in Chinese political culture.

Comparative Distinctions in Political Culture and Socialization Among Noncompetitive States.

All three noncompetitive states discussed here—the Soviet Union, Egypt, and the People's Republic of China—are countries that traditionally were governed in an authoritarian manner, experienced a revolution in which one leadership group was overthrown by another, and established another authoritarian system but this time devoted to economic modernization.

Beyond these gross similarities there are some distinctions among the three. The USSR is the most highly developed and has been most committed to mobilization of the people over a long period of time. The Soviet political culture is thus more uniform on a national basis than that of the other two states, but so too are Soviet processes of political socialization. The Soviet network of party, mass organizations, and educational establishments reaches the population down to the lowest level and in the remotest regions. This physical investment in social mobilization is unmatched in Egypt and the PRC.

Egypt and the PRC remain largely traditional countries in which most people dutifully obey their leaders according to traditional precepts. Both regimes are committed to modernization and thus are interested in uprooting some cultural habits they regard as contradictory to modern economic activity. Of the two, however, Egypt retains less of a commitment to modernization than to what it conceives of as a national identity. Egyptian nationalism has a strong Islamic flavor, and Egypt thus has not attacked the traditional authority structure so much as it has used it. In contrast, the PRC has fluctuated greatly in policy on cultural matters. At times the regime has permitted some freedom of communication, as in the "Hundred Flowers Bloom" period of the 1950s; at other times it has attacked critics of the regime in an almost violent manner (as in the Great Proletarian Cultural Revolution of the 1960s). Neither Egypt nor the PRC are nearly as mobilized as the USSR, however.

POLITICAL CULTURE AND SOCIALIZATION: COMPARING COMPETITIVE, FRAGMENTED, AND NONCOMPETITIVE STATES

All states utilize similar institutions of socialization: all children are raised by families and learn their attitudes and beliefs through contact with institutions permitted by the prevailing society. However, important differences in the processes of socialization exist in competitive, fragmented, and noncompetitive states.

In competitive states people tend to believe politics should be open, decisions shared, and groups heard. In these countries people thus have many group loyalties but they have developed an overriding national consensus that makes political violence unthinkable. Basic loyalty to the system is spread through institutions such as schools, political parties, and volunteer groups and these institutions reinforce the consensus on political competition already prevailing throughout society.

In fragmented states, while groups retain subloyalties over and above their national loyalties, national socialization processes do not exist that can effectively overwhelm these subloyalties. As a result these countries are only superficially united and their governments lack widespread legitimacy. Such countries are always fending off secessionist movements, partisan claims by special groups, and possible revolution.

Noncompetitive states have definite patterns of political culture that tend to support authoritarian rule and work against the establishment of free group activity and open political competition. In such states all institutions serve the interests of an established elite and rest on a dutiful population used to accepting authority from above.

NOTES TO CHAPTER 3

1. See, for example, Gabriel A. Almond and Sidney Verba, *The Civic Culture Political Attitudes and Democracy in Five Nations* (Princeton: Princeton University Press, 1963); David E. Butler and Donald Stokes, *Political Change in Britain: Forces Shaping Electoral Choice* (New York: St. Martin's Press, 1969).

2. James Petras, *Politics and Social Forces in Chilean Development* (Berkeley & Los Angeles: University of California Press, 1969).

3. Ibid., pp. 146-7.

4. Lowell G. Noonan, *France, the Politics of Continuity in Change* (New York: Holt, Rinehart & Winston, 1970). pp. 101 ff.

5. Ibid., p. 74.

Chapter 4

Political Participation

ISSUES IN POLITICAL PARTICIPATION: A FRAMEWORK FOR COMPARISON

The political participation process is the means by which people develop
and express their political beliefs and recruit, train, and select their leaders for
the future. It is a direct application of a political culture to a specific area of
activity. That is, the aims, values, and beliefs of a people will determine their
own actions in politics and will restrict the types of persons selected to be
political leaders.

The process of political participation must be accomplished by every
political system, whether competitive, fragmented, or noncompetitive. Government policy must always be based on the actions and activities of persons both in
and outside the political sphere so that policy can realistically be formulated
and executed. This directly and indirectly involves the broad patterns by which
people individually or organized in groups participate in politics.

The primary means by which people participate in politics in competitive
systems is through elections. By casting their ballots the mass of citizens can
express their opinions about both specific and general political ideas. However,
some systems allow for more direct participation than others and elections can
mean different things in different countries.

In some countries mass participation is also achieved by the free organization of politically minded groups. These groups can be permitted direct entry
into the political system by lobbying within political parties, legislatures, or
administrative bodies. On the other hand, in some systems individual groups
that appear to be agents of popular participation can be controlled by other
agencies, for example, a head of state or a monolithic political party.

POLITICAL PARTICIPATION IN COMPETITIVE STATES

Patterns of Similarity

Great Britain, India, and Chile are, or until recently have been, competitive
systems which permit free elections and free group activity. In all three

countries political leaders are selected by political parties which are, in turn, open to free mass membership by all citizens. The populations in all three countries are free to join political parties and to support other groups with narrower political aims. These groups establish a kind of interplay and balance through competitive bargaining and negotiation. Their activities also produce the leaders upon which the entire political structure rests. Beyond these generalizations, there are significant differences among the three countries.

Three Case Studies: Great Britain, India, and Chile

GREAT BRITAIN

The British political system is characterized by a free, open, and intense interplay of political groups and individuals. The level of popular participation is extremely high, both in terms of general turnout at national elections, vocal expression on political issues through free group activities and the media of communication, and in the actual practice of individuals who formulate political opinions and seek to advise their fellows and their governments of these views.

Group Activity and the Recruitment Process in Great Britain

The British system is often described as being dominated by a highly organized party system that recruits, trains, and promotes the nation's political leaders. However, it is also true interest groups are at work at a much more fundamental level in similar pursuits. British political parties have always maintained strong links, if not always official alliances, to coalitions of groups representing special interests in society at large. The justification for these relationships is sometimes called the "Whig Theory of Representation," attributed to the great eighteenth-century politician, Edmund Burke. The concept can be traced back to medieval practices that afforded special economic groups direct representation in the houses of Parliament. British political representatives have thus always been viewed as spokesmen for segments of their community. Conversely, these economic groupings (sometimes called "corporations") have enjoyed direct participation in the political process through their links to members of Parliament. The early division of the British Parliament into a House of Lords (representing landholders) and a House of Commons (representing more commercial interests) is evidence of the long-standing recognition in the country of the right to political participation of different kinds of economic groups.

The importance of political groups in the British political process cannot be overestimated. No country in the world has a more virulent Society for the Prevention of Cruelty to Animals; in no other nation could actions of government trigger so many instantaneous organized responses from interested groups of citizens. Today, the group process, while overshadowed by the political parties at the national level, is thoroughly institutionalized. Members of Parliament from all major parties can legally be retained by special groups to represent the views of that group within Parliament. Thus the British television industry, for example, will pay fees to members of Parliament so that the interests of the industry will be defended within the legislature. An MP accepting such a retainer is not viewed as having a conflict of interest; he is simply thought of as a representative of a special constituency within his own party. In the case of today's British Labour party, all members of certain special groups are automatically inducted into the party. Thus all trade union members are automatically members of the Labour party, unless they "contract out." Their union dues are used to support the party unless union members officially demand they not be. Trade unions directly sponsor a large number of MPs: usually at least one-third of the Labour party representation in Parliament is held by union members and leaders representing the union interests. Thus groups not only voice demands in Great Britain, they are actively involved in the process of recruiting political leaders. (See comments on the "Working Class Today" in Chap. 5.)

All policy and legislation in Great Britain reflects the interplay of the population as organized into recognized groups. From group proposals politicians try to create their own political programs. Group lobbying before political parties at party conferences is thus a major instrument of direct popular political participation. Here people with special demands can voice their interests to politicians who make national policy. On the other hand, politicians are kept responsible by these groups, which make their demands public to their members, to the parties, and to the people at large. Groups can decide whether to support or to withhold support from a political party based on the record of the party in office; some groups (like the trade unions) can directly affect the outcome of national elections by their willingness to produce active support in terms of money and workers at particular moments. In addition groups can influence the decisions of administrators by providing them with information and presenting their views on specific policies.

Processes of Communication in Great Britain

Such group activity and massive popular participation could not take place if Great Britain were not a highly literate country, well endowed with a modern communications network and with a long tradition of respect for differing political opinions. The British population reads more newspapers than any other public in the world. The British press, which is not government controlled, reflects the great partisan divisions of the political system. There are several large families of newspapers: one owned by Cecil King (the *Mirror* is his best known newspaper) tends to support the Labour party; another owned by Lord Thomson (among them the *Times* of London) is generally conservative; a third great magnate, Lord Beaverbrook, controlled the *Daily Express*, and his organization during his life time and since his death, has generally continued to be pro-Conservative. In addition, there are some other very well-known newspapers—the *Guardian*, which tends to support the small Liberal party; the *Observer*, which is independent, though sometimes pro-Labour; and the *Daily Mail*, which avidly supports the Conservative party. All these newspapers have a broad national readership. Indeed, the *Daily Mirror*, with a daily circulation of 5 million in a country of 54 million, has no equal in terms of popularity in any country with a free press.

In addition to newspapers, the British public is kept informed by the other mass media—radio, television, books, and films. Radio and television were for a long time monopolized by the British Broadcasting Corporation (BBC). This is a government corporation that, though supported by tax dollars, is extremely neutral on political matters. British mass communications are scrupulous in their political objectivity and are not even permitted to sell television time for political purposes except as regulated by a very stringent law. Today, Great Britain also has an Independent Television company (ITV), which is privately owned, but it too has retained the tradition of political objectivity and neutrality. Partisanship is promoted primarily by groups using their own propaganda; by the press; by individual artists in plays, films, and books (all widely read and circulated); and by individuals in face-to-face contact with one another.

Freedom of speech has always been deeply respected in Great Britain, and possibly in no other country is it so widely used by so many people. The institution of Hyde Park Corner is symbolic of this tradition: in a section of this large London park any person, for any reason, can address and reach a wide audience on any subject of interest and concern. He is not restricted in anything he might say; he can be honest and rational or stupid and malignant, but he will be heard, applauded or shouted at, and protected. Great Britain has always permitted even the most extreme views their right to a public hearing, without the introduction of public investigations, security checks, and police surveillance. Communists and Fascists have been free to speak, to organize, to run for office without being hampered by any special burdens or restrictions. This tradition seems to be well engrained and deeply respected throughout the British community.

Electoral Participation in Great Britain

As already noted British society has for a long time been class based, with a well-educated elite running most spheres of activity while the majority of the people, the working masses, passively accept lesser roles. The process of political participation in Great Britain has reflected this class basis, but since World War II there has been an increasing movement of working-class people into groups and parties that represent their views in the political process. The general level of political participation, as measured by activity in the electoral structure, reflects the fact that political activity is national, widely distributed, and not confined to a particular class. Fully 80 percent of the British electorate identifies with some political party, and normal voter turnout is usually between 70 and 80 percent of those eligible. It is true that educated persons of middle- and upper-middle class backgrounds dominate the leadership positions of most political groups (including the Labour party), but political activists are drawn in large numbers from all classes. This is revealed in Table 4.1, which presents comparative social characteristics of members of Parliament in Great Britain, 1951-1966.

Table 4.1. Social Characteristics of Members of Parliament, 1951-1970

Characteristics	Party	1951	1959	1966	1970
University Education	Lab.	41 %	39%	51%	59%
	Con.	65 %	60%	67%	69%
Working-Class Occupation	Lab.	37 %	35%	30%	30%
	Con.	--	--	--	--
Professions or Business	Lab.	44 %	48%	52%	54%
	Con.	77 %	76%	75%	76%
Median Age	Lab.	52	55	50	50
	Con.	47	48	48	48
Women MPs	Lab.	11 %	13%	19%	10 %
	Con.	6 %	12%	7%	15%

SOURCE: Reprinted with the permission of R.M. Punnett, *British Government and Politics* (New York: W.W. Nortòn, 1971, p.91, and Heinemann Educational Books, Ltd., London).

As can be seen both parties are represented mostly by university-educated men, largely from the professions and business. Both parties, however, have large minorities of MPs who are not college graduates and the Labour party has many members who are manual laborers. This is evidence of political participation drawn from a wide social spectrum, despite the carry over of traditional class attitudes in British society.

INDIA

India is by law and practice a country of open and democratic political patterns, though not nearly so open as Great Britain. However, since independence the process of participation has broadened in India and more people than ever before are today active in Indian political life.

Group Activity and the Recruitment Process in India

While the official Indian political structure shares many structural and institutional processes with the British—both countries have cabinet-parliamentary systems responsible to a broad national electorate—the cultural patterns underlying the British group process is quite different from that underlying the Indian. British party organizations dominate political decisionmaking and draw their basic support from coalitions of active interest groups; in India, interest groups tend to be weak and inactive. The Indian party structure is consequently less informed and less capable of efficient decisionmaking than the British. Because Indian constituencies are not well organized, Indian politicians must take more of the political process personally upon themselves. They must invent policy on grounds other than group demands. In the past Indian public policy has often been drawn from abstract statements of socialist ideology. Also because of the relative weakness of the group process, Indian politicians have not easily been held responsible for their actions. Individual politicians with magnetic personalities have come to dominate groups and parties and approach a charismatic level of appeal.

Despite this broad general comparison to the British system, some interest groups do function within India and serve as channels of participation and leadership recruitment. Immediately following independence all political power in India was concentrated in the hands of the Western-educated elite who ran the Indian National Congress. Led by Jawaharlal Nehru, the Congress dominated every phase of Indian politics. However, with the death of Nehru and the passing of the group who surrounded him, power has begun to shift away from the nationalist elite to leaders of local organizations who are politically pragmatic, rather than ideological and utopian. Today power is shared in India; local personalities have developed their own followings and in many areas have supplanted the nominated representatives of the national political parties. These rural bosses have, in some cases, become charismatic personalities in their own right and as such represent the aspirations and desires of their traditionally minded following. Through these new provincial leaders, the aims of rural India, the great mass of the Indian people, are voiced to national politicians and the nation at large. However, because such politicians normally have had weak organizations, the desire for more expression and participation on the part of the people has not always been satisfied. India is thus still a nation of violent uprisings in the face of political discontent; the group process is still so inefficient that in times of crisis, such as famine, drought, and the like, persons are as likely to riot as to make demands upon politicians. Indians still feel politics and government are not broadly responsive to their wishes; this results from the relative difficulty in establishing organizational links between the government and the population at large.

Certain groups within the more literate, educated urban sector in India function in much the same way groups do in highly developed competitive systems. In these areas, most people are politically aware and trained to respond to political events. Thus, the workers in Indian cities are generally organized into labor unions, which are usually part of the Congress party (in legal terms), just as the British trade unions are part of the British Labour party. However, throughout India there is a surplus of labor and unions generally are weak bargaining units because employers can always hire nonunion workers for low wages. Thus unions in India really serve only a limited economic function; they are agencies largely sponsored and subsidized by the Congress party (or in some cases, one of the Indian Communist parties) for purposes of mobilizing public opinion. The relationship of interest group to political party in India is quite in contrast to that in Great Britain: in Great Britain, interest groups can sponsor party members and support the party of their choice; in India, the party creates and subsidizes the interest group. In the first case, the group has demands based on the wishes of its members that it communicates to the political elite; in the second case, the political elite attempts to create this communication link by sponsoring the group. Economic interest groups are weak in India mainly because India is an economically underdeveloped country.

However, groups other than economic ones can also serve as agents of political participation. In India there are a large number of community associations that reflect the complex ethnic and linguistic divisions in the Indian population. These groups have developed intense political aims, normally demanding some sort of special protection or treatment for their cultural individuality. Although such aims may be criticized as being narrow and provincial, they still serve as a connecting link between traditional peoples and the national political system.

In addition to communal groups India also has agrarian and student groups. These are both mostly elite oriented, reflecting the educated and wealthier segments in Indian society. Some agrarian groups have led uprisings in various regions. Indian Communist parties have led in organizing landless peasants in rebellion against wealthy landlords. While these uprisings reflect a certain parochialism, they also represent the growing politicization of the Indian peasantry and their increasing willingness to participate in political activities. Similarly, student organizations have been involved in "antiestablishment" protests. In India there is a severe shortage of jobs for college graduates and student organizations act as safety valves for students' discontent with their economic prospects. They thus permit students to express their discontent through demonstrations when they might otherwise riot or enter into longer range subversive activities.

Processes of Communication in India

Seventy percent of India's population is illiterate and the process by which people learn their political facts and develop their opinions is much more informal than would be true in a highly literate, industrial society.

There are newspapers of course. These circulate among the urban elite—perhaps 25 percent of the people—and they can be quite influential since power is still heavily concentrated in a relatively small number of hands. While the Indian press is usually described as free from government control, there have been instances in which the government has closed down opposition newspapers and imprisoned their editors. These actions have been taken within the country's legal framework (every country has laws against libel and scandal), but it is nevertheless true Indian newspaper editors have to be more careful about what they write about their government than their British counterparts. Indian newspapers are simply not as institutionalized as British newspapers, and a government move against a newspaper in India does not produce a national outcry as it undoubtedly would in Great Britain.

With respect to the mass of the Indian population, radio communication is probably the most important source of political information. Every village has a radio that broadcasts the programs of the government-controlled network in the language of the region. The government controls all radio and television communication, and it is undoubtedly true in some cases radio explanations of government policy turns out to be a defense of that policy.

Opposition groups in India do not have equal access to the major communications media; the government, invariably led by the Congress party, has always had the upper hand in this area. Also because of the limited development of the country, television reaches few people and the arts, films and literature among them, are enjoyed only by a small elite. Government dominance and censorship therefore favors the Congress party at the expense of other political organizations.

Probably the most prevalent form of political communication in India, among people at the lowest levels is face-to-face discussion. In this context, the prestige of local personalities can have great influence in interpretations of political information coming from outside. Local groups can sway large numbers of citizens by their ability to express political beliefs for their members, and the government can exercise little control over what is discussed and how issues are resolved. There is no doubt Indian political opinion, as expressed in the electoral process, has shifted away from the Congress party, despite its ability to control the formal communications media. This shift of opinion can only be the result of face-to-face political discussions.

Electoral Participation in India

The political participation process is quite complex and disparate in India, which has local, state, and national levels of government and political elections at all levels. The system is dominated by national authorities, and despite

Table 4.2. Voting Behavior of the Indian Electorate in 1967 as Compared to 1962

Type of Voter	% of 1967 Electorate*
1. Voters with Regular Voting Habits	
a. Voters for Congress in both 1962 and 1967	26.3
b. Voters for opposition parties in both 1962 and 1967	7.8
2. Voters Who Defected from 1962 Choice	
a. Voted for Congress in 1962; voted for opposition parties in 1967	12.1
b. Voted for opposition parties in 1967; voted for Congress in 1967	2.7
3. New Voters	
a. Did not vote in 1962; voted Congress in 1967	15.1
b. Did not vote in 1962; voted opposition parties in 1967	18.0
4. Dropouts	
a. Voted Congress 1962; did not vote in 1967	6.2
b. Voted for opposition in 1962; did not vote in 1967	1.4
5. Apathetics: Did not vote either in 1962 or 1967	10.3
Total	99.9

SOURCE: Adapted from Samuel J. Eldersveld, "Elections and the Party System," *Asian Survey* (November 1970), p. 1017.

*Those eligible to vote in 1962 and 1967 and about whom both 1962 and 1967 voting behavior information was available.

widespread illiteracy, the Indian public has continually demonstrated an expanding and sophisticated knowledge of politics. The growth of participation in elections has led to the emergence of many new political parties and to the decline of the Congress party as the overwhelming force in Indian politics. About 55 percent of those eligible to vote turn out at Indian elections. The number of candidates and parties have continually increased, and voters have shifted allegiances among individual politicians as well as from party to party. (This shifting in party preference is presented in Table 4.2.)

As can be seen, approximately only 34 percent of the electorate voted the same way in 1967 as in 1962. Almost 15 percent of the electorate defected from their earlier preference and about 7 percent dropped out of the system. There were 30 million new voters in 1967 (33 percent of the electorate). This great influx of people into the electorate, which was in no way predictable or controllable by the parties in power, insures that India will remain an open competitive system with fairly broad patterns of participation.

CHILE

Chile, which is not so economically developed as Great Britain, but not nearly so underdeveloped as India, has a small, literate, compact, and generally urban population that views itself in national terms. Chileans conceive of themselves as members of classes within the same social system, much as the British do. Chile, unlike India, does not have the problem of assimilating different linguistic and cultural groups. However, although Chile enjoys a general social homogeneity, the country is going through an important social upheaval in which interest groups play an important part.

Group Activity and the Recruitment Process in Chile

Unlike Great Britain and India, Chile has had a presidential system of government in which power has been divided among legislative, executive, and judicial branches. Chileans, like Britons, have been able to participate either directly or indirectly in politics by supporting interest groups. However, because the Chilean system provided for more points of contact through which groups might enter the system, Chilean political groups have been at once more vocal on many different points of view, but less organized (since some groups may find themselves in one position with the legislature and in another with the executive) than British groups. This outward appearance of incoherence is compounded by the fact that Chile has a multiparty system in which no particular political group or even coalition of groups can be certain of a majority behind any special set of policies. Government has been carried on through deals made among different parties in Congress at one level, and through negotiations between Congress and the president on another. In these circumstances groups have had to maximize their influence by selecting particular strategies. Thus some groups may have supported candidates of opposing parties, at different times or for different offices, merely on the basis of group demands. It has been possible in Chile to elect a president from one party and a majority for his opposition in Congress. This poses a great dilemma for individual groups: whom should they support and how avidly, if they are to attain their goals?

Recently segments of the working class have been striving for a redistribution of income through direct, organized political activity. Agrarian groups have been operating within the political system for over a decade; until the military coup they had seized rural estates for their members and redistributed lands despite the actions and pronouncements of all of Chile's political leaders. In the same vein, supporters of the Christian Democratic party have staged massive street demonstrations under their own leadership, without the direct organizational activities of the party. Labor groups also actively supported the Socialist party and President Allende, until these groups (and parties) were outlawed by the military in 1973.

Thus, while some of Chilean interest groups may be described as more like the Indian (i. e., sponsored by parties with little grassroots support), many Chilean groups have wide community support.

It can thus be said that in Chile the process of political participation has matured. Groups voicing the real demands of the public have brought these demands to the politicians. Chile's government has had to respond to these demands or risk being defeated at elections. Since 1964 and the Frei administration, Chile's leadership has generally attempted to pursue its responsibility to the lower classes, undoubtedly because of the ever-increasing organization of this population. It can be said then that these groups transformed Chile's political parties and the programs that they have sought to pursue, until the advent of the military coup.

While Chilean political participation has been broadened by the increasing activity of the group structure, Chile's politicians are still very much derived from the elite. They are urban, literate and professional, seeking support from the lower classes. Some working-class members have been chosen to represent special districts by the more radical parties, but the top leaders of all parties—Left and Right—are from the traditional Chilean elite.

Processes of Communication in Chile

Until the Allende presidency legally Chile had a free process of political communication. Private companies published the country's newspapers, Chile's most influential day-to-day medium for the distribution of political information. Of Chile's adult population 80 percent is literate and newspapers receive a much wider distribution here than in India. They are widely read in the urban areas where the elite is concentrated. However, Chile's newspapers are usually quite partisan; more like in India than in Great Britain, the Chilean government has moved against particular editors and publications. President Allende had particularly singled out the Christian Democratic press in this regard. In addition, the move of his government to take control of paper manufacturing interests had aroused some concern among the opposition press, before the military coup. Now, since the coup, the Socialist and Communist press has been outlawed.

It must be emphasized that Chile has a thriving cultural life in addition to newspapers and political periodicals. She has world-renowned novelists and poets, a wide audience for theater, films, and the other arts. and a broad distribution of the arts throughout the country. Chilean producers import foreign films and television programs, and make a broad appeal to urbane and cosmopolitan sectors of the population. In this the Chilean people still experience a varied and free interplay of ideas and information.

Electoral Participation in Chile

The growing activity of political groups in Chile has served to transform the base of Chile's political electorate. As new voters have come into the system, new interests and demands have been generated. Elections have been, until the military coup of 1973, the primary means by which most Chileans have participated in politics.

In Chile there have been separate popular elections for the Congress and the president. Thus some elections are waged by local parties on the basis of local issues; others are entirely national. Chile's law states that all citizens over the age of twenty-one who pass a literacy test are eligible to vote. (This accounts for about 80 percent of the adult population.) Chile's legal system also requires that all who are eligible to vote must vote subject to a fine and/or prison sentence of up to sixty days. This is a fairly difficult law to enforce; however, other regulations, such as the requirement for proof of voter registration to do business with banks or government agencies, are more effective in inducing Chile's citizens to register and to vote. (Table 4.3 summarizes voter participation in Chile from 1945 to 1961.)

Table 4.3.   Voter Participation in Chile, 1945-1961

Year	Type of Election	% of Population Registered	% of Registered Who Voted
1945	Congressional	11.9	70.1
1946	Presidential	11.5	75.9
1949	Congressional	10.4	79.5
1952	Presidential	18.4	86.6
1953	Congressional	18.1	71.5
1957	Congressional	19.1	68.4
1958	Presidential	21.5	83.5
1961	Congressional	25.1	74.5

SOURCE: Adapted from Federico G. Gil, *The Political System of Chile* (Boston: Houghton Mifflin, 1966), p.213.

About one-half the population of Chile is under the age of twenty-one; the low proportion of the population registered to vote reflects this fact. Table 4.3 shows that there has been a consistent increase in the proportion of voters registered. Of those registered, more people vote in presidential than in congressional elections, but even so there is quite a high proportion of eligible voter turnout in Chile.

Participation rates vary from region to region in Chile; the urban areas, which have a higher rate of literacy than the rural areas, have proportionately high rates of voters. Women could not vote legally in Chile until 1949 except in municipal elections (they voted in Great Britain at age thirty in 1918; all British women were eligible to vote in 1928; in India women have been eligible to vote since independence). The registration of women today in Chile still lags far behind that of men, though the trend has been toward greater registration of women. In Chile male voters outnumber female voters by a ratio of 3:2, even though there are more women in the Chilean population than men and the literacy levels of the two groups are roughly the same. In the few presidential elections in which women have participated, they have favored Christian Democratic candidates much more than men have. Overall, women appear to be far more conservative than men in their voting habits. In 1970 Allende received 45 percent of the male vote, but only 28 percent of the female vote. Women were also very important in the demonstrations that preceded Allende's downfall. The growing participation of women in Chile's political life can thus mean some important changes in party strength and political developments for the future.

Comparative Distinctions in Processes of Political Participation Among Competitive States

Processes of political participation differ among competitive states largely because their traditions and levels of economic development differ. Great Britain, the most highly developed of the three competitive states discussed here, also has the most complex, developed, and widespread institutions of political participation. Great Britain has a powerful, vocal, and partisan press that is distributed widely among and read by her highly literate population. The British habit of forming interest groups for specific political purposes is very widespread and considered legitimate throughout British society. Modern media of communication—radio, television, films—also bombard the public with many varied opinions and views of a specific and general type. Government does not propagate the views of the governing party, and any gross violation of the tradition of political neutrality by government-controlled media would be deeply resented in Great Britain. In addition, electoral interest and voter turnout is extremely high throughout the country.

This highly developed pattern of political participation is made possible by Great Britain's high level of economic development, which allows the British people to become educated, to develop political interests, and to devote time and energy to political organizations. The complexity of the economic system also leads to a situation in which most Britons belong to more than one group whose individual special interests overlap. Thus, interest groups in Great Britain do rot (as they sometimes do in India) provide an alternative symbol of loyalty to political parties or the state itself. Group leaders are perceived of as having a narrow cause and do not generally acquire an elaborate charismatic status with the population.

In India the group and communication processes are not nearly so developed as in Great Britain. In India, because of the generally low level of economic development of the country, there are comparatively few literate people and a correspondingly low level of press and book distribution. Also, modern media of communication are relatively limited. Group activity, because Indians have fewer economic pursuits and less contact with modern communications than Britons do, is also less developed. Indians in cities are aware politically, join political organizations, and vote, but to a much greater extent than their rural compatriots. Most Indians live outside the cities, and in the rural areas processes of communication and participation tend to be traditional, based on face-to-face contact, with much respect and influence afforded local personalities. There is much less overlap in group activity in India than in Great Britain and much of it is artificial (i. e., sponsored by the political parties rather than springing spontaneously from public needs). However, political participation and voter turnout seem to be increasing as the country's political and economic development progresses.

Chile's processes of political participation were widespread and increasing in their impact at a rapid rate until the military coup of 1973. Chile has a literate population, a widely distributed partisan press, and a network of interest groups, which reinforced the basic partisanship of this transitional country. Unlike Britons, Chileans have not developed overlapping allegiances to many groups, nor has there been quite so much respect for opposition viewpoints. In Chile there has been a relatively rapid shift in power from an entrenched upper-class elite to newer middle- and working-class groups, while poorer, less educated segments of the working class have been less able to improve their positions in Chilean society. Recent political resentments deriving from conflicts between the more impoverished workers and the new Chilean middle class have been deep compared to class antagonisms in Great Britain. However, Chile compared to India has had a widespread level of political participation: Chileans have a national awareness and their groups have been allied to national, not local or traditional, organizations.

POLITICAL PARTICIPATION IN FRAGMENTED STATES

Patterns of Similarity

In fragmented states patterns of political participation tend to reflect the basic disunity of these societies. Group loyalties tend to override national ones, and citizens' loyalties to narrow pressure groups, or to regional and tribal organizations, often override their national loyalties. Formal processes of communication are, as a consequence, often controlled by the government in an attempt to counteract the natural centrifugal tendencies of each society's pattern of political participation. However, voter turnout and public awareness can vary significantly even among fragmented states and are affected by such variables as national tradition and level of economic development.

Three Case Studies: France, Indonesia, and Zaire

FRANCE

France is a modern industrialized society with a literate and politically alert population, a complex economy, many highly organized interest groups, and a multiparty political system, which, on paper, would seem to involve widespread popular participation in a great variety of political activities. However, the political structure in France (unlike that in Great Britain), has not long been dominated by large mass political parties, which are natural points of contact to political interest groups.

Group Activity and the Recruitment Process in France

In France, society has been fragmented into many competing groups that often take on a broad political character rather than the defense of some special interest. Political interest groups tend to be diffuse in their goals and have difficulty in articulating them; the fragmentation of the party system had also meant that groups are not clear about where to exert their greatest efforts. In the Fourth Republic, French parties could not stay unified behind a coherent program very long, and cabinets were continually unstable. In the Fifth Republic the legislature and the parties have considerably diminished in importance, and major decisions have been made by administrators working for the president of France. In both instances, interest groups have had difficulty in establishing clear relationships with persons in power. They may speak for their constituents, but they have difficulty in making themselves heard before those who make the real political decisions. Thus, they are quite weak and ineffective when compared to British interest groups.

Part of the difficulty facing interest groups in France is the nature of the groups themselves. France is still very much a country of small communities, and "political" groups have a much more informal character than they do in Great Britain. They are not as highly organized and do not develop specific planks and objectives very easily. Also, compared to interest groups in other Western countries, French interest groups tend to be quite small: for example, only 15 to 20 percent of French wage earners are organized into trade unions (42 percent of the British civilian labor force is unionized); only 25 percent of French farmers belong to any agricultural group (90 percent of British farmers belong to the Nation Farmers Union). It is probably correct to say that informal associations in France, such as wealthy families and religious alliances, are more influential than the more highly structured political interest groups.

Compared to British interest groups, French interest groups are therefore not as important in the political recruitment process.

Persons can, however, still participate in politics through the group system. Groups were normally involved in political campaigns in the Fourth Republic, when they provided funds for certain candidates. This influence has declined considerably in the Fifth Republic because the importance of the National Assembly has also declined. Since 1958 organized groups have attempted to influence national referenda and presidential elections. Most interest groups have been opposed to the Gaullist regime because the new system has deprived them of their usual channels of influence. However, group activity has not been very successful, as the Gaullists continue to rule the country.

Interest group activity, despite these defeats, has increased in France since 1958 particularly aimed directly at the French administrative structure. In addition, agitation by groups in agricultural areas has spilled over into rural riots and violence. Labor organizations, though fragmented and disorganized, have been able to paralyze the country on occasion by resorting to strikes. In the Fourth Republic such violence took place, largely because of the government's inability and weakness in resolving important questions. Today these riots are more the result of bitter opposition against a regime that wishes to insulate itself from public opinion.

Processes of Communication in France

The fragmentation and weakness of France's group structure is reflected in the country's media of communication. France has a generally free press, with publications in circulation reflecting every point of view. However, France ranks relatively low in newspaper circulation—well behind most other developed nations in the world and far behind Great Britain, where more copies of newspapers are sold every day than any country in the world.[1] The nonpartisan press—*France-Soir* and *Parisien Libéré*—has a much greater readership than the partisan press. Indeed, *Humanité*, the Communist party newspaper, now has a circulation of only 200,000, compared to some 2 million for the nonpartisan newspapers, (compared, for example, to 5 million sold by Great Britain's highly partisan *Daily Mirror* each day). This represents a tremendous loss of readership to the Communist press, which in 1945 and shortly thereafter published two dailies for almost 1 million daily readers. Other French newspapers are also generally declining in circulation. In 1964 Paris had 14 daily newspapers, compared to 28 in 1946; outside Paris, the number of papers had dropped from 175 to 93 in the same period. Since the advent of the Fifth Republic the press has become much more nonpartisan and nonpolitical.

Many persons within the French press and the political elite have demonstrated widespread dissatisfaction with the information they receive about their government. This criticism is not basically directed at the press but at the Fifth Republic's concerted policies of government secrecy. French newspapers are not censored or controlled, but under the Fifth Republic access to information has been severely curtailed. French newspapers have generally been critical of this government practice, but to little avail. President de Gaulle's press conferences were characteristically staged to the most minute detail: the president answered only questions he wished to answer and these were given to him in advance. Free interviewing and free reporting were quite limited in scope in this situation. President Pompidou also remained insulated from press scrutiny.

In addition, radio and television in France are not as politically neutral as they are in other Western competitive systems. Indeed, some persons have described the Fifth Republic as "de Gaulle plus television." In France, recent presidents have used radio and television extensively to campaign for their positions in both national referenda and presidential electoral campaigns. This use of the media has been denied to the opposition, giving the government an extremely important electoral advantage. Since almost all French homes have a radio and a television set, this constitutes one of the major political issues raised by the opposition against the government. Some reforms have been instituted in the administration of radio and television, but they seem to have had little effect. Today, a minister appointed by the president no longer directs the radio and television systems; rather a relatively apolitical Board of Directors has been given broad powers, among them to check on accuracy and fairness. This board represents civil servants, the public, the press, and the government agency in charge of radio and television (Office de Radio Diffusion - Télévision Française or ORTF). However, ORTF is government appointed, and the actual management of the industry is still directed by the government.

It should be noted that even with governmental control of the media, the French population has exhibited considerable independence of mind in elections and referenda. General de Gaulle did not win a popular majority in the first ballot of the 1965 presidential election (he did win a majority in the runoff in which there were only two candidates). Indeed, he resigned his presidency because of a defeat in a national referendum in 1967. Exposure on television can thus sometimes be detrimental to the aims of the government, if government representatives deport themselves poorly. The precise impact of television on French opinion is of course difficult to measure.

Electoral Participation in France

France has extensive grassroots political participation, especially in her local governmental structure. France is still very much a country of small communes (rural villages of less than 2,000 inhabitants). These small units are administered by local elected councils of between nine and thiry-seven members. With 38,000 communes, there are almost one-half million local office holders in the country—nearly 2 percent of the electorate.

Most municipal officials are active members of political parties, so most dues-paying members of parties in France have a good chance of holding political office on the local level (e. g., it is estimated that one-half the dues-paying Socialists in France have at one time been municipal councillors).

In addition to this direct form of political participation, the French population voices its active political interest through elections and the vote.

However, as in most other countries this form of participation is unevenly used by different groups in the population. In the Fourth Republic, France had a legislative system characterized by very complex party competition for legislative seats; the Fifth Republic has direct presidential and legislative elections, but only the president has been powerful politically. It is thus difficult to compare voter turnout in the Fourth Republic to voter turnout in the Fifth Republic.

Table 4.4.   Referenda in the French Fifth Republic 1958-1972

Date	Abstentions: % of Registered Voters	Pro-Gaullist: % of Votes Cast	% of Registered Voters	Anti-Gaullist: % of Votes Cast	% of Registered Voters
9/28/58	15.1	79.2	66.4	20.7	17.4
1/8/61	23.5	75.3	55.9	24.7	18.4
4/8/62	27.0	90.7	64.9	9.3	6.6
10/28/62	27.0	61.7	46.4	38.2	28.8
12/19/65	28.2	54.5	44.8	45.5	37.4
4/28/69	79.4	46.7	36.7	53.2	41.6
4/23/72	39.5	67.7	36.1	32.3	17.2

SOURCE: Adapted from H. Ehrmann, "Politics in France," in Gabriel A. Almond, ed., *Comparative Politics Today: A World View* (Boston: Little, Brown, 1974), p.215.

Table 4.5.   Breakdown of the Vote in the 1965 French Presidential Election, Second Ballot

Segment of Electorate	% of Total Vote Received De Gaulle	Mitterand
Men	49	51
Women	61	39
Ages:		
Voters both men and women, between 20 and 34	49	51
Voters, both men and women, above 34	55	45
Farmers	59	41
Businessmen	67	33
Workers	45	55
Rural Areas	57	43
Paris	51	49
Towns of more than 100,000 (excluding Paris)	57.5	42.5

SOURCE: Adapted from Henry W. Ehrmann, *Politics in France* (Boston: Little, Brown, 1968), p.91 (taken from *Sondages* poll taken between the two ballots, which accurately forecast the election results.)

In addition, the Fifth Republic has carried out plebiscites on important political issues, something the Fourth Republic never did. In a plebiscite the voter decides the issue directly on the basis of his own opinion. Thus, in plebiscites the direct political participation by most Frenchmen in governmental decisions has been massive and little direct influence of interest groups, parties or elected officials have been evident. Voter turnout on French referenda is summarized in Table 4.4.

It can be seen that more than 70 percent of French eligible voters voted in all referenda. In 1958 the referendum on the Fifth Republic constitution was voted on by almost 84 percent of the electorate. France, at this time, had universal suffrage and no property qualification for voting.

As in other countries some segments of the electorate participate to a greater extent than others. In France men vote more often than women and the urban educated population votes more than the rural population. There are also very few women in French political life as almost all party officials are men. The party preferences of different groups is summarized in Table 4.5.

It can be seen that in 1965 men more than women voted for the leftist candidate; that rural areas, farmers, and businessmen favored de Gaulle, while workers preferred Mitterand (a Socialist). The young were almost evenly divided about de Gaulle; the middle-aged and elderly supported him. However, all groups participated at high rates: 85 percent of the electorate voted in 1965.

INDONESIA

Indonesia, like India, is an economically underdeveloped country with a weak interest group structure. Political groups in Indonesia, rather than supporting the system in the manner of open interests in an open system, usually have a regional or ethnic base and demand special privileges from the regime. However, Indonesian ideology has always emphasized the importance of representation for all groups in the community and conceived of the aims of all special interests as theoretically unified in the Indonesian nation. All groups that have political aims are seen as legitimate so long as they support the nationalist elite.

Thus, beneath an ideological facade of national unity, Indonesia's great cultural fragmentation not only exists but has become institutionalized. In Indonesia, even in the period of free political activity (from 1945 to 1957), there was never a clear sense of the leaders being bound by the people. The Indonesian parliament was a place for leaders to confront one another—not as representatives of interests in the community, but as spokesmen for different ideologies; the object of such confrontation was not compromise among disparate interests, but clarification of thought. This was to be done through the traditional methods of *mufakat* (deliberations), in the spirit of *gotong rojong* (mutual aid). This odd contradiction of theoretical respect for the representation of interests while politicians and groups are only weakly organized continued through the period of Guided Democracy to the present day.

In 1957, Sukarno announced his "conception" (later labeled "Guided

Democracy") of the solution to the problems with which Indonesia had been grappling since 1950. Blaming the major difficulties of governmental weakness and instability on the adoption of "Western style liberal government," which, he said, was based on a concept of opposition contrary to Indonesian tradition, Sukarno proposed the establishment of a new series of state councils that would replace the elective bodies of state. From 1959 to 1960, Sukarno, using the same justification, dismissed the elected Constituent Assembly, deactivated the elected parliament, dissolved the major opposition parties, and suppressed the major opposition press. In place of these, Sukarno appointed a National Advisory Council as well as a *Gotong Rojong* Congress, choosing the membership himself, on a "functional" basis. Today, there still is no free participation process, despite the later overthrow of Sukarno by the military.

Group Activity and the Recruitment Process in Indonesia

The new councils set up by Sukarno were supposed to be more "representative" than the previously elective bodies of state, because they were selected on a functional basis. The groups selected to be represented were trade unions, youth movements, the intelligentsia, religious leaders, farmers and peasants, journalists, women's organizations, artists, veterans of the revolution, foreign-born citizens, Indonesian business circles, and certain state institutions such as the police and armed forces. The members in the new National Council, whose function was to give solicited and unsolicited advice to the government on principles, not details, were to be nominated by the functional groups but appointed and discharged by Sukarno himself. As in India, then, the groups were sponsored by the government, their members were recruited by the government; they were not the spontaneous outgrowth of grassroots politics.

Although the National Council was to be representative of the population and was to have certain advisory functions, its major value was seen in its capacity to instruct the people in the goals of the state—not the other way around. One of the presumptions of the system of Guided Democracy, as stated by Sukarno, was "the progress of (the) state should come first, then the progress of the wider society, and only then should we think of the smaller groups."[2] The National Council was seen as one institution that would place the interests of the state before those of any other individual or group or even combination of groups in Indonesia. Thus the regime explicitly permitted groups and communications only so far as they would support the regime in power.

All actions under Guided Democracy had been taken under the slogan of NASAKOM (Unity of Nationalists, Religious People, and Communists), a phrase that has been described as "a shibboleth since guided democracy was introduced in 1959, espoused by the PKI [the Indonesian Communist Party] with the President's support."[3] Under NASAKOM, Sukarno had attempted to use the Communists as a balance against both the army and the other remaining nationalist politicians. Ideologically, NASAKOM was taken to mean a situation in which the "progressive segments" (i. e., those in Sukarno's favor) in the Indonesian community were represented. Under this concept Sukarno had attempted to include the Communists in the major organs of state, though this

had generally been opposed by non-Communist politicians and the military.[4]
The non-Communists therefore responded with an ideological grouping of their
own, an organization called "Supporters of Sukarnoism." This latter group also
claimed to represent the totality of all "progressive" groups in Indonesia, though
it actually included only the major non-Communist groups that wanted to keep
the PKI in check.[5] All groups claimed to represent best the totality of the
Indonesian community even though, like the earlier political parties, they were
urban-based elite associations having little contact with the general population.
Their claims of being representative were merely asserted ideologically,
without really widespread attempts to build support within the Indonesian
community. Although they claimed to represent the nation, both Sukarno via
NASAKOM and the "Supporters of Sukarnoism" were strongly motivated by
political considerations.

NASAKOM, it should be emphasized, exemplified the general approach to
participation of Guided Democracy in much the same fashion as did the new
"functional" councils. Like the councils, NASAKOM was put forward as a
reflection of the totality of Indonesian society—a society that, even though
composed of diverse elements (nationalists, religious people, and Communists
as defined by NASAKOM), was still capable, by traditional Indonesian methods, of coming to a harmonious consensus. Consensus or unanimous agreement,
similar to the Rousseauist concept of the "general will," was ideologically held
to be attainable and characteristic of Indonesian behavior, and NASAKOM was
the slogan under which it was held to be reached. This consensus was, by
implication, to be "guided" by Sukarno, who was the originator and articulator
of the slogan. As in the functional councils, the elements represented under
NASAKOM were not selected by the population at large, but by Sukarno by
virtue of his role as the leader of the nation who instinctively knew the
composition of his people and who could, therefore, by his own mystical
abilities, establish the institutions that best reflected the national will. Representation and participation was therefore to be achieved under the guidance
and direction of the state ideology that Sukarno formulated.

This approach has not been substantially changed since the coup of 1965.
General Suharto has replaced the Communists and Sukarno's supporters with
others loyal to himself. He has maintained the practice of nominating groups and
persons loyal to himself for government office, while endowing them with
slogans to legitimize them. He has even permitted a parliamentary election (the
first since 1955), in which ostensible opposition parties were permitted to
compete, though not the PKI, which is outlawed and considered treasonous. Yet
there has not been a presidential election, and it is the president who wields the
power.

Processes of Communication and Electoral Participation in Indonesia

Political participation in Indonesia is thus still limited to the urban elite and
special groups within the military. The economy is weak as are all economic
groups. Communication is difficult and all media of communication—the press
and radio—are completely controlled by the government. There still is only

limited contact between the national government and outlying regions, and very few channels of contact between government policymakers and persons with political aims in the Indonesian community exist. There is thus little political participation by the mass of Indonesians: they do not have a free press; they vote only in controlled elections and are not free to support political groups for their own interests. All these activities are subject to government control. On the other hand, the government does not really mobilize the total population through coercion. Rather the natural fragmentation of Indonesian society is respected and permitted to continue so long as Indonesians do not threaten the regime's aims, which have been precarious and limited. Under General Suharto, the primary goals have been the gradual restoration of the Indonesian economy, control of inflation, and attraction of foreign investment. To accomplish these, Indonesia has not felt it necessary to transform her political processes or increase the level of political participation of her people.

ZAIRE

In Zaire political participation, perhaps more than in any other state considered in this book, has directly reflected the very basic tribal fragmentation of the national community. Where French and Indonesian politics have both reflected many conflicting groups and goals, in Zaire there has not long existed either an attempt at coalition (as in France) or an ideological scheme for unity (as in Indonesia). Only Patrice Lumumba made an early, though short-lived, attempt at creating a national political party and received some important support. However, since Lumumba's death, politics in Zaire has consisted of a state of war among several reasonably large tribal groups and the military. Since independence these groups have been able to develop political aims, but many of these aims have been contrary to the concept of any national system. Political groups have not had any experience in working together or in reaching political compromises. They had not worked in colonial-sponsored political bodies, nor did they have the opportunity of learning to trust one another within the confines of an organized nationalist movement. In Zaire, after independence and Lumumba's death competition for leadership among the different tribes emerged, resulting in a prolonged and complicated civil war. Politics quickly became not a practice of persuasion and compromise within well-defined rules, but rather individual groups going their own way. It is true that France and Indonesia evidence similar traits, for in them too violation of constitutional norms is characteristic of group behavior. However, Zaire, more than the other two, has barely had any experience with peaceful political participation. In Zaire group tactics forever continually spill over into violence, and the process of political participation has basically been a process of military confrontation.

Group Activity and the Recruitment Process in Zaire

Zaire has many political groups that, since independence, have sought to protect the interests of their members. These groups include, for example, military subunits whose main mode of participation has been through the army mutiny. The dissension among army subgroups has led to much of the anarchy that has plagued Zaire since independence since the army has been the only means by which the new state could hope to ensure the protection and security necessary to a peaceful political process. With the army in tribal disarray, the rest of the country soon followed suit. Only since the reestablishment of a unified military under General Mobutu in 1965 has anything like a national political system emerged in Zaire. Since 1965 group violence has been submerged while administration of the country has stabilized under military auspices.

In addition to the military, other groups in the country have sought special interests. There has been violence among ethnic groups, among religious groups, among provinces, and among tribes. There have been full-fledged insurrections as in the secession of Katanga province; there has also been the fragmentation of provinces into subprovinces.[6] All these have been somewhat overcome by the military, but through much bloodshed.

Thus, political participation in Zaire exists, but through different channels than in other states. The political process does not really evidence the free interplay of interest groups. An interest group normally has a specific narrow goal it is trying to achieve within a recognized political system; in Zaire groups have, in general, sought broad unlimited goals: they have sought to overthrow the system or to transform their position within it; they have not aimed for special policies—rather, they have tried to represent their people or their region for all things at all times. Such groups are really communal groups similar to small nations; they are not interest groups in the sense of a modern political process.

Interest group politics is preeminently a politics of compromise, in which groups are willing to trade support for special favors and in return establish the legitimacy of the political leaders. This is a recognized fact even in France and Indonesia where compromise is also extremely difficult. In Zaire no important political leader has ever recognized this fact. From Patrice Lumumba, the murdered nationalist who wished to establish a mobilized militant state, to General Mobutu, who has monopolized all power in his own hands, there has never been an acceptance of free political interplay. Different groups simply do not trust each other well enough.

In Zaire, if a tribal group gives into another in an area of special importance, it is giving up its reason for being. The surrender of a group's self-concept—its subnationalism—is impossible unless reinterpreted within some broader national framework that all groups accept. Consequently, the fragmentation of the community has been so severe no national society can authentically be said to exist. Groups have been so fearful of one another and so antagonistic toward all national policymakers the political system at the national level has become immobilized under the military, even though violence has stopped.[7] If this immobility were to subside, a more modern politics would be less likely to emerge than another civil war.

Thus, political participation takes place in the narrow confines of traditional group activity. Tribal leaders, who are respected for their traditional positions, have at times been able to mobilize their particular popula-

tions behind special aims through informal processes of communication—discussions and tribal meetings. The practice of the military of
kidnapping and murdering opposition leaders has been successful in achieving
at least a nominal loyalty of different tribal groups to the national system.
However, this does not mean that the different tribes trust each other or actively
support the regime. Under these circumstances the recruitment of nationally
minded leaders is at best only accidental, at worst nonexistent.

Processes of Communication and Electoral Participation in Zaire

There is no national system of political participation that has any meaning
for the population of Zaire. Newspapers are confined to small elites in urban
areas and are quite unimportant in the overall process of communication since
they do not reach a sizeable public. Subsequent to General Mobutu's takeover
the press, despite its limited significance, came under government censorship.
Limited radio and television communication is also completely under government control.

Elections have been staged under General Mobutu and, even though rigged
and controlled, they constitute the most promising means by which the people
can be involved in a national political life. Though the outcome is a foregone
conclusion, it is nevertheless true that a national election brings the concepts of
nationhood and national politics closer to people who are used to thinking
exclusively in tribal terms. In a sense, elections constitute an educational
process, which is, also, a mode of participation. The people are instructed in the
aims and identities of national leaders, over and above tribal matters. This same
process takes place in all tribes, no matter how hostile they are to Mobutu. The
fear that the individual groups have of military action is enough to allow this
minimal cooperation with elections. How deeply national politics has
penetrated tribal groups is immeasurable, but it is likely to be very weak at this
moment.

Elections in Zaire do not produce representative politics. All parties
support President Mobutu and no group as yet has dared to challenge or
contradict him. The legislature is thus not really a link between the government
as personified by Mobutu and the community. It is a facade through which only
supporters of the president can enter. The community at large, for the moment,
remains outside the political process—passive, immobilized, and inactive. This
is more out of fear of anarchy and military violence, than out of any genuine
acceptance of President Mobutu's policies.

Comparative Distinctions in Processes of Political Participation Among
Fragmented States

As in competitive states, processes of political participation in fragmented
states reflect levels of economic development as well as the cultural and
political traditions of these states. Of the three fragmented states considered
here, France is by far the most highly developed economically and the least
fragmented politically.

In France political participation takes many forms and is quite widespread, reflecting the country's long tradition of popular, though divided, representative government. The French electorate directly elects the national legislature and the president and participates in policy through voting on referenda. However, although elections are well-established procedures in French politics, elected officials are not as closely tied to group politics as they are in competitive states.

In France groups tend to have a separate existence from the national political party framework. They are not, as for example in the British political party system, integrated behind particular politicians into coalitions that determine policy on a national basis, nor do they lobby so much in the legislature since that body is no longer the major policymaking institution in France. They, instead, take their special demands directly to administrators, who are quite insulated from legislative and popular pressures.

France, in addition, has a literate population, a widely distributed press and modern media of communication—i. e., radio, television, and films. The press in France is not so well circulated as that in Great Britain and many widely read newspapers are nonpartisan. However, radio and television are government controlled, reducing the opportunities for airing opposition viewpoints. Despite this, French citizens appear to maintain a strong interest in and are informed about politics; they demonstrate this through high voter turnout in elections and a willingness to complain directly (via strikes, riots, or other demonstrations) to the government over matters of vital concern.

In comparison to France, both Indonesia and Zaire have less developed processes of political participation. In the latter two countries most of the population is rural, basically uneducated, and living in traditional communities. People do not have a very clear conception of the national political system, though they are aware of their special tribal and regional identifications. Thus they do not form pressure groups that make demands and inform the national government so much as they follow traditional affiliations out of their feelings of community and respect for local leaders. Indonesia and Zaire also do not have highly developed communication processes. Radio, television, and newspapers are government controlled in both states and are important only in the cities. Political communication outside the towns is carried on traditionally, by word of mouth, tending to perpetuate traditional political conceptions.

Indonesia and Zaire are somewhat different from each other in that Indonesia has established institutions that are intended to reflect the many groups and sectors in society, at least as ideologically predetermined. Although representatives in these institutions are generally responsible to President Suharto rather than to the electorate, elections to a legislative assembly have been held and the people have had some opportunity to choose from a number of political parties. Opposition groups, i. e., groups that are not government sponsored, have a small representation in the Indonesian legislature. The institutions of Zaire are not so elaborate; in Zaire elections have also been staged but the government has been careful to see that all national groups and parties are loyal supporters of President Mobutu. Elections, as well as the limited communications media available, tend to be used to establish and reinforce national above tribal loyalties.

POLITICAL PARTICIPATION IN NONCOMPETITIVE STATES

Patterns of Similarity

Noncompetitive states have similar processes of political participation in that they restrict the political process in the real sense to those considered "qualified" according to some partisan or ideological standard. Thus in Marxist states like the Soviet Union or the People's Republic of China all communications and group activity are sponsored by the governing Communist parties. Meaningful participation by the mass of the population does not exist, except as expressly organized and permitted by the party and its subsidiary organizations. In Egypt, another noncompetitive state, the military-bureaucratic leadership is deemed qualified to lead by virtue of its traditional standing as well as its role in the nationalist revolution. As in the Soviet Union and the People's Republic of China, all groups and media of communication in Egypt must be approved by the government leadership in order to function.

Three Case Studies: The USSR, Egypt, and the PRC

UNION OF SOVIET SOCIALIST REPUBLICS

Group Activity and the Recruitment Process in the USSR

The Soviet Union is committed to the maximization of political participation by her citizens within the framework of her noncompetitive structure. This is in deep contrast to Indonesia and Zaire where the regimes have purposefully limited participation, owing to fear of structural collapse of the political system. In the USSR, real participation is desired and real recruitment takes place, but only within strictly defined boundaries and without free interest group activity, open communications, and free elections. The state and all its institutions rest on a monolithic ideology that does not recognize any value in open criticism and dissent. Political participation thus must take place behind a facade of party unity and ideological purity.

Soviet politics can justly be described as oligarchic since the preponderant number of decisions are made by a very small number of people who occupy the top positions in the Communist party bureaucracy. However, within this formally noncompetitive structure interest groups, composed of people who are also part of the Communist elite, do exist and do compete for influence. These groups do not have the open-structured organization of their counterparts in competitive systems; rather, they take the form of informal factions within the party bureaucracy or the state administration.

In the USSR all economic affairs come directly under state control. The efficiency levels of production, working conditions, and wages are all set by government bureaucrats advised by professionals and specialists. When agricultural policy, for example, is established, it is based not merely on the whims of party bureaucrats, but on the information they receive from these institutionalized groups. When the USSR establishes a defense policy, it reflects the information presented by the military and the advice of those involved in defense production, as well as the wishes of top party leaders. This is not substantially different from policymaking, in its most general way, in other states. In the USSR, however, the influence of special interests are entirely informal. Groups and interests are represented by individuals in secret face-to-face contact with political leaders who never formally admit to being pressured. There are no open institutions for complaints or lobbying, which take place behind closed doors.

In the USSR then interest group participation is present and the success or failure of interest groups depends upon their access to the decisionmaking process. Military factions obviously have direct links to the top leadership through both state and party bureaucracies, and these have been very influential and successful. Industrial groups, represented by specialists who are responsible for economic planning, have also succeeded in achieving places of contact in the government machinery.

It is possible, on occasion, for large groups to fail in achieving a position in the hierarchy. When their demands go unmet, these groups do not have the option, which in competitive systems acts as a safety valve, of going to the people through the open communications media. On very rare occasions, because of the relative narrowness of the avenues of political participation, political demands in the USSR have taken the form of riots and violent outbursts. Such outbursts occurred in the 1960s over difficulties in the agricultural sector, but clearly reflected different political interests on the part of bureaucrats who opposed Nikita Khrushchev's reorganization of the agricultural bureaucracy. This activity was not revolutionary, i. e., aimed at the overthrow of the state; rather, it was the reflection of the political viewpoints of individuals who had been defeated by persons in authority and therefore had no other means to express themselves within the monolithic structure of the state.

In the USSR the state has never been satisfied with passive obedience. The Soviet leadership is constantly seeking to stir up the support of its people, to get them into the political and social life of the state, and to recruit the best people for party positions. Its recruitment of leaders takes the form of a centralized civil service system to which entry is controlled on the basis of both politics and ability. Politicians are created out of this system. The USSR is governed by an interlocking system of jobs that is described in detail in administrative textbooks. Promotion from a lower rank to a higher one is supposed to be based on merit as well as tenure in office. Because of the interlocking relationship between the CPSU and all other institutions of importance in the state, it is almost a certainty all persons in all positions of importance are party members. The party bureaucracy is then the most important institution in determining who shall enter politics and who shall not in the USSR. In addition to recruitment through the civil service, the CPSU foments participation through massive political education programs. Indeed, since the death of Stalin, emphasis has been placed more and more on recruitment through education than on fear and repression. In 1960 an entire educational system devoted to Marxist-Leninist studies was instituted with more than 20 million people—party members and nonmembers—enrolled. These people were to be trained as propagandists who would be capable of carrying the CPSU's message to the mass of the people. Soviet citizens were exhorted to give up the fear and apathy so characteristic of them under Stalin and to be diligent in their work and loyal to their state.

Processes of Communication and Electoral Participation in the USSR

Although all communication is state controlled in the USSR, a conscious effort is made, as in the political education program, to create interest and excitement among all Soviet citizens. The Soviet press, though an arm of the party and completely subject to party bureaucrats, has since the death of Stalin more and more reflected differing points of view among military, industrial, and intellectual leaders in the community. The regime has been unpredictable in the limits it has permitted in the voicing of dissent; certainly government interference in cultural and intellectual matters under CPSU General Secretary Leonid Brezhnev and Premier Alexei Kosygin is somewhat more repressive than under Khrushchev. On the other hand, the fact that the USSR has two major information organs—*Pravda*, the CPSU paper, and *Izvestiya*, a Moscow newspaper—makes it possible for different points of view to be expressed even among the same elite. Many Soviet citizens consider *Pravda* to be more liberal than *Izvestiya*, though the differences are not clear cut. In recent years journalists as a professional group have become something of an interest group in their own right. A large number of Russians work on small local papers and participate actively in the party's propaganda activities.[8] Also, today the USSR has a number of special interest journals that reflect differences in Soviet elite opinion. *New Times* and *International Affairs*, for example, represent the generally moderate views of the diplomatic elite. In contrast, *Red Star* propounds the more conservative, doctrinaire views of the military leadership. Differences on specific issues among publications such as these can reflect the actual conflicts on policy that may occur within Soviet decisionmaking bodies.

The Soviet press excites interest and participation among citizens by providing a forum for the airing of justifiable grievances—as long as those grievances are not threatening to the foundations of the regime itself. Examples of criticism of local government or middle- or lower-level bureaucrats in the press are common. In the USSR the government and party bureaucrats are sensitive to public opinion on the local level.

The press is not the only means by which the party exhorts Soviet citizens actively to support the party line. In addition, party workers are regularly involved in oral presentations to groups exhorting them to work harder and to become more actively involved in the party's goals. While it is true that elections in the USSR have very little significance, a kind of political participation is brought about by the CPSU election campaigns, which promote face-to-face contact among party leaders and the people. Party members, in lecturing workers to increase their productivity, see the workers on a personal basis. The average citizen thus comes into contact with a political worker who represents the party line. For example, every factory has a party cell within it, and before elections leaders of these cells call meetings of workers to instruct them and discuss the issues. In this situation electoral processes and political recruitment come together.

Political Participation in the USSR, Indonesia, and Zaire

Although participation processes in the USSR are restricted by comparison to those of highly developed countries with open, competitive groups and parties, in comparison to the people of Indonesia or Zaire many more Soviet citizens know about politics, are touched by it, and can participate in it. In the USSR the population is literate and employed in a highly developed economy. Children from their earliest years are exposed to CPSU teachings and encouraged to join CPSU organizations. Party functionaries meet people on a face-to-face basis in their places of work to exhort them to support the party line. Citizens are pressured to better themselves by participating in CPSU education programs, and they are kept informed about political matters by a large number of newspapers and magazines which fall directly under party control. This is in great contrast to Indonesia and Zaire where few people can read, few know about national politics, and few organizations can reach them.

EGYPT

Although Egypt can be described as a dictatorial, authoritarian state, Egyptian politics, like Soviet politics, is described by Egyptian leaders as national, active, and dynamic. The Egyptian people, like the Soviet people, are urged to participate in politics, to enter political organizations, and to inform themselves on political matters. Similarly, the processes of participation and information are restricted by a governing elite. However, Egypt is not a Marxist state dedicated to ideological uniformity and the Egyptian population has a deeper tradition of public participation in politics than exists in the USSR. The result is a pattern of political participation that is at once similar to, but then quite different from, the Soviet model.

Group Activity and the Recruitment Process in Egypt

The Egyptian political system does not permit free, open lobbying and interest group activity. However, the Egyptian revolution was not carried out by a small band of guerillas who lacked basic organizational support in the community. In the USSR the CPSU was a small minority, which had achieved a military dominance in the country after the collapse of the tsarist regime in World War I. The CPSU established its political branches throughout the country, controlling all groups and all means of education in order to create widespread political support for its aims. The approach to political participation taken by the CPSU reflects these origins: the party instructs and controls; the citizens are expected to conform in detail to party dictates. In contrast, when the Egyptian army overthrew King Faruk they were fulfilling desires that had been expressed vocally by many Egyptian political groups since the 1920s. The

Egyptian military thus had a broad base of popular support and no pressing need to establish a massive totalitarian party of the Soviet type.

The major groups supporting the contemporary Egyptian regime are the military, the bureaucracy, rural merchants, and the *ulema* (the Moslem religious hierarchy).[9] The government, as originally established, was operated by a Revolutionary Command Council (RCC) headed by President Nasser. Until 1957 all decisions in Egypt were made by this small military elite, with no formal institutions in which representatives of the public could voice their interests and concerns. In this period, political participation was restricted to informal meetings among the revolutionary leaders with persons they believed to be influential in the community. The Egyptian revolution severely attacked those who were most privileged under the previous regime—the old upper class and foreign residents—but these attacks stopped short of an all-out purge of the Soviet type. Rather, the old groups lost their influence to new middle-class groups, and the old elite suffered an attack on their economic positions. Politics in Egypt, as in the USSR, was almost entirely bureaucratic. Decisions were made by an administrative elite under the Revolutionary Command Council. Political participation by Egyptians took the form of individual petitions to bureaucrats concerning specific complaints. There was no direct participation by Egyptians in the decisionmaking process itself, except informally and therefore haphazardly.

In 1956 President Nasser and the RCC determined to expand the possibilities for political participation in Egypt. They published a new constitution and submitted it to a popular referendum. Also, General Nasser formally ran for president (though no one opposed him). In both cases, more than 99 percent of the electorate voted "yes." The RCC was abolished, and Nasser became president and appointed a new cabinet. The constitution of 1956 provided for the establishment of a National Union (NU), a sort of super political party. It conducted elections to the Egyptian National Assembly in 1957, the first broad political activity in which Egyptians could directly participate since the revolution.

Unlike those in the USSR, candidates for political office in Egypt did not have to be ideologically trained and pure. In the 1957 elections the National Executive Committee of the National Union acted more as a censor of the political process than as a totalitarian instigator. The committee screened candidates who sought political office and could eliminate them from the contest; it did not train and sponsor all the candidates. In practive, however, the NU acted primarily as a rubber stamp for the bureaucracy and permitted only candidates who were loyal to the government.[10] Egyptians, consequently, were given a very limited choice in the election.

The National Union dissolved in 1958 when the United Arab Republic (UAR)—a union of Egypt and Syria—was established. The new political system as applied to both regions followed the format of the NU, but the system never worked to unite the new country and Syria seceded in 1961. Real politics and a real fusion of interests had not taken place in the UAR, and except for the fact of Nasser's personal popularity in Syria there was no basis for political unity in the new nation.

In 1961 the Egyptian government determined that it needed to open its political process further, and constituent groups of the Egyptian community were recognized as having a legitimate place in the political process. A national congress of 1,750 members was convened to draw up the charter for the next general elections. Groups such as organized labor, professional associations, and community organizations were permitted to elect delegates to the congress. President Nasser presented his proposals, which were widely publicized by the press and television, and the congress was permitted to debate and discuss the charter. However, despite the legal right to disagree with Nasser, no one in the congress used the situation to challenge the president's wishes. His charter was adopted unanimously and the National Union (which had lasted only five years) was replaced by the Arab Socialist Union (ASU), the main governing group in the country today.

Electoral Participation in Egypt

On paper, the charter of 1961 permits widespread political participation. The structure is officially based on organizations at the grassroots level, which are directly elected by universal suffrage. The basic units of the Arab Socialist Union are a combination of local parties in towns and villages and other popular committees elected in workshops, factories, and businesses. In legal terms, then, all Egyptians (voting is compulsory for all men over eighteen years of age, optional for women) elect their own representatives to the Arab Socialist Union. This is the only political organization permitted in the country; it represents a kind of fusion of all groups that would be interest groups or political parties in other systems.

Egyptians then are required to participate in politics to further the ends of the revolution. They do so by elections to the Arab Socialist Union and to the National Assembly. Since it is unclear how independent these institutions are in decisionmaking, interest in elections can become quite cynical. Certainly the military, which is not elected, has tremendous influence over decisionmaking. However, the importance of other constituent interest groups has substantially increased since the revolution, partly reflecting the regime's success in modernizing the country. Today business and labor groups represent some economic power and seek to be heard in their areas of interest. How clearly they are heard is still obscured by the monolithic structure of the ASU. The groups are a constituent part of the system, but do not have clear access to legislation as in systems with open party systems and open legislative bargaining. The overwhelming power in Egypt is still held by the president, and political participation consists of getting as close to him and his bureaucracy as possible.

Compared to politics in the USSR, however, Egyptian politics is more open and seems to be opening up more rapidly, but it is still not competitive. Thus elections in both countries are today quite meaningless—in both nations the important decisions are made by insulated bureaucratic elites and participation in the real sense is limited to those who can enter or influence the elite. In the USSR, however the avenues to the elite are much more rigidly defined and structured than in Egypt. In the Egyptian sphere there seems to be an authentic commitment to eventual establishment of a really representative political system. The ASU is not conceived on the same model as the CPSU; it is certainly a monopolistic political organization, but its aims appear to be more toward representation of the present groups in Egyptian society rather than in rooting out all differences and all possible ideological opposition. The CPSU is a self-appointed elite dedicated to governing the USSR according to a state-established dogma; the ASU strives to become a mass majoritarian organization which can speak for all Egyptians in all their complexity.

Processes of Communication in Egypt

Other areas show similar differences in detail between the USSR and Egypt. For example, the Egyptian press is freer than the press in the USSR. Egypt still has individual papers and editors who are only indirectly controlled by the government; the Egyptian government does not directly produce all the country's communications. In Egypt, journalists may make political points and risk being censored; in the USSR, journalists are employed to further the party line. Egyptian communication is thus controlled by the government, but much more indirectly than in the USSR.

In addition to the press, Egypt has an elaborate broadcasting apparatus which is directly controlled by the government. Indeed, Egyptian overseas broadcasts are more extensive than any other country's except the USSR's.[11] Films, however, are not controlled at all, and the Egyptian public is exposed to most Western film products. Egyptian television also imports many American "canned" programs for its entertainment list. Most communications media in Egypt are extremely nationalistic, patriotic, and reflective of the government's line. However, compared to those in the USSR they are more varied and less ideological.

Political Participation in Egypt and the USSR

Egypt's political elite remains pragmatic and opposed to intellectual dogmas; it has not constructed a mass party for its base but relies on a bureaucratic elite for decisionmaking. The elite has made some motions to involve the public, as in the ASU, but real power is still in the hands of the bureaucrats. Open participation thus remains restricted, though there is some as yet vague desire to achieve a form of Egyptian populism in government.

PEOPLE'S REPUBLIC OF CHINA

As with the USSR and Egypt, the People's Republic of China is a highly mobilized state demanding active and dynamic support of all her people. Also like the other two noncompetitive states, the PRC has a bureaucratic tradition that supports the rule of a tightly knit elite. The leaders of the Chinese Communist party constitute the top leadership of the government and, as such, head all the major hierarchies in Chinese society. As in the USSR, the party organization in the PRC has an overwhelming position in fomenting massive public participation in all political activities. Again, as in the USSR, all groups in the PRC are commanded by the party and its leadership—an elite group, endowed by the special legitimacy of Marxist ideology to tutor the people in the political program of their state.

Group Activity and the Recruitment Process in the PRC

China is relatively underdeveloped economically and has fewer strong economic and occupational groups than the USSR. Group organizations within the Chinese system represent regional and other subnational entities, as they do, for example, in India. The superficial structures established by the CCP to correspond with Soviet mass organizations have little national strength; rather, they directly reflect the strength of party penetration in given areas. Thus, there is much greater political participation and recruitment in urban areas where people tend to be more literate and more in contact with political ideas than in rural areas. This is a marked contrast to the USSR where the entire nation is roughly equally mobilized, owing to the far-reaching police and communications systems. Political mobilization in Egypt, a much smaller country than the PRC in size and population, is also conducted on a national level, primarily owing to the massive broadcasting industry.

The People's Republic of China nevertheless maintains a system of mass organizations, paralleling the party and the government, which blankets all sectors of society. For example there exist the All-China Association of Industry and Commerce, the All-China Federation of Trade Unions, the All-China Student Federation, All-China Federation of Literary and Arts Circles, and others. These organizations are major instruments of political participation linking the people at the lowest level to the party and the government. Each group, while controlled from the top, nevertheless holds congresses that meet for long intervals and formally make policy. Party members always occupy the key leadership positions in these organizations, but membership in them is very broad and gives an impression of wide public support for the CCP. Meetings are held, study groups established, and vigorous indoctrination occurs in much the same fashion as in similar groups in the USSR. These groups work on welfare and cultural matters, promote recreational activities, perform services in hospitals, and produce many books and pamphlets. Primarily, however, their work is educational, instructing the people in the aims of the government. They tutor the population in the party line and receive government aid and representation in the People's Congresses at the various administrative levels.

In the PRC mass organizational activity is carried down to the lowest possible level. Local police stations and street committees (block organizations in the large towns) are organized under party auspices to further the party program and smoke out opposition. The Chinese Communist party, then, by virtue of its policy line and its penetration of the government and mass organizations has full control over political participation, recruitment, and the decisionmaking functions of the Chinese political system. However, the economic and geographic units that serve as the base of the national administration still allow certain interests to originate not only within the party, but at the various administrative levels of the government. and even from the larger society.

In the People's Republic of China, while the CCP has attemped to develop a centrally controlled system of social, political, and economic mobilization after 1949, the party has never been able completely to monopolize all political activity. The country has long been partially urbanized and industrialized, and Western ideas, attitudes, and values are fairly widespread through the urban, educated Chinese population. The new regime in 1949 was obliged to develop new political structures, for after the Nationalist revolution in 1911, there remained political parties, associational interest groups, and some communications media that had been used by the old system. The governmental apparatus of the Chinese Communist party tried to harness this old infrastructure to its own uses; it did not wish to use up all its resources in establishing new groups. It aimed at national control, and made many bargains with the established groups provided the latter professed loyalty to it. Thus even small businessmen could operate in the new Marxist state, for a time, under the canned label "National Bourgeoisie."

The semiautonomous groups permitted by the PRC tend to be of the regional type. Some recognition of separate subnationalities is demonstrated by the fact that the CCP permits the existence of several small political parties in China (all loyal to CCP directives), merely for the purpose of expressing the identities of the subnational groups. These groups have no importance in political decision-making, but they do give their constituents a feeling of being represented and thus create support for the regime.

In China there exist some interest groups that are organized for specific purposes, such as trade unions, civic groups, and businessmen's groups. However, because of the party's penetration of the government and mass organizations, these groups' demands and interests also are defined for them. The party structure thus controls affiliated interest groups, rather than simply communicating the demands that are originated by the latter.

Processes of Communication and Electoral Participation in the PRC

In addition to direct person-to-person control of interest groups (party members directly instruct the interest associations in their activities), the CCP controls and employs to its own advantage the channels and means of access to the leadership and the public in general. Elections are controlled at all levels. The electorate at best can only reject a few candidates; they are given no direct role in the nomination process. The educational system and the press are monopolized. Any idea not approved by the party cannot find public expression. To assure this, the party can resort to propaganda and persuasion, and ultimately, terror. Rectification campaigns to remold the cadres (party leaders at the local levels) and the intellectuals have on occasion led to purges of men not loyal to the party line. Huge physical demonstrations extolling Mao Tse-tung and his interpretation of socialism have occurred with the help of the mass organizations. These and other actions are designed to make people enthusiastic about the regime. They also aid in implementing party policies. By insisting, or forcing the Chinese people to become politically active, the party politicizes all areas of life into which its authority penetrates, and the range of political life is very great. For example, there is the "socialist pact," an agreement among neighbors in a locality to observe certain standards of conduct in which interests of the state or "socialist construction" are involved.[12]

In a way, therefore, almost all of China's population is exposed to CCP guidelines. As a result, Chinese society appears to be extremely conformist. However, there are groups that have become somewhat disenchanted with the system: students, intellectuals, technicians, and bureaucrats. Deviation among these persons has generally been prevented by extensive programs of "reeducation," as well as by a system of terror headed by the Public Security Ministry within the State Council, and the Public Security forces within the People's Liberation Army. For those found guilty of political crimes, one of the most common forms of punishment is forced labor ("reform through labor"). Political deviants are conscripted for the building of communication networks—roads and railways—throughout the country.

Patterns of Participation in the PRC, Egypt, and the USSR

Thus, political participation in China is entirely mobilized and directed by an elite, utilizing an administrative apparatus within the party structure. The system is widespread and penetrating. The Communist revolution was a popular nationalist movement and is still supported by a large majority of Chinese. Popular support for the CCP is derived from this fact. The participation of millions of Chinese in their political system is to a large extent commanded by the elite, but the People's Republic of China is a traditionally bureaucratic society and the Chinese have no strong heritage supporting free and open political competition. As in Egypt, the people in the PRC tend to be passive and expect their leaders to make the decisions.

It is noteworthy that the People's Republic of China, despite Marxist ideology and a strong Communist party apparatus, has suffered little of the brutality and mass murder so characteristic of the Soviet regime under Stalin. More like Egypt, the PRC's lack of competition rests on a popular basis—a cultural homogeneity, widespread nationalism, and the tradition of accepting leadership from administrative elites.

Comparative Distinctions in Processes of Political Participation Among Noncompetitive States

Noncompetitive states are different in their processes of political participation to the extent that their levels of economic development and political traditions are different. Of the three countries discussed here, the USSR is the most highly developed and most intensely committed to mobilizing political support for her regime.

The USSR has a widely distributed and carefully controlled apparatus for generating political participation throughout the country. All groups are government sponsored and all communications, written and electronic, are under strict government control. The Soviet government does not merely censor communication; it creates it through government-controlled devices. All education and channels of information reflect the current party line. No group or newspaper is permitted to propagate anything other than this line except on matters of detail or of limited concern to the regime. The law is strictly enforced by a party-controlled police system on a national scale. Soviet organs of political participation are thus massive and ubiquitous, reflecting the country's vast investment in national political and educational organizations.

The PRC and Egypt are less politically mobilized than the USSR, but for different reasons. The PRC, which is as committed as the USSR to reforming the political views of her population, does not have the physical and economic resources of the USSR. Thus the PRC has been unable to establish the police apparatus characteristic of the USSR nor has she a comparably vast array of party-sponsored mass organizations and groups. The Chinese people have generally obeyed the regime, but more often out of a traditional sense of duty than out of a system of enforced uniformity by the state. The People's Republic of China has had several upheavals, but the government has not responded in the manner of the Soviet regime of the 1930s, which "purged" its opponents by police methods. The population of the PRC is far more rural and traditional than that of the Soviet Union, and the Chinese regime has been able to make some use of traditional patterns of political participation.

Egypt is not so mobilized as the USSR or PRC, partly because it is poor economically, but also because it is less ideologically committed to total mobilization. The Egyptian regime rests on traditional loyalties and has not attempted to attack them so much as use them. Thus while the press, radio, and television are government controlled in Egypt, the public gets to see Western films and an occasional Western-made television program. Egyptians can travel much more widely than their Soviet or Chinese counterparts, and although the government has the power of censorship, interest groups do exist within Egypt that are essentially private and not government sponsored. The regime attempts to retain the loyalty of these groups, and Egyptians support their leaders more out of a feeling of traditional respect and loyalty than out of a conscious calculation of political interest.

POLITICAL PARTICIPATION: COMPARING COMPETITIVE, FRAGMENTED, AND NONCOMPETITIVE STATES

Competitive, fragmented, and noncompetitive systems have different approaches and concepts of political participation.

In competitive states, where group conflict is considered normal and desirable, many institutions are established to protect the free interplay of the group process. Elections are safeguarded and many different kinds of groups may participate. Also, the press and other communications media that are necessary to political communication are protected from undue interference by government or other institutions. Groups in these states generally see themselves as part of a national political system and use their ties to politicians to affect national policy. They are an integrated part of the process, informing politicians of group interests and demands and watching the actions of politicians for their members.

Fragmented states, because of the prevalence of deep subnational loyalties among their populations, tend to develop systems in which group organization and communication are less free from government interference. Because they fear disintegration of the state, the governments of fragmented states will often seek to retain definite advantages over their opposition by, for example, maintaining control over the press and/or electronic media. This is usually deemed necessary because in these states free group activity often leads to unreasonable demands on government and groups often do not have a strong national perspective that overrides their narrow special interests. In some fragmented states the government attempts strictly to control the group process.

In noncompetitive states, populations participate in politics to the extent that they are mobilized behind their respective regimes. Governments neither idly permit groups and individuals to participate as they will, nor are they merely content to control the media. In noncompetitive states, governments, normally supported by traditionally obedient populations, generate and create mobilized political participation through state organs. All opposition is stamped out, often through police or terrorist techniques. Interest groups and communication media exist, but must adhere to the wishes of government leaders. People are required actively to support the regime, not merely passively to obey it.

NOTES TO CHAPTER 4

1. Bruce M. Russett, *World Handbook of Political and Social Indicators* (New Haven: Yale University Press, 1964), p. 108. France here is ranked nineteenth in newspaper circulation.

2. Subandrio, *Indonesia on the March*, vol. 2 (Djakarta: Department of Foreign Affairs, August 1964): 21.

3. Ewa T. Pauker, "Has the Sukarno Regime Weakened the PKI?" *Asian Survey*, vol. 4, no. 9 (September 1964): 1058.

4. For detailed information on the political aspects of Guided Democracy, see Ibid.

5. Herbert Feith, "President Sukarno, the Army and the Communists: the Triangle Changes Shape," *Asian Survey*, vol. 4, no. 8 (August 1964): 969-80 and Herbert Feith, "Dynamics of Guided Democracy," in Ruth T. McVey, ed., *Indonesia*, Southeast Asia Studies, Yale University (New Haven: HRAF Press, 1963), pp. 309-409.

6. M. Crawford Young, "Domestic Violence in Africa: The Congo," in Charles Anderson, Fred Von der Mehden, and Crawford Young, eds., *Issues of Political Development* (Englewood Cliffs: Prentice-Hall, 1967), pp. 120-44.

7. David Apter, *The Politics of Modernization* (Chicago: University of Chicago Press, 1965), p. 362.

8. Fredrick C. Barghoorn, *Politics in the USSR* (Boston: Little, Brown, 1966), p. 176-7.

9. Leonard Binder, "Egypt: The Integrative Revolution," in Lucian W. Pye and Sidney Verba, eds., *Political Culture and Political Development* (Princeton: Princeton University Press, 1965), p. 399.

10. Peter Mansfield, *Nasser's Egypt* (Baltimore: Penguin Books, 1965), p. 196.

11. Binder, "Egypt," p. 432.

12. James R. Townsend, *Political Participation in Communist China* (Berkeley & Los Angeles: University of California Press, 1966), p. 92.

Chapter 5

Political Parties

*

POLITICAL PARTIES: A FRAMEWORK FOR COMPARISON

All political systems contain politically minded groups that state the interests of their members and, in so doing, act as agents of political participation. In some systems these groups remain open and free from government control. When this is so, they are great articulators of public policy and thus perform the important functions of informing the population and the politicians of the needs for political action in certain areas. On the other hand, in states in which political groups of this sort are weak, they are often sponsored by the government in the hope they will eventually develop into independent political groups.

Political parties are special kinds of political groups. Whereas interest groups concern themselves with narrow programs for special populations, political parties seek national goals: in competitive states, they nominate candidates for national office; they help elect their chosen candidates; and once officials are chosen they seek to influence the implementation of national programs. In order to maximize their influence political parties must put together the articulated interests of many different groups within the population. This is sometimes referred to as the process of "interest aggregation." In contrast to interest groups which articulate specific and limited demands, political parties attempt to aggregate these many special demands in a national framework.

Undoubtedly, political parties state and articulate demands as well as aggregate them. Most particularly in noncompetitive states, political parties are often great articulators, usually directing the activities of all other political groups. In fragmented states, on the other hand, political parties may not be very successful in aggregating national programs and thus may tend to remain quite narrow, reflecting the many divisions of society. In competitive states, the function of aggregation is usually most evident because of the stable consensus that is normally characteristic of these states. Usually a relatively small number of political parties are agents of competition, with each party representing a different aggregation of interests—each usually having some national claim and scope.

POLITICAL PARTIES IN COMPETITIVE STATES

Patterns of Similarity

In competitive states elections normally constitute one of the most important political activities in the country, since it is through the electoral process competing groups determine which among them will fill the government offices and legitimately direct government policymaking for a legally established time period. For this reason, political parties—those organizations that directly participate in elections by nominating candidates, developing national programs, and soliciting votes—are extremely important and well developed. Political parties in competitive states, because they strive to run the national government, attempt to develop a national base of support behind their programs and candidates. Often, because such parties (or coalitions of parties) seek to be national, there can be considerable overlap in policy among them and compromise is possible once the election is over. Beyond that, political parties reflect the cultural and political values of their individual countries and to that extent differ from parties in other countries.

Three Case Studies: Great Britain, India, and Chile

GREAT BRITAIN

National politics in Great Britain has, for a very long time, been merged in the public mind with a concept of party competition in an institutionalized two-party system. In Great Britain, the party in power establishes the government while the largest party that lost the last general election is euphemistically referred to as "Her Majesty's Loyal Opposition." The relationship of the two parties is aptly described by the traditional dictum "The Government governs, the Opposition criticizes."[1] The major functions of an opposition party are to raise questions and objections and to hope for victory in the next general election. Historically the party framework has been able to aggregate the basic demands of the general population so that large-scale social and political movements have not appeared outside the party system. Third parties have, for most of the twentieth century, been very small though, at present, the small Liberal party appears to be gaining in strength, having received nearly 20 percent of the vote in the February 1974 national election. The important political opposition in Great Britain is voiced by politicians working within the major political parties; other groups in society pursue their demands by patronizing sympathetic politicians and not by establishing political groupings of their own.

The British political system rests on a stable legal and social basis. For over one hundred years Great Britain has had a mass electorate accepting the constitutional system which, while providing that there should be no formal limit to the power of a government with a parliamentary majority, still

establishes the rights, privileges, and duties of an accepted legitimate opposition. For this period the basic two-party framework has popularly been
conceived of along class lines, with each major party being viewed as theoretically representative of some major social class.[2] A third small party, the
Liberals, has generally been viewed as falling somewhere between the two
large parties in its approach to issues.

Since World War II the British party system has continued in the traditional
framework, but has undergone many important structural and strategic changes.
Such factors as religion and regionalism are not now and for a long time have not
been central in British elections, and the status system upon which the British
class structure has long been based has also begun to erode. The postwar period
has seen the appearance of a governing Labour party with an effective popular
and parliamentary majority—a new event for Great Britain in which the
Conservative party has long been representative of a British elite that ruled the
country both socially and politically. All these recent trends question the
traditional interpretation of British politics as being class based.

The Role of Political Parties in Great Britain

Over the years, the British electoral system has become based on highly
organized political parties that permeate the entire legislative and executive
character of British government. British political parties have very tight control
over their recruitment practices and very strict procedures by which members
are promoted or demoted. It is virtually impossible to get ahead in British
politics without being a loyal member of one of the established parties.

In a British election campaign the national parties present their policies in
the form of fairly specific programs. The electorate is conceived of as giving a
mandate to one program over the other so that once a party is elected it attempts
to have its program carried out. Parties normally succeed in accomplishing this
because they are highly disciplined.

The competing parties in a British election are organized into "shadow
governments," a designation of members in the opposition party to cabinet posts
so that when a party wins an election, i. e., takes a majority of seats in the House
of Commons, it automatically elects its leadership to the important positions in
the government. Thus the prime minister does not really win a competitive
election in the Commons; he is already normally the head of the majority party
there. The cabinet is composed of the other high-ranking politicians of the
majority party and together with the prime minister forms a steering committee
that is responsible for making government policy. Cabinet members also head
the administrative departments, which carry policy out. The British cabinet
does not lose votes on important issues; structurally the whole system depends
on the government retaining its majority throughout its term of office, and in
practice this is what generally occurs. This is due to the fact British political
parties are highly organized and highly disciplined. There also are really only
two national political parties in Great Britain, so it has not been mathematically
difficult (except temporarily as in February 1974 when a "balance of power"
was achieved by the Liberals) for one to achieve a majority.

In sum, the major political structures in British politics reflect the character of British political parties, which are strong, disciplined, and cohesive. They produce the national programs and the leaders and therefore conduct the essence of politics in the country. If Great Britain is to be regarded as a competitive state, it is because she has competing political parties that are willing to run against each other in highly regulated election campaigns. In reality, however, the parties constitute a true sociopolitical elite, exaggerated by the fact that between elections, one party has the unquestioned upper hand at all levels of government. It does not usually share decisions with its opposition; it is merely criticized by it.

The Social Basis of Party Strength

The evolution of a two-party framework in Great Britain is demonstrated by election returns since 1900 (see Table 5.1). From the late nineteenth century to the end of World War I, British government was dominated by either the Liberal or the Conservative party. In the 1920s the Labour party supplanted the Liberal party as the second major party. Except for that period of transition from Liberal to Labour (from 1922 to 1931), the two leading parties have attracted 90 percent or more of the vote between them. Great Britain has not generally had a situation, common for example in Fourth Republic France, where it is necessary to have two or more parties pool their seats in Commons to elect a government between them (i. e., to establish a coalition).

As can be seen from Table 5.1, the Conservative party has been the only British party that can be described as a "major" party throughout the twentieth century. It is also the only party ever to have received a majority of the popular vote in all this time. From 1900 to 1974 Conservatives have participated in cabinets for more than fifty of those years; Conservatives have clearly dominated the government for more than forty years. This record must be viewed in conjunction with the fact the Conservative party has visibly been the party of an upper class and has been controlled by individuals who have, in a sense, been trained to govern by the "best" schools and "best" families in the country. It has never been a party that had to establish itself, through electioneering techniques, as fit to govern. Since World War II, however, the Conservatives have lost their position of overriding dominance: the twenty-nine years since 1945 have seen Labour in power for about twelve years and the Conservatives (Tories) in control for about seventeen—and Labour is now again in power. This is a roughly equal division of power.

Much has been written about the British phenomenon of the "working-class Tory,"[3] that laboring voter who, despite his occupational status, decides to vote Conservative rather than for the Labour party. The ability of the Conservative party to attract voters of all classes has variously been attributed to the deferential characteristics of British society—that is, the lower classes as much as the upper strata have presumably shared the belief that the aristocracy should govern—and via the Conservative party. Of course, it also is true Conservative success with the working-class vote has reflected certain organizational failures and deep divisions within the British Labour movement. Never-

Table 5.1. General Elections in Great Britain, 1900-1974

Parliament	Length of Parliament Yrs.	Mos.	Party in Power	% of Total Vote Won by Party in Power	% of Vote Held by Major Opposition Party	MPs Elected by Party in Power
1900-1906	5	1	Conservative	51.1	44.6	402
1906-1910	3	9	Liberal	49.0	43.6	400
1910	-	9	Liberal	46.9	43.2	275
1910-1918	7	9	Coalition	Lib. 43.9: Cons. 46.3		272: 272
1919-1922	3	8	Conservative	32.6		335
1922-1923	-	11	Conservative	38.2	29.5	345
1923	-	9	Labour	30.5*	38.1	191
1924-1929	4	5	Conservative	48.3	33.0	419
1929-1931	2	3	National (Coalition)	Cons. 38.2: Lab. 37.1		260: 288
1931-1935	3	11	National** (Cons. dom.)	67.0		554
1935-1945	9	6	Conservative	53.7	37.9	432
1945-1950	4	6	Labour	47.8	39.8	393
1950-1951	1	7	Labour	46.1	43.5	315
1951-1955	3	6	Conservative	48.0***	48.8	321
1955-1959	4	3	Conservative	49.7	46.4	344
1959-1964	5	0	Conservative	49.4	43.8	365
1964-1966	1	5	Labour	44.1	43.4	317
1966-1970	4	3	Labour	47.9	41.9	363
1970-1974	3	7	Conservative	46.4	43.0	330
1974-	0	8	Labour****	37.5	38.3	301
1974			Labour	39.3	35.7	319

SOURCE: Taken from David Butler and Jennie Freeman, *British Political Facts, 1900-1967* (London: Macmillan, 1968), pp. 141-4; *British Record*, BIS, no. 7 (June 25, 1970): 1; *Washington Post*, March 2, 1974; *British Record*, BIS, New York, October 16, 1974, p. 1.

*Labour governed with Liberal support.

**Conservatives dominated this government; Labour remained a major opposition party.

***Labour received a higher popular vote, but fewer seats (48.8 percent of the vote, 295 seats).

****Labour governs, though a minority party. Smaller parties (Liberals, particularly) pledged support.

theless, over a long period of time the Conservative party has shown strength on a national scale from all classes at the polls, while its own leadership has generally been drawn from the uppermost segments of British society. The recruitment of members of Parliament from the ranks of the privileged has until the present continued to be a Conservative practice.

The sources of Labour party strength have been somewhat broadened since World War II, but most of Labour's strength has historically been and still is drawn from the working class; the Labour party today is still heavily dependent on the trade unions. Its recent rise to majority party status seems to be associated with a statistical decline in working-class conservatism (the conversion of many working-class Liberals and Conservatives to Labour) in recent years and its ability to attract a working-class vote that in the past had been quite unpolitical, that is, unaffiliated with any party. Labour has, with the decline of its ideological base, also begun to attract some more middle-class votes. The class alignment of both parties, however, seems to be aging, and new voters of different class backgrounds appear to be entering both major parties.[4]

Party Organization Since World War II

The Labour party grew up in the early part of the twentieth century as a coalition of socialist societies and the trade union movement. Structually and theoretically there are more limitations on the power of the leadership of the Labour party than is true of the Conservative party. For example, when the party is out of power a Labour leader must face reelection annually (in 1960 Hugh Gaitskell was opposed by Harold Wilson and in 1961 by Anthony Greenwood); such an occurrence until 1965 had no place in the Conservative party framework since that party has a much more hierarchical internal organization than the Labour party has had. Despite this, in practice Conservative leaders have been forced out of the prime ministership before serving their full terms more often than Labour leaders have;[5] for example, Anthony Eden and Harold Macmillan both resigned their offices. No Labour leader since World War II has had to do this.

Today the trade unions are the most important element in the Labour party, accounting for five-sixths of the party's membership and most of the party's funds. The National Executive Committee (NEC), which supervises the party outside Parliament, consists of twenty-eight members (the leader, deputy leader, twelve trade union delegates, seven constituency delegates, five women, and a treasurer elected by the Annual Conference). Normally, the MPs have a small majority in the NEC, though trade union votes have an influential position both here and in the Parliamentary Labour party (PLP). Generally, the leader of the party is able to maintain control over the NEC with the aid of union votes.[6]

The leader of the Conservative party, until the reforms of 1966, was always the recognized leader of the party in the House of Commons and had attained this position through long experience in that body. The leader historically was selected by acclamation without any formal balloting. In the early period of the party's history in the early nineteenth century, frequently an individual was designated to be prime minister by the monarch and was only subsequently elected leader of the party. Of course, by then the choice of leader was obvious to all party members.

In technical terms, the party leader was selected at a meeting of the party's members in the House of Commons. In 1922, this procedure was broadened and Conservative peers and prospective candidates were invited to participate in the selection of the leader. In 1937 the Executive Committee of the National Union, the organization within the party that represents the party's national constituent units,[7] was also invited to participate.[8] In formal terms, the party at large thus selected the leader, but, in practice, the leader had already been coopted by the tight elite that traditionally ran the party; new leaders were produced under the patronage of old leaders, and the party meeting merely legitimized this selection process.

Between 1945 and 1951, when they were the opposition party led by Winston Churchill, the Conservatives maintained their traditional party structure and organization. Churchill, as leader, behaved in the accepted almost absolute manner and his choice of successor in 1955, Anthony Eden, was very much a personal choice concurred in by other members of the party at all levels. Churchill's leadership of fifteen years spanned a period of opposition and of government; under him no great changes occurred in terms of party personnel and structural organization. Party leadership, drawn from the wartime cabinet, was traditional in outlook and no great challenge to traditional decisionmaking processes occurred. The party gradually absorbed new members and made way for new leaders through traditional recruitment procedures.

This situation changed radically in the 1960s. The end of Conservative rule in 1963-1964 was marked by the Profumo scandal, an event of extravagant proportions for the Tory leadership. This scandal, which called into question the integrity of certain Conservative members of subcabinet rank, coincided with the succession problem created by the retirement of Harold Macmillan in 1963. The government, considerably weakened according to the public opinion polls, resorted to its traditional tightly controlled selection processes. In 1963 the top leadership in the party selected Sir Alec Douglas-Home as Macmillan's successor in a meeting closed to the press and the general public. Home was then a peer but resigned his seat in the Lords to run for a seat in the Commons. His government (from 1963 to 1964) generally lacked popular support and found it necessary to avoid calling a general election until the legal maximum limit, thus creating the only five-year Parliament since the World War I coalition government. The Conservatives lost the ensuing election, though by a small margin.

The selection of Home and the close loss in the 1964 election called the traditional Conservative party organization into question, and, later, in 1966, after a large Labour victory in the general election, a new procedure was adopted to choose Home's successor; Home himself was instrumental in bringing about the change. Under the new procedure, the persons eligible to vote for leader remained the same—Conservative MPs, Conservative peers, and candidates for and members of the National Executive Committee of the National Union—only this time, the process of election was fully publicized at the Parliamentary party level.[9] In the first such election Edward Heath defeated Reginald Maudling; Heath became leader and Maudling, deputy leader. Other changes accomplished at this time also affected Conservative policy and election strategy.

The shift in the leadership selection procedure in 1966 was accompanied by attempts to broaden the base of the Conservative party in other ways to include the new professional groups that had emerged as important voting blocs in the 1950s. Rather than focusing attention on the aristocratic elements among their traditional supporters, the Conservatives began to emphasize expertise and youth advantageously to distinguish themselves from old line Labour party men, who remained in public view; the average age of Labour party MPs has consistently been older than that of Conservatives and the Tories wished to point up this difference.

In addition, the Conservatives established new groups of experts to help focus the party program in specialized areas. A clear choice of strategy was made: no longer would campaigns be dominated by electioneering slogans, but by specific proposals. The new specialists were supposed to "systemize and sharpen Opposition action on particular measures"[10] (notably the Finance, Steel, and Transport bills). The new strategy also entailed the upgrading of salaries of professional party agents, and the party set a goal of 20 percent as an increase in the membership of young Conservatives.

Electoral Trends and the General Elections of February and October 1974

The February 1974 general election was held during one of the worst British industrial crises since World War II. The immediate issue causing Conservative Prime Minister Edward Heath to dissolve Parliament and call the election was a prolonged strike by coal miners that had resulted in severe power shortages and the adoption of a three-day work week by much of the nation. In addition, the country had been suffering from one of the worst periods of inflation in recent years, and the prime minister sought to tie the issue of higher wages to rising prices, claiming that the coal miners' demands were inflationary.

The Conservative government, after attempting to bargain with the miners union under the nation's new Industrial Relations Act (coal mining is a nationalized industry in Britain), offered them a wage package and claimed that anything higher would be inflationary and a bad example to other workers given the weak state of the British economy. The miners' union rejected this government offer as too low comparative to wages for miners throughout Europe, as well as too low to support a decent living standard in Great Britain. Heath called the election to gain a public mandate for dealing with the coal miners' demands.

The election results did not produce the mandate for which Heath hoped; indeed, his party lost twenty-six seats and its majority in Parliament. Labour gained fourteen seats, but not enough to form a majority. The small Liberal party gained three seats, and the support of its small delegation of fourteen in the House of Commons was needed by the Labour government. Despite this, Liberals were not represented in the new Labour cabinet.

A number of unusual features appeared in the February 1974 election returns. The two major parties were still quite close—Labour received 37.5

percent of the vote while the Conservatives received 38.3 percent—but the smaller number of Labour voters elected a larger number of MPs than their Conservative rivals, owing primarily to the redrawing of district lines. Another unusual result lay in the Liberal party vote: the Liberals took 6 million votes or 19.3 percent of the popular vote (up 11.7 percent in four years), though they still had only fourteen seats in the House of Commons. Liberals thus became the second party in many electoral districts, and some observers credited the party with a real chance of establishing a much more important electoral presence in the political system. In addition to the Liberals, other minor parties also did fairly well, particularly the Scottish Nationalists, who captured five seats in the House of Commons. The most important unusual feature in the February 1974 returns, however, lay in the election of the first minority government in Great Britain in forty-five years. Prime Minister Wilson had less than a majority in his own party and had to rely on the votes of the Liberals on critical issues. He therefore called another general election in October 1974 in which Labour won eighteen additional seats—a majority of only three seats, but enough to govern without minor party support.

Despite these unusual election results, Great Britain remains with its general political system intact. The country retains an extraordinarily stable alignment in this crisis situation—a governing party with less than one-half the vote, confronted by an organized opposition very close in electoral strength to the government. The Conservative party today is the only national opposition and its electoral position is such that a slight swing in voter sentiment could again bring it to power.[11] The class basis of the parties is still there, but continues to erode. Labour voters, as well as Conservative voters, seem apathetic about the major parties' rigidities on the industrial issue. Voters of both persuasions have been attracted by the Liberal party's moderation on the questions of prices, wages, inflation, and industrial organization. British voters thus are not pre-determined by class or ideology, but by the policies and issues of the day. British opposition, however, remains party opposition, but the positions and traditional appeals of the major parties now appear to be in question to a larger portion of the electorate than at any time since World War II.

INDIA

The role of political parties in India is not significantly different from their role in other competitive states. They create and sustain the interest of the citizens in politics. Not only do they make politics lively for most people, they make issues intelligible for them. In the developing societies such as India political parties also serve as vehicles of modernization and aid the process of nation building.

The National Congress Party and Its Relationship to Other Parties in India

The striking fact about the National Congress, India's largest political party, is that historically it was the national movement. It had no rivals worth mentioning. The Communist party, which was founded in 1925, consisted of only a small band of revolutionaries engaged in conspiratorial tactics and did not make effective appeals to the people. Other groups like the Swarajists and the Congress Socialist party remained within the Congress party. The major exception was the Muslim League. However, the league was communal and therefore even it could not claim the national appeal of the Congress party.

This situation began to change after independence. By the time of the first Indian general election Congress had to face opposition from half a dozen political parties whose number and strength grew in the ensuing years. These parties fell under four broad, overlapping categories:

1. Marxist parties;
2. Democratic Socialist parties;
3. Rightist parties; and
4. Communal parties.

The relationship of the Congress party to each of the parties in these categories differs.

Marxist parties. The two important Communist parties in India today are the Communist Party of India (CPI) and the Communist Party of India-Marxist (CPIM). The CPI's cooperation with Congress during the struggle for independence was minimal. The Communists condemned Congress as an agent of the bourgeoisie and were contemptuous of Gandhi. In 1942 they collaborated with the British when Congress was fighting the latter. These experiences conditioned the attitude of Congress to the CPI. Further, in 1948 the CPI made a vain attempt to overthrow the government by organizing armed revolts in some parts of India. This led to the banning of the party in some states. Surveying the Nehru government's policy toward the Communists during the first decade of independence, Overstreet and Windmiller wrote that "it has been as anti-Communist as the rules of the parliamentary system would permit, and on a few occasions has breached the spirit if not the letter of the rules in an effort to inhibit the activities of the C.P.I."[12]

Government policy toward the Communists has included close police surveillance of the party, its auxiliary organizations, and their foreign contacts; restriction on the travels of Communists to and from India; limitation of delegations to international Communist-front organizations; extensive use of preventive detentions against Communists; and occasionally repressive measures. In 1959 the Nehru government dismissed the Communist ministry in the state of Kerala at a time when the ministry had the support of the majority in the legislature. The same device was resorted to, apparently with greater justification, to get rid of a Communist-dominated united front ministry in West Bengal in 1967. The Shastri government, armed with the power of the Defense of India Rules (1962), made large-scale arrests of Communists in December of 1964 and though some of those arrested were subsequently elected to the Kerala legislature in 1965, the national government refused to release them. Instead, the state governor—an agent of the national government—dissolved the legislature.

The CPI changed its tactics and constitution at the party's Amritsar Session in 1958. The new constitution declared the party would strive for "full democracy and socialism by peaceful means." It also promised that under the regime of the party "there will be the widest possible extension of individual liberty, freedom of speech, press and association, including right of political organization."[13] The conversion of the Communists did not convince Nehru. In a document prepared for the Congress leaders, he expressed his admiration for many of the achievements of the Soviet Union but noted that Communists, who had "no moorings in the land of their birth," always resorted to violence and bloodshed in foreign countries. Their vision of the world was therefore tainted by the means they employed.[14]

Such denunciations of the Communists were also motivated by political considerations, since the Communists were highly critical of Nehru's domestic policies, especially his economic policies. Two developments, however, have helped to narrow the gap between the Congress and the CPI. These are the Congress's unequivocal commitment to socialism at the Bhubaneshwar Session and the CPI's commitment to democratic ways at the Amritsar Session. The CPI on its part believes that there are far darker forces in India today than the Congress party—the communal and rightist parties. Consequently, the attitude of the Congress party toward the CPI also has mellowed.

The CPI is distinguished from the CPIM (India's other Marxist party) in the implacable hostility of the latter to the Congress. The CPIM does not make any unambiguous commitment to peaceful means for the achievement of its goals. Congress, therefore, treats the CPIM not only as a powerful opponent, but as a source|of possible danger for the country.

Democratic socialist parties. The two important democratic socialist parties in India today are the Praja Socialist party (PSP) and the Samyukta Socialist party (SSP). The interesting thing about these two parties is that almost their entire leadership was active in the Congress party in the preindependence period.

The Praja Socialist party was established in 1952 as the result of a merger of two other socialist parties whose leadership had broken away from the Congress party over personal disputes with Congress party leaders. The ideological basis of the PSP is a mixture of Gandhiism—an emphasis on village development along the lines established by India's great national leader, Mahatma Gandhi—social democracy, and Marxism.

In the early years of independence, the Congress party was dominated by conservatives. The only one person in the top leadership who genuinely believed in an orthodox form of socialism was Jawaharlal Nehru, but his influence was effectively contained by the conservative forces ably led by Sardar V. Patel. When Nehru established his supremacy in Congress he opened a dialogue with the leadership of the PSP with a view to achieving cooperation. The negotiations, however, broke down, partly because Nehru could not meet some of the programmatic demands made by the PSP. On the other hand, the PSP leadership itself was divided on the issue of cooperation with Congress. At the Avadi Session (1955), Congress declared a socialistic pattern of society as its goal, and in 1964, at the Bhubaneshwar Session, Congress adopted socialism by peaceful means as its goal. Since then many Congress party members have expected the Praja Socialists to return to their parent organization. However, Praja Socialists insist the Congress party's declaration of socialism is a political gimmick and does not put socialist principles into practice, especially in the economic sector. Only at the state level have there been instances of limited cooperation between the two parties.

The Samyukta Socialist party was formed in 1965 by some of the radical leaders of the old Praja Socialist party. It is doubtful whether there are any significant ideological differences between the Samyukta Socialists and the Congress party. However, since its birth the Samyukta Socialists have shown a deep antipathy toward Congress, which, in turn, has shown no warmth of feeling for this party.

Rightist parties. At the national level the most important rightist party is the Swatantra, which was formed in 1959 to stem "the tide in political life towards Socialism frought with danger to the liberties of the people and disaster to the economy of the country."[15] The economic policies of the Swatantra party are similar to those of the British Conservative party. In foreign policy, it seeks to make a pro-Western stance. The Swatantra and the Bharatiya Kranti Dal (a recent off-shoot) have many things in common, though, on the whole, the Dal is less conservative than the Swatantra.

The formation of the Swatantra party was a source of worry to the Congress party. Its ideology and program, which stressed the rights of private property and attacks on socialism, were repugnant to Nehru and to all socialist-minded Congress party members. It threatened to deprive the Congress party of both its traditional sources of voters—the middle class and white-collar workers—and financial support. Further, it threatened to win the support of feudal elements, whose "pocket boroughs" had hitherto returned Congress candidates to the national and state legislatures. Despite such threats, many Congress leaders secretly sympathized with the causes the Swatantra championed. The left wing of the Congress party, represented by Nehru, Krishna Menon, and others was uncompromisingly opposed to the Swatantra both for political and ideological reasons; the right wing was ambiguous in its attitude to the Swatantra party.

Communal parties. The Jan Sangh and the Muslim League are the prime examples of communal parties (parties that seek to advance the interests of religious, ethnic or linguistic communities, as opposed to parties with national programs) in contemporary India. The Jan Sangh, a fast-growing party in the Hindi heartland of India, is militantly nationalist, antisecular, anti-Communist, and anti-Pakistani. The Muslim League is a force only in the state of Kerala, on the southern tip of the Indian subcontinent.

Congress's attitude to communal parties has been one of uncompromising opposition. Both communal parties are rightist in their economic philosophy. Thus, both are opposed to two of the pillars of the Congress party—socialism and secularism. Both communal parties are traditionalist and, therefore, obstacles in the path of modernization—a goal to which Congress is dedicated. Con-

gress also fears the activities of communal parties will exacerbate the relation between the majority community (Hindu) and the minority communities. Hindu-Muslim relationships are especially delicate and the Jan Sangh
only inflames the situation.

There are also cold political calculations behind the Congress party's
unconcealed oppostition to the Jan Sangh. The Sangh is rapidly gaining
popularity in the traditional centers of Congress power. Its appeal to the lower-
middle class and small shopkeepers is particularly effective. In the past these
classes constituted a large part of the Congress party's electoral support. Thus
political principles and electoral considerations make the attitude of Congress
to the communal parties one of hostility at the national level. At the state level,
occasional and short-lived deviations might be noticed.

Organizational Structure of the National Congress Party

In preindependence India the organizational structure of the Congress
party coincided with administrative units of the country. This old organizational
structure has been retained, and Congress today still is organized around
districts of local government rather than according to electoral constituencies.

The constitution of the Congress party says that the party organization will
consist of the annual and special sessions of the national Congress, and various
committees, among them the All-India Congress Committee (the governing
committee of the Congress party at the national level), the Working Committee,
Pradesh Congress Committees, District/City Congress Committees, Bloc Congress Committees, and lower committees at the grass-roots level determined by
the Pradesh Congress Committees. To these elements must be added the
president of the party, general secretaries, the leader of the legislative party
(who, in the event the party gets a majority, becomes the prime minister), the
Parliamentary Board, and the Election Committee.

At the national level, the most important officials in the structure are the
president and the members of the All-India Congress Committee (AICC). The
president is elected by the Congress delegates for a two-year period to preside
over the sessions of the party and to exercise the powers of the Working
Committee when the party is not in session. Consequently, he can exercise
substantial powers. For the three or four decades before independence the
office—whose powers and influence were considerable—was occupied only by
men of the highest caliber in national life. But in the postindependence period
both the power and influence of the office began to decline, mainly because of
the birth and rapid growth of the office of prime minister. In the early years after
independence some bitter clashes occurred between the Congress president
and the Congress prime minister. Partly because of the towering personality of
Nehru, then prime minister, and partly because of the very logic of the
parliamentary form of government, the prime minister emerged triumphant.
Since then the prime minister has generally remained predominant.

In preindependence days, especially during the Gandhian era, the Congress
party had a highly organized, disciplined hierarchical structure, but at that time
it was fighting against British rule and had an overriding purpose in the
achievement of independence. Personal ambitions, parochial loyalties, and

particularist demands were subordinated to the national goal of liberation from British hegemony. These were the years of struggle and sacrifice, not of bargaining or self-seeking. Hence, Congress, as the embodiment of national will and aspiration, could win the undivided allegiance of patriotic Indians. At this time it functioned as if it were a monolithic structure.

Tight discipline within the Congress party structure did not last long because its rationale was lost when independence was won. The common enemy withdrawn, the overriding goal achieved, and the consuming passion satisfied, new forces, previously submerged or suppressed, began to appear in invigorated form. Gandhi, who accounted for so much of the unity, discipline, and resolution of the party, wanted to convert it into a social service agency in the wake of freedom. He was ignored on this point. The introduction of universal adult franchise gave politics a new dimension. Political power, then, became the key to most things for which men yearn in the material world. It became the object of personal ambition and effort. Political parties became the instruments to build influence and win power. One consequence of these developments, as far as the Congress party was concerned, was the emergence of factions within the party and the proliferation of conditions favorable to their growth. Externally, the very structure of federalism created two entities competing for citizens' loyalty. State politicians were quick to learn that the effective means of expanding and consolidating their power was not to toe the line of national party or the national government. The creation of linguistic states in a way legitimized parochial forces, despite fierce and frequent denunciations of them from Delhi. Meanwhile, the great heroes of the struggle for freedom gradually departed: Gandhi was assassinated in 1948; Patel died in 1951; Rajendra Prasad was effectively lost to the party after his election as the president of the republic in 1950; Nehru's popular appeal began to dwindle after the Chinese attack of 1962. Few of the next generation of politicians could boast of a national stature. Those who were catapulted to the national arena could only camouflage their parochial proclivities. Open identification with the parochial forces would have brought them discredit and eventually resulted in their own fall. But if they were reluctant to champion parochialism at the national level, an action that would contradict their own role, they had at least to accommodate it operating in the system and shaping the contours of its politics. Those who operated at state levels either by choice or in a mood of resignation also found it hard or unnecessary to strike at the roots of parochialism. Some of these people were the products of that force; others were unscrupulous enough to feed and exploit it to further their own personal and political ambitions. Those who perceived its potential evils were afraid to annoy the masses and to run the risk of political ostracism. The net result of these developments in the organizational discipline of the Congress party has been a growing decentralization, with more and more power now in the hands of local leaders.[16]

Electoral Support for the National Congress Party

Since there are no comprehensive studies of Indian voting behavior, it is difficult to pinpoint the sources of the Congress party's electoral support. Two things about the Congress are remarkable: it is India's only truly national

party—its organizational network spreads every district of India, a country
continental in size. In all states Congress still remains a sizeable force. Neither
of these characteristics is shared by any other Indian political party. The Jan
Sangh derives its strength from the Hindi heartland. The Communist strength is
confined to only three or four states and some industrial centers. The Swatantra,
the Praja Socialist, and the Samyukta Socialist parties also get their support from
certain isolated pockets. But the Congress's support is territorially so well
distributed that in no geographical region, in no state, can it be considered as a
negligible political force. In the first three elections after independence (1952,
1957, and 1962), its votes veered around an impressive 45 percent; while not a
single opposition party during any of these elections could secure even one-
quarter of this figure. Even in 1967, when Congress was "routed" in many states,
the party polled about 41 percent of the national electorate, while its nearest
rival, Jan Sangh, could muster only a bare 10 percent. These figures indicate the
sources of Congress's electoral support cut across regions, classes, and castes.
This is because, for most people, Congress is the party that won independence
for the motherland. It is the party of Nehru and Gandhi—two names they have
most frequently heard. Again, Congress was the ruling party at the national
level, in the states, and in the vast majority of local government units. From the
very beginning the party forged close links with the administration—a luxury
denied to all its rivals. This aspect of Congress strength, which explains a large
part of its grassroots support, is stressed by Weiner:

> The local Congress party aids its membership and its supporters in
> the countryside in their efforts to influence tax enforcement, to get the
> necessary permits for the purchase of cement, fertilizers, and other
> commodities, and to influence local administration in its appointments
> and myriad activities. The party is concerned also with the coercive
> powers of local administration. Though the administration of justice is
> generally apolitical, many individuals feel that influence in the local
> party will protect them in dealing with local police.[17]

Generally speaking rural areas—and about 70 percent of India's people live
in rural areas—constitute the bastion of Congress support. Here lives the
"average" Indian—illiterate, fatalistic, credulous, and easily manipulatable. As
these conditions change Congress's power is also being eroded. This is not to say
Congress is the "villain" in the democratic drama of India. In the urban centers
there is not only deeper discontent, but a determination that things can be made
better. The beneficiaries of this attitude are very often the radical parties.
Congress, in any case, is the victim.

A continuing source of support for Congress since independence has been
India's religious minorities, who constitute 15 percent of the present population.
There are some exceptions—the Muslims for example, in the Malabar part of
Kerala—but the general pattern of minority voting behavior in India is to
support Congress, partly because Congress has been the party in power and
partly because it has shown a genuine concern for the minorities. The party also
gets some support from the working class through its affiliate, the Indian
National Trade Union Congress (INTUC)—India's largest trade union.

Trends in recent elections.   A decline in Congress votes in the 1967 general election was expected. Economic conditions had grown from bad to worse, and many states were on the verge of famine. It was for the first time Congress had to face the people after the death of Nehru. Further, in most states the party was torn from top to bottom by factional struggles made acute by the selection of candidates, and in some states parallel Congresses were formed by dissident party members. At the same time, in many states opposition parties had formed unified fronts and were determined to make Congress's distress their golden opportunity. Under such circumstances some losses in the political fortunes of Congress were predicted. What surprised everybody was the magnitude of its losses. (Table 5.2 summarizes the results of elections from 1952 to 1971.)

Table 5.2.   Elections to the Lok Sabhas, 1952-1971

Year	% of Seats of Congress Party	% of Seats of Largest Opposition Party	% of Votes of Congress Party	% of Votes of Nearest Opposition Party
1952	74.4	3.3	45.0	10.6
1957	75.1	5.4	47.8	10.4
1962	73.1	5.9	46.0	10.0
1967	54.4	8.5	40.7	9.4
1971	67.2	4.8	43.1	10.5

SOURCE: Adapted from R.L. Hardgrave, Jr., *India: Government and Politics in a Developing Nation* (New York: Harcourt, Brace and World), 1970, pp. 159-60; Ramashray Roy, "India 1972: Fissure in the Fortress," *Asian Survey* (February 1973) pp. 231-45.

NOTE: Not including independents.

The table shows two things. First, even in 1952, when Congress had numerous advantages over the opposition parties, it did not win an absolute majority of votes. Secondly, in the four consecutive elections since, twice (1957 and 1971) Congress votes rose; in the two other elections they fell. In terms of seats, which is far more important for practical reasons in a parliamentary system, the losses in 1967 were very heavy indeed. In the first election (1952) Congress had won 364 of 489 seats—nearly 75 percent. In the 1967 election Congress could win only 284 of 520 seats—about 55 percent.

These results have been confirmed by results at the state level.[18] Congress was also humbled at the local and national levels by the defeat of several of its stalwarts, among them the party president, several party bosses, several former central cabinet ministers, and four former state chief ministers. The trend was thus clear in all of India's elections. Voters were turning away from Congress in large numbers to the benefit of leftist parties.[19]

The split of the National Congress party.   The first half of 1967 showed that Congress had learned some lessons from its defeat in the elections. When it came to choosing the party's leader, the leadership succeeded in averting an open contest. Indira Gandhi was chosen as leader of the party and thus became the prime minister. Within the party Mrs. Gandhi soon began to establish her ascendency; in this she sought and got the support of its younger leaders. A feeling of estrangement began to develop between her and the party bosses—the syndicate—who had chosen her in the hope she would be pliable.

In July of 1968 the Central Parliamentary Board nominated N. Sanjiva Reddy, speaker of the Lok Sabha, as the Congress candidate for the presidency of the Indian republic. Reddy was a former member of the Syndicate and his relations with Mrs. Gandhi were very cool. Moreover, he was nominated against the wishes of Mrs. Gandhi, who had wanted her supporter, Jagjivan Ram, to be nominated as the Congress candidate. Both Reddy and Ram were senior Congress leaders and both had impressive credentials. In choosing Reddy, the Syndicate was motivated by the thought it would be a demonstration of their strength vis-a-vis the prime minister. The prime minister, however, retaliated by relieving Morarji Desai of his finance portfolio, without any prior consultation with him. This left him with no alternative but to resign, which he did. Desai's forced resignation was a blow to the Syndicate, with which he was closely identified. In another swift move Mrs. Gandhi nationalized the leading Indian banks. This move, calculated to win the support of the vociferous, leftist younger members of Congress, was interpreted as another snub to the conservative Syndicate. After the Desai episode the division between the supporters of the prime minister and the Syndicate deepened, with acrimonious criticism from both sides. This division was reflected in the presidential election. Two supporters of the prime minister, who were also senior Congress leaders, wrote to the Congress president, S. Nijalingappa, questioning the propriety of his consultations with rightist parties and accusing him of conspiring with them to secure the victory of Sanjiva Reddy and topple Indira Gandhi from power later. This was followed by heated assertions and denials from the two sides. Already, a prominent Congress MP, another supporter of the prime minister, had openly challenged the Congress high command by declaring his support for the opposition candidate, V. V. Giri. The prime minister on her part refused to cooperate with all Syndicate efforts designed to assure the election of Reddy. Specifically, she refused to call a "whip" (i. e., a party line vote on Reddy's election), though this was specifically requested by the Congress president and thus emboldened many Congress legislators, who had been clamoring for the right to vote according to their conscience in the presidential election. Her open quarrels with the Syndicate thus resulted in the division of the party and the defeat of Reddy, the official Congress party candidate, in the election.

In an open letter to Congress party members, dated November 8, 1969, Indira Gandhi described the conflict between herself and the Syndicate as one "between those who are for socialism, for change and for the fullest internal democracy and debate in the organization on the one hand and those who are for the status quo, for conformism and for less than full discussion inside the Congress." [20]

On November 12, the Syndicate group in the Congress Working Committee met. Of the twenty-one members, eleven were present and they decided to suspend Mrs. Gandhi "from the primary membership of Congress." Their resolution said they had "to choose between Indira Gandhi and everything the Congress stood for; and it has rightly decided in favour of the latter." In another resolution the committee charged Mrs. Gandhi for attempting to "capture the Congress machinery first at the top level and then at other levels."[21] But the Congress parliamentary party met on November 13, and expressed its confidence in Mrs. Gandhi. Through a resolution it declared that the action of the Working Committee was "invalid and unjustifiable."[22]

The Syndicate group in parliament met separately and elected Dr. Ram Subhag Singh as the leader of the group in the Lok Sabha. This group, with a strength of sixty to sixty-five members in the Lok Sabha, was recognized as the official opposition, for which minimum strength of fifty-two members is required. No party had been able to achieve this since the country conducted the first election in 1952. For the first time in India's history the Congress party lost its absolute majority in the national legislature. The first trial of strength for the ruling group of Mrs. Gandhi came when the Swatantra party moved an adjournment motion against the government on November 17. It was rejected by 306 votes to 143. Those who voted against the motion included, besides the ruling party, the two Communist parties, some communalists, and many independents. The motion was supported by the Swatantra party, the PSP, SSP, Jan Sangh, the Nigalingappa group, and a few others.[23]

In 1971 Mrs. Gandhi called for a general election and the Congress split was placed before the Indian electorate. In the confrontation Mrs. Gandhi roundly defeated the Syndicate, taking about two-thirds of the seats in the Lok Sabha. Individual leaders of the Syndicate were sent to their defeat. Mrs. Gandhi appears once again to be the undisputed leader of India's only dominant national political party.

CHILE

Unlike Great Britain and India, Chile, before the overthrow of President Allende, had developed an open, competitive political system in which the branches of government could be separately controlled and managed. Thus the president of Chile, who was popularly chosen in a national election, could represent one party, or group of parties, while the national legislature—also chosen through popular election—could be controlled by entirely different parties. In contrast, in Great Britain and India the chief executive, the prime minister, is chosen by a majority in the legislature. In these two countries a great premium is placed on strong party organization, because a party victory can mean overwhelming power. In Chile, a party victory in one contest did not necessarily indicate party power in the future, for some other party could win in another separate contest. Chilean politics thus became a process of permanent negotiation among parties, each of which might have some influence in some part of the system, but none of which could gain the overwhelming dominance enjoyed by a majority party in a parliamentary regime. This was made particularly acute since Chile had a multiparty system in which it was difficult for any party to achieve a popular majority over any long period of time.

Political Parties in Chile From Left to Right

The Left.   The Chilean Left (now outlawed by the current military junta) consisted primarily of two large parties—the Communists and the Socialists—and a large number of smaller, more radical groups. For example, there existed a Maoist group—the Partido Communista Revolucionario (PRC)—that was expelled by the Communists and insisted on guerrilla warfare as the only means by which the left wing could take over. In addition, there was the Movimiento de Izquierda Revolucionaria (MIR), which, while headed by a socialist, had been influenced by the Cuban revolution of Fidel Castro and drew its main support among student groups. The MIR, while not engaging in full-blown guerrilla warfare, had carried out terrorist activities in some of Chile's major cities. The MIR had robbed banks and planted bombs, but not to as great an extent as other Cuban-oriented groups in Latin American countries.

The Chilean Communist party was much larger than these more radical offshoots and had long occupied an important place in the country's political affairs. The party, founded in 1912, rose to a dominant place in Chile's labor movement by 1921; it was weakened by internal strife during the 1920s and 1930s but made considerable gains among urban workers in the 1940s. In the late 1940s the party was outlawed, and its strength among workers declined, though internal party organization remained intact. In the 1950s the Communists supported candidates of other parties and struck an alliance with the Socialists, which lasted till the overthrow of Allende. The party's influence had increased among urban workers, and under Allende, a Socialist, the party enjoyed greater influence than it ever had before.

In ideology and organization the Chilean Communists resemble other world Communist parties. The party was always closely allied to the Communist International (Comintern), an organization of world communist parties dominated by the Soviet party (CPSU). The Chilean Communist party's doctrines are interpretations of Marxism-Leninism, but its program is decidedly more reformist than revolutionary. Chile's Communists have pushed reforms of the educational and electoral systems to broaden popular participation; they also have favored greater government intervention in the economy. However, the party has not advocated total nationalization of all industries or dismantling the Chilean democratic structure. It has catered more to the aims of "middle-class" workers and has opposed mass mobilization of all of Chile's poor. Rather, the Communists presented their program as an improvement on existing procedures, and within the middle-class Chilean frame of reference. As is true of many other Moscow-oriented Communist parties in Latin America, Chilean Communists have consistently adhered to a "popular front" strategy —cooperating with other parties of the Left (and, sometimes, of the Center or Right) to attain specific short-term objectives.

The Chilean Communists, until disbanded, were supported mostly by workers and the party directly controlled a number of Chilean trade unions. Workers were given opportunities to participate in party affairs, though, as in other countries, the party was tightly organized and highly disciplined. The Chilean Communist party was governed authoritatively by a Central Executive

Committee that called all party meetings and nominated all candidates for office. This committee was elected by the party conference, which was normally packed with supporters of party leaders.

The Chilean Socialist party, Chile's other major left-wing party, had old roots in the Chilean system; some authors date it back to the middle nineteenth century. Recently, Chile had a Socialist president—Allende—elected with the aid of the Communists, but for most of Chile's history the party was not a dominant group.

Compared to similar groups in other countries the Chilean Socialists were, in ideological and policy matters, nearly as radical as the Communists and in some cases even more extreme. Socialist ideology was generally Marxist and anticapitalist, but the party was thoroughly nationalist and sought a peculiarly Chilean form of socialism. It was not affiliated with the international Communist movement, though it was allied with the Chilean Communist party. It rejected foreign influence—both of the Soviet and American varieties. Compared to the Chilean Communists, the Socialists were more sympathetic to the views of Cuban leader Fidel Castro, as well as to those of the Chinese Communists.

The party advocated agrarian reform and broadening popular participation in government. Its main support was derived from intellectuals and the urban working classes, with little support from agrarian groups. Like the Communist party, the Socialist party was run by professional politicians. The party had a strong centralized administration that was dominated by a Central Committee which, in turn, called all party meetings and nominated all candidates. Compared to the Communists, however, discipline was not as strong below the highest levels of the party. Under President Allende, the Communist party had been a far better organized and reliable supporter of the regime than the Socialists, despite the fact that the president was himself a Socialist.

The Center. Unlike the leftist parties, Chile's center parties are not tightly organized around ideological principles. Chile's Christian Democratic party, the largest center party, is generally considered to be left of center. It came into existence in 1938 as an offshoot of the more right-wing Conservative party, and by 1963 it had become the most popular party in Chilean history.

In 1964 Eduardo Frei, a Christian Democrat, was the first person ever to be elected president of Chile with an absolute popular majority, over two rivals. In 1965 the party attained an absolute majority in the Chamber of Deputies, the first time this feat had been accomplished in over 100 years. This popularity has receded in recent years—a measure of the country's response to the success of the party's program. The Christian Democrats have also suffered because Frei, barred by the Chilean constitution from seeking a second consecutive term as president, could not lead his party in the 1971 presidential election.

The Christian Democratic government led by Eduardo Frei, was elected on a program that was broadly reformist and promised much to Chile's rural and urban workers. The party pledged it would enact a law permitting legal unionization of rural workers and it would carry out an agrarian reform. It also promised to "Chileanize" the country's mining industry, to stimulate economic growth and industrialization, and to control inflation, a long-standing economic difficulty facing the nation. The government's success in carrying out its promises was quite uneven, and the Christian Democrats lost some supporters because of this fact.

The Frei government actively promoted the unionization of rural workers and put into effect two broad agrarian reform laws. The government expropriated much land from wealthy landholders and redistributed it to formerly landless peasants. These actions brought the Christian Democratic party the support of the rural masses, which had not, even under President Allende, effectively been challenged by the more leftist parties.

Frei also developed much support for his party among miners and mining interests, by "Chileanizing" foreign-owned mine fields. The Frei administration obtained important concessions from the Anaconda, Kennecot, and Cerro de Pasco companies which ran the mines as well as the nitrate firms.

The Christian Democrats, however, failed in their promises to urban labor and did not succeed in curbing inflation. Inflation hurt the employed urban worker most, so this voter was drawn to the more radical pledges of the Marxist parties.[24]

The Christian Democrats are a basically pragmatic, centrist party, devoted to socioeconomic reform and progress. The party, neither Marxist nor anti-Marxist, would undertake broad and far-reaching programs if these were believed correct. The Christian Democrats have some ties to the Catholic church, but these have been considerably eroded in recent years. The party, which still exists today, is quite secular, nationalistic, and devoted to gradually increasing participation of the masses within the confines of Chile's democratic system. Its main support is from the Catholic middle class and the rural masses. It is also a highly centralized party, governed by professionals, and remains the single largest Chilean political party.

In addition to the Christian Democrats, Chile had a right-center party, the Radical party, which was banned by the military junta because it supported President Allende. This party had both left- and right-wing factions, with some members favoring radical reforms while others favored more moderate approaches. The Radicals were willing to coalesce with other parties, no matter what programs they espoused. The Radicals were lacking in consistent ideological commitments and had suffered by comparison to the Christian Democrats in this respect. Before 1964 the Radical party was the major center party, participating in most governments between 1938 and 1952. It had since lost this position to the Christian Democrats.

The Radical party varied in composition, included mostly small farmers, some professionals and skilled workers, and many government workers. The party was internally the most democratically organized of Chilean parties, exercising little discipline over its members and placing few obstacles in the path of organizational advancement.

The Right.   The Right consists of two of the oldest parties in Chile, which governed the country for most of its history before the reformist regime of Eduardo Frei. Today Chilean right-wing parties have been permitted to exist by the military, which may mean their eventually recapturing some of the strength that they seemed to be losing.

The two parties are the United Conservative party (UCP) and the Liberal Party (LP). The Conservatives, composed primarily of upper-class landholders and aristocrats, are pro-Catholic, favor private enterprise, and are opposed to the expropriation of property.

The Liberal party is the party of the urban commercial classes, supported primarily by wealthy businessmen. It is more open to change than the Conservative party and has no pro-church ideology. This party is somewhat torn by factionalism, but it tends to be quite uniformly upper class. Both the UCP and LP are highly centralized and run by professionals, with little internal party democracy. Since 1965 the two parties have been formally combined and now run as a single organization, the National party.

Trends in Recent Elections

A summary of voting returns in Chilean presidential elections is given in Table 5.3:

Table 5.3. Presidential Election Returns in Chile, 1946-1970

Year	Winning Candidate	Party	% of Total Vote
1946	G. Gonzalez-Videla	Radical	40.3
1952	C. Ibanez	---	46.8
1958	J. Allesandri	Liberal	31.6
1964	E. Frei	Christian Democrat	55.6
1970	S. Allende	Socialist	36.7

SOURCE: Adapted from Federico Gil, *The Political System of Chile* (Boston: Houghton-Mifflin, 1966); *New York Times*, Sept. 12, 1873; *The Economist*, March 10, 1973.

*Ibanez was supported by parties of both the Right and the Left, and his victory is widely regarded as personal, not partisan.

As can be seen, no party has won two successive presidential elections in Chile since World War II. However, the trend in elections seemed to be moving gradually to the Left, with winning candidates in successive elections emerging from increasingly left-wing coalitions every time.

Some authors, before the military coup, saw a consistent trend in Chilean presidential politics based on these facts. These writers believed Chilean presidential election campaigns raised public aspirations for economic improvement, and that presidents, in the last few elections, began their terms with great public support and expectation.[25] The early period of a Chilean administration was thus characterized by public confidence, which in a few years eroded as a result of economic difficulties and internal factionalism. In time, a new presidential election was held and the administration was replaced by a

leader of a different party, which again promised a little more than the
government was able to deliver.

In contrast to the results of presidential elections, electoral trends as
evidenced in Chile's legislative elections showed a tendency for parties of the
Center to dominate. This indeed has been the case since 1949 (see Table 5.4).
Politics in Chile of the 1970s did not consist of the manipulated coalitions of the
1950s, which lacked programmatic commitments. Rather, recent coalitions have
been characterized by tendencies to a moderate left-center ideology and
program, thus contributing a definite style and cohesion to Chilean politics until
the advent of the Allende presidency.

Table 5.4.   Election Returns for the Chamber of Deputies in Chile, 1949-1973

Year	Largest Party	% of Votes Won by Largest Party	% of Seats Won by Largest Party
1949	Radicals	22.5	22.7
1953*	Nationalists		
1957	Radicals	22.5	24.0
1961	Radicals	22.0	26.7
1965	Ch. Dems.	42.0	56.3
1969	Ch. Dems.	30.0	37.5
1973	Ch. Dems. in Coalition**	54.7	58.0

SOURCE: Adapted from Federico Gil, *The Political System of Chile* (Boston:
Houghton Mifflin, 1966), pp. 232-3, 234-7, 307-11; *The Economist*, March 10, 1973.

*Between 1952 and 1958, Chile was governed by a coalition of parties whose
support was pledged to President Carlos Ibanez. Ibanez's party, the Nationalists,
no longer exists in Chilean politics and had few roots before his candidacy. His
regime is considered to be based on his personal popularity.

**In 1973 parties opposed to President Allende ran as a coalition called the
Democratic Confederation.

The basic conflict between Chile's center-dominated style of legislative
politics and the tendency for the electorate increasingly to support more left-
wing presidents of course contributed to the immobilization and eventual
overthrow of the Allende regime. It should be noted that Allende, while he
received more popular votes than any other presidential candidate in 1969, was
elected president only because the Christian Democrats supported his candidacy in the Congress. (Under the Chilean constitution of 1925 a candidate who
receives less than a majority of the popular vote, a normal result given the large
number of political parties in Chile, can become president only if he is elected
by the Congress, which must choose between the two candidates who received
the greatest number of popular votes. The Chilean Congress has in every
presidential election since 1946 selected as president the candidate with the
highest popular vote.) Allende had personally received only 36.7 percent of the
popular vote in the 1969 presidential election and never held a majority in the
Chilean Congress throughout his term. In 1973, just before the coup, the Chilean

Congress was dominated by an anti-Allende coalition of parties, led by the Christian Democrats, who held 58 percent of the seats in the Chamber of Deputies and who were instrumental in bringing the military into the government.

Comparative Distinctions in Political Parties Among Competitive States

Political parties reflect the cultural and political habits of the countries in which they operate. As these cultural patterns vary from state to state, so also do their respective political party organizations and systems.

Great Britain, with her long-established two-party system, has developed a very balanced competitive party structure. Each major political party (Labour and Conservative and now the Liberals) represents different social groups to a certain extent, but they all overlap considerably and tailor their appeals to a growing middle sector that does not automatically support either the traditional left- or right-wing approach to politics. The third small party, the Liberals, fits somewhere between the two large parties and has tended to support the cohesion of the system in times of crisis, rather than becoming a source of instability. Both major parties in Great Britain are also very close in electoral strength, both are highly structured internally.

In contrast, although India has a quasi-parliamentary form of government, she has a large number of competing political parties. However, only one party—the Indian National Congress—has been able to dominate the political life of the country since independence on both the national and state levels. Because of this fact, one of the major channels of competition in India is among leaders and factions within the Congress party; this competition is often more important in terms of its effect on national policymaking than the rivalry among parties. Indeed, most minor parties in India were originally factions within the Congress party. India's great regional and cultural diversity puts constant pressure on governing groups, and minor parties spring up in an attempt to represent some of these more parochial views and interests. However, there is little chance that these minority parties will attain national leadership, in view of the comparatively narrow base of their support.

Chile is unlike both Great Britain and India in that although Chile has a large number of parties, they do fall into natural coalitions with a national, not parochial, outlook. Thus (until the military coup of 1973) Chilean politics has generally consisted of a relatively flexible center-left coalition of parties facing a center-right coalition, with each group trying through its programs and electoral appeals to enlist the support of new voters. Chilean parties have been highly organized and Chilean competition has definitely been interparty competition.

POLITICAL PARTIES IN FRAGMENTED STATES

Patterns of Similarity

Fragmented states are generally characterized by the kind of group politics that makes it difficult to develop political parties with a national base of support.

In fragmented states, political parties tend to represent narrow regional, economic, or ideological interests and tend to be relatively unsuccessful in building coalitions among groups. Thus they have difficulty aggregating the various articulated interests in their respective countries in a manner comparable to political parties in competitive states. Beyond this basic similarity, political parties in fragmented states reflect their nation's respective cultural habits and differ from one another because of this.

Three Case Studies: France, Indonesia, and Zaire

FRANCE

France has long been a country with a deeply fragmented party structure. Political party organizations are numerous, and no single party has long been able to aspire to majority status either in terms of the popular vote or of legislative strength. Rather, French political parties have represented the deep schisms in French public opinion and their multiplicity and intransigence are merely reflections of deep divisions in French society.

Political Parties in France From Left to Right

As in Chile, political parties in France are normally grouped into left- , center, and right-wing categories. These are historic designations in France which have, over time, changed in specific meaning. At the time of the French Revolution, "left" meant "republican," while "right" meant "monarchist"; in the nineteenth century, "left" meant "egalitarian" in economic matters, while "right" signified "authoritarian" in this area. The twentieth century, however, has seen the emergence of groups that are in favor of economic egalitarianism but are at the same time authoritarian. Thus many designations are today quite arbitrary and do not necessarily reflect the ideological positions of the parties by any objective standard.

The Left.   The largest left-wing party in France, the Communist party, gets a mass vote (between 20 and 30 percent during the post-World-War-II years in almost all elections). It claims to be descended from a long line of leftist political parties within France and appeals to the traditionally left-wing voter. In policy, however, the party has been obedient to Moscow and has at least until recently been true to the international Communist line.

Communist voters in France are not all dedicated Communists but vote for the party for a variety of reasons. The party, for example, has been able to present itself as most closely identified with the industrial working class. It also receives some support from poor and landless peasants. A great deal of support accrued to the Communists because of their active role against the Germans in World War II. By being the representative of the traditional left wing, the party also receives a great deal of left-wing intellectual support. In addition, since it is the most outspoken antireligious party, the Communists attract an anticlerical vote. Overall, the Communists have represented the wishes of those who are generally discontented with both the French social establishment and the political system. The party therefore receives the negative votes, and Frenchmen tend to view the Communist party as a legitimate institution for just this purpose.

In organization, the French Communist party is similar to other Communist parties. It is tightly controlled by professional party workers who determine party policy and choose the candidates. Communist deputies in the National Assembly return over two-thirds of their salary to the party. Since many Communist leaders come from working-class backgrounds, they are dependent on the party for financial support in elections.

The French Communist party is a good example of an organization that is more interested in its own narrow programs than in achieving national support for a national program. It has been a major contributor to the basic fragmentation of the French political system since World War II because its willingness to cooperate with other political groups has been limited and completely opportunistic. Communist opportunism, in turn, has caused the other parties to mistrust alliances with the Communists, thus making a strong left-center or leftist coalition on a permanent basis (as in Chile) difficult to achieve, at least until recently.

This can be seen by viewing the development of Communist political strategy since World War II. In the period from 1944 to 1947 the French Communists participated in a "Popular Front"—an alliance of leftist and center groups dedicated to the overthrow of fascism and the restructuring of France on a more egalitarian basis. Communists were admitted to cabinet positions and participated in the framing of the constitution of the Fourth Republic. However, in 1947 the Soviet Union directed all world Communist groups to be intransigent opponents of the "Capitalist" West. From 1947 to 1953 the French Communists obediently opposed all measures undertaken by the Fourth Republic, voluntarily dropping out of all coalitions. Since 1953 (after the death of Stalin, and consequent changes in the international party line), the Communists have attempted to reestablish themselves within the French party structure, but with only limited success. In the 1960s, after General de Gaulle came to power, the Communists supported a Socialist candidate in a presidential election (1965) and also agreed to enter the Socialist Federation, a coalition of leftist parties in the 1967 legislative elections; they also cooperated with other left-wing groups in the referendum of 1969 that toppled General de Gaulle. However, in each case the coalition collapsed after the election; the 1969 presidential election saw the Communists abstain, though a new attempt at coalition for the 1973 legislative elections was carried out. This 1973 coalition was successful in reducing the majority of the Gaullist party, which now governs with the support of two small centrist parties. Although the leftist coalition lost the election, it has picked up considerable strength since 1969.

The French Socialists, unlike the Communists, are devoted to political democracy. The Socialist party is also more moderate than the Communist party on economic questions and is generally supported by middle-class salaried voters. The Socialists, who since World War II have lost many working-class voters to the Communists, are not now a mass party in France; they receive on the average about 15 percent of the vote in most elections.

The Socialists have long been hostile to the Communists in France and rather than participating in left-wing alliances that the Communists would dominate, the Socialists have chosen to support moderate to right-wing cabinets and coalitions. In the Fourth Republic Socialists participated in every cabinet, except for the period 1950 to 1954, and generally accepted more conservative policies than they really liked. In 1958 they supported General de Gaulle for fear of an even more right-wing government coming to power.

Overall, the French Socialists generally support a politics of compromise and aggregation, but they have gradually lost strength to the moderate Center and to the more radical Left. In organization, the party is centralized and disciplined, but it has been unable to attract many new members. Thus, while they would favor a competitive party system, the Socialists do not have much strength in bringing this about.

The Center.   There are two major center parties in France—the Radical Socialists party and the Democratic Center party. The Radical Socialists were the leading party of the Third Republic (from 1870 to 1940). Traditionally republican and secular, the party's main support today is in rural areas and small towns. Frenchmen view it as a rather old-fashioned, small business party, and it has received only from 10 to 13 percent of the vote in most elections since World War II.

The Radical Socialists are a loosely organized group with little ideological commitment. The party has normally been willing to support coalitions of either the Right or Left, for the pragmatic purpose of achieving some political influence. During the Fourth Republic (from 1945 to 1958), Pierre Mendès-France became leader of the left wing of the party and managed to give it a more activist image; indeed, the party ran in coalition with the Socialists during this time. However, Mendès-France soon lost influence and the party moved back to the Right-Center during the early years of the Fifth Republic. Today, it is a left-center party again, running in alliance with the Socialists. However, like the Socialists, it is a weak party and seems to be declining.

The Democratic Center party (CDP), a new party (since 1968) consisting primarily of the Popular Republican party (MRP), which was formed after World War II, and a number of other smaller center parties, is distinguished from other French parties by its pro-Catholic stance on church issues. In economic policy it favors moderate reform. The MRP was strong during the Fourth Republic (from 1945 to 1958), participating in most cabinets and usually being the governing party. At this time it was a left-center party, in favor of European integration and measures to improve the living standards of the poor. It also had been active in the resistance against the Germans and was closely associated in the public mind with General de Gaulle. However, the MRP became associated with the major failures of the Fourth Republic and lost votes to both left- and right-wing parties. It lost fully half its deputies in the decade between 1948 and 1958.

The party is fairly well disciplined and was held responsible by the French electorate for its actions. Thus, today the CDP has lost most of its left wing and is usually described as being a right-center party and has supported the Gaullist coalition in the National Assembly. It receives roughly 10 percent of the vote at elections and has only a weak voice in French political affairs.

The Right. On the Right are the Independents and the Gaullist parties. The Independent Republican party is Catholic, conservative and devoted to republicanism. It represents urban conservatives, such as business and white-collar workers.

Like the Socialists, Radicals, and the Democratic Center party, the Independent Republican party, which is fairly loosely organized, is weak in electoral strength. It usually receives as little as 15 percent of the vote, and finds it difficult to dominate any coalition; thus, it represents a further fragmentation of the French political system. The Independents must be courted by other parties but they retain their individual commitments and freely pick and choose alliances. President Valéry Giscard d'Estaing is an Independent Republican but was elected and governs only with the support of the UDR, the Gaullist party.

Parties associated with General de Gaulle have punctuated the history of France since World War II. In 1948 the Rally of the French People (RPF) was organized under de Gaulle's personal aegis, but the party did not compete in an election until 1951, when it received 21 percent of the vote. In 1953 de Gaulle denounced this party because its deputies acted like other French politicians in shifting support among weak coalition governments. The party then split and did poorly in the 1956 legislative elections. In 1958 General de Gaulle was brought to power as president of the new Fifth Republic. A new party, the Union for the New Republic (UNR) was established to support the personal leadership of General de Gaulle. In 1967 this party changed its name to the Union for a Democratic Republic (UDR).

The UDR has been the most powerful party in the Fifth Republic, maintaining constant dominance in the legislature and, until the election of Giscard d'Estaing in 1974, being the party of the president. Even President Giscard d'Estaing, an Independent Republican, was elected only with open UDR electoral support. In the Fifth Republic, the president dominated the political system, and there has been very little attempt to develop any alliance with leftist and left-of-center groups. Coalitions in the National Assembly really serve little purpose, since the president legally can impose his will on the legislature.

The UDR under President d'Estaing is supported by a generally conservative group of voters who wish strong executive leadership and fear a Socialist or Communist government coming to power. Giscard d'Estaing governs only because the UDR supported his candidacy in the 1974 run-off election after its own candidate, Jacques Chaban-Delmas, was eliminated on the first ballot. The UDR's voter thus showed they preferred a conservative, even if not of their own party, to the Socialist candidate, François Mitterand.

Electoral strength of the Gaullist parties has fluctuated somewhat as demonstrated by the election returns of the Fifth Republic (see Table 5.5).

As can be seen in the table, despite the fact that the UDR remains a doctrinally conservative party and has made little attempt to placate its

Table 5.5. Election Returns for Gaullist Parties in the Fifth Republic, 1958-1973

Presidential Elections	Leading Candidate	% of Popular Votes on 1st Ballot	% of Popular Votes on 2nd Ballot
1958	DeGaulle*	---	---
1965	DeGaulle	43.7	54.5
1969	Pompidou	44.0	57.5
1974	Giscard d'Estaing**	33.0	50.1

Legislative Elections	Leading Party	% of Seats after 2nd Ballot	% of Votes on 2nd Ballot
1958	UNR***	35.6	26.5
1962	UNR	48.9	40.5
1967	UDR	56.2	42.6
1969	UDR	67.7	47.0
1973****	UDR	49.0	40.1

SOURCE: Adapted from Henry Ehrmann, "Politics in France," in Gabriel A. Almond, ed. Comparative Politics Today: A World View (Boston: Little, Brown, 1974), pp. 215, 231. New York Times, May 19, 1974; New York Times, March 4, 1973. Giscard d'Estaing received the support of the UDR after he came in ahead of the UDR candidate, Jacques Chaban Delmas, on the first ballot while Francois Mitterand, the Socialist came in first. Chaban Delmas by coming in third was legally eliminated from the second ballot runoff.

*DeGaulle was elected by Fourth Republic Assembly, 329 to 224 votes as premier of the Fourth Republic. He was then indirectly elected president by an electoral college composed of local officials. He recieved 77.5 percent of the votes in the electoral college.

***UNR governed with help of Independents.

****The UDR retains a majority of seats with the assistance of the Independent Republicans and the Democratic Center party. Together the three parties are a government coalition.

opposition in terms of program and policy, the Gaullist regime increased its percentage of the vote in every French election from 1958 to 1973. What is not evident in the table is the margin enjoyed by the Gaullist parties over the opposition. For example, in 1967 when the UDR held slightly more than 50 percent of the seats in the National Assembly, the party's margin was very slim compared to a united leftist opposition. In 1958 the UNR was supported by other parties such as the Independent Republicans and though Gaullist representation itself was small, its coalition was strong. From 1969 to 1973 the UDR had a powerful numerical majority alone, for the first time in French legislative history. In 1973 the success of the UDR apparently forced the French Left to coalesce and the result was another, though narrower, victory for the Gaullist coalition. If these two coalitions show some endurance, France may well be on the way to ending the perennial fragmentation of her national politics. As yet, however, there is little indication that this will in fact come about. The leftist coalition has managed to stay together for two consecutive elections—the 1973 election for the National Assembly and the 1974 presidential race. They were narrowly defeated in both and still have not demonstrated whether they can win an election or if they can stay together if they should win.

INDONESIA

Like France, Indonesia is a nation that has produced a multiplicity of political parties, each responsible to a narrow constituency and few really either capable or interested in pursuing national goals and policies. Until 1957 Indonesia had a freely operating party structure; since that time parties have been agents of other powers in authority. Under Sukarno (from 1957 to 1965) only a few political parties could exercise any influence and since Sukarno's overthrow by the military (1965) to the present all parties have been subject to the power of General Suharto. Although a facade of representative elections has been maintained (a legislative election was held in 1971), Indonesia no longer truly has a free party system and final authority today rests with the military. However, the superficial appearance of a party structure is maintained.

The Spectrum of Political Parties in Indonesia

Indonesian political parties include some old, established organizations that, as in France, have had strong regional and occupational constituencies developed over the course of the twentieth century. Before the onset of Guided Democracy and the end of open party competition,Indonesian parties could be divided into several ideological categories: religious, nationalist, and Marxist. Within each category different kinds of parties could be found. Among the religious-oriented parties was the Masjumi, a group of Islamic, problem-oriented reformists interested in economic development and efficient administration, which contrasted with the Nahdatul Ulama, a more traditionalist Islamic group that originally had split off from the Masjumi. Among the nationalist parties was the PNI, some of whose leaders were interested in efficient administration and policy problems, but some of whose members wished to carry on the nationalist revolution on an ideological level with little concern for such things as economic development. Among the Marxist parties there could be found the social democratic parties, such as the Partai Socialis Indonesia (PSI), which were moderate and concerned with administrative tasks and problems, and the Communist party (PKI), which was a revolutionary party dedicated to mobilizing the people behind the utopian goals of proletarian revolution. All these parties were removed from the people and debated their disagreements in ideological terms. The main issue in the 1955 election, for example, was not the government's record or policies; it was rather a dispute over ideological symbols between an out-party, the Masjumi, which stood for Islam, and the PNI, the in-party, which emphasized the appeals of nationalism. Each party claimed its position best represented the nation by virtue of the correctness of its ideology.[26] It should also be mentioned different parties drew their strength from different areas: the Islamic parties were strong in the Outer Islands and rural areas; the nationalist Marxist parties did well in urban areas on Java.

The Role of the President and Political Parties in Indonesia

In the parliamentary period Sukarno, the great nationalist hero, occupied the post of president to which he was not elected but appointed by a Revolutionary Committee during the Indonesian revolutionary war against the Dutch in 1945. As head of state, he could appoint the *formateurs* of cabinets. As the foremost leader of the revolution and as ceremonial chief of state, he therefore occupied a preeminent position: the 1950 constitution, though it set up a parliamentary form of government, made him inviolable, and cabinet ministers were made responsible for his actions. Thus, Sukarno could exercise a great deal of influence but was in no way responsible to anyone; he could criticize government policy and the cabinets without really being held accountable for his opinions, even though the cabinet was responsible for his acts.[27] Having been placed in such a position he managed to keep himself above party politics, while he presented himself as the ideological spokesman for the entire nation. Although he saw himself as the bridge between the elite and the masses, he placed the responsibility for carrying on the activities of government squarely on the leaders of the political parties—not on himself. As he put it:

> Our state is based on democratic principles. The wishes of our people determine the structure of the Government and the policy it follows. This is founded on the hope and belief that in this way our country will get the best administration. The political parties—to be more exact, the leaders of the political parties—bear the responsibility of proving that hope and belief are true.[28]

Indonesian political parties, divorced from the people, expected to work wonders for the people—and not feel bound by them. The justification for all this was seen in the claims of the nationalist elite: as leaders in the fight for independence, they felt themselves to be qualified to know what was best for the people. It was assumed elections would eventually confirm this, but, at the moment, politics was a matter for the urban educated class. Sukarno, placing himself above politics, saw himself as the unifying element of the nation. While other members of the government tended to view their leadership tasks quite legalistically, he emphasized the importance of uniting the people behind a mystical ideology. The result was conflict between those who wanted to tackle immediate government problems (the Islamic reformist and democratic socialist parties) and those who, like Sukarno, wished to pursue the utopian goals for which the revolution had been fought (the nationalist and Communist parties). Neither group had a clear concept of representation: both would act, unbound, in the interests of the undifferentiated "people," without necessarily investigating empirically what the "will of the People" might be. In other words, the parties were not capable of or interested in carrying out the aggregation functions normally attributed to political parties in competitive political systems.

Parliamentarianism and Political Parties in Indonesia

Thus, from 1949 to approximately 1957, Indonesia maintained what has generally been described as a multiparty parliamentary system on the European model. The 1955 general election for the national legislature was the only free election ever held in independent Indonesia; it yielded a highly fractionalized representation in the legislative body. Elected on the basis of an extreme form of proportional representation, the Indonesian legislature allowed seats for twenty-six separate parties. No single party received more than 22 percent of the popular vote and a parliamentary majority depended on an alliance of a minimum of three parties in any coalition (and generally more since party discipline was weak). Cabinet instability, a plague on Indonesian politics before the 1955 election (when representation in the legislature consisted of the various revolutionary groups that had opposed the Dutch), became an established and unavoidable fact after the 1955 election. (The results of this election are shown in Table 5.6).

Table 5.6. General Election Returns in Indonesia in 1955

Party	% of Total Valid Vote*	Seats in National Legislature
PNI	22.5	57
Masjumi	20.9	57
Nahdatul Ulama	18.4	45
PKI	16.4	39
PSII	2.9	8
Parkindo	2.6	8
Partai Katholik	2.0	6
PSI	2.0	5
IPKI	1.4	4
Perti	1.3	4
Others*	9.6	24
Total	100.0	257

SOURCE: Adapted from Herbert Feith, *The Decline of Constitutional Democracy in Indonesia* (Ithaca: Cornell University Press, 1963), pp. 434-5.

*Sixteen other parties received less than 1 percent of the vote and were rewarded with either one or two seats in the national legislature.

As can be seen from the table, the two strongest parties, the PNI and Masjumi, each with 57 seats, were both quite far from receiving a majority in the legislature, which would have required 117 seats. Neither party, even with the support of the third party, Nahdatul Ulama, would have had 117 seats. The only way to achieve a majority would have been to include three of the four top parties, but they were very far apart ideologically and could not agree on a program. Thus, with this legislature, Indonesia was doomed to unstable government.

Indonesian parliamentarianism was the creation of the Westernized Indonesian elite. These men, who had never been united in any single nationalist association, were ideological and rigid in their disagreements. However, despite their parliamentary factionalism, they voiced the desire to achieve a consensus or harmony of interests, and they phrased this desire in terms of concepts derived from the traditional Indonesian village. A legislature was conceived of as a place for political leaders to confront one another—not as representatives of interests in the community, but as spokesmen for different ideologies; the object of such confrontation was not successful compromise among separate interests, but clarification of thought. This was to be done through traditional methods of deliberation (*mufakat*) in the spirit of mutual aid (*gotong rojong*), which would yield a consensus of opinion (*musjawarah*) to which all parties would unanimously agree regardless of their ideological leanings.

The result of this concept of parliamentarianism was a paralysis of the legislative process. Party differences, compounded with regional and ethnic problems, became so rigid compromise in any real sense became impossible. The attempt to find ideological unanimity had led to a practice of endless unresolved committee discussions with the avoidance of final decisionmaking. The resultant inability of the government to cope with the nation's problems led to regional rebellions and unrest and the country seemed to be disintegrating.

Guided Democracy and Political Parties in Indonesia

The Indonesian parliamentary structure was therefore forcibly ended by Sukarno, who suspended the constitution of 1950 and the opposition parties with the aid of the military and the Communists. The purpose of the new system, called Guided Democracy, it was said, was to bring order to the state by instituting traditional Indonesian methods of reaching agreement; the essence of these methods was to achieve unanimity of opinion, not to have one side vote down another. The concept was Rousseauist: somehow or other there was a "general will" that, in the course of consultations, could be found to unite all participants in the discussion. *Musjawarah*, the method of deliberation, was described as "deliberating upon a question until such time as it is resolved by unanimous agreement, with all views and opinions and interests considered . . . and . . . the result of such deliberations must always be unanimity."[29] Thus, only those parties that actually supported the official ideology were allowed to operate—because unanimity of decision could be found only among them.

Difference of opinion was not to be tolerated outside the bounds set by the state. Parties and individuals could have their own outlook, but they had to participate actively in "carrying out the program of the Revolution."[30] The new councils were not representative in the sense they could independently voice the desire and interest of constituents to whom they were responsible; rather, they were to be a "reflection" of the nation, organized in the image of the greater society, though not really appointed by the latter or responsible to it. This is reminiscent both of the Dutch-sponsored Colonial Council, the Volksraad, and of the old Hindu concept of the state as reflection of a cosmic reality.

Clearly the system as perceived could be dictatorial in practice—a tutelary, not a representative government. The aim was "to carry on the Revolution" and for this, it was said, unity of thought and purpose was necessary; the government was therefore demanding the unanimous support of all the people. All the evils of the parliamentary period—excessive adherence to individual leaders, provincialism, and playing at councils—were blamed on the liberal system of government, which "allow[ed] each man to act as he like[d] and in addition also received encouragement and assistance from foreign subversion."[31] However, the possibility of elections in Indonesia in the future was not denied.

By far the most important political party under Guided Democracy was the Indonesian Communist party (PKI). This party, which originated in the early twentieth century, was always an extremist underground group, outside the mainstream of the Indonesian nationalist movement. It had never been involved in any direct manner in governing the country. By 1960 the other major opposition parties and the press had been outlawed in Indonesia and a new series of councils, whose membership was selected by Sukarno, had superseded the old legislature as representative organs of government. Sukarno, fearful of losing influence to the military whose prestige and power had increased by virtue of its role in putting down regional rebellions, sought political allies through the Guided Democracy apparatus whom he could use to counterbalance the military so as to retain some freedom of action for himself. For this purpose he patronized the PKI, which like other parties in Indonesia, was comprised mainly of urban intellectuals.

In 1965 the PKI claimed 4 million party members and, on October 1, 1965, attempted to stage a coup against the Indonesian military in order to allow the government under Guided Democracy to shift to the Left. The Communists managed to kill six top Indonesian generals but missed their major target, Defense Minister Abdul Haris Nasution; in twelve hours the coup was effectively suppressed by the army under General Suharto. The military and the PKI had been the two major weights in the Guided Democracy balance. When the PKI moved against the military and lost, the armed forces responded by moving against the PKI. Each side was ruthless in its determination to do away with the other. Some observers believe the Indonesian army has since that time murdered up to one-half million Communist sympathizers. Despite this, however, Indonesian political rhetoric has shown a strong continuity with the past: the military is playing the political game in the same way the civilians did before them.

By moving against the Communists the army effectively cut out its major rival for power in Indonesia. President Sukarno still had some popular support (which could not accurately be measured since he had never run for election), but the military did not trust him, believing he had been involved in the abortive coup. Thus the military set about to take political power for itself, but in the Indonesian style—by allowing revolutionary actions to appear traditional and moderate, and by causing a maximum shift of power to be accompanied by a minimum loss of face. The main political thrust of the military was directed against the Communists and President Sukarno.

The army's first move was against the PKI, and this was primarily carried out by military means under General Suharto's direction. To provide the appearance of popular support for this move the army allowed (or perhaps induced) mass rallies to demonstrate opposition to the PKI and to demand its destruction. The army then placed fifteen cabinet ministers under "protective custody." These actions were taken in order to diminish the power and legitimacy of President Sukarno's rule, but they were also taken with Sukarno's official approval. Sukarno insisted he retained full presidential powers; therefore, it was he who gave General Suharto full authority to "insure the security of the nation."

After these preliminary official maneuvers, President Sukarno consented to a purge of leftists from the Indonesian government. By presidential decree the PKI was legally banned and all other parties were forbidden to accept former Communists as members. The fifteen ministers held in protective custody were dismissed and a new cabinet was appointed—all in the name of President Sukarno. Theoretically the governmental system was the same: Indonesia was still being governed under the 1945 revolutionary charter; only the personnel was being changed. However, now it was the military which, through the new appointments, controlled government policy as well as the entire Indonesian communication system, including the radio and the press. Sukarno was still president and Great Leader of the Revolution in name, but the military was already in effective control.

At this point the new military rulers set about to create the semblance of popular support for the changes they were making. Student groups, nonexistent before the abortive coup of the PKI, emerged to demonstrate their vocal opposition to Communism and, later, to President Sukarno. The military were not about to move in an obviously unconstitutional manner: President Sukarno's power was going to be reduced, but within the context of Indonesian political institutions. Rather than forcing the situation the army waited for the People's Consultative Congress, Sukarno's own highest legislative body, to legitimate what already had been accomplished in practice. In the meantime press curbs were relaxed and former Sukarno opponents were released from prison. These measures precipitated a barrage of criticism of the president. Similarly, the announcement of a new economic policy that would curb socialism underlined the gross economic failures of the past. These moves were calculated to demonstrate an apparent popular desire for change in Indonesia. Finally, in June of 1966, a full eight months after the attempted coup, the People's Consultative Congress approved the government decrees against the PKI, and lacking any Communist membership, the legislative body supported the army without any opposition.

By the middle of 1966 Sukarno was president in name only. His policies and pet projects lay abandoned, while he was forced to consent to measures he had previously opposed. On July 5, 1966, the People's Consultative Congress stripped him of his title of President for Life. The congress also ruled he could no longer issue decrees, and it ordered a review of all decrees he had issued since 1959, the year he had suspended the 1950 constitution and reinstated the 1945 constitution. The congress also called for an election to be held in 1968. All decisions of the congress were unanimous, in accordance with the traditional concepts of *mufakat, gotong rojong,* and *musjawarah.* Finally, in 1971, after Sukarno had died while under house arrest, the election was held. Parties pledged to President Suharto won fully 70 percent of the seats, and as under Guided Democracy, they now exercise little influence. The facade of a party structure remains, and freedom of the press has been restored, but the ultimate power is today in the hands of the military. Indonesian society thus remains fragmented, held together more by military force than political structure.

ZAIRE

As in India and Indonesia, political parties in Zaire primarily originated in a movement for national independence. In Zaire, as in Indonesia, the basic tribal divisions of the nation prevented the emergence of a unified mass party that could consolidate nationalist groups to the extent the Congress party did in India. In Zaire, politics remained tribal politics, and most parties were direct representatives of different regional and tribal groups.

Nationalism and Political Parties in the Congo

Congolese nationalism developed in five partially overlapping stages.[32] First there were primary resistance movements (armed opposition to the colonial power, usually led by traditional rulers). Congolese colonial history recorded many regional armed insurrections from which the second stage of nationalism eventually developed—the emergence of messianic religious sects which supported broader, less localized claims. Some of these sects showed the influence of Christian teachings but at the same time exhibited antagonisms toward colonial authority. The third stage, that of urban riots, developed contemporaneously and reflected the complaints of the nontraditional urban worker. All three early stages were of massive character but lacked clear organization and specific demands.

There was no articulate, educated Congolese elite until the development of the fourth stage, the emergence of prepolitical associations. These included labor unions, alumni groups, and tribal associations. Since Belgian colonial policy made it difficult for these groups to organize and it severely restricted their political activities, the tribal associations, which alone were able to develop truly mass memberships, became the most important of these groups. The fifth stage, the development of political parties, came very late in Congolese history. The origin of political parties can be traced only to 1957 and the first Congolese legislative elections. Even Indonesia's parties had some thirty- to forty-years experience and some chance at representative participation in colonial councils before independence. In the Congo, this experience was limited and restricted to only a few years.

Political parties reflected general political development in the country. Most parties were tribal and regional in character; their leadership tended to think in traditional terms; no common thread or ideological coherence existed among them; in addition they were only weakly organized and tended to be short-lived. The natural result was a highly pluralistic system with no single party representing a majority viewpoint.

Early Congolese political parties fall into two categories: tribal and nationalist. As we might expect, the tribal parties were many. The first party, the Alliance des Bakongo (ABAKO), led by Joseph Kasavubu, was centered in Kinshasa. Another, the Partai Solidaire Africaine (PSA), led by Antoine Gizenga, was centered in Kwilu District. This Kwilu tribal group had support and leadership drawn from urban groups in Kinshasa. Other early tribal parties included Centre de Regroupement Africaine (CEREA), which represented the Kivu tribe and Moise Tshombe's Confederation des Associations Tribales du Katanga (CONAKAT), centered in Katanga. In addition to these large parties, there were a large number of local parties centered about each provincial capital. The basis of organization for all these groups was the ethnic and tribal character of the leadership. They were exclusive in membership, non-national in viewpoint, and rather uncompromising in position.

In this early period of organization there were some nontribal parties that drew most support from urban intellectual and elite groups. These nationalist parties tended to have strong European ties and failed to develop mass followings. One such party was Action Socialiste, a socialist party that was originally organized by Belgian socialist groups. Another was the Union Congolais, also originally established by Belgians, which stressed Catholicism as a basis for its structure. Both parties were viewed as too closely tied to the colonial power, though their specific policies found some appeal in the early period.

Independence and Political Parties in Zaire

The only really nationally oriented party to enjoy support that cut across some tribal lines was the Mouvement National Congolais (MNC), led by Patrice Lumumba. However, even this party structured itself along tribal lines, having separate branches for Lulua and Baluba tribal interests. In the May 1960 elections, the results of which are presented in Table 5.7, the MNC was more successful than all others, when viewed on a national scale. Two conclusions emerge from the table. First, the MNC was the only party to win seats in the legislatures of all six provinces. It also captured the largest number of seats in both houses of the national legislature. However, it received nowhere near a majority vote, having less than one-third the seats in the Chamber of Deputies and less than one-fourth the seats in the Senate. As a result of the election, a coalition, which would have had to include a minimum of four parties, would have to govern. Predictably it was difficult to retain this coalition for long as the parties themselves were undisciplined and lacked a uniform political outlook. Second, each party tended to be strong in its own particular region and did not have to worry about compromise with other political groups on the local level. In

Table 5.7. Returns of the May 1960 Election in the Congo (Seats Won)

Party	National Assembly		Provincial Assemblies					
	Chamber of Deputies	Senate	Leo-pold-ville	Equa-teur	Orien-tale	Kivu	Katanga	Kasai
MNC/L (Lulua)	41	19	2	10	58	17	1	25
MNC/K (Baluba)	8	3	35	--	--	--	1	21
PSA	13	4	35	--	--	--	--	--
CEREA	10	6	--	--	--	30	--	--
Cartel Katangais	7	3	--	-	--	--	23	--
ABAK	12	4	33	--	--	--	--	--
PUNA	7	7	--	11	--	--	--	--
UNIMO	1	2	-	8	--	--	--	--
PNP*	15	3	--	5	6	5	--	4
CONAKAT	8	6	--	--	--	--	25	--
Other	15	27	20	26	6	18	10	20
Total	137	84	90	60	70	70	60	70

SOURCE: Adapted from M. Crawford Young, *Politics in the Congo* (Princeton: Princeton University Press, 19650, p. 302.

*The PNP was a coalition of local tribal groups.

general most provinces elected no more than two large parties to the local assembly.

As already described, soon after independence in 1960 the central government in Zaire (then called the Democratic Republic of the Congo) collapsed into a civil war of rival regions and rival parties. Lumumba, the only potential national leader, was murdered, and the 1960s saw the subdivision of the country into twenty-one provinces (from six) with rival tribes aiming for particularistic goals within each new region.

Twice during the early 1960s civilian politicians attempted to reconstruct politics along civilian party lines. Cyril Adoula was for a short time premier and established the Rassemblement des Associations Congolaises (RADECO), a coalition of groups that included various tribal loyalties. Moise Tshombe also became premier for a short while and established the Confederation Nationale des Associations Congolaises (CONACO), another coalition. Both these umbrella parties proved undisciplined and weak. Finally in 1965 General Mobutu seized power in a military coup and ended the free activity of all political parties.

Today, the constitution of Zaire stipulates the maximum number of parties in the country shall be two. However, the only party operating is the Mouvement Populaire de la Revolution (MPR), a new group pledged to support Mobutu and organized directly under his patronage.

All political sanctions and authority have shifted into the hands of the military, and while the MPR provides a facade of civilian government, it too exists under the ultimate sanction of the military. Today Zaire, like Indonesia, is a fragmented nation, tenuously held together by military force. Free party organization and politics have been ended, and the only semblance of a party is an arm of the government. However, the reaction of General Mobutu's government to political fragmentation goes considerably further than that of General Suharto's regime in Indonesia: in Indonesia, many more constitutional symbols have been retained; political groups and parties have freedom to organize and voice their opinions, though under Suharto's view. In Zaire, the only open political activity is that which is permitted and supported by General Mobutu.

Comparative Distinctions in Political Parties Among Fragmented States

France, Indonesia, and Zaire all have histories of numerous political parties dividing their respective political systems and making it difficult for strong national policies and leadership to emerge. The three countries have reacted to this common difficulty in different ways.

France has centered most of the authority of its government in the hands of the president (an elected official), thus reducing the effect of the parties, which must compete for representation in the legislature, on policymaking. This has compounded the frustration of the opposition, and parties that in the past had refused to cooperate with one another have been able to unite against the entrenched government coalition. These opposition coalitions have been rather short-lived, however, and French parties have not been able to build national bases of support. They remain, for the most part, collections of regional and economic groups whose parochial interests generally override their national aims. Only the Gaullist party, the UDR, could by itself claim until recently to have a national appeal, and since the death of President Pompidou and the election of President Giscard d'Estaing, an Independent Republican, its future has become a matter of speculation. The UDR does not now have a majority in the National Assembly as a result of the 1973 elections and the president of France belongs to a small minority party. However, France remains a democratic country with free elections, widespread communication, and a widely read press. French government is civilian government, though it rests more on a professional administration than it does on political parties.

Indonesia and Zaire both had developed extremely difficult party systems with which to govern their respective countries. Both countries had numerous political parties, most of which were tied to regional or tribal interests and attached very little importance to governing their respective countries from a national perspective. In both states regional divisions led to a state of civil war, while political parties were unable to compromise their differences. The result for both states has been the establishment of military rule, though some symbols of party government have been retained.

POLITICAL PARTIES IN NONCOMPETITIVE STATES

Patterns of Similarity

Political parties in noncompetitive states are alike in that they are not primarily agents of political competition; in these states, elections are not the principal means by which political leadership is determined. In countries in which political decisions are not openly challenged, all political institutions—including political parties—serve the interests of an established elite. Parties in these nations are educational enterprises, bringing the message of the leadership to the mass of the population. They serve as a communications network between local and national politicians and help to recruit new members and leaders for the future. Within these broad outlines, however, the importance of political parties varies considerably even among noncompetitive states.

Three Case Studies: The USSR, Egypt, and the PRC

UNION OF SOVIET SOCIALIST REPUBLICS

The Soviet Union is a one-party state. As such, it absolutely denies the possibility for political competition and, therefore, is different from the other states with which we have dealt.

The Communist Party of the Soviet Union (CPSU) originated as a small conspiratorial, underground revolutionary group. Although since 1917 the composition and organization of the party have radically changed, it has remained a highly selective group; its membership, while quite large, fluctuates between only 4 to 6 percent of the population. Because of this it is considered a great honor, in the USSR, to be allowed to become a member of the CPSU.

The Soviet Communist party has attempted to remain true to the concepts enunciated by Lenin in the early revolutionary period. This has colored its recruitment and socialization processes. A member of the CPSU is not just an ordinary voter interested in party victory; he is a political leader, part of an elite bringing the Communist truth to unenlightened or ignorant masses. Therefore, he has a duty to obey the party leadership, which is considered to be ideologically more enlightened than he is.

Recruitment and Membership in the CPSU

In practice recruitment of a party elite in the USSR occurs in a highly centralized and highly politicized bureaucratic system. Party members are recruited through the party apparatus, which permeates all organizations in Soviet society. For example, all institutions of higher education in the USSR give courses and examinations in Marxist-Leninist political theory. Of those students eligible to take these examinations, approximately one-third are admitted to KOMSOMOL, the party youth organization. This is the first stage of recruitment into the CPSU; only a minority of KOMSOMOL members finally ascend to party membership. Similarly, party cadres in factories and farms actively instruct and recruit members, adhering to rigidly established ideological standards. The final selection of party members is a political one, made by party activists at the lower levels.

Party committees at all levels maintain a list of key posts that they must fill. The selection of individuals for these posts, even at the lowest levels, is often affected by political feuds among higher-level party officials. The Soviet system is thus characterized by a very high rate of turnover at all levels, reflecting changes among top party leaders on policy matters.

Many procedures intended to rationalize the process of party membership selection in the USSR have been introduced, but much that actually occurs is still quite unsystematic and highly political. It is clear, for example, certain kinds of individuals have definite advantages, while others are discriminated against. Thus while 20 percent of local CPSU leaders are women, there are only a few women members of the Central Committee and none in the Politburo. Also, discrimination has occurred along nationality lines. Non-Russian, particularly non-Slavic, nationalities have always been underrepresented as have rural populations in general. The Great Russians as a nationality dominate the CPSU.

The CPSU comprises a political-social elite, which is primarily urban, industrial, and educated. About 50 percent of the CPSU membership has university educations, much higher than the national Soviet average of 7 percent. The party is dominated by industrial managers, professionals, technicians, and executives of Soviet society. Its general composition, despite the political turmoil of the twentieth century, has been fairly consistent in these characteristics. It is probably true CPSU membership in the USSR is a prerequisite for success in any field, with the possible exception of science.

Power Structure of the CPSU

The CPSU, as a governing party, has undergone some changes in internal structure and policy. Under Stalin the police were used to enforce party discipline but since the 1950s the terror has been lifted to a considerable extent. This means the CPSU is now willing to permit discussion and some competition, at least within its own administrative structure. Other institutions, for example, the military and the industrial managers, are heard and considered on matters of public policy. The CPSU today relies on the Soviet educational system to produce its adherents, and the early ideological fanaticism of the revolution seems to have become moderated.

Power struggles within the leadership. Although the CPSU has a membership of several million people, many of its procedures reflect its origins as a conspiratorial group. All decisions are still made by the top leaders in secret; the mass of the people and the mass of the party learn decisions later, if at all. Top leadership maintains firm discipline over the organization, and terror was seen as a legitimate instrument of control until the death of Stalin in 1953.

Over the past forty years there have been some savage struggles for power among the top elite: at times one man ruled over everything; at other times there seemed to be a kind of sharing of power. Especially in the 1930s and 1940s terror and murder were used by party leaders to maintain their authority over their opponents (much as the tsars had done in the past).Throughout, however, the concept of "democratic centralism" has been used. This is a guiding organizational principle for all Communist parties and, in formal terms, means the following:

1. elections must be held for all party governing bodies from bottom to top;
2. periodic accountability of party bodies to their party organizations must be given;
3. strict party discipline and subordination of the minority to the majority is be enforced; and
4. decisions of higher bodies are unconditionally binding upon lower ones.

Within the CPSU, "democratic centralism" is a euphemism for willing acceptance by lower-ranking Communists of dominance by superiors. The CPSU has, when united at the top, always been able to carry the mass party with it. Thus there has not been open competition either within the party or on a national scale.

Under the cover of euphemistic ideological slogans, politics does exist in the USSR. It takes the form of unofficial factional rivalry within the framework of the CPSU. It is never out in the open as in freely competitive elections, or even as in a one-party system's nominating processes. The people who get to the top in the USSR are those who gain the support of their colleagues through unobserved backroom deals and manipulations. For example, under Lenin, the party was held together basically by loyalty to him personally, but when Lenin died, a period of jockeying for support emerged—between Stalin and Trotsky. Stalin won out in this struggle and instituted a regime based on force and terror to deal with his competition. He murdered many of his political opponents, including Trotsky. Since Stalin, the use of terror has diminished and ousted leaders no longer are killed. Political in-fighting in the USSR is therefore cruel and bitter, for once the leader can dominate the party, it offers him an efficient bureaucracy through which the country can be controlled.

Today, it appears unlikely one-man rule will again emerge in the USSR. While there is no formal method of succession within the CPSU, some precedents have been established. Political struggles now seem to be confined to the top levels of the party, never going below the Central Committee. Also, certain special interest groups, such as the military, are consulted and approve the final choice of leaders. There seems today to be a consensus leadership should be shared by a committee and not concentrated in the hands of one person. The single most important Soviet leader today is Leonid Brezhnev, general secretary of the CPSU, who holds no government post. Also important are Alexei Kosygin, the chairman of the Council of Ministers (premier), who holds no party post. Other important figures are Mikhail Suslov, the secretary of the Central Committee of the CPSU, and Nicolai Podgorny, a member of the CPSU Politburo and president of the Presidium of the Supreme Soviet (i. e., the Soviet legal head of state). (Chart 5.1 summarizes the formal organization of the CPSU.)

The Party Congress. Theoretically, the Party Congress is the supreme body of the CPSU. Delegates to the congress are elected according to a ratio to the total number of party members. Congresses are supposed to be held every four years, but in practice there has been no regularity in meetings.

Practically speaking, congresses are held to legitimize political changes that have already occurred elsewhere in the system. Their main formal function is to hear the report of the Central Committee, which is delivered by the acknowledged head of the party. There are a variety of other routine matters—other reports, audits, mandates, greetings of other Communist parties—that are carried out by the congress, but these are of little consequence.

The Party Congress, with over 4,000 members, cannot possibly become a deliberative assembly. It is too large to organize and assert itself and, consequently, has followed the leadership and direction of the Central Committee (or other structures at different times).

The Central Committee. While the Party Congress is theoretically the supreme body in the CPSU and the Central Committee is theoretically its executive required to carry out the will of the congress, these functions have varied at different times in Soviet history.

The Central Committee before Stalin was an elite group of Soviet leaders

Chart 5.1.   Formal Organization of the CPSU

The CPSU is central to all government in the USSR: the major decisions are made within the party, not within government institutions. Until 1966, called the Presidium.

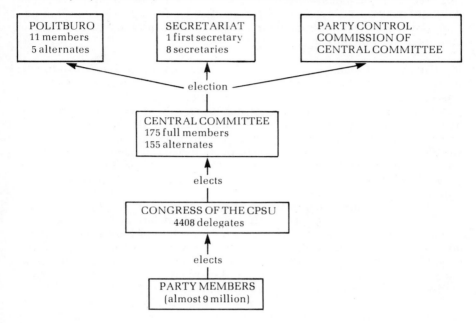

who made most important political decisions. Stalin changed that by increasing the size of the body so that it, like the congress, also became unwieldy for executive decisionmaking. Power then shifted to Stalin as chief executive of the party and the government.

Since Stalin's death the Central Committee has again become more important, but mainly because the USSR has not seen the extreme unification of its executive leadership as it existed under Stalin. Today, the leadership of the Politburo, the executive committee of the Central Committee, is united, thus downgrading the importance of the Central Committee itself. If there is competition among various factions, the Central Committee is used as an arena to resolve the problems.

The Politburo.   Theoretically, the Politburo is the top executive policy-making branch of the party. It is basically a small executive committee within the Central Committee ("Politburo" stands for Political Bureau of the Central Committee), and members of this group are the top elite; the Central Committee in comparison consists of underlings and proteges of members of the Politburo. Under Stalin, the Politburo became the center of power in the party: all decisions were made here under his personal dictatorship. Then, the Politburo consisted only of Stalin and his lieutenants.

After Stalin's death the Politburo was renamed the Presidium and its size enlarged. Its membership became more mixed, reflecting the emergence of a shared leadership in the party. Shifts in personal or factional power are reflected in the personnel shifts in the Presidium. (The Presidium was renamed Politburo in 1966.) Today, some men are holdovers from previous periods and some are relatively new. Promotions and demotions constantly take place in an atmosphere of dark intrigue.

Party control organs.   A "control organ," whose function is to make sure the party line is observed throughout the party hierarchy, is necessary to oversee a noncompetitive, nonresponsible institution. Stalin used the secret police to penetrate bureaucratic control organs and, through them, the entire party. Thus he created a terrorist system of rooting out opposition—in fact, Stalin came to power through his dominance in the party control network. This has all changed since 1953: Stalin's secret police have been abolished. The control apparatus no longer has an independent political role; it has been placed under the Central Committee, where its work is carried out by bureaucrats who review the work of party branches.

The Soviet state police instrument today, the KGB, is, however, still a terrifying institution of political control to Soviet citizens, party members, and nonmembers alike. After all, it is the latest in a line of police organizations dating back to tsarist times that in the past arbitrarily and ruthlessly interfered in political processes. Since the death of Stalin the KGB has been directly under party control, but many Soviet citizens still fear and distrust it. It has acted as a kind of special interest group and has been quite visible.

Since 1953 the Soviet police has not been used to instill terror over CPSU functionaries. Forced labor and exile have been dropped as major instruments of national economic policy, and thousands of persons have been released from internment camps. However, because the KGB is under political control, the entire Soviet judicial apparatus has reflected the policies of leaders in power. The public trials of leading writers—critics of the regime—testifies to the fact the CPSU leadership views itself as above reproach within its own legal system. An individual can be arrested and tried for political convictions, despite the liberal and open language of Soviet legislation, because the KGB is still at the disposal of Soviet political leaders.

The Secretariat.   The Secretariat is the communications center of the party: the first secretary is generally the most powerful man in the country, and he has the dominant voice in making policy since he is the chief administrator. Under Stalin, the Secretariat effectively dominated the whole party. After Stalin's death, the Soviets were so concerned about the concentration of policymaking power in the Secretariat they abolished the office of general secretary (Stalin's post). After Lavrenti Beria, the chief of the secret police, was liquidated, Khrushchev became first secretary but never was as powerful as Stalin. Today, Leonid Brezhnev is general secretary but again must share his power with others and does not approach Stalin's level of authority.

Overall Operation of the CPSU

The apparatus of the party works in such a manner that the larger supposedly representative bodies have little power, while decisions are made by a small unchecked clique of leaders who informally establish their relations with each other—without any kind of procedure or constitution to guide them. Through intraparty wrangling and personal manipulations, leaders come to the top. However, these leaders do represent particular approaches to policy, and, indirectly, entire spheres of activity in Soviet social, economic, and political life. Thus, while they are not chosen in open elections they still represent important interests in the Soviet community. When the CPSU chooses its leaders and national policies it is, in effect, aggregating and realigning the aims and approaches of important groups in the USSR. In this broad sense it functions as a political party in any other system: it aggregates a national policy out of constituent groups and produces a national leadership.

EGYPT

Egypt is a noncompetitive state in which the institution of political parties has always been regarded as suspect by the current ruling elite. The Egyptian revolution was carried out by the military, which maintained a generally low estimation of the ability and integrity of civilian politicians. Also, unlike the Communist revolution in the USSR, the early stages of the Egyptian revolution professed no ideologies that would call for the establishment of civilian political organizations. Thus, political parties have been late in their establishment in Egypt; the regime has refused openly to label political groups as political parties, and, even compared to other one-party, noncompetitive states, Egyptian civilian political organizations have been relatively weak and of little purpose to the regime.

The Spectrum of Political Parties in Egypt

Egypt has seen the establishment of three successive civilian political organizations: the Liberation Rally, the National Union, and the Arab Socialist Union. Each of these organizations has acted as the civilian arm of the military ruling groups and can thus be described as political parties. The Liberation Rally was established immediately after General Nasser overthrew General Naguib (1954). General Naguib had been supported by the older political parties including the Wafd, and General Nasser hoped to limit the participation of these groups in his new regime.[33] Thus, the Liberation Rally was to develop the support of the peasant masses and downgrade the political position of urban intellectuals whom Nasser did not trust. The party was to mobilize the mass of the population; members of the military leadership—the Revolutionary Command Council—enlisted local authorities and established branches throughout the rural areas. However, besides blocking the formation of other major parties, the function of the Liberation Rally was to approve of Nasser's ouster of Naguib and little else.

The Liberation Rally was superseded by the National Union (NU), an organization mentioned in the constitution of 1956 but not established until 1959. The National Union was also supposed to be national in scope and was organized on a regional basis. In theory, every village was included in the system; the NU had committees on the smallest local level to help elect local leaders. Under the NU rural representatives tended to come from the same traditional leadership groups as they had before the revolution and they far outweighed representatives from the urban centers in proportion to the population. The NU organized the parliamentary elections of 1957 (and, after the union with Syria, the UAR Parliament of 1960). These parliaments were one-party affairs, with all members pledged to the regime. The NU and the parliaments neither formulated policy nor legitimized it. The true function of these institutions was to mobilize a generalized national support for Nasser after the Suez invasion of 1956 by Britain, France, and Israel. However, the NU was more of a national organization than the Liberation Rally since it did conduct elections and recruit persons for office.

After Egypt's separation from Syria in 1961, the National Union was permitted to fade away. The Egyptian government now stated its active interest in mobilizing the population behind development projects. Neither the Liberation Rally nor the National Union had been used for developing public support and participation in development projects. The new interest in development coincided with the new ideological commitment to "Arab Socialism," a concept that required the establishment of mass civilian political organizations. These were not necessarily to be of the Soviet type, but the presence of Marxist thought was evident in the new structures.

In 1962 a Congress of Popular Forces met to establish the Arab Socialist Union (ASU), a new political organization conceived on Marxist lines to be a leadership group. As such it was a contrast to the National Union, in which every Egyptian citizen had been considered a qualified member. The Arab Socialist Union was a mass organization, but not structured completely on regional lines. Only persons who applied to it could become members. Occupational groups were also represented. Government agencies, schools, and factories were represented and this change greatly increased urban representation compared to the NU. This was necessary for the new development goals of the regime. Most persons with modern skills and investors with capital were concentrated in the urban areas, and the regime wished to mobilize these groups and increase their strength. The NU, which represented the country regionally, tended to overrepresent the traditional agricultural sector since Egypt's peasants constitute a vast majority of the population. Under the Arab Socialist Union the dominance of the rural population was downgraded, and the new party now represented the development aims of the governing elite.

Organization of the Arab Socialist Union

The Arab Socialist Union, as a political party, now has branches both throughout the country regionally and in all of the country's major enterprises. The highest representative body of the party is the Egyptian parliament, since the party has not established a separate party national legislative body. The parliament is a one-party body, and all representatives in it are members of the ASU. Members of parliament are elected on a regional basis, and the only meaningful distinction among members is their occupational background. Most are administrators and professionals, who support the ruling elite. As in previous parliaments, the representatives do little to initiate policy and merely legitimize the wishes of the government.

Internally, the Arab Socialist Union has levels of party organization that are elected both regionally and occupationally. The party charter stipulates that one-half the seats on its elected bodies at all levels must be occupied by workers and peasants. The category "workers" includes anyone who belongs to a trade union (and therefore includes teachers and civil servants); "peasants" are defined as small landholders, but they include the rural middle class as well. The ASU is now a large organization with over 5 million members, but as already mentioned it is primarily a rubber stamp for an entrenched elite.

Operation of the Arab Socialist Union

Political parties are thus quite weak and undeveloped in Egypt, even compared to those in other noncompetitive states. In the USSR the civilian party bureaucracy mobilizes the population behind specific projects and is the highest political institution in the state. In Egypt, the party is a facade behind which separate leadership groups hide. Political manipulation and maneuver do not take place within party institutions. These occur within the military itself and among military and civilian groups on an informal basis.

PEOPLE'S REPUBLIC OF CHINA

Political power on mainland China, as in the USSR, is dominated and monopolized by a single party. The Chinese Communist party (CCP) has established a tripod of power—party, government, and army—each arm of which has its own central and subsystem organizations; but the latter two arms—the government and the army—are penetrated by party leaders. The CCP is the unifying thread in Chinese society. Having rapidly increased in membership since 1949, its 1961 membership was approximately 17.1 million. Today, it is estimated to have more than 20 million members. More significant, it is organized hierarchically by territory, with industrial and agricultural units at the lowest level. By establishing committees within the units of all other social systems—government bureaus, schools, farms, and military units—the CCP dominates all other institutions. The linkage between the party hierarchy and the economic and social institutions it penetrates is strengthened by the fact that many of the leaders of factories, farms, and similar units are CCP members.

Organization of the Chinese Communist Party

Before the Cultural Revolution there were four levels of party organization established by the party constitution of 1956:

1. The national or central;
2. Provinces and autonomous regions;
3. The *hsien* (counties), autonomous counties, and the cities; and
4. The basic cell level of the production or residential unit.

The National party Congress was theoretically the most important group of the party, but its function was mainly a legitimizing one, that of adopting long-range policy guidelines and ratifying appointments and changes in the Central Committee, wherein the real power lies. (See Chart 5.2 for a summary of the formal organization of the CCP.)

The Central Committee met in plenary sessions once or twice annually to discuss vigorously current social and economic trends and to adopt new policy lines. Having ninety-four members as of 1962 and including the ruling elite of the party, these plenary meetings could be attended by provincial party leaders or local cadres, or even select personnel from outside the party when the issue(s) being debated concerned certain territories and/or economic sectors. For example, in the early 1950s, local cadres were consulted as to how to proceed with collectivization of agriculture.

Within the Central Committee, top power was exercised by the Politburo, whose nineteen members provided, in number and ideological viewpoints, a good framework in which to formulate policy lines. Within the Politburo was the Standing Committee of seven members headed by the chairman of the party. Much of what is known about the Politburo and Standing Committee must be based on the speculation of China watchers and their knowlege of the membership. It has been assumed that various members of both the Politburo and the Standing Committee have lost power and influence in the manner and frequency in which their views were adopted, even though they may have retained their formal positions.

Other groupings elected by the Central Committee included the Secretariat, which was the party's administrative arm, maintaining contact with provincial and local party leaders. The Secretariat has not existed since the Cultural Revolution.

In addition, a Military Affairs Committee along with the general political departments helped to enforce the implementation of party doctrines within the army and the governmental agencies. The latter have become especially important since the Cultural Revolution in executing policies in the economic sector. Although relatively little is known about the specific structure and dynamics of these various committees, they do seem to participate in policy formulation and policy implementation.

Before the Cultural Revolution, there were other groupings that were attached to the Politburo. The National Party Control Committee (abolished since the Ninth Party Congress of 1969, after the Cultural Revolution) helped to maintain internal unity and discipline by overseeing the work of lower-level party groups. Party committees composed of Central Committee members penetrated the bureaucracy and other public bodies and made basic administrative decisions for the latter. The departments and committees of the formal

Chart 5.2. Formal Organization of the CCP (1956-1969)

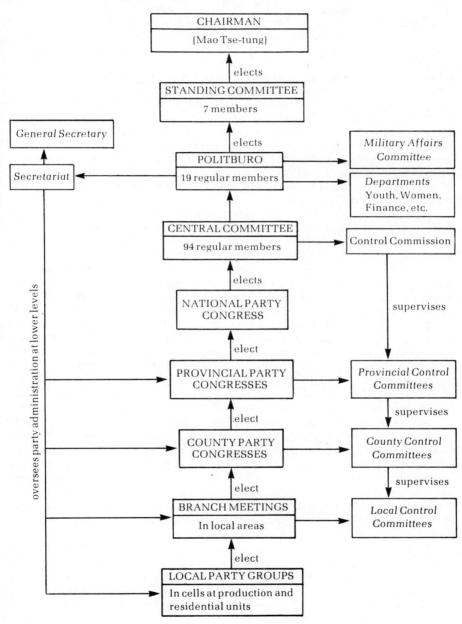

PRC governmental structure were thus in constant contact with the bureaucracy of the Central Committee of the CCP.

Constituting a hierarchial organization aside from the CCP itself were the Party Control committees (now also nonexistent since the Cultural Revolution). The central committees of the party congresses at each level could establish Party Control committees, those below the National Central Committee being subject to approval by the next higher echelon. These special purpose committees were supervisory and investigative. They prevented a high degree of subsystem autonomy and maintained discipline at their respective levels; they dealt only with intraparty affairs. Technically controlled by corresponding party committees, a higher-echelon control committee could investigate those below it. Therefore these constituted an organization parallel to the party. They were ended by the Cultural Revolution, which attempted to weaken the bureaucratic aspects of the CCP and strengthen local officials who were loyal to Mao. All local political authorities today are still within the CCP, but party organization is not so hierarchically organized. The 1969 party constitution has not provided for a secretariat or control committees (though it has not ruled them out). Also it is not now clear how the new bodies are produced, as there is no provision for elections.[34] (See Chart 5.3 for a summary of the formal organization of the CCP after the Cultural Revolution.)

The central party organization before the Cultural Revolution included central bureaus which, though located in certain provinces, were subject directly to the Central Committee. They assured against regionalism by various local or provincial parties. Unlike the USSR, the PRC permits the organization of small regional parties so long as they support CCP policy. These regional parties were and are now granted narrow representation in the National People's Congress, in the hope that this will foster greater identification of outlying regions with the national government. Regionally based parties are thus unimportant in terms of national policy formulation and are not genuine competitive bodies. Some regional groups loyal to Mao have been reestablished since the Cultural Revolution, but they remain of limited importance.

Party organization within the CCP between the highest and lowest levels before the Cultural Revolution followed the same pattern as that of the Central Committee. There were party congresses, but real authority lay in the committees. Plenary meetings were held to discuss policy and to decide how to place national directives within the framework of local conditions. Also as important, these intermediate-level organizations maintained direct contact with the Central Committee; in November of 1960, for example, the first secretaries of all provincial and county party organizations were either full or alternate members of the Central Committee.

Provincial party committees directed party committees in local government agencies, but in county and local government branches the committees were not subject to county or local party control. Provincial party committees became somewhat more autonomous of national party direction because of an emphasis upon pragmatism, which led to decentralization. This was especially true of the periods just before and after the Great Leap Forward. However, party leadership prevented an outburst of regionalism by empowering only men who

Chart 5.3.   Formal Organization of the CCP After the Cultural Revolution (1969-   )

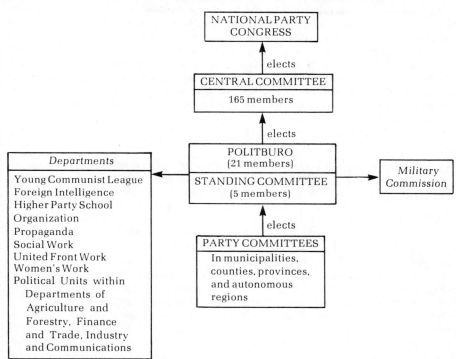

firmly believe in the party line. The Cultural Revolution was a reaction against this capturing of central control over the country by the central party bureaucracy. Today the relationship between the CCP and its local branches is not highly organized and more power is left to local party groups loyal to Mao, rather than to a central party machinery.

Party organization in the cities was never subject to direct Central Committee control, but to control of the local county and provincial committees of the areas in which they lie. This has been ascertained through accounts of meetings at the lower levels of the party. In them the cadres made their presence felt. Usually party members at the lowest levels, the cadres, are thoroughly indoctrinated by party ideology, disseminate to the factory workers and farmers the "mass line," and participate in vigorous group discussion at party meetings.

The lowest level of party organization at the local production or residential unit, though at the bottom of the pyramid, was and is perhaps most important in carrying out policy directives, for this is where state and society meet. The nature and size of these cells vary according to the unit of production—farm or factory, the territory and the administrative structure in the government, to which it is subject. Organization has become complex in these units. Hierarchical as are those of upper levels, a local party cell may contain three or four echelons, with the leadership in the party committee, usually a small group. They function similarly to the national party with limited decisionmaking powers and have continued to be of importance since the Cultural Revolution.

The largest local-level organizations are the communes. This was especially true during the period of the Great Leap Forward, when party committees could be distinguished from the administrative committees of the communes. In the commune the party organization has always been fully in control of policy formulation and implementation. Today commune party cells loyal to Mao are still powerful.

The CCP thus has been organized as:

> an alter ego to society. At top, middle or bottom, wherever there is an organized group of men, for example, as an office or factory, inside of that group will be a committee or group of Party members. These Party members hold positions in the larger organization, but at the same time, they work in the Party, and they work hard. . . . In short, the Party embraces the active leadership elite of the country.[35]

Since the Cultural Revolution the local strength of the party has probably been strengthened, though it is not now so hierarchically structured. The CCP is the only national political organization that sets national goals and carries them out. Like the USSR and unlike Egypt, China is a noncompetitive *party* state, mobilized on civilian political party lines. There seems to have been less resort to terror and murder in the PRC since 1949 than in the USSR (few people died during the Cultural Revolution compared to the number who died in the bloody Soviet party purges of the 1930s), but then less is known about the inner politics of the CCP than of the CPSU.

Comparative Distinctions in Political Parties Among Noncompetitive States

The Soviet Union and People's Republic of China are both one-party states in which all institutions of political life are responsible to and permeated by each country's single governing party. Thus, in both these states the party produces the leadership, educates the population in the aims of the political elite, and, in general, holds the country together. Institutions of state—executives, legislatures, and judiciaries—are responsible to and controlled by the party.

The USSR and PRC are somewhat different from each other, owing to varying traditions and levels of economic development. The Soviet Union is politically far more mobilized than the People's Republic of China because the former has a more centralized and highly developed economic system, with a higher rate of literacy, and a more effective police apparatus. Also, the Soviet Union's legacy of the use of political terror has affected the attitudes of its population toward politics. The USSR has had more violent factional disputes and bloody purges than the PRC has.

While Egypt is a noncompetitive state, it has not relied on political parties as major instruments of legitimate government authority. Some organizations have been established that resemble political parties, but the elite remains centered in the military and the bureaucracy.

POLITICAL PARTIES: COMPARING COMPETITIVE, FRAGMENTED, AND NONCOMPETITIVE STATES

Political parties serve somewhat different functions in the three different kinds of state, though they are also similar in important respects. In competitive, fragmented, and noncompetitive states, political parties are educational institutions, seeking to inform the public of the rightness of their political views; they act as links between the governed and their rulers; and they are symbols of political representation. Even where political parties are not powerful in the sense of affecting government policy, they act as agents of legitimacy. However, there also are important distinctions among different types of political party systems.

In competitive states, political parties are essential participants in the political process. They act as aggregating agencies converting individual and group demands into national programs and policies. Thus they moderate these narrow demands and in so doing render their nations governable. In addition, by selecting and training candidates, they are a major agency for developing future leaders in their respective countries. In competitive states, therefore, political parties are essentially agents of political competition. They regulate the process and establish the rules by which competition may successfully be conducted.

In fragmented states, political parties are generally ineffective institutions. Because of the basic divisions of these societies, political parties are unable to aggregate individual and group demands and to present national programs and leaders with broad national support. They are thus weak and generally remain ineffectual vis-a-vis other institutions, i. e., the military or bureaucracy.

In noncompetitive states, political parties can be extremely powerful, but they are not agents of political competition. In competitive states, government has to moderate among rival demands, and political parties are important in this moderating (aggregating) process. In noncompetitive states, parties do not so much aggregate as instruct. They present the views of an elite to a population organized to follow. They can become more important than the very institutions of state, because they essentially have no competition and constitute the primary organizing structure in society. In some noncompetitive systems, i. e., as in the USSR, the party can exercise monolithic control over the entire political life of the state.

NOTES TO CHAPTER 5

1. For a detailed discussion of the traditional British concept of opposition, see Sir Ivor Jennings, *Cabinet Government* (Cambridge: University Press, 1965), Chapt. 15.

2. Allen Potter, "Great Britain: Opposition with a Capital 'O'," in Robert A. Dahl, ed., *Political Oppositions in Western Democracies* (New Haven: Yale University Press, 1966), Chapt. 1.

3. *See* R. T. McKenzie and Allen Silver, "Conservatism, Industrialism and the Working Class Tory in England," in R. Rose, ed., *Studies in British Politics* (London: Macmillan, 1966), pp. 21-33.

4. David E. Butler and Donald Stokes, *Political Change in Britain: Forces Shaping Electoral Changes* (New York: St. Martin's Press, 1969), Chapts. 4, 5, 11.

5. R. M. Punnett, *British Government and Politics* (New York: W. W. Norton, 1971).

6. Ibid.

7. The Conservative Party National Union consists of advisory committees for local government, trade unions, political education, young Conservatives and women's organizations.

8. "The Party Organization," mimeographed (Westminister: Conservative and Unionist Central Office, August 1964), p. 3.

9. "Some Recent Developments," mimeographed (Westminister: Conservative and Unionist Party, February 1968), p. 1.

10. Ibid., p. 1.

11. The swing vote in 1974 was 12 percent, quite a bit higher than the mean national swing in British elections between 1950 and 1966, calculated by Butler and Stokes, which varied between 0.7 and 3.5 percent. *See* David Butler and Donald Stokes, *Political Change in Britain*.

12. Gene D. Overstreet and Marshall Windmiller, *Communism in India* (Berkeley & Los Angeles: University of California Press, 1959), p. 536.

13. Ibid., p. 545.

14. *See* Appendix in Vincent Sheean, *Nehru: The Years in Power* (New York: Random House, 1960), p. 292. Quoted in Michael Brecher, *Nehru; A Political Biography* (New York: Oxford University Press, 1959), p. 604.

15. M. Ruthinaswamj, "Swatantra Party" in M. Pattabhi-ram, ed., *General Election in India, 1967* (Bombay: Allied Publishers, 1967), p. 38.

16. Stanley A. Kochanek, *The Congress Party of India: The Dynamics of One Party Democracy* (Princeton: Princeton University Press, 1968), p. 299.

17. Myron Weiner, *Party Building in a New Nation* (Chicago: University of Chicago Press, 1967), pp. 463-4.

18. R. L. Hardgrave, Jr., *India: Government and Politics in a Developing Nation* (New York: Harcourt, Brace & World, 1970), pp. 160-1.

19. *The Hindu*, February 19, 1969.

20. Ibid., November 12, 1969.

21. Ibid., November 13, 1969.

22. Ibid., November 15, 1969.

23. Ibid., November 18, 1969.

24. *See* Robert J. Alexander, "The Left Wing Opposition and the Chilean Democratic System," in B. McLennan, ed., *Political Opposition and Dissent* (New York: The Dunellen Co., 1973).

25. For example, see Thomas G. Sanders, "Allende's First Month," *American Universities Field Staff Report on Chile: West Coast of South America*, vol. 18, no. 2 (April 1971).

26. Herbert Feith, *The Decline of Constitutional Democracy in Indonesia* (Ithaca: Cornell University Press, 1963), pp. 122-45, 353-66.

27. A. K. Pringgodigdo, *The Office of President in Indonesia as Defined in the Three Constitutions in Theory and Practice*, Modern Indonesia Project, Cornell University, Ithaca, 1957, p. 43.

28. Sukarno, "Order-Peace-Prosperity," *Indonesian Review*, vol. 1, no. 4 (July-September 1951): 247.

29. Sukarno, *For Liberty and Justice* (Djakarta: 1960), p. 12.

30. *Political Manifesto, Republic of Indonesia, August 17, 1959* (Djakarta: Department of Information, 1960), p. 8.

31. Ibid., pp. 51-2.

32. M. Crawford Young, *Politics in the Congo* (Princeton: Princeton University Press, 1965), p. 281.

33. *See* Leonard Binder, "Political Recruitment and Participation in Egypt," in Joseph La Palombara and Myron Weiner, eds., *Political Parties and Political Development* (Princeton: Princeton University Press, 1966), pp. 218 ff.

34. D. P. Whitaker et al., *Area Handbook for the People's Republic of China* (Washington, D. C.: Government Printing Office, 1972), pp. 284-9.

35. Franz Schurmann, "Party and Government," in Franz Schurmann and Orville Schell, eds., *The China Reader*, vol. 3, *Communist China: Revolutionary Reconstruction and International Confrontation—1949 to the Present* (New York: Vintage Books, 1966), p. 113.

Chapter 6

Political Processes and Public Policy

POLITICAL PROCESSES AND PUBLIC POLICY: A FRAMEWORK FOR COMPARISON

Every political system formulates and enforces public policy in a manner that reflects its general culture as well as the institutional strength of the various politically oriented groups and individuals within the state. All interest groups and political parties, whether in competitive, fragmented, or noncompetitive states, are concerned with achieving government action in their respective areas of concern. They accomplish their aims through their behavior in the established formal institutions of their respective societies (described in Chap. 2), as well as through informal methods by which influential persons meet and decide on their future activities.

POLITICAL PROCESSES AND PUBLIC POLICY IN COMPETITIVE STATES

Patterns of Similarity

In competitive states, various political groups tend to be integrated into special institutions in which they can openly pursue their aims. Thus, decisions are relatively openly arrived at through the interaction of persons in such formal structures as interest groups, political parties, legislatures, administrative agencies, courts, and local governments. Power is shared, much as the political culture of these states supports a regulated system of rules by which many groups and individuals can legitimately participate in politics. However, among competitive states, the specific institutions that are important in the political process can vary from state to state.

Three Case Studies: Great Britain, India, and Chile

GREAT BRITAIN

In Great Britain a great many services are provided directly by the government. Such areas as education, the construction and maintenance of highways, the radio and television industries, welfare measures such as national health care, old-age insurance, and workmen's compensation are all provided wholly or partly by the government. In addition, the British national government builds and maintains housing, supports the arts in various forms, and operates within its cabinet ministries some of the major industrial enterprises in the country through a series of nationalized industries acts. The coal industry, the airlines, the railroads, the post, telephone and telegraph agency, electric and gas utilities, and central banking are all government enterprises. Thus the national government in its day-to-day activities directly touches the lives of all British subjects.

The Civil Service and Public Policy in Great Britain

The every day work of the national government is carried out by a professional civil service, directed in only general terms by the cabinet and the Parliament. As described in Chapter 2, the major institutions that develop public policies, both foreign and domestic, are the political parties. A party that has a majority in Parliament elects the prime minister and enacts his legislative program. However, the actual execution of the program—the process by which these formal, legal dictates that are passed by Parliament are translated into actions affecting the public—is carried out by a highly respected and carefully trained bureaucracy, which in formal terms is governed by cabinet ministers and subcabinet officers organized into separate departments.

It is the bureaucracy that raises government funds by collecting taxes and that enforces the national law by establishing agencies and corporations with specified tasks. The administrative bureaucracy also investigates the operation of the legal structure and suggests innovations and improvements to officials in the cabinet. Technically, cabinet officials direct the administration and speak for the ministries in Parliament. However, most administrative activities themselves are today considered to be relatively nonpolitical.

The actual processes of government in Great Britain are thus carried out at the national level, in the subcabinet offices of the civil service. It is there the country's major interest groups are most influential. Special interests have close relationships with the specialized segments of government, which are established to deal with their problems. If there is a competitive system in Great Britain in this respect, it is among competing groups for the favor of the civil service and the ministries that specialize in their affairs. At the highest levels of government, especially in the area of new public policy, politicians can and do affect the work of the bureaucracy because the cabinet, a political body, directs the administration. In practice the members of the British cabinet, who legally head the ministries, are concerned primarily with the formulation of new policy. They generally leave the details of implementation to the lower-level bureaucrats. They thus do not interfere in the vast majority of bureaucratic decisions and question them only if there is some scandal or gross displeasure with its treatment by the civil service expressed by a major group. On occasion, for example, an espionage scandal has brought public criticism of the basically old-fashioned, informal system of control in the British bureaucracy. The British, however, are not beset with widespread problems of corruption and, even yet, have not established separate agencies for investigating bad administration. This tendency to leave details to the bureaucracy of course increases the actual discretion of civil servants over areas that can sometimes be unprecedented or political.

In Great Britain the central bureaucracy is permanent, since senior civil servants and those who work for them are legally guaranteed security of tenure in office. The change of cabinet from one party to another does not lead to changes in the civil service. Thus, bureaucrats can become more important to specialized groups, over time, than any politician.

British civil servants tend to be very well educated, since they must pass fairly difficult examinations to get into the bureaucracy or to be promoted within it. These individuals have developed a strong informal sense of community within the civil service and have also developed an image of efficiency and fairness that is widely respected by the public of all major parties. For example, it should be noted most bureaucrats in Great Britain are from middle- to upper-class backgrounds and are more likely to support the Conservatives than the Labour party politically. This caused great concern among Labour party supporters in the 1940s when the first major socialist legislative program was enacted. However, the civil service carried the program out effectively and, in the 1950s under the Conservatives, continued in pretty much the same mold. Thus, the faith of the British public in the nonpartisanship of the administration has been enhanced. The administration is in general immune from political criticism, and since it operates efficiently it is also usually out of the public eye.

Local Government

Besides the national civil service much public policy in Great Britain is enforced by authorities at the local level. This is done even though the country is a unitary state (with several exceptions), with authority vested legally in only one central government.[1] Local power is legally granted by the national Parliament to local units by legislative enactment. However, local activities are controlled, as are administrative activities, by ministries headed by members of the British cabinet. The major ministers who deal with local government are the Minister for the Environment, the Secretary of State for Scotland, and the Secretary of State for Wales.

The central government controls local units by auditing their finances, by controlling grants and loans to them, and by special legal powers. The consent of the relevant cabinet minister is required for certain important local actions—for example, the appointment of some officials, certain building plans, and even specific matters with respect to police, fire, and educational services. The central government, through an appropriate ministry, has the broad authority to remove a local government if it neglects its duties.

Despite these legalistic considerations, in practical political terms local government is important and influential in Great Britain. Local governments today plan and maintain their area's roads, they provide street lighting, drinking water, recreational facilities, and sanitation. In general, police and fire protection are provided at the local level by local government. Education, libraries, child welfare clinics, day nurseries are all provided by local government under legislation passed by Parliament.

The main local administrative unit is the county, which is divided into boroughs, urban districts, and rural districts. In general, the county provides the broader services (such as police and fire protection), but the districts take care of more local matters, such as street lighting. All local units are headed by elected councils, which in turn elect the local mayors. Mayors are nonpartisan chairmen who preside over council meetings. In different units of local government (boroughs, rural districts, or urban districts) there are varying terms of office for council and mayor, but local government in Great Britain at all levels is elected by the citizenry, not appointed by the central government.

Local political offices are unpaid, and the kind of people these offices attract varies considerably from area to area. Often individuals who are interested only in local prestige will run for office, though sometimes people go into local government as a first step in a political career. The level of quality and competence varies greatly from one local leadership group to another.

Overall, despite legal restrictions, local government and county councils are competitive public bodies that are open to the press and to the local citizens. Local authorities are free in the conduct of their internal affairs, and they meet regularly (about four times a year in public session) to do so. Usually, localities will produce governments that generally support one of the major political parties, but not all councils are run on party lines. Party labels in local elections have come into use only recently, but many persons in local politics are independents. The Labour party usually has a more direct role in local party elections than the Conservatives, but other organized groups, which reflect Conservative policy, though not the party directly, are active at the local level.

Compared to national politics, local politics in Great Britain is looked upon with apathy. Voting turnouts in local elections are usually between 30 and 40 percent of the electorate, compared to between 70 and 80 percent of the electorate in national elections. This is possibly due to the fact local governments deal with comparatively unimportant issues. However, interest group activity at the local level is highly organized and influential. Trade unions representing individuals in the public services (e. g., teachers) can be extremely important here, though much less so at the national level. Also, various groups concerned with all aspects of housing (in terms of both construction and occupancy) are influential at the local level but can be lost at the level of the national party or administration.

The Nature of Policymaking in Great Britain

In summary, British political decisions are made every day at the local level in local governmental units, and at the national level within the civil service. Both levels are fairly obscure to the public, which accepts them with a fairly high degree of apathy. Interest groups, however, have been able to establish themselves at both levels, and they exert the major pressures for innovation and change in current policy. These pressures eventually can influence decisions made by ministers at the cabinet level. However, day-to-day policy generally remains hidden in obscure administrative committees and local councils, only to become political when the public becomes genuinely excited and aroused. This is very rare in Great Britain, and, overall, the political parties seem able to create new policy without too much concern for local or administrative opinion. The public seems to support this system of decisionmaking, concerning itself much more with party confrontation than the day-to-day problems of policy enforcement.

INDIA

India is a large, federally organized state in which decisions are shared in formal terms among local, state, and federal authorities as well as among legislative, executive, and judicial branches of government. India is also a poor, economically underdeveloped country in which the government is heavily involved in development planning and attempts directly to finance new enterprises as well as provide public services. The burden upon the Indian civil service, in terms of day-to-day policymaking, is thus very great and the gap between legal policy and its actual enforcement is much greater in India than in Great Britain.[2]

The Civil Service

The Indian civil service (now called the Indian Administrative Service) was established by the British when India was still a colony. During the colonial period and the fight for independence, the civil service acted as an arm of the mother country, and while it was regarded as efficient, its loyalty to the new state was questioned by the nationalist elite. The habit of viewing national civil servants as enemies has persisted to the present day, and Indian states tend to resist the expansion in decisionmaking power of the national bureaucracy. Each state in India maintains its own separate civil service that is concerned with local problems. The federal bureaucracy handles specified areas of national policy mentioned in the Indian constitution. These include the foreign service, postal service, and collection of national revenue.

As with the British civil service, the Indian Administrative Service is a bureaucracy based on an examination system that is supposed to be immune to political control and manipulation. Indians must pass written and oral tests to be admitted into the service, and promotion within the bureaucracy is based on merit demonstrated and time served within each rank. Compared to their British counterparts, Indian bureaucrats constitute a definite social elite because the Indian population is generally so poor and uneducated while the bureaucracy is manned by bright university graduates. This is especially so at the highest levels, where official cooperation is essential to the success of any policy legislated by the political branches of government. Elitism has led to a sense of common interest among the bureaucrats but also to charges of arrogance and high-handedness from others who must deal with the administration. This situation can be damaging to Indian plans for development, where broad social upheaval can be an expected result. Because the populace and important political groups deeply distrust and fear the bureaucracy, they have withheld support even for those development projects that have been likely to help them directly. In return, the Indian bureaucracy has remained rigidly upper class and formalistic in its approach to problems. These factors have reduced the capacity of individual bureaucrats to demonstrate any initiative within the service and have also kept popular participation and recruitment into the service on a very narrow basis.

In India, then, the civil service is highly trained and capable, but quite distant from the population. This makes the bureaucracy in India more vulnerable to political attack than it is in Great Britain. In any political system (but especially one bent on economic development), for policy to be efficiently formulated and enforced there must be a relationship of mutual trust and respect among politicians of all parties and the civil service. The laws passed by the legislature must be enforced in the spirit in which they were passed, regardless of the distribution of votes among parties on individual bills. In addition, politicians must trust the bureaucracy's ability and intentions. If a bill does not achieve its legislative purposes in India, this is almost always blamed on "corrupt" or "inefficient" bureaucrats. The enforcement of legislation is not always perfect in any political system, but in countries with highly regarded civil services politicians look to the bureaucracy for advice and information on how to improve legislation from an administrative viewpoint. In India the basic gap between politicians and bureaucrats makes this difficult.

India has been governed by a single political party, the Indian National Congress, since independence. Top bureaucrats and top Congress party leaders have been able to work together to a certain extent, because of their long experience in dealing with one another. Most charges against the bureaucracy in India have been leveled by political opponents of the Congress party, though even Congress has launched an anticorruption drive.

The national government has not suffered a collapse in its policymaking ability, which could occur if a weak coalition were to come to power. If this occurred, it would be possible for the political bodies to remain paralyzed and decisions on long-range, as well as day-to-day, matters would have to be made by the bureaucracy. The level of trust that the general public has in the civil service would have to be high in such a situation, for if both political and administrative branches of government could not operate the country would collapse in chaos. In some states (e. g., in France, from 1958-1962), the bureaucracy has been called upon to act in this manner and has performed with relative success. The national Indian bureaucracy has as yet not been tested.

Federalism in India

Unlike Great Britain, India is a federal state whose constitution centers power in a federal government but assures special powers to state governments as well. The federal government, as well as the state governments (see Chap. 2), are elected and are accepted by the people as legitimate agencies of authority. In general, the Indian constitution divides power between the federal and state governments in a manner comparable to the division of power in the United States. There are areas (ninety-seven items are listed in the constitution) over which only the federal government may legislate; these include defense, foreign affairs, and currency. There are matters over which only states may legislate (sixty-six items are enumerated in the constitution); these include such things as police protection, welfare services, and education. There is also a Concurrent List of forty-seven items over which the federal and state governments share authority; these include the civil and criminal law and socioeconomic planning. When in conflict, federal law prevails over state law, and the Indian Supreme Court is the final interpreter of the constitution. As described in Chapter 2, the courts in India are legally part of the political process but have not been as actively involved in it as courts in the United States have been.

In India, the federal government has been able to dominate the states by political as well as constitutional means. Under the constitution, it can create new states, change the boundaries of existing states, and even abolish states by ordinary legislation, without a constitutional amendment. Such power represents no idle threat, for the Congress party has generally had an overwhelming majority of votes in the national legislature and has, in fact, created new states. In addition, the Indian constitution permits the federal government to direct state governments if the states fail to comply with laws enacted by the national legislature. In a number of cases the federal government has also taken over state governments (e. g., West Bengal in 1968) under an emergency power provision when parties in opposition to Congress have either refused to cooperate with the national leadership or when state governments have had such weak coalitions they were unable to make policy decisions.

It should be noted however that such extreme measures have been relatively rare and do not represent the norm by which power in India is exercised. In political terms, generally state governments have been dominated by the Congress party as much as by the federal government (e. g., in 1972, Mrs. Gandhi's new Congress party had 70 percent of the seats at both the national and state levels). In the normal instance the federal government has depended on and cooperated with the states for the implementation of much national policy. State political leaders are elected independently of national leaders and retain an independent base of support. Even if they are Congress party members, they can bargain with the national leadership because they are not selected by a closed elite of party officials. The federal system involves much bargaining and negotiation, and Indian states have much more to say about the final implementation of national policy than local governments in Great Britain do.

Local Government

Local politics in India is an important area of party confrontation. At the national level, there is no viable alternative to the Congress party, but at the state level power has alternated among different parties and coalitions. Compared to the British public, the Indian public is not apathetic about local politics. In a real sense, local politics is one of the most direct means by which groups that oppose central government policy can win an official position in the Indian system. State elections are thus hotly contested, and the resolution of these contests can often determine the success or failure of national policy within the separate states.

Local government, in terms of administration, is also important in understanding the final resolution of Indian policy. Every Indian state has its own administrative service, with many levels of internal government. This is necessitated by India's large population; many states in India are as large or larger than European countries. In addition, fully 80 percent of the Indian population is rural and lives in small agricultural villages. These villages are units of local government and can be quite independent of party control since leaders are elected at this level because of their local social standing. Thus, effective local administration with support of local politicians is essential if India is to convert national policy directives into actions affecting her people.

Local government in India is elected at the *panchayat* (village) level and is quite close to the people. Local interests and complaints are heard here. Local governments in some areas have been traditionally oriented, opposing national and state government development plans. While local elections have increased voter awareness and raised the aspirations of the people, local units are poor in resources and laden with traditional habits of thought. The result has been a growing frustration, which makes it difficult for state and national policymakers.

The Formulation of National Policy in India

Thus the Indian system is one of compromise and negotiation. Leading politicians talk about development and mobilization of the people, but decisions in the final analysis are the product of competing forces representing many levels and interests in Indian society. National policy can be stated clearly in the Lok Sabha, but it may be implemented quite differently in the *panchayat*.

CHILE

The Chilean constitution, until the overthrow of the Allende government in 1973, established a system of separation of powers in which president, legislature, and judiciary were legally independent of one another. Such a system is in contrast to that of both Great Britain and India, parliamentary countries in which the effective executive, the prime minister, is elected by the legislature. At the present time a new Chilean constitution is being written that may alter Chile's traditional policymaking machinery.

Decisionmaking in Chile has (until the military coup) technically been shared among the branches of government, each responsible to different constituencies for differing lengths of time. In practice, however, the Chilean system had allowed the president to dominate the system both in terms of initiating policy and seeing it was carried out. It should be noted, however, that in Chile's system normally the president and the majority in national legislature would have been of the same political persuasion. If a president of Chile did not receive a majority of the popular vote in a popular election, he had to be elected by the Chilean legislature. The legislature would not elect a president whom it thought it would oppose at every turn. Thus, when Allende became Chile's first Socialist president and had to deal with a Christian Democrat legislature, he had to reach significant compromises with his opponents. He, more than any of his predecessors, had to cajole and compromise in order to get the legislature to support his legislative program; in the end he gave up the effort and failed in this regard.

Central Government

Chile is not a federal system and all general policy decisions are made at the level of national government under the direction of the president, who usually dominates both the legislative and administrative process. He initiates the formal legislative program and, through a variety of executive powers, may issue ordinances that can change existing laws without legislative concurrence. He may also suspend the Congress temporarily. Although he is commander-in-chief of the armed forces, this is only a formality. Until the Allende presidency Chile did not have a strong tradition of the military interfering in politics and presidents did not generally meddle with the military. However, late in Allende's administration the president appointed military leaders to head the civilian cabinet, paving the way for the military junta now still in power.

Chile had a civil service based on the merit principle, which was organized under prescribed laws passed by Congress. As in other states, the efficiency and support granted to the bureaucracy affected the final ability of the government to carry out its aims. In comparison to the bureaucracies of Great Britain and India, the relative importance and effectiveness of the Chilean bureaucracy fell somewhere in between. In Great Britain, the bureaucracy provides a great many services quickly and efficiently and, as a result, is almost taken for granted by the people. In India, the bureaucracy is mistrusted and is unable fully to carry out government directives. As a result the Indian population fears and criticizes the administration. In Chile, the civil service efficiently carried out existing law, but many citizens wanted to see many more initiatives taken by government. Criticism was thus not directed at the bureaucracy as such, but directly at the political branches of the government. Chileans widely assume that if a law is passed, it will be fairly and efficiently enforced in a nonpolitical manner. Today the military government controls the bureaucracy by having placed its men in strategic positions in the civil service.

Chile, while it has a civil service, is a somewhat complicated state because the system has permitted the establishment of semiautonomous agencies, which in the past could resist presidential and legislative pressure and still affect the administration of Chilean law. Thus Chile had an office of comptroller general (Contraloría General de la Republica), which was responsible for supervising national property and overlooking the government's budgets and accounts. The comptroller audited all expenditures of public funds and pronounced on the constitutionality of executive decrees. He could require the president to reconsider a decree, though if the president resubmitted it the decree became law. The comptroller in Chile was independent, with a guaranteed tenure of office, similar to a Supreme Court judge in the United States. In practice, from the establishment of the office in 1952 until the military coup, the comptroller was active and aggressive in his role as guardian of the public funds and had challenged many presidential decrees.

In addition to the comptroller, the Chilean Supreme Court and the judicial system in general have been active participants in decisionmaking. This differs from the judiciary in Great Britain and India where parliamentary traditions have left the courts a narrowly defined legal role. The Chilean Supreme Court has constitutionally been endowed with the power of judicial review—the authority to decide whether acts of other branches of government are constitutional. This power has been interpreted narrowly in that the Chilean court has always refused to become involved in partisan disputes and has always restricted itself to decisions in well-presented legal cases, as the United States Supreme Court has. The Chilean court has thus refused to consider, on jurisdictional grounds, cases considered too political or explosive. Nevertheless, the court's very presence within the system as a last resort and its guaranteed independence has affected the decisions of both the executive and the legislative branches of government. The military government has not touched the Chilean court system.

Besides the comptroller and the courts the Chileans have established several other semi-independent agencies that were able to resist presidential and legislative pressure. The government maintained a development corporation, for example, usually referred to as CORFO (Corporación de Fomento de la Producción). This organization was managed by a board of twenty-one members, in which labor, management, and government were represented. CORFO, like a British nationalized industry, was technically connected to a ministry but it is not a subgroup within the ministry (as would be the case in Great Britain). Rather, the Chilean government participated in CORFO's decisions through its representatives within CORFO's management. This management was guaranteed a security of tenure, so that while the government could change the membership by its appointment power, it could not get rid of the whole organization at once; it had to observe the set terms of office for each member. The government then had to negotiate with CORFO; it could not automatically get all its policies adopted. This was true also for a large number of other agencies (e. g., in the fields of commerce, housing, aviation, maritime services, and banking).

Chile, like many other Latin American countries, has a very large proportion of persons on the government payroll—many more than either Great Britain or India has, in proportion to their respective populations. More than one-fourth of all persons in the Chilean work force are government employees. These workers, while literate and low paid, are basically nonrevolutionary in their outlook, since their livelihood depends on the current government establishment. On the other hand, because there are so many civil servants in Chile they have relatively low prestige, compared to civil servants in Great Britain and India. The Chilean civil service is so bloated that it is generally not very efficient or responsive, and with so many Chileans in the government service performing basically nonproductive jobs, the bureaucracy is itself a great drain on the country's economy.

Local Government

All local government officials in Chile are members of a bureaucracy appointed by the president. Thus, unlike local officials in Great Britain and India, local Chilean officials are not elected and are not responsible to separate constituencies. Chilean local government officials are responsible to and dependent on the president, who nominates and appoints them to their respective offices, though for set terms. Today local officials in Chile are appointed by the military.

Although there are no elected local executive officials, local Chilean authorities can be divided into two groups—political and administrative. The political group is responsible for seeing the spirit of national policy is communicated to the people; the administrative group implements the law. Thus, all mayors of cities and governors of provinces in Chile are politicians (or military men, today) appointed on the basis of their recognized political abilities. In contrast, administrative officials are selected through the merit system. Local populations do elect legislative assemblies—cities elect councillors and provinces elect provincial assemblies—but all the executive power at the local level is in the hands of presidential appointees and bureaucrats. Thus local areas have little real autonomy and maintain the Chilean tradition of looking to the central government for all decisions.

In recent years rural discontent with national development policies has demonstrated that local feelings are not completely dead in Chile. However, this activity has taken the form of violent outbursts but has not led to attempted takeover of local assemblies. Chileans have long recognized the need for greater local responsibility, but in practice local officials have expected and accepted national rule. Chile lacks both the British tradition of local responsibility and the Indian excitement about it. In Great Britain and India, interest groups and/or concerned members of the local community can make successful appeals at the local level; in Chile, all appeals must go to the national capital. Thus, Chileans tend to be apathetic about local government, and local authority is of very minor importance. Decisionmaking authority in Chile has been vested in the president, who has tremendous dominance, but who must take into account the general feeling of the Congress as well as of some semi-independent agencies at the national level. With these accommodations, public policy is made in Chile.

Comparative Distinctions in Political Processes and Public Policy Among Competitive States

Great Britain, India, and Chile all utilize a variety of political structures in the enforcement of their day-to-day political process. The structures used differ from one another as the levels of economic development and cultural traditions vary from country to country.

Great Britain is a highly developed country with a long-established civil service that is highly trained and carries out day-to-day policy at the national level. This bureaucracy has a high degree of public trust for its efficiency and nonpartisanship; it has served governments headed by either major party equally well. Local government also is important in Great Britain on narrow local issues. The public at large seems largely unconcerned about practical policymaking, reserving its most intense interest for national partisan conflicts. Practical policymaking in Great Britain is, however, affected by organized interest groups at both the national and local levels.

Indian political processes are much more affected by partisan political considerations than British processes are. In India the great social gap between elitist bureaucrats and comparatively middle-class politicians makes policy difficult to enforce to the satisfaction of either group. This is exaggerated by the fact that policy in India, aimed at the broad economic development of the country, is comparatively grandiose, requiring high levels of official and public support. Local politics is also much more partisan and hotly contested in India than it is in Great Britain and tends to complicate national policymaking further since local politicians have quite different perspectives than national ones. However, both India and Great Britain basically have parliamentary systems and broad national initiatives are made in both states by the governing party, headed by the prime minister and the cabinet.

Chile, with its structure of separation of powers and its tradition of concentrating power in the hands of the elected chief executive, develops and executes policy in a manner distinct from that of Great Britain and India. In Chile the president (and now, the military junta) has direct responsibility for the the formulation and execution of policy, retaining great authority over the initiation of programs. The president needed the support of the Chilean Congress, which could have been controlled by a party other than his own. In addition, the civil service, the courts, and certain other official agencies retained a certain independence of the president and could influence policy. Local officials in Chile, unlike those in Great Britain and India, were not elected but are presidential appointees. Today, the Chilean Congress is suspended and the military leadership has taken the place of the president, ruling over the Chilean bureaucracy and local governments as he did in the past.

POLITICAL PROCESSES AND PUBLIC POLICY IN FRAGMENTED STATES

Projecting Similarities

In fragmented states, the political process in formal institutions does not always reflect the actual distribution of power among groups within the community. Thus, far-reaching decisions can often be avoided, or if formally made, not carried out. This is because the fragmentation of society in these states produces a government of tenuous influence and/or of limited expected longevity. For governments to stay in office in these states, the powers in office must avoid the open hostility of major groups in the community, and these are usually so strong and entrenched that any government decision is likely to produce destructive forms of opposition. Compared to competitive states, then, fragmented states generally try to insulate their processes of public policy from public view and, as a result, these processes can often be only weakly institutionalized in the system. Any change in temporary power relationships among important groups shifts the manner and place in which political decisions are finally made.

Three Case Studies: France, Indonesia, and Zaire

FRANCE

National policymaking is politically in the hands of the president of the French Fifth Republic, who is a directly elected official and chief of state. Although the constitution places policymaking legally in the hands of the premier, who is elected by the legislature (as in the Third and Fourth Republics), the great personal popularity and political skills of President de Gaulle caused power to shift into the hands of the presidents. The Fifth Republic has never been dominated by a premier; this practice continued under President Pompidou, another Gaullist who, like his predecessor, was able to formulate and execute policy without much fear of interference by the French legislature. It is not clear how President Giscard d'Estaing, an Independent Republican, will manage his relations with the legislature, but he has begun his presidency very much in the de Gaulle-Pompidou tradition of a strong presidency.

Central Government

The president of France has a cabinet of advisors and a General Secretariat, both of which are in charge not only of the formulation of public policy, but its execution. Within these groups are included the high-level civil servants representing the elite of the French administrative bureaucracy. There is a close relationship between presidential advisors and the various ministries that carry out French law. In practice, then, while France has both an elected legislature and an elected executive, there are neither separation of powers nor checks and balances within the French system. In Chile's presidential system the president had to deal with both the Congress and some semi-independent agencies and, in close elections, was elected by and responsible to the legislature. In France, real authority is in the hands of the president who is not connected to or checked by the legislature in any way. Legislative elections in France, which involve the component groups and parties in society much more directly than presidential elections do, have in the Fifth Republic been hollow exercises. The people may vote for representatives to the National Assembly, but this has achieved little in terms of policy. Presidents have submitted plebiscites directly to the people in order to bypass the legislature and to deny it a role in decisionmaking. While it is possible for the National Assembly to dismiss a premier and to pass laws, and for referenda to fail, the practical effect of these acts on day-to-day public policy is more theoretical than real. In France, no member of the parliament may hold office in the executive branch as his counterpart may in parliamentary systems like Great Britain and India. Members of the National Assembly who are selected for cabinet positions must give up their legislative seats. The Fifth Republic thus tries to overcome the bad effects of fragmentation, by ignoring the fragments and denying them power. In so doing, the Fifth Republic has become almost entirely an administrative state. Long-range decisions are made and executed with the participation of high-level civil servants; day-to-day policy processes are carried out by lower-level bureaucrats. Bureaucrats smoothly and efficiently gather information, run nationalized enterprises, and carry out public services without being confronted by legislative politicians or factions that have been selected by the people to represent them. Bureaucrats even draw up policies in detail without consultation with the legislature. On the other hand, the president has demanded loyalty from the administration and has overruled technical decisions made by bureaucrats on political grounds. In some areas administrative officials must thus serve the president, but in others much is left to the bureaucracy.

Because of the great power that is now exercised by civil servants, interest groups have transferred their greatest efforts from legislative lobbying to the administration. In France the bureaucracy has to deal with unaggregated demands, since political parties and legislatures are so powerless they no longer can operate as agents of compromise. Instead, ministers are buffeted by conflicting points of view, and when policies have been controversial the bureaucracy has itself become divided. Such questions as European integration and socioeconomic planning have seen one administrative agency pitted against another, with little chance for the resolution of conflict.[3]

The French bureaucracy is highly respected, and the higher grades are considered to be extremely competent and efficient. Capable administration is a tradition dating back hundreds of years, to well before the French Revolution of 1789. Aspiring sons of the best French families have always wished for good positions in government service, and they have to survive a difficult preparation in specialized schools to achieve their aims. Unlike Great Britain where entry into the civil service is based on an examination open to anyone, in France there are two specialized universities (the National School of Administration and the École Polytechnique) that train persons for government service. The final examinations at these universities determine admission to the bureaucracy and the rank at which the entrant may be placed. Only the best students can hope to advance to high-level positions in the French civil service.

In France the judicial system is operated as part of the administrative structure and French judges and courts are staffed in a manner similar to other areas of the bureaucracy. Lawyers are trained in the French law codes in special schools; prospective judges are trained in court administration as well. Each who would be lawyer or judge thus must receive a specialized education. A candidate to be a lawyer must pass a final lawyer's examination; a candidate for a judgeship must pass a judge's examination. A student who gets a good grade in these examinations, which are administered by the Ministry of Justice, will be assigned a good starting position as lawyer or judge. Judges in France are thus not semipolitical figures as they are in Anglo-Saxon countries. Good lawyers do not aspire to be judges and politicians are not appointed as judges. French courts are very much like bureaucratic agencies and judges are bureaucrats.

The judicial system is held in great esteem in France, much as is the rest of the administration. Today the French maintain two separate judicial structures—a regular court structure, which hears normal civil and criminal cases, and an administrative court system, which hears cases involving disputes with the government. Each system has a separate Supreme Court and is insulated from the other. The level of efficiency and justice in both is very highly regarded.

Local Government

Local government in France is also heavily influenced by the central administration, though in recent years there has been a revival of interest in developing local responsibility and initiative. There are two basic units of local government in France—the commune and the department. The country has about 38,000 communes, and they average about 1,300 inhabitants. However, there is great variation in size among them. The small communes elect small municipal councils; the large communes (e. g., Paris, Lyons, and Marseille) elect larger councils. The councils elect the mayors of the respective communities. In general terms, the council adopts public policies while the mayor executes them. If there is a conflict between mayor and council, the national government can call new municipal elections. In general, the matters dealt with at the commune level are quite minor and excite little political interest.

The other important unit of local government in France is the department. The country is divided into ninety-five departments, each of which also elects a general legislative council. The executive authority at the department level is vested in the prefect, an administrator appointed for each department by the national government in Paris.

The institution of the prefect is peculiarly French. The individual who serves as prefect must be loyal to the national administration but is the direct target of pressure in all important local matters. The role of the prefect is to see national policy is implemented in the region to which he is assigned. He thus must carry out decisions made by the relevant national ministries. As national ministries have increased in size they have more frequently dealt with the department through their own bureaucracy, bypassing the prefect. This has led to a gradual decline in the power of the prefect, a phenomenon that has also been accelerated by the growth of popular interest in local politics. As local politicians on the elected councils of their departments achieve public support, the prefect as an appointed official must seek to compromise with and persuade them. He can not very easily command them in the name of the Paris government. The specific powers of the prefect vis-a-vis the council are great: in technical terms, he is responsible only to the Ministry of the Interior; in practice, however, he wants a smoothly run department and for this needs local political support.

Local government can thus reflect the varying approaches and ideologies natural to the French community. While services are nationally administered in form through government servants, the prefects, in fact the local region has much to say about the details of national policy implementation. Since the institution of the Fifth Republic efforts have been made to accelerate decentralization in many fields. Regional councils, a basic threat to the power of individual prefects, have been appointed to deal with questions of economic development. Many services in France that are now administered by the national government (e. g. police, education) would be administered by the local government in Anglo-Saxon nations. Accordingly, there has been some attempt to consolidate the communes into more effective units vis-a-vis the national government. However, the police are still nationally administered; despite the student riots of 1968 educational reforms have been limited, leaving most decisions with respect to higher education in the Ministry of Education in Paris. Indeed, de Gaulle resigned from the presidency when he lost a popular referendum on a question that would have allowed greater autonomy to Brittany and Normandy. Overall, then, despite some real efforts to develop stronger local government the French tradition of centralized administrative authority still dominates the Fifth Republic and superficially covers over the basic rifts and conflicts in French society.

INDONESIA

Indonesia's Colonial Inheritance

Indonesia's political processes are today dominated by the military under President Suharto. More than the French, Indonesians have in practice abandoned any real attempt to use the representative body of state—the elected legislature—in the process of decisionmaking. The Indonesian legislature can meet and legislative elections have been held. Today, in addition, there is a relatively high degree of freedom of communication and organization compared to the period of Guided Democracy (from 1957 to 1965). Most of the political parties that were outlawed by President Sukarno have been reestablished, and the press may now, within limits, freely report and comment upon the doings of the government. However, the president and his government monopolize real decisionmaking; Suharto and his cabinet draw up the programs and try to see them implemented. As in France, the attempt has been made in Indonesia to create an administrative state whose president can achieve political unity and coherence, which the competitive party structure has been unable to do. The political parties can talk and organize, but they cannot block or even share in the decisions made by the executive. The basic fragmentation of political opinion is thus superficially recognized as it was under Guided Democracy. The conflicting groups that compose Indonesian society are given symbolic positions within the system; they do not, however, participate in the essential work and details of politics.

In one very important respect Indonesia differs from France, and that is in its level of economic development and the consequent capabilities of its administrative structure. France is a highly developed country in which the civil bureaucracy is extremely well trained and highly respected throughout the community. Before the advent of President de Gaulle, the administration was frequently described as the only institution that held the country together, for in this period governments were weak and indecisive and left many problems to bureaucratic judgment. Indonesia also suffered a period of government weakness in its short-lived parliamentary system (from 1952 to 1957). Unlike the civil service in France, the civil service in Indonesia was not very well trained or highly respected. The result was a collapse of government services, the cessation of government control over outlying areas, and a general descent into anarchy. This, of course, eventually culminated in a series of political dictatorships—first by Sukarno, then by Suharto. Political freedoms are limited now in comparison to the parliamentary period, but because of Indonesian administrative weakness this has not led directly to strong government in practice.

Indonesia's administrative problems are, like India's, partially the product of the country's colonial past. Under Dutch rule very few Indonesians were trained for administrative positions, and those who were trained were confined to the lowest ranks of the bureaucracy and exercised only limited responsibility. As in India, a basic conflict emerged in Indonesia between administrators and nationalists upon independence. At that time, the few native administrators in the country were suspected by the nationalists of harboring loyalties to the Dutch, simply because they had been trained by and worked for the Dutch in colonial projects. The comparison between India and Indonesia, however, should not be drawn too closely, because British rule was much more direct in India than Dutch rule was in Indonesia. In India, the civil service administered most of the country and was highly trained at the upper levels; only a small part of Indonesia was directly governed by a Dutch-led bureaucracy. Outside of Java (most Dutch investment was concentrated in Java), the country was led by traditional regents, who technically only took "advice" from Dutch officials assigned to their areas. Most Indonesians in the outlying areas never saw a European or understood they were being served by an organized system other than their traditional chiefs and sultans. While some modern services did eventually come to the outlying regions in the form of roads and health measures, these were relatively minor and generally decreed through the established local authorities. Not until well into the twentieth century did the Dutch colonial administration begin to serve Indonesia on a national basis and then in only narrow areas of public policy.

The Administrative Structure Today

Contemporary administration and policymaking in Indonesia reflect the inbalances of the colonial period. Immediately after independence the government tried to equalize salaries for bureaucrats and, consequently, lowered the pay for higher-level civil servants, while increasing the wages for the lower ranks. Today, persons with even a little education can do much better in terms of monetary reward working for private industry than working for the government. Over the years, as a consequence, many fairly skilled persons have left the civil service for other jobs, leaving many relatively uneducated persons to rise slowly in the ranks simply by staying in their jobs for a long period of time. Fully one-half the government budget in Indonesia has gone to salaries for military and civilian officials, leaving little revenue for the actual implementation of programs. Despite this high cost of bureaucracy the best people have left government service anyway and the service, poor to begin with, has deteriorated badly.

Administration in Indonesia thus barely exists in practice and one of the major problems facing President Suharto is the establishment of a government service that can effectively carry out government policy. On paper, the Indonesian civil service is based on a merit system similar to European bureaucracies. In practice, it has been corrupt, incompetent, and unwilling to take government directives. This has left most of Indonesia without real national government, and traditional local authorities have made most of the decisions affecting the people. Local rebellions have raged since independence, and today the level of public service provided at the national level is probably still less than that which the Dutch delivered before 1940: roads and airstrips are in a bad state of disrepair, hampering the country's transportation system; mines and plantations have closed down, owing to poor delivery of supplies and lack of protection from local bandits; and poor fiscal policies have led to an inflation so great that people in Indonesian cities have to spend mountains of paper money for their groceries. Under President Sukarno, Indonesia, because of incompetent administration, managed to achieve something few countries ever achieve—a declining per capita income. In other words, the Indonesian economy could not at this time keep pace with its own rate of population growth, much less expand production and raise the standard of living. Overall, especially under Sukarno's Guided Democracy (when government administration seemed to collapse entirely), Indonesian unity was a fiction and not a reality. Whatever government decisions were made in the country were carried out by local elders in the traditional village units. National government was a facade of elaborate councils, which conversed for hours but could not enforce any resolution because the system had no trustworthy enforcement machinery.

One of the reasons for Indonesian inefficiency and corruption is that the salaries of government employees, which are fixed by government regulations and do not vary with the cost of living, are simply insufficient to keep them alive. To make ends meet a bureaucrat must take bribes and develop clients who will support him. This, of course, means gross violation of the law, but a bureaucrat living in an economy with a very high rate of inflation has little choice (in Indonesia, the value of the rupiah has declined by more than 100 percent since 1967, by official export exchange rates, though the rate of depreciation has lessened to some extent since 1971).[4] The problem facing contemporary Indonesia is that habits of corruption and bribery have become almost institutionalized and are thus difficult to eradicate.

President Suharto has begun to move directly in the area of the administrative service, through a large number of presidential directives. The ultimate sanction behind these directives lies in the power of the military, which is personally loyal to the president. The military maintains the country's internal security, providing protection against banditry and has continued in its efforts to crush Indonesia's seemingly permanent regional rebellions. The president's directives have been aimed at promoting economic development and internal security in the hope of attracting some foreign investment. Many individual administrators have been replaced and a new "Development Cabinet" appointed. While the military in practice governs the country, the Development Cabinet is dominated by civilians and its goal is to institute policies that will enable the reestablishment of an effective civilian administration.

The Development Cabinet was appointed in 1968 to implement a five-point program, labeled *Pantja Krida*.[5] These points were stated as follows:

1. Achievement of political stability;
2. Implementation of the Five-Year Development Plan;
3. The holding of general elections;
4. The maintenance of security; and
5. The improvement of the state apparatus.

The program emphasized the improvement of administration so that development plans could be carried out. The president revoked over fifty decrees made by President Sukarno and ordered a complete restructuring of all government units and departments. The number of departments within each cabinet ministry was altered to ensure development plans would receive first priority. Many complaints have been made about the government's inability to reduce corruption, but wholesale personnel changes have been made in an attempt to placate criticism. President Suharto has noted mass dismissals of civil servants would be both illegal and impossible. His hopes for improving Indonesian processes of public policy formulation lie in reorganization and upgrading of certain programs at the expense of others. For this he needs widespread support from many sectors in Indonesian society.

The legislative election of 1971 returned General Suharto's allies in force and his cabinet continues today, possibly with greater legitimacy than before. Indonesia is a naturally pluralistic society, which has existed on the verge of anarchy for nearly twenty years. The present leadership consists of a pragmatic group of military men and politicians that must create the actuality of government out of a heterogeneous, uneducated, and impoverished society. The president's cabinet appears to be the major institution that attempts to accommodate the different interests at stake in national policymaking. It is undoubtedly true most Indonesians today are governed primarily by local elders in the old way, but the continued stability of the presidential regime and its ability to adjust the interests of varying groups and enforce its policies should soon begin to impinge on Indonesian village life.

Reestablishment of Policymaking Processes in Indonesia

Since 1965, much has been done in Indonesia to re-create the official structures of national politics, and some accommodation of interests has now been accomplished. Probably the greatest single achievement along these lines has been the 1971 elections. Political parties can now organize and the press is relatively free, though these remain confined to the cities where only a minority of the people live. Indonesian fragmentation undoubtedly remains deep, though great efforts have been made to develop a form of national consensus under General Suharto's strong civilian-military cabinet system. In Indonesia, unity and consensus are probably far weaker than they are in France, where the people are united by common history, culture, language, modern economics, an excellent administration, and numerous popular elections. Indonesia has few of these advantages, but her leaders know what they must accomplish and are working hard in this direction.

ZAIRE

Zaire's Colonial Inheritance

As with other recently independent states, political processes in Zaire reflect the institutions and concepts introduced by the mother country, Belgium, when Zaire was the Belgian Congo. Congolese colonial history—briefer and more chaotic than the histories of most other colonized states—reveals that the inherent fragmentation of the area was only superficially and temporarily reduced.

Belgium did not assume responsibility for policymaking in the Congo before 1908. Until that time, decisions concerning domestic socioeconomic policies and general economic planning and development were left to private investors, their corporate employees, as well as to Catholic missionaries. When Belgium decided directly to administer the colony, she left any concessions already granted to the large companies and the church within their own spheres of interest. Thus the Union Minière du Haut Congo continued to control Katanga's copper mines; Forminière maintained its monopoly of the diamond trade; missionary activity continued as before. Belgium thus shared political authority with these other groups, leaving them extremely powerful in their own regions.

Nor did Belgium promote, or even permit, the development of free political activity among the native population. The Congolese were not trained to organize interest groups for purposes of stating specific aims, and party politics was permitted only in the 1950s. When political parties did emerge, they had very weak links to the people, except on an ethnic basis. Neither did they reflect interest group activity, nor did they speak in national terms.

Although many Congolese received a primary education and could read, higher education was almost completely denied to them. The only university in the Congo, Lovanium University, was not founded until 1954, and natives were not permitted to go to Belgium for higher studies. Since higher education was a general prerequisite for entry into the Belgian civil service, these posts were reserved for Belgians, except at the very lowest levels.

Administrators in the Congo, whether European or Congolese, were directly responsible to the Belgian cabinet and legislature and looked to Brussels for ultimate sanction. Despite not being responsible to a Congolese constituency, Belgian administrators efficiently provided a great number of services to the colony over most of the twentieth century. The Congo had modern roads, a high level of health care, a great deal of primary education, and a very high level of foreign investment compared to most other colonial areas. On the other hand; without the Belgians the country had only a limited sense of national unity and most Congolese did not perceive the services provided by colonial authority as meant for their personal benefit. The Belgian administration was not widely respected in the Congo and was viewed as foreign and untrustworthy by the Congolese nationalists; it was seen as of minor importance compared to the missions and the companies by the average Congolese.

When the Belgians left the Congo in 1960, the country—without a well-trained native civil service to counteract her inherent political fragmentation—collapsed. The civil service ceased to operate; all public services were discontinued; a sense of responsibility to general public authority vanished.

Not only did civil authority cease, but military discipline (also a product of training and modern administration) also collapsed. The Congolese military became beset with mutinies by soldiers who would not recognize the authority of ranking officers. Only by hiring mercenary soldiers and paying them could the new native government develop any sense of public security, even for its own officials. When from 1964 to 1965, 170 mercenaries rebelled, there was no loyal native force that could deal with them. The inability of the government to crush the mercenaries led directly to the coup by General Mobutu. It is interesting to note that despite the fact he came to power because of a mercenary uprising, Mobutu has kept the mercenaries on. He still regards them as the best trained and disciplined troops in Zaire.

The Administrative Structure Today

The present government of President Mobutu is the strongest since independence. The problems facing the regime are much greater than those facing President Suharto in Indonesia. Indonesians have a common culture and sense of nationality, despite great regional problems. There are many Indonesian leaders who have popular constituencies and the Indonesian military has a sense of camaraderie and discipline. None of these factors are present in any great degree in Zaire. President Mobutu must develop both the spiritual feeling of nationality and all the civilian and military institutions that could make that spiritual sense actual in any important way.

President Mobutu has chosen to approach his mammoth problem by adopting an outwardly nationalistic, anticommunist and anticapitalist ideology. Fully aware of the inherent weaknesses of any regime in Zaire, he has personally decreed most of the nationalist symbols now ubiquitous in the country. Thus, colonial place names have been replaced by native ones. Citizens have been directed to drop European first names and to take native ones. Mobutu has attempted to take an outwardly independent or neutral stance on international questions, though he has welcomed European investment. (He is viewed by other African states as under the influence of the United States.) Out of his nationalism has also come an attack on the Catholic church, which has criticized his directive against Christian first names.

This nationalist drive has been used by the present regime to promote support for Mobutu against the more particularistic groups, the church, and foreign concerns. In the last analysis, however, Mobutu cannot govern directly because he lacks a real administration to carry out his orders. Government in Zaire consists of presidential decrees communicated to the citizens; there is no institution of government workers to see that the decrees are actually carried out. There is only a fear the military may discover infractions and take physical reprisals. The government of Zaire thus is an African-style one-party civilian superstructure, which is kept under control by the threat of military sanctions. Weak though the military may be, it is still strong enough to frighten the civilians.

Mobutu has attempted to establish the beginnings of a real civilian authority, but these moves have not gone very far as yet. During the chaos that followed independence, provinces multiplied from six to twenty-one. Mobutu has reconsolidated the provinces so that now there are only eight. He has also established a civilian political party, the Mouvement Populaire de la Révolution (MPR), which in practice is the only civilian national group in the country. This party popularizes Mobutu's nationalist schemes and tries to develop public support for the president. Today, Zaire officially has an administrative structure consisting of territorial administrators, district commissioners, and provincial governors. These officials comprise an official bureaucracy directly under the president and his cabinet. The MPR designates all these officials and they are formally appointed by the president. Mobutu has consciously directed appointments not be made on a regional basis, and persons from one part of the country can become officials in a different geographic section. This is part of an overall strategy aimed at reducing the influence of narrow tribal and regional groups.

Mobutu seems to have been successful in stabilizing the Congolese economy, but he has done this by granting foreign (especially Western) enterprises many concessions over his own people. He has attempted to maximize his personal authority by constantly shaking up his cabinet to keep rival politicians off balance. In so doing he has retarded the development of important political groups in the country outside his own MRP. This is of course intentional; Mobutu feels without his own strong hand the basic forces tending toward disintegration of Zaire may again get the upper hand. At present, they are at least under superficial control.

Comparative Distinctions in Political Processes and Public Policy Among Fragmented States

Of the three fragmented states dealt with here France, because she is the most highly developed, is the only one capable of developing national policies and effectively enforcing them. In France, a highly trained and respected bureaucracy makes sure basic public services are carried out: the roads are paved, mail delivered, police and fire departments staffed, and schools open. All these services are centrally administered with little emphasis on local or regional considerations. France is a well-to-do country by world standards and her administrative bureaucracy has traditionally held the country together, despite the nation's history of social and political fragmentation.

In Indonesia and Zaire, countries with poor economies, administrative services are weak, poorly staffed, and have only limited traditions. Thus, while Generals Suharto and Mobutu may try to develop national policies and programs, they have only weak government services for bringing these policies to the people. Both countries rely on the military as the ultimate sanction, but this is not sufficient for the enforcement of policy on a day-to-day basis.

POLITICAL PROCESSES AND PUBLIC POLICY IN NONCOMPETITIVE STATES

Patterns of Similarity

In noncompetitive systems, usually one group of people monopolizes all the political influence in the state. This group, an elite, thus can overwhelm all the established formal institutions, and decisionmaking becomes a kind of informal jockeying for power behind elaborate formal structures. Political activity can thus become hidden from public view, but it can also result in forceful decisionmaking and enforcement, since the state and its governmental arms are basically unified and cohesive. The political maneuver that occurs in noncompetitive states in general reflects competition for office among individuals in the elite; it does not reflect any deep fissure in society. Decisions once made, then, can actively be enforced.

Three Case Studies: The USSR, Egypt, and the PRC

UNION OF SOVIET SOCIALIST REPUBLICS

In the USSR, policy is the product of discussions held among top members of the Communist party hierarchy, many of whom also hold important positions in the government. The USSR has a long and elaborate constitution that establishes a federal system and a parliamentary structure (described in Chap. 2). However, all governmental structures have always been facades behind which the CPSU has monopolized real power. The party controls both major bureaucracies in the country—the CPSU apparatus and the state administrative officials—forming a kind of interlocking directorate with party functionaries. Stalin, the most powerful leader ever to have emerged in the USSR, was never a government functionary. His most important office was that of general secretary of the Communist party, and he gathered his power through his control of the party's bureaucracy. Even today it is undoubtedly true that real decisionmaking power is limited to the top members of the CPSU hierarchy.

The Administrative Structure Today

The USSR is both a party state and an administrative state.[6] The country is organized on bureaucratic lines fully. For persons within the Communist party to rise in political influence they must be able to affect this party structure. This does not mean that politics, in the broadest sense of that term, does not exist. The Soviet Union is a large, highly complex country in which many different kinds of policies have to be formulated. Underneath the facade of party conformity a real factionalism exists. The Soviet system involves a confusing system of infighting and maneuvering among regional party organizations, subordinates of the party at the national level, and professional specialists who are given important positions for their technical expertise. This factionalism is often described as a kind of brutal power struggle among individual personalities and groups which support them.

In the USSR, the top members of the CPSU hierarchy are extremely powerful. They control the military and police power of the state, make all public policy decisions for all regions, and control the entire communications structure. Politics in the USSR at the highest level therefore becomes a process by which party subordinates seek the favor of those in the highest positions, while high officials attempt to outmaneuver one another. When Stalin was alive he personally controlled the entire party bureaucracy by his use of terror and the secret police. Party functionaries who maneuvered for policies other than Stalin's own were in great personal danger. The highest levels of the CPSU were most fearful of Stalin's "purges," but they also were the most important officials in the country; a high bureaucrat in favor with Stalin could hope to effect real policy changes.

Much has changed in the USSR since the death of Stalin. Today, it appears that less power is now monopolized by personal dictators who can in effect control and terrorize the country's administrative structure. Compared to Stalin's regime, contemporary Soviet leaders appear to have moderated their political tactics and have attempted to institutionalize specific procedures by which policies are now made. Today more than ever before top party functionaries consult with the lower party apparatus in reaching specific decisions. In a real sense interest groups representing economic, occupational, and regional configurations are consulted by party functionaries. Except for the military, these groups remain amorphous and disorganized compared to their counterparts in competitive systems. However, compared to Stalin's era they are active contributors to the policymaking process. In the USSR today, economists contribute to economic planning, teachers' groups can bring about educational reforms, and lawyers can contribute to general legal policymaking. Where top leaders have strong commitments to particular policies they can still overlook these groups, but in recent years the top Soviet leadership has become more pragmatic. They now consult with technicians and use their expertise, even though specialists can be relatively low in the hierarchy.

Increasing pragmatism has also led to a different form of Soviet power struggle, in which those on top no longer resort to violence against those who oppose them. Today it is possible for Soviet leaders who lose in power struggles at the top to be retired peacefully, with little fear of murder or imprisonment. This is a vast change from the days of Stalin. Khrushchev was instrumental in introducing this policy of "de-Stalinization." Since his downfall, de-Staliniza- tion has been a lesser priority with the present Brezhnev-Kosygin leadership, but basic pragmatism seems to prevail over ideology, and there has been no reinstitution of Stalin's main instrument of repression, the secret police.

Compared to most other countries (competitive, fragmented, and noncompetitive), the Soviet political apparatus is both more centralized at the national level and also more involved in day-to-day administrative activities. Party policies at the highest levels can determine decisions made in courts, in low-level administrative offices, and in the regions and provinces. In formal terms the Soviet doctrine is that the party leads, but government administers. After 1917 a full-fledged civil service was recruited for purposes of implementing party policy, but under Stalin the bureaucracy was oppressed and frightened and served the dictator's wishes. The administration became weak, inefficient, and corrupt internally, but obedient externally. With Stalin gone, the USSR was left without a force to mobilize this bureaucracy. Khrushchev felt that in these circumstances the party had to take direct responsibility for reorganizing the administration, for if it didn't other forces in the community might appear. Today there are a series of agencies in Moscow, dominated by party functionaries, which oversee the entire Soviet bureaucracy. Their function is to see the administration efficiently implements CPSU policy. In general, these agencies, called "control organs," oversee both national and regional levels of administration.

Day-to-day decisionmaking in the USSR, while under ultimate party control, still involves a complicated administrative process comparable to that in other highly developed nations. Law can be enforced in the final analysis only at the lowest levels, where bargaining and consultation with those who will be affected by the policies must take place. If the party were to replace all the administrators in this sense, it would simply convert itself into another bureaucracy. This is a goal that the leaders of the CPSU would like to avoid. They have thus attempted to influence and control state bureaucrats through the use of force and "voluntary" organizations to take over some administrative special functions. In the main, however, the USSR remains a bureaucratic state in which most citizens seem to accept administrative decisionmaking passively and apathetically. The system is responsive to the party's demands, and public opinion is neither organized nor respected as legitimate within the Soviet ideological framework. There is thus little probability that policymakers will, in the foreseeable future, be brought under control by public grievances. Only party control organs seem operable.

The Soviet administrative structure is much more ideological in its rhetoric than bureaucracies in most other countries. Administrative decisions are generally explained in terms of Marxist-Leninist doctrine, and these decisions cover a vast variety of activities. The Soviet bureaucracy has a broader reach than bureaucracies in other states because it represents the ideological vanguard and monopolizes all force in the state. There is no sharing of authority with local powers or branches of government. The bureaucracy is the agent of the CPSU, the only legitimate governing agency in the state, and administrators are directly responsible to the party because of the latter's ability to control the organization, recruitment, and promotion policies within the administration.

Policymaking in the USSR

Marxist theory has always held that government is an instrument of oppression by one class over another. The government (i. e., the administrative bureaucracy and other formal institutions) was supposed to disappear once the working class took power. The Soviets have thus always attempted to deprive governmental institutions of any true legitimacy; they have instead attempted to vest power in the party, hoping government would "wither away." This has not succeeded in practical terms. The CPSU is the great maker of public policy and Soviet politics is an internal party matter. However, the USSR is a vast bureaucracy and will unquestionably remain so. No other system exists in the USSR for converting party doctrines into real decisions with practical effects.

EGYPT

Formulation of Public Policy in Egypt

Decisionmaking in Egypt is concentrated in the hands of a political, military, and bureaucratic elite whose maneuvers and tactics are, as in the USSR, not open to public scrutiny. However, unlike the USSR, Egypt is not a party state. The power of the Egyptian regime, while still exercised in an authoritarian manner, is not so broad and massive as that of the Soviet regime. The Egyptian elite has not attempted to overwhelm and transform its population; instead, the government rests upon the passive support of major elements in traditional Egyptian society.

On the surface Egypt, like the USSR, is a revolutionary state dedicated to uprooting the economic inequities of the past. Egypt has a single political party, the Arab Socialist Union, that acts as a connecting link between the elite and the rest of the country. However, in terms of actual political processes, the ASU is a facade behind which the constituent groups in Egypt's elite may operate. These groups include the military, the civil bureaucracy, political party leaders, and, to some extent, leaders of economic interest groups such as trade unions. Competition among these groups is amorphous and difficult to discern. However, there is in Egypt as in the USSR, a difference of opinion over important policy among different groups within the elite. This leads to a kind of disguised factionalism, which constitutes the essence of politics in Egypt.

The process of formulating public policy in Egypt has for most of the country's recent history revolved about the personality of President Nasser, who governed the country from 1952 to 1970. President Nasser was revered as a great hero by most Egyptians and his appeal was certainly of charismatic proportions. Nasser was able to dominate all formal institutions in the Egyptian system personally, and not through any political party or ideological movement. He did this despite his own apparent wish to establish an institutionalized system of government in the country that could exist independent of the personalities involved.

Nasser did not come to power in Egypt because of his organizational ability. He was the leader of a military coup that overthrew a weak, ineffective, and unpopular monarchy. His background was thus more bureaucratic than political. He was used to making decisions in closed meetings with his immediate allies and colleagues. There was never any sense of political representation of the Egyptian community in these meetings, and the government reflects this disdain for the representative process today. Decisions are made by an insulated elite behind closed doors and are enforced by a civil bureaucracy responsible to the elite and not to the public.

The Egyptian regime, while authoritarian, has never seemed to be as absolute or dependent on terror as the regime of Josef Stalin in the USSR. The Egyptians have conducted purges of top leaders and maintain a secret police to help supervise the bureaucracy. However, there have been no mass mobilizations or murders, and little irrational fear of the top leadership among the Egyptian elite. It appears Egyptian leaders have developed a strong sense of *esprit de'corps* and a consensus has existed among them against the excessive use of internal violence. The police apparatus is necessary to make certain the bureaucrats are carrying out government policy and lower-level politicians are obedient. There are no independent interest groups or legislative investigations that could perform these functions in Egypt.

The Administrative Structure Today

The Egyptian bureaucracy is not, in comparison to the bureaucracies in India or Indonesia, a product of a recent colonial past. Egypt never was directly ruled by a European power and the country always maintained the fiction of traditional self-government until Nasser's coup of 1952. Traditionally, the civil service always acted as the main enforcer of the law without the interference of representative bodies. This means that as far as day-to-day policy was concerned the bureaucracy not only enforced the laws, but also (through its power of enforcement) interpreted and amended them. The traditional Egyptian bureaucracy was regarded as the representative of the king and therefore was viewed as internally corrupt. Egyptian civil servants' main task was to collect taxes; often not all this revenue went back to the national government. The corruption of the regime at the highest level was seen as a reflection of the deeper problems of ineffectiveness and veniality, which were widespread throughout the administration. The traditional bureaucracy was completely subservient to corrupt rulers and internally corrupt itself.

The contemporary Egyptian system has inherited many problems from the past. In 1952 many bureaucrats in Egypt were foreign-born (these have now been replaced with native Egyptians). Many, however, still are European educated and have fit into the hierarchy in a manner quite similar to their predecessors. The Egyptian bureaucracy remains a generally conservative force within a regime that is outwardly revolutionary. Traditionally subservient and never a great source of legislative initiative, the civil service in Egypt has been slow to transform itself into a revolutionary force comparable in any way to the CPSU apparatus. It is still more comparable to the Soviet state bureaucracy—relatively weak and subject to the whims of top political leaders. Indeed, it should be emphasized Egypt has really not attacked many old institutions (including the bureaucracy) because of a basic commitment of the leadership to Egyptian nationalism. For example, Egyptian law codes adopted in the 1950s were not revolutionary inventions, but were adaptations of Islamic precedents to the modern age. Similarly, the personnel of the bureaucracy has been "Egyptianized" (as has the private economic sector), but the manner of business itself is not very different from before.

Revolutionary fervor, the use of the secret police, and reliance on the military in some civil areas have affected Egyptian bureaucratic behavior to some extent, however. Today, Egyptian administrators are more efficient and less corrupt than those under Faruk because the former must compete with other factions within the elite. The regime's commitment to economic growth has meant administrators are closely watched and evaluated when they are involved in important economic projects.

The stress on economic policy has had an important effect on the Egyptian bureaucracy in other ways. The recruitment of economic specialists in recent years has meant the relative decline of the old-fashioned bureaucratic "gentleman" within the administration itself. Today new administrators in Egypt must have some technical expertise, and if they wish to climb the hidden hierarchy to power, they have to impress the modernizing segments of the Egyptian elite—the military and nationalist politicians. This has led to greater activity among bureaucrats in economic planning and implementation. It is clear that today these new modern bureaucrats have increased in influence compared to the old administration and are a key element in the regime of President Sadat. They have gained in influence because they have successfully introduced and enforced broad economic and social reforms in Egypt.

Policymaking in Egypt Today

Egyptian government and policy processes are today in a state of rapid transformation. In the past the country has been ruled in an authoritarian manner with the people passively accepting rule from above. Politically, this state of affairs is probably still a fairly accurate picture of the policymaking process in Egypt. However, the regime is committed to economic planning and an increase in the country's standard of living. In carrying out successful economic and social reform it has raised the expectations of many groups of people. All these activities are being carried out without the monolithic control of thought and activity characteristic of the USSR. Today, Egypt has a small elite that makes and carries out the major policy decisions and includes only a small number of factions. Already, however, substantial changes in the participation process have occurred. The Arab Socialist Union, while not a totalitarian party compared to the CPSU, now has branches at the local level. It represents many different groups in Egyptian society. Since the death of President Nasser, power is in the hands of President Sadat—a politician with a civilian, not a military background. Politics is still hidden and controlled, but groups never important before are emerging. Overall, Egypt remains a noncompetitive state, but not so monolithic or pervasive in her authoritarianism as the Soviet Union.

PEOPLE'S REPUBLIC OF CHINA

As is true of the USSR, the PRC is a party-dominated state in which the CCP and the government bureaucracy are closely interlinked and top party officials make most important day-to-day and long-term decisions. Although both countries claim to be Marxist-Leninist systems and both emphasize ideological rhetoric, political processes are somewhat different in these two noncompetitive states.

The Administrative Structure Today

Despite tight centralization in the Chinese Communist party hierarchy, there has always existed a more provincial autonomy in the PRC than in the USSR. The provincial governments have become especially important since 1957, with the creation of the party political bureaus at this level.

Viewed from the top Chinese government has been divided into major functional systems dealing with agriculture and forestry, culture and education, finance and trade, foreign affairs, industry and communication, and political and legal affairs. These are headed by vice premiers of the State Council, many of whom are members of the Politburo. Theoretically, directives flow from the top down, but certain lower-level branches have shared decisionmaking with national party committees. As in the USSR, the formal position of the Chinese system is that the party sets the policy and the government agencies carry it out, supervised by party committees. In carrying out policy the Chinese government has been quite pragmatic in outlook and has emphasized technical over ideological considerations, frequently disregarding party guidelines. The political departments of the party's Central Committee try to ease friction between ministries and party committees. However, as seen in 1957 at the time of "Hundred Flowers," and even more so during the Cultural Revolution, the party has tried to "rectify" intellectuals and technicians and transform their thoughts into the mold of the party line. This was done primarily by propaganda and terror, though overall the Chinese system has not engaged in the massive use of violent purges so characteristic of the USSR. Even the Cultural Revolution led to replacements of individuals in particular political positions, and not mass murders.

As in the USSR, Chinese top ranking party officials occupy the highest positions in the governmental structure and bureaucracy. The CCP maintains committees—the "fractions"—within many parts of the bureaucracy at lower levels. Also, policy directives are often jointly issued by the Central Committee and the State Council with prior Politburo approval.

The Chinese governmental structure is parliamentary on paper and as the CCP dominates the government, the executive dominates the other branches of government. Legislating is done by the Politburo of the Central Committee, the National People's Congress, and the State Council. Justice has, as in the USSR, been reinterpreted to serve the interest of the party. Courts and laws serve "the People," via a hierarchy of "People's Courts." Laws have remained largely uncodified and changeable with regard to particular circumstances; criminal acts are today dealt with in the traditional manner, but political offenses are dealt with more harshly. As in the USSR, the actual development of policy processes in the PRC are a reflection of ideological wranglings among the top leaders.

Democracy is ideologically defined by the Chinese Communists in terms of its functions for the party. First, individual party members and local party organizations are to develop creative and positive thought by vigorous discussion—both prerequisites for leadership and decisionmaking ability. Second, democracy implies the strengthening of ties between the party and the masses, enabling the latter to have a true role in public policy formulation. Last, the broadened intraparty democracy should give more autonomy to regional organizations, which can better meet local needs.

These principles taken together allow for flexibility; however, the underlying theory of contradictions developed by Mao prevents widespread deviation from the party. According to the chairman, the PRC was subject to two types of contradictions—antagonistic and nonantagonistic. The former are those contradictions between "the People" (arbitrarily defined as workers, peasants, and bourgeoisie), and the bourgeois-capitalist classes. These struggles are today said to be unimportant since the Communists have firm political control. There are, however, also struggles within the ranks of "the People"—between, for example, the "nation" and individuals, the leaders and the masses, and ideology and pragmatism. These contradictions must be resolved, and, according to Mao, the correct resolutions to them lie within the fundamental consensus as to "the People's" interests. He reasons that only the party, as the Leninist vanguard of "the People," can guarantee solutions to these problems. They are to be found and implemented by rectification of the cadres and the intellectuals via discussion and criticism, and adherence to the Marxism-Leninism and party directives.[7]

Recent Upheavals in Public Policy

These underlying principles of organization are the ideological bases upon which the CCP seeks to unify the state and society. The party-government leadership had, however, before the Cultural Revolution diverged into two alternative policy lines. This was a partial result of the great economic failures of the Great Leap Forward, which produced much public dissatisfaction. This party split, which pitted Mao against Liu Shao-chi, another high-ranking Central Committee member, was made public in 1966 and constituted the major political confrontation of the Cultural Revolution. Mao's personal dominance had to be demonstrated, and this was done after 1966 through youth groups and cadres ideologically loyal to the chairman. The cadres loyal to Liu were overthrown.

In terms of the country's revolution and modernization, Mao has stressed the moral pursuit of justice and virtue while Liu emphasized the need for technical planning and new progress. The policy dispute was between the view that the voluntarism of the people, once mobilized, could foster the revolution; and the view that the material base of society, the relations of production, would have to be changed before the superstructure—political, social, and cultural life—could also be changed.

There are additional instances of the policy conflicts. For example: (1) the mass line versus party building—Mao wanted the cadres to serve the people, indoctrinating them with revolutionary spirit; Liu and other pragmatists preferred to subordinate this party struggle to party unity, stressing the training of party members and cadres to become a new elite that could guide social transformations; (2) village versus city—Mao idealized the man of the soil, disdaining city life. He hoped for a self-sufficient countryside of farmers, craftsmen, and militia soldiers. However, practical party leaders recognized the need for industrialization and an urban elite of educated and professional people. These were required to hasten the path toward modernization; (3) Red

versus expert, the politically trained versus the professionals and technicians—In the final analysis, the matter has come down to whether the PRC
should alter her goals and become revisionist or maintain the continuous
revolution of struggle within "The People." It now appears that the conflict has
not been entirely resolved. The Cultural Revolution saw the displacement of
Liu's pragmatists by Mao's idealists; today, however, the regime once again
appears to be veering on a pragmatic course under the leadership of Premier
Chou-en-lai.

Policymaking in the PRC

As in the USSR and Egypt, the process of decisionmaking and leadership
selection in the PRC usually is well hidden among factional groupings within the
top party elite. Despite the fact there are regional and military groups that are
not integrated into the party structure as directly as their counterparts in the
USSR, the party is a powerful administrative tool that commands mass loyalty. It
is not a weak facade as the ASU is in Egypt.

The People's Republic of China is a poor, developing country. Effective
implementation of the laws is very difficult under these circumstances. The
Chinese Communist party lacks the physical power of the CPSU to mobilize and
reeducate its total population. Its reach is narrower, and the Cultural Revolution
was clear evidence the party was not so unified at the top that factional splits
could not spill over into great public upheavals. The Chinese government must
bear great pressures from a people taught to expect and forced to work hard for a
higher living standard. Because of the accepted state ideology, participation in
the political process remains limited to the elite. More than similar pressures in
the USSR and Egypt, these pressures in the PRC and the party's inherent
factionalism have spilled out into the open. This does not mean that the PRC is
any more open to free political debate and discussion than the other two
countries; it does mean that factionalism may be deeper or more difficult to
confine within party circles.

Comparative Distinctions in Political Processes and Public Policy Among Noncompetitive States

Political processes in noncompetitive states vary in accordance with each
state's level of economic development, devotion to traditional political practices, respect for regional diversity, and commitment to national modernization
programs.

Of the three noncompetitive states discussed here the Soviet Union is the
most highly developed, has the strongest commitment to national mobilization,
and is least concerned about local traditional habits or provincial rights. Thus
the Soviet Communist party dominates the nation's policymaking and enforcement processes down to the lowest levels and in all regions. The CPSU,
maintaining control over the military and police, has been able to develop and
enforce policy, at times using quite violent tactics. More than politics in Egypt
and the PRC, Soviet politics is confined to elite party circles in which the nation's
major policy decisions are made.

While the People's Republic of China is also a Marxist state governed by a
fairly centralized political party that has strong local links, provincial and

regional considerations affect policymaking more than in the USSR. In the PRC, because of general poverty and the low level of economic development, government does not always have the resources to enforce its will on local political units. Also, the regime professes to respect a certain degree of regional autonomy (a traditional concept in the PRC), and seeks the cooperation of constituent parts of the Chinese state. Chinese government has not been as prone as Soviet government to use violence and terror to ensure the enforcement of national policy. On the other hand, factional disagreements over approaches to policy among the Chinese elite have erupted into public upheavals like the Cultural Revolution. Overall, however, as in the USSR, political processes in China are dominated by a small elite governing through the top levels of the Communist party.

Egypt is unlike the USSR and PRC in that policy in Egypt is not made and enforced by a tightly organized elite, governing through a mass political party. The Egyptian leadership group formulates public policy through informal closed door meetings in which representatives of competing civilian and military elites bargain with one another. Policy decisions are enforced by a relatively traditional bureaucracy, which has always been subservient to the prevailing political leadership. While Egypt is, like the People's Republic of China, a modernizing state devoted to raising the living standards of her people, she permits local and traditional leaders to bargain within the circles of the elite. As in the other two states, policy processes in Egypt are controlled by a small elite in an authoritarian manner, but (unlike the other two states) these processes are not hierarchically and centrally organized in a party structure.

POLITICAL PROCESSES AND PUBLIC POLICY: COMPARING COMPETITIVE; FRAGMENTED; AND NONCOMPETITIVE STATES

Competitive states have highly institutionalized political processes. In such states, rival groups compromise their differences in reaching policy decisions through open electoral politics, representative legislatures, and open interest group activity. Day-to-day activities are carried on by bureaucracies sheltered to some extent from politics, but local government and organized private groups can represent differing points of view and affect policymaking at the national and local levels. Competitive states tend to be quite effective in reaching and legitimizing policy decisions, but their capacity for enforcing these decisions varies with their respective levels of economic development and consequent effectiveness of their administrative services.

Fragmented states do not have strong policymaking institutions because the constituent political groups in these states that seek to affect policy are generally unable to moderate their differences. Thus elections and legislatures are generally unable to produce majorities or coalitions capable of legitimizing policy decisions. The result is the atrophy of representative institutions, with the concentration of decisionmaking authority in the hands of an executive who strives to govern through an insulated bureaucracy or military establishment. These states retain their group differences, however, and leaders in such states tend to keep their policies moderate and noncontroversial in order to avoid aggravating group conflicts. Political processes thus are relatively weak in terms of the government being able to initiate new programs. In terms of enforcement, as in competitive states, day-to-day government activities depend on the level of development of the state's administrative services.

In noncompetitive states the established elite makes the public policy decisions, consulting with technical experts to some extent. In this sense an informal group process can affect policy decisions. However, there are no open institutionalized processes by which the elite can be challenged on policy decisions. As in other states, the ability of a state to execute its policy decisions depends on the effectiveness of its administration and its basic level of public support and legitimacy.

NOTES TO CHAPTER 6

1. Scotland, Wales, Northern Ireland, the Isle of Man, and the Channel Islands all have some degree of autonomy.

2. *See* Robert L. Hardgrave, Jr., *India* (New York: Harcourt, Brace & World, 1970) pp. 64-77.

3. Henry W. Ehrmann, *Politics in France* (Boston: Little, Brown, 1968), Chapts. 9, 10.

4. *International Financial Statistics* (Washington, D.C.: International Monetary Fund, May 1974), pp. 184-5.

5. In *Review of Indonesian and Malayan Affairs*, vol. 2, no. 2 (April-June 1968): 72.

6. Frederick C. Barghoorn, *Politics in the USSR* (Boston: Little, Brown, 1972), Chapts. 7, 8.

7. H. F. Schurmann, "Organization Principles of the Chinese Communists," in Roderick MacFarquahar, ed., *China Under Mao: Politics Takes Command* (Cambridge, Mass.: MIT Press, 1966), pp. 87-90.

Chapter 7

General Assessment: Comparing Different Political Systems

ASSUMPTIONS OF THIS STUDY

We have begun our study of modern political systems, on the basis of certain assumptions, outlined in Chapter 1. We have defined politics as the actions and behavior patterns taken by citizens (in every kind of state) in attempting to arrive at joint policies and decisions. Implicit in this definition is the proposition that politics is a universal human phenomenon—that all human beings, no matter who they are or how they live, will in fact seek joint policies and decisions. We have thus assumed that all political structures have a social basis and they strive to attain the same goal—the maximum legitimacy and efficiency in converting each system's conception of public expectations and demands into reality.

Despite the generality of these assumptions, we have noted particular political procedures vary from place to place and time to time, because politics is a reflection of particular social orders, and the latter are also hypothetical structures that are quite variable. Thus people are assumed to interact with one another in all systems, but some societies from this point of view are much more highly integrated than others. Integrated societies have strong cultural links; these communities in general have a broad consensus on social values, they usually have a well-defined language and literature and a great degree of ethnic homogeneity. In addition, they are often highly integrated economically, with a well-structured division of labor. This usually implies an established organization for training and educating their populations, both for general culture and for technical skills. In contrast there also exist societies that are weakly integrated, and this also is reflected in their political structures.

Societies which vary considerably in important respects, are often theoretically analyzed into subgroups. We have in this study assumed all societies have leadership groups that are more active than other social entities in the political sphere. We thus have assumed every social system has some kind of political elite, though again elites can vary from one another in many ways. They can differ in style of decisionmaking—emphasizing traditional, bureaucratic, or charismatic appeals. They can also differ in background—in the manner in which they have been socialized and recruited into their respective systems. All elites, however, must attain legitimacy in the opinion of the important groups within their societies. They must be able to demonstrate they are the most appropriate and "correct" leadership groups for their particular political units. The manner in which elites attempt to achieve legitimacy again varies considerably among systems.

These broad theoretical generalities do not tell us a great deal about particular political systems unless we further categorize the general ideas in terms of more specific concepts. Thus we have theoretically subdivided the political process into three stages: inputs (where social demands and supports are felt); outputs (where political decisions are carried into effect arousing public opinion); and conversion processes (where inputs are transformed into outputs by politicians and administrators, working through particular governmental structures). In doing so, we have assumed all political systems attempt to convert inputs into outputs and, in general, all systems must solve the same basic problems, though they may choose different structures for accomplishing this. The final choice of legitimate political process is a reflection of the basic social fabric itself and the deep-seated public beliefs and values that this fabric implies.

Finally, in addition to subdividing the political process for analytic purposes, we have also categorized political systems into three major theoretical types, each corresponding to a particular style of society and value system. We have labeled these three kinds of system, competitive, fragmented, and noncompetitive, each type referring to the subgroup system, the type and level of political inputs, and the nature of the conversion processes it uses. We have assumed all political systems must fall into one of these three categories, though we have recognized in the real world all political systems have certain features in common. Because we have defined the nature of the political process, we assume the three types can be compared.

We have thus made a great number of assumptions and have accepted a great many general propositions. Now we must assess what we have learned at least in a general sense from all of this. How do the three categories of states compare with one another in terms of political efficiency? How are policy processes affected by such general phenomena as ideology and economic development? Can we predict anything about future political development or transformation from one type of system to another? How do particular variables (i. e., interest groups, socialization patterns, levels of political participation, political parties, policy processes) affect our general conclusions about these types of systems? The following is an attempt to provide some answers to these questions.

COMPETITIVE STATES

We have analyzed the political processes of three competitive political states—Great Britain, India, and Chile. Each state represents a different religious and cultural background, a different level of economic development, and broad geographic and population differences. However, all have some important similarities in their political structures.

First, despite their sharp religious and cultural differences, each country's social structure has a coherence and internal unity that is well recognized by its citizens. In terms of the pattern of political socialization and recruitment in each state, there are great differences in magnitude: Great Britain is a highly literate, educated state; India has low levels of mass education and literacy; and Chile falls somewhere in between. However, all three states (with the exception very recently of Chile) have had a highly educated, unified elite that runs the political system of the country and that exemplifies the values of the politically aware in each system. Thus we can say competitive states have political elites that believe in open discussion and debate and in preserving the competitive rules of the political game. This was also true for Chile for most of the time she was a competitive state. In observing these three states, we can also say competition appears to be related to a sense of unity within the elite—a broad consensus and mutual trust and understanding of basic issues—and a similar unity linking the elite to most of the mass public. All three countries have (again, except for Chile) strong national identifications, little tradition of relying on force and violence in enforcing political decisions, and a strong strain of conservatism when it comes to changing political procedures. When we make these general comments, the election of President Allende in Chile becomes an interesting example of the difficulty of maintaining competitive politics when an elite losses its unity of purpose. President Allende was the first chief executive since World War II to be freely elected in an open competitive system with major support from ideological, nondemocratic groups. The issue of the Allende presidency was whether it was possible for a regime committed to Marxist economic and social reform to retain for long an open, competitive electoral process that permits the equal participation of non-Marxist groups. The election of Allende split Chilean political circles on this question, and his presidency lost the unity of political support from the middle classes necessary to maintain Chile's constitutional processes. The result has thus been a military coup, but it is as yet unclear what sort of permanent regime will eventually be restored.

The question of economic development and change is thus a basic one for these societies and is directly related to political activities in all three states. It appears as a political issue in election campaigns, and its presence is felt at all levels of society. These three states are extremely different in terms of overall economic development: Great Britain is highly developed; Chile is moderately developed; and India is very poor. Because Great Britain's economy is highly developed and her people are well fed, educated, and trained, that country has a widespread system of political recruitment and participation; Chile's economy is only moderately developed, and many Chileans are not yet fully part of the country's political process; in India, probably a majority of the people are not effectively heard in the political system at all.

Economic development also seems to affect the output of the systems in terms of policymaking. Because Great Britain has a high per capita income and is well developed technologically, government servants are well trained and confident; they have good communications facilities and other resources and can convert government policy into action with great efficiency. Chile is only moderately successful in this, and India is not very efficient at all.

Despite the differences in economic levels, all three states have had one achievement in common—strong civilian political party organizations dedicated to achieving popular support and progress. All three states have had elite political groups that, through interest groups and communications structures, attempt to enlighten and persuade the public to their views. In particular form the three countries are somewhat different: Great Britain basically has a two-party system; Chile, even after the coup, has a multiparty system; and India is one-party dominant. However, the major parties in all three countries have generally been committed to negotiation and compromise and have sought mass support. They have played an overriding role in the political system, because they have made political competition real and because they have drawn the broad masses of the people, in all their differences, into political decisionmaking. In Chile the bringing of the masses into politics by the Marxist parties made competition and negotiation difficult because this meant a new sharing of power with groups in Chilean society that did not wish to share. Thus, rapid popular mobilization of the poor was resented by the middle classes and contributed to the instability and eventual overthrow of the Allende regime.

FRAGMENTED STATES

The three fragmented states discussed in this book—France, Indonesia, and Zaire—also are an extremely varied group of countries culturally. Each is situated on a different continent and represents a different background and value system: France is a modern secular state with a Roman Catholic tradition; Indonesia is poorly developed and Islamic; and Zaire is poor, tribal, animist, with only limited Christian influence.

In all three states, subgroup loyalties are very strong; people feel their families and/or tribes and villages (and, in France, political movements) are more vital to their personal identifications than the nation. France, in particular, has had great difficulty through centuries of political violence in achieving a stable national identity within her population; Indonesia and Zaire have also had poorly unified nationalist movements and occasional outbreaks of physical violence in times of national political crisis.

Unlike competitive states, these three countries have not been able to establish unified cohesive leadership groups capable of speaking to the values of the mass of their respective populations. Rather, each nation's elite has been subdivided into warring factions, incapable of compromising their positions and subsequently dividing the population behind them. In these nations, subgroups recruit and socialize their members to political actions and beliefs; there is no single system by which the people are drawn into politics in such manner that they can agree on basic constitutional norms.

As with elites in competitive states, elites in these countries tend to emphasize varied appeals. Leaders attempt to project themselves variously as traditional, bureaucratic, or charismatic. However, because these societies are so fragmented and traditional norms tend to work against unity, leaders usually attempt to project themselves as charismatic, promoting their own personalities as symbols of national identification. Usually this is done while relying on some bureaucratic structure—either a civil or military administration—for needed practical support.

These political systems all proclaim themselves to be representative of their people, and, indeed, France is (unlike the other two) a state that holds open competitive elections. However, the pressing needs of national unity are so great in all three states the governing groups tend to create great advantages for themselves in all political exchanges with their opposition. Thus in France, the president legally dominates the mass media, can bypass the legislature, and can carry on the government through his administration no matter what opposition parties do. Indonesia's leader, General Suharto, has gone considerably further. He has permitted some semblance of party competition, but his adminsistration has been directly involved in his achieving an overwhelming majority of seats in the national legislature. Zaire, the most extreme example, has only one party, that which is pledged to President Mobutu. France is thus ruled by a civilian elite that governs through the civilian administration; Indonesia and Zaire both have military leaders who, though they have established some superficial civilian institutions, dominate the political structure because of their support within the military.

The political output of these three countries varies, as it does in competitive states, partly because of their differing levels of economic development. France is a highly developed country with a well-trained administrative service. In France, when political decisions are made, they are effectively carried out; the public is aware of this and can react in a manner obvious to political leaders. Both Indonesia and Zaire are highly illiterate countries with poor means of communication and inefficient civil bureaucracies. In these two states, many policies never reach much of the population, who live in tribal groups cut off economically from the capital cities. In such states, the military is generally a more far-reaching bureaucratic structure than the civil administration (i. e., it covers a wider geographic area of the country). There is often no way for many people to react to government in these states in a manner that can have any political effect, except perhaps mass rioting.

Thus we can see despite great individual differences there are certain patterns of similarity in the manner in which fragmented political systems perform their functions. In terms of political socialization and recruitment, these states tend to lack a national structure. Political beliefs and values are generally communicated by separate and discrete subunits, many differing over the concept of nation and nature of politics. Political recruitment also occurs through the subgroups—the tribes, the villages, the regional political parties. Persons active in politics begin as provincial leaders, usually retaining their provincial loyalties above all else. The national state is a weak object of loyalty, when compared to its position in the attitudes of elites in competitive political systems.

Fragmented states vary in levels of political participation, largely owing to varying levels of economic development. France is a highly literate country with a large newspaper-reading public. She has many political organizations, and French people are aware of and alert to political issues. French elections have wide voter turnouts and people often demonstrate their beliefs in the street. Both Indonesia and Zaire lack the aware publics and the organizational and communications facilities that make wide public participation possible. In this sense, it should be noted France also has a much more highly organized interest group and political party structure than the other two countries, for many of the same reasons. In France, public demonstrations are usually the work of organized groups; in Indonesia and Zaire, riots tend to be amorphous and disorganized with little or no specific purpose.

As already noted, France is much more effective in policymaking and enforcement than either Indonesia or Zaire because of her great economic advantages. However, all three countries share the fundamental problem facing all fragmented societies: political cohesion is weak and temporary so that far-reaching decisions frequently are avoided rather than made. These states must make every effort to avoid alienating and antagonizing important elements in society. The tendency for all three states is thus to be relatively conservative on policy matters, especially domestic policy, which directly bears on the internal population. When domestic policy initiatives are made, these countries often have great difficulty in enforcing them because of the relative lack of public support behind the regime. Thus, governments in these states are generally weak and short-lived; they generally avoid decisions, but when they try to make policy, they often are threatened with coups and are overturned.

It should be noted the French Fifth Republic today presents an interesting attempt to break out of the fragmented mold into a more unified competitive system. Gaullist government in France has been strong government (but almost entirely in the realm of foreign, not domestic, policy), attaining its will by using special advantages over its electoral opposition. While quite conservative, it has lasted more than fifteen years and has therefore not been short-lived. President Giscard d'Estaing, following President Pompidou, must make his government appear effective, constitutional, and supported by a majority of the population. His party, a small minority, must attempt to restructure traditional French socialization and recruitment processes so that the French public learns to view its governing coalition as a truly "national" leadership. It is as yet unclear whether the Gaullist-conservative coalition will retain its ruling majority status, now with the passing of the two Gaullist presidents—de Gaulle and Pompidou. Gaullism today appears dead in France, but it is uncertain what sort of politics will take its place.

NONCOMPETITIVE STATES

Our three noncompetitive states—the USSR, Egypt, and the PRC—are as varied a group as the states in the other two categories. The USSR is a European state with a Christian background, though today it professes a pronounced atheism; Egypt is a North African state with a pious Islamic population; and the PRC is the seat of the ancient Chinese Empire with its complex population makeup and Buddhist-Confucian ethic. The cultural and value structures in these states differ in many respects, but as with cultural and value structures in competitive and fragmented states, they show certain patterns of similarity.

All three countries have a very long history of being unified states. While not equally homogeneous in terms of ethnic makeup, all three have a national language, a national literature, and a concept of legitimate national state that overrides subgroup loyalties.

All three have highly unified elites that try to achieve a definite ideological uniformity that can be communicated to the rest of the population. Tremendous emphasis is placed in all three states on absolute unity within the elite; while some form of conflict is inevitable in every human system, the cultural norms in these noncompetitive nations cause leaders to cloak and disguise their differences by manipulating their rhetoric and by using vague ideological slogans.

Styles of leadership do vary among these states: tradition and charisma, for instance, is far more evident in elite appeals in Egypt than in the other two states. However, all three, because of their emphasis on elite unity and ideology, are fundamentally bureaucratic states whose elites are highly organized in a hierarchical manner.

Despite these great points of similarity, the three political systems do afford some major contrasts in the manner in which they perform their political functions. The USSR, which is most highly developed of the three states economically, has the most far-reaching system of political socialization and recruitment. Every Soviet citizen is part of the socialization process through the vast array of schools, mass organizations, and party cells that permeate all of Soviet social and industrial life. Egypt and the PRC strive to achieve the same result as the USSR, but they have been less successful. It should be noted Egypt is not quite as committed to total mobilization as the USSR is. Also, large populations in Egypt and the PRC are still not closely tied to the country's communication structure and are, therefore, outside the socialization process. Many persons in these two countries are illiterate and find politics to be quite remote.

Political participation is a very important function in all three states, and all have established mass political parties and large numbers of organizations and groups that serve a double purpose: they educate the people as to the desires of the elite and they foment support for the regime. In many respects they actually override the civil bureaucracies in these states, since bureaucrats must be more concerned about the party line than about any dictates of particular government officials.

In terms of political output, as with the other two categories, much is dependent on levels of economic development. All three noncompetitive states are dominated by their bureaucracies. Of the three, the Soviet bureaucracy is the strongest, most highly developed, and most effective in making and enforcing policy. The Soviet administrative structure is vast and well-trained and reacts to every whim of the party elite. In contrast, the Chinese bureaucracy has been a source of conflict, since there are so few trained administrators in the PRC that they cannot readily be replaced. Chinese politicians seek support among bureaucrats, because the PRC is still a vast and underdeveloped nation difficult to administer. Policy is not easily carried to the poorer regions in which people are still mostly living on subsistence agriculture. Politicians must cajole and persuade the Chinese bureaucracy, and though they use many of the techniques of the Soviet Communist party, they generally stop short of violence and terror. Egypt is also a bureaucratic state that has had some of the problems of the Chinese, but Egypt is a smaller country, and most of her people are concentrated in a small geographic area. Policy in Egypt (as in the PRC) is fairly efficiently administered in urban areas but is not very effectively enforced in outlying areas.

COMPARATIVE POLITICS AND WORLD POLITICS

What have we learned from our observations of the three types of political system? We have seen all systems have inputs, outputs, and conversion processes. However, the degree of competition and fragmentation in a state affects the inputs to which leaders must react.

When a state is fragmented, it is internally weakened. Its policies are the results of compromise among deeply opposed groups and often so are its actions. In contrast, a country with a unified noncompetitive elite can reach forceful decisions and bring them to effect, whether they are empirically correct or not. This kind of system has little opportunity of testing policies and relatively poor methods of holding public officials accountable for their efficiency, honesty, and competence in office. Thus the choice of a bad policy may go undetected until it results in a catastrophic event—an internal riot or the loss of a foreign war, for example. Internal control and criticism are thus more vital to noncompetitive states than to competitive states, where control and criticism are integrated into the political processes.

Highly competitive states can appear to be weak and divided but, in fact, can often have effective policymaking procedures. Once a policy in such a state has been debated and adopted it normally will have been modified according to open criticisms and will have achieved wide public support. In contrast, leaders in fragmented and noncompetitive states can only guess as to their levels of support and must always protect themselves by various legal and control measures in case of great misjudgments.

It is obvious from these theoretical generalizations interactions among these different kinds of states can be quite difficult. Fragmented and noncompetitive states may reach policies on an often nonrational basis. The former depend on compromises among weak political groups; the latter, on compromises among hidden factions in a closed elite. Open rhetoric in these states may not correspond to reality, and other states must beware of assuming too much about them. In these differences can be found the seeds of international distrust, a problem the world still must resolve to the advantage of all political units, no matter their internal organization.

Different states must have relations with one another because of the necessity for international trade and the drive of all political units for military security and political influence. Foreign political relations, indeed, constitute an important demand or input in every political system. International conflict and competition is thus normal, but today in the age of nuclear weapons, it has become recognized this competition must be regulated and controlled. Today we must therefore learn as much as possible about the internal workings of all kinds of political systems so that we can try to harmonize our policies and avoid costly wars.

Selected Bibliography

CHAPTER 1: THE POLITICAL SYSTEM

Almond, Gabriel A., and Powell, G. Bingham. *Comparative Politics: A Developmental Approach*. Boston: Little, Brown and Co., 1966.

Almond, Gabriel A., and Coleman, James S. *The Politics of the Developing Areas*. Princeton: Princeton University Press, 1960.

_____, et al., eds. *Crisis, Choice and Change: Historical Studies of Political Development*. Boston: Little, Brown and Co., 1973.

Anderson, Charles W., Von der Mehden, Fred W., and Young, M. Crawford. *Issues of Political Development*. Englewood Cliffs, N.J.: Prentice-Hall, 1967.

Apter, David E. *The Politics of Modernization*. Chicago: University of Chicago Press, 1965.

Aristotle. *Politics*. Translated by Benjamin Jowett. New York: Viking Press, 1952.

Bentley, Arthur F. *The Process of Government*. Chicago: University of Chicago Press, 1908.

Bill, James A., and Hardgrave, Jr., Robert L. *Comparative Politics: The Quest for Theory*. Columbus, Ohio: Charles E. Merrill, 1973.

Binder, Leonard, et al. *Crisis and Sequences in Political Development*. Princeton: Princeton University Press, 1971.

Blondel, Jean. *An Introduction to Comparative Government*. New York: Frederick A. Praeger, 1970.

Dahl, Robert A. *A Preface to Democratic Theory*. Chicago: University of Chicago Press, 1956.

_____. *Modern Political Analysis*. Englewood Cliffs, N.J.: Prentice-Hall, 1963.

Down, Anthony. *An Economic Theory of Democracy*. New York: Harper and Row, 1957.

Easton, David. *The Political System.* New York: Knopf, 1953.

_____. *A Framework for Political Analysis*. Englewood Cliffs, N. J.: Prentice-Hall, 1965.

Galbraith, John Kenneth. *American Capitalism: The Theory of Countervailing Power*. Boston: Houghton Mifflin, 1956.

Inkeles, Alex. "Soviet Union: Model for Asia?," *Problems of Communism* (November-December 1959): 30-8.

Lipset, Seymour M. *Political Man*. Garden City, N.Y.: Doubleday, 1960.

Locke, John. "Second Treatise on Civil Government." In *Readings in Political Philosophy*. Edited by F.W. Coker. New York: Macmillan Co., 1942.

Marx, Karl. *Capital and Other Writings*. New York: Modern Library, 1932.

Organski, A.F.K. *The Stages of Political Development*. New York: Knopf, 1965.

Pitkin, Hannah F. *The Concept of Representation*. Berkeley and Los Angeles: University of California Press, 1967.

Plato. *The Republic*. Translated by Benjamin Jowett. New York: Random House, 1952.

Pye, Lucian W. *Aspects of Political Development*. Boston: Little, Brown and Co., 1966.

Rousseau, Jean-Jacques. *The Social Contract*. Chicago: Henry Regnery Co., 1954.

Truman, David B. *The Governmental Process*. New York: Knopf, 1951.

Weber, Max. "Politics as a Vocation." In *From Max Weber*. Edited by H. Gerth and C.W. Mills. New York: Oxford University Press, 1946.

CHAPTER 2: STRUCTURAL AND INSTITUTIONAL DIFFERENCES AMONG POLITICAL SYSTEMS

Andrews, W. G., ed. *Constitutions and Constitutionalism*. Princeton: Van Nostrand, 1961.

Armstrong, John A. *Ideology, Politics and Government in the Societ Union*. New York: Frederick Praeger, 1967.

Barnard, C. I. *The Functions of the Executive*. Cambridge, Mass.: Harvard University Press, 1971.

Blondel, Jean. *Comparative Legislatures*. Englewood Cliffs, N.J.: Prentice-Hall, 1972.

Brzezinski, Zbignieu, and Huntington, Samuel P. *Political Power, USA/USSR*. New York: Viking Press, 1965.

Chapman, Brian. *The Profession of Government*. New York: Humanities Press, 1966.

Duchacek, Ivo D. *Comparative Federalism*. New York: Holt, Rinehart and Winston, 1970.

Frank, Elke, ed. *Lawmakers in a Changing World*. Englewood Cliffs, N.J.: Prentice-Hall, 1966.

Janowitz, Morris. *The Military in the Political Development of the New Nations*. Chicago: University of Chicago Press, 1963.

Jennings, W. Ivor. *Cabinet Government*. Cambridge: Cambridge University Press, 1959.

Kornberg, A., ed. *Legislatures in Comparative Perspective*. New York: David McKay, 1973.

Kornberg, A., and Musolf, L. D. *Legislatures in Developmental Perspective*. Durham, N.C.: Duke University Press, 1970.

La Palombara, Joseph, ed. *Bureaucracy and Political Development*. Princeton: Princeton University Press, 1963.

Meacham, J. Lloyd. "Latin American Constitutions: Nominal and Real," *Journal of Politics* (May 1959): 258-76.

Pennock, J. Roland, and Chapman, J. W. *Nomos X: Representation*. New York: Atherton Press, 1968.

Rae, Douglas W. *The Political Consequences of Electoral Laws*. New Haven: Yale University Press, 1971.

Scarrow, Howard A. "Parliamentary and Presidential Government Compared," *Current History* (June 1974): 264-7, 272.

Shils, Edward A. "Political Development in the New States," *Comparative Studies in Society and History*, vol. 2, no. 3 (March 1960): 265-92; no. 4 (June 1960): 379-411.

Wahlke, J. and Eulau, H., eds. *Legislative Behavior: A Reader in Theory and Research*. Glencoe, Ill.: The Free Press, 1959.

Wheare, K. C. *Federal Government*. London and New York: Oxford University Press, 1963.

——————. *Legislatures*. London and New York: Oxford Univerisity Press, 1963.

——————. *Modern Constitutions*. London and New York: Oxford University Press, 1966.

CHAPTER 3: POLITICAL CULTURE AND SOCIALIZATION

Adorno, T. W. et al. *The Authoritarian Personality*. New York: Harper and Row, 1950.

Almond, Gabriel A., and Verba, Sidney. *The Civic Culture: Political Attitudes and Democracy in Five Nations*. Princeton: Princeton University Press, 1963.

Apter, David E., ed. *Ideology and Discontent*. Glencoe, Ill.: The Free Press, 1964.

Bendix, Reinhard. *Nation Building and Citizenship*. New York: Wiley, 1964.

Bluhm, W. T. *Ideologies and Attitudes: Modern Political Culture*. Englewood Cliffs, N.J.: Prentice-Hall, 1974.

Dennis, Jack, ed. *Socialization to Politics: A Reader*. New York: Wiley, 1973.

Deutsch, Karl, W. *Nationalism and its Alternatives*. New York: Knopf, 1969.

Easton, David, and Dennis, Jack. *Children in the Political System: Origins of Political Legitimacy*. New York: McGraw-Hill, 1969.

Edinger, L. J., ed. *Political Leadership in Industrialized Societies*. New York: Wiley, 1967.

Greenstein, Fred. *Children and Politics*. New Haven: Yale University Press, 1965.

Hoffer, Eric. *The True Believer: Thoughts on the Nature of Mass Movements*. New York: Harper and Row, 1951.

Johnson, Chalmers. *Revolutionary Change*. Boston: Little, Brown and Co., 1966.

Lipset, Seymour M. "Some Social Requisites of Democracy,"*American Political Science Review* (March 1959): 69-105.

Nordlinger, Eric A., ed. *Politics and Society: Studies in Comparative Political Sociology*. Englewood Cliffs, N.J.: Prentice-Hall, 1970.

Putnam, Robert D. *The Beliefs of Politicians*. New Haven: Yale University Press, 1973.

Pye, Lucian W., and Verba, Sidney, eds. *Political Culture and Political Development*. Princeton: Princeton University Press, 1965.

CHAPTER 4: POLITICAL PARTICIPATION

Bachrach, Peter. *Political Elites in a Democracy*. New York: Atherton Press, 1971.

Broomfield, J. H. *Elite Conflict in a Plural Society*. Berkeley and Los Angeles: University of California Press, 1968.

Butler, David E., and Stokes, Donald. *Political Change in Britain: Forces Shaping Electoral Choice*. New York: Macmillan Co., 1969.

Clark, J. M. *Teachers and Politics in France*. Syracuse, N.Y.: Syracuse University Press, 1967.

DiPalma, G. *Apathy and Participation*. New York: The Free Press, 1970.

_____. ed. *Mass Politics in Industrial Societies: A Reader in Comparative Politics*. Chicago: Markham Publishing Co., 1972.

Eckstein, Harry. *Pressure Group Politics: The Case of the British Medical Association*. Stanford: Stanford University Press, 1960.

Edinger, L. J. *Political Leadership in Industrialized Societies*. New York: Wiley, 1967.

Ehrmann, Henry W. *Organized Business in France*. Princeton: Princeton University Press, 1957.

_____. *Interest Groups on Four Continents*. Pittsburgh: Pittsburgh University Press, 1958.

Hamilton, R. *Affluence and the French Worker in the Fourth Republic*. Princeton: Princeton University Press, 1967.

Lane, Robert E. *Political Life: Why People Get Involved in Politics*. Glencoe, Ill.. The Free Press, 1959.

Lasswell, Harold D., et al. *The Comparative Study of Elites*. Stanford: Hoover Institution Studies, 1952.

Marvick, Duane. *Political Decision Makers: Recruitment and Performance*. Glencoe, Ill.: The Free Press, 1961.

Milbrath, Lester W. *Political Participation—How and Why People Get Involved in Politics*. Chicago: Rand-McNally Corp., 1962.

Millen, Bruce M. *The Political Role of Labor in Developing Countries*. Washington: The Brookings Institution, 1962.

Nordlinger, Eric A. *The Working Class Tories*. Berkeley: University of California Press, 1967.

Putnam, Robert D. *Comparative Political Elites*. Englewood Cliffs, N. J.: Prentice-Hall, 1974.

Rokkan, Stein, ed. *Approach to the Study of Political Participation*. Bergen: The Chr. Michelsen Institute, 1962.

Skilling, H. Gordon, and Griffiths, F. *Interest Groups in Soviet Politics*. Princeton: Princeton University Press, 1971.

Verba, Sidney, and Kim, J. "The Modes of Democratic Participation: A Cross-National Analysis." Sage Professional Papers in Comparative Politics, no. 01-013, 1971.

Weiner, Myron. *The Politics of Scarcity: Public Pressure and Political Response in India*. Chicago: University of Chicago Press, 1962.

CHAPTER 5: POLITICAL PARTIES

Alford, Robert. *Party and Society*. Chicago: Rand-McNally Corp., 1963.

Beck, C. et al. *Comparative Communist Party Leadership*. New York: David McKay, 1973.

Beer, Samuel H. *British Politics in the Collectivist Age*. New York: Knopf, 1965.

Campbell, Angus, et al. *Elections and the Political Order*. New York: Wiley, 1966.

Chambers, W. N. *Political Parties in a New Nation: The American Experience, 1776-1809*. New York: Oxford University Press, 1963.

Coleman, James S., and Rosberg, C. G. *Political Parties and National Integration in Tropical Africa.* Berkeley and Los Angeles: University of California Press, 1964.

Dahl, Robert A. *Political Opposition in Western Democracies.* New Haven: Yale University Press, 1966.

——————. *Regimes and Oppositions.* New Haven: Yale University Press, 1973.

Duverger, Maurice. *Political Parties.* London: Methuen, 1954.

Epstein, Leon D. *Political Parties in Western Democracies.* New York: Frederick A. Praeger, 1967.

Huntington, Samuel P., and Moore, Clement. *Authoritarian Politics in Modern Society: The Dynamics of Established One Party Systems.* New York: Basic Books, 1970.

Jennings, W. Ivor. *Party Politics.* Cambridge: Cambridge University Press, 1962.

La Palombara, Joseph, and Weiner, Myron, eds. *Political Parties and Political Development.* Princeton: Princeton University Press, 1966.

Leiserson, Avery. *Parties and Politics.* New York: Knopf, 1958.

Lipset, Seymour M. and Rokkan, Stein. *Party Systems and Voter Alignments.* New York: The Free Press, 1967.

McLennan, Barbara N., ed. *Political Opposition and Dissent.* New York: The Dunellen Co., 1973.

Neumann, Sigmund, ed. *Modern Political Parties.* Chicago: University of Chicago Press, 1955.

Rokkan, Stein. *Citizens, Elections, Parties.* New York: David McKay, 1970.

Weiner, Myron. *Party Politics in India, The Development of a Multi-Party System.* Princeton: Princeton University Press, 1957.

——————. *Party Building in a New Nation: The Indian National Congress.* Chicago: University of Chicago Press, 1967.

CHAPTER 6: POLITICAL PROCESSES AND PUBLIC POLICY

Argyris, C. *Understanding Organizational Behavior.* Homewood, Ill.: Dorsey Press, 1960.

Armstrong, John A. *The European Administrative Elite*. Princeton: Princeton University Press, 1973.

——————. *The Soviet Bureaucratic Elite: A Case Study of the Ukrainian Apparatus*. New York: Frederick A. Praeger, 1959.

Barnett, A. Doak. *Cadres, Bureaucracy and Political Power in Communist China*. New York: Columbia University Press, 1967.

Berger, M. *Bureaucracy and Society in Modern Egypt*. Princeton: Princeton University Press, 1957.

Braibanti, Ralph. *Asian Bureaucratic Systems Emergent from the British Imperial Tradition*. Durham, N.C.: Duke University Press, 1966.

Downs, Anthony. *Inside Bureaucracy*. Boston: Little, Brown and Co., 1967.

Eisenstadt, S. N. *The Political Systems of Empires*. New York: The Free Press, 1963.

Eldersveld, Samuel J. *The Citizen and the Administrator in a Developing Democracy*. Chicago: Scott, Foresman and Co., 1968.

Hyneman, Charles S. *Bureaucracy in a Democracy*. New York: Harper, 1950.

La Polombara, Joseph, ed. *Bureaucracy and Political Development*. Princeton: Princeton University Press, 1963.

Lowi, T. J. *The End of Liberalism: Ideology, Policy and Crisis of Public Authority*. New York: W. W. Norton, 1969.

Parkinson, C. N. *Parkinson's Law and Other Studies in Administration*. Boston: Houghton Mifflin, 1957.

Prybula, J. S. *The Political Economy of Communist China*. Scranton, Penna.: International Text Book Company, 1970.

Suleiman, E. N. *Power and Bureaucracy in France: The Adminstrative Elite*. Princeton: Princeton University Press, 1974.

CHAPTER 7: GENERAL ASSESMENT: COMPARING DIFFERENT POLITICAL SYSTEMS

Almond, Gabriel A., and Powell, G. Bingham, eds. *Comparative Politics Today: A World View*. Boston: Little, Brown and Co., 1974.

_____. *Comparative Politics: A Developmental Approach.* Boston: Little, Brown and Co., 1966.

Blondel, Jean. *An Introduction to Comparative Government.* New York: Frederick A. Praeger, 1970.

_____. *Comparing Political Systems.* New York: Frederick A. Praeger, 1972.

Deutsch, Karl W. et al. *The Nerves of Government.* New York: The Free Press, 1963.

Friedrich, Carl J. *Constitutional Government and Democracy.* Boston: Ginn and Co., 1950.

Groth, Alexander J. *Comparative Politics: A Distributive Approach.* New York: Macmillan Co., 1971.

Holt, Robert, and Turner, John, eds. *The Methodology of Comparative Research.* New York: Wiley, 1970.

Huntington, Samuel P. *Political Order in Changing Societies.* New Haven: Yale University Press, 1968.

Scarrow, Howard A. *Comparative Political Analysis: An Introduction.* New York: Harper and Row, 1968.

Schumpeter, Joseph. *Capitalism, Socialism and Democracy.* New York: Harper and Row, 1950.

Glossary of Abbreviations

ABAKO   Alliance des Bakongo. Early tribal-based political party in Zaire.

AICC   All India-Congress Committee. Important committee within the Indian National Congress party.

ASU   Arab Socialist Union. Egypt's governing party.

BBC   British Broadcasting Corporation. Nationalized radio and television network in Great Britain.

CCP   Chinese Communist Party. Governing party in the PRC.

CDP   Centre Pour la Democracie Progressive. French political party.

CEREA   Centre de Regroupement Africaine. Early Tribal-based political party in Zaire.

CONACO   Confédération des Associations Congolaises. Early coalition party led by Moise Tshombe in Zaire.

CONAKAT   Confédération des Associations Tribales de Katanga. Early tribal-based political party in Zaire.

CORFU   Corporación de Fomento de la Producción. Chilean development corporation.

CPI   Communist Party of India.

CPIM   Communist Party of India-Marxist. The more radical of the two Indian Communist parties.

CPSU   Communist Party of the Soviet Union. The only legal political party in the Soviet Union.

ITV   Independent Television Corporation. Privately owned television network in Great Britain.

KGB   Committee of State Security. Soviet secret police organization.

KOMSOMOL   All-Union Lenin Communist League of Youth. Soviet Communist party youth organization.

LP   Liberal party. Chilean liberal political party.

MIR   Movimiento de Izquierda Revolucionaria. Left-wing, revolutionary Chilean political party.

MNC   Mouvement National Congolais. Early political party led by Patrice Lumumba in Zaire.

MP   Member of Parliament. Term used in Great Britain and India.

MPR   Mouvement Populaire de la Revolution. At present, the only legal political party in Zaire.

MRP   Mouvement Républican Populaire. French political party important during the Fourth Republic.

NEC   National Executive Committee. Important committee within the British Labour party.

NPC   National Party Congress. Governing congress of the CCP before the Cultural Revolution.

NRA   National Rifle Association. Powerful American interest group.

NU   Nahdatul Ulama. Traditionalist Islamic Indonesian political party.

ORTF   Office de Radio Diffusion - Télévision Français. Nationalized French radio and television network.

PCR   Partido Communista Revolucionario. Maoist Chilean Communist party.

PKI   Partai Kommunis Indonesia. Indonesian Communist party.

PLP   Parliamentary Labour party. Labour members of Parliament.

PNI   Partai Nationalis Indonesia. Indonesian Nationalist party.

PPCC   Provisional People's Consultative Congress. Indonesian legislative body under Guided Democracy.

PRC   People's Republic of China

PSA   Partai Solidaire Africane. Early tribal-based party in Zaire, led by Antoine Gizenga.

PSI   Partai Socialis Indonesia. Indonesian Socialist party.

PSP   Praja Socialist party. Indian political party.

RADECO   Rassemblement des Associations Congolaises. Early Congolese coalition party, led by Cyril Adoula.

RCC   Revolutionary Command Council. Military council through which Nasser governed Egypt in the early years of his regime until he established the National Union in 1956.

RPF   Rassemblement du Peuple Français. Party established under the aegis of Charles de Gaulle in 1948.

SSP   Samyukta Socialist party. Indian political party.

SST   Supersonic Transport airplane.

UAR   United Arab Republic. Union of Egypt and Syria, 1958-1961.

UCP   United Conservative party. Chilean conservative political party.

UDR   Union des Democrates pour a Vè République. New name for Gaullist party (UNR); changed in 1967.

UNR   Union pour la Nouvelle République. Party of President de Gaulle in the Fifth Republic (1958-1967).

USSR   Union of the Soviet Socialist Republics.

Glossary of Concepts

Antithesis.   The opposite; Hegel and Marx viewed history as progressing from the conflict of opposites; i. e., the clash of thesis and its opposite, the antithesis. See also *Thesis* and *Synthesis*.

Arab Socialism.   Guiding philosophy and principles of Egypt's major political party, the ASU. Under President Nasser, Arab socialism had a pan-Arab thrust.

Archipelago.   An island group; as the Indonesian archipelago.

Aristocracy.   A class of persons holding high rank and privilege; to Aristotle, "aristocracy" was the best form of state; i. e., it was a state in which the "best" people governed.

Bolshevik.   A member of the more radical majority of Russian revolutionaries that staged the October Revolution of 1917, overthrowing the more moderate revolutionary group, the Mensheviks (minority).

Boxer Rebellion.   An unsuccessful uprising in 1900 by a Chinese secret society, directed primarily against foreign legations in Peking; was crushed by an international expeditionary force.

Brahmin.   The most prestigious caste of the Hindu religion; referring traditionally to priests and their descendants.

British Commonwealth.   An international organization consisting of Great Britain, a large number of former British colonies, which are now independent, and Great Britain's dependent territories.

Bureaucracy.   An organization of administrators structured hierarchically into ranks, with established functions for each rank, and established rules for promotion among and tenure within these ranks. "Bureaucracy" was one of Weber's sources of legitimate authority.

Cadre.   A group of persons trained and qualified to lead a large organization; as the CPSU is a cadre party, being trained and qualified in ideological terms, to lead the USSR.

Capital.   The wealth, whether in property or currency, that is used through investment to produce more wealth.

Capitalism.   An economic system based on the private ownership and organization of wealth and production by individual persons, the capitalists.

Caste system, Hindu.   The procedure by which the Hindu religion subdivides Hindu society into rigid, inherited social groupings.

Censorship.   The act of a government in looking through books, magazines, films, or other material to suppress parts it deems objectionable.

Censure.   Disapproval; a vote of censure taken in a parliamentary system notes disapproval of the government by the elected legislature and normally would lead to the resignation of a premier or prime minister.

Centralism, democratic.   Guiding organizational principle of Communists parties, which dictates that the decisions of higher bodies are binding on the lower ones, and that all party members must support the party line.

Charisma.   A special personal quality of an individual that gives him the gift and power to become a leader. Weber saw "charisma" as a source of legitimacy for a government.

City-State.   A political system that is small, centered on a city, but retains its independence and power of self-government; as in ancient Athens.

Coalition.   A combination or alliance of groups; as a "coalition government" in a parliamentary system that consists of an alliance of political parties.

Common Market, European.   An organization of nine European nations (France, Germany, Italy, Belgium, Netherlands, Luxembourg, Great Britain, Denmark, and Ireland), whose function is primarily to reduce trade barriers among the nine and develop common economic policies among them.

Commune.   The smallest administrative division in France. France has over 38,000 communes. Also, the large collective farm unit in the PRC. See also *Paris Commune*.

Communism.   The theory and political movement that is based on the writings of Karl Marx. The theory is based on the belief that eventually all social classes will be abolished and all property will be owned in common. The USSR and the PRC have both adopted versions of this theory and their governmental systems reflect this.

Communist International (Comintern).   A radical organization (1919-1943) founded in Moscow, whose major aim was to attain political power for Communist parties throughout the world through violence and revolution.

Confidence, vote of.   Expression of approval of the government by the legislature in a parliamentary system.

Control organ.   Organization within political parties in noncompetitive states whose function is to make sure the party line is observed throughout the party hierarchy.

"Corporations."   Traditional term, derived from medieval usage, to designate economic sections of the community that should be represented, at least indirectly, by MPs in the British Parliament.

Coup.   An overthrow of government by forcible means, usually overthrowing the constitutional system as well.

Cultural Revolution.   Political upheaval in the PRC in 1965-1966, resulting from a conflict among factions within the CCP and involving the activities of the Red Guards, a youth group.

Culture, political.   The complex of behavioral norms, attitudes, and beliefs that relate to politics in a given society.

Decentralization.   Shifting of political power away from the central directorate
of leaders to lower ranking, more local personalities, as for example with
the Congress party in India.

De-Stalinization.   The practice, followed by Communist parties since 1956, of
eradicating the memory and works of Josef Stalin; as in the destruction of
monuments and the renaming of public places.

Divine Right of Kings.   The claim made by monarchs, generally before the
eighteenth century in Europe, that they ruled by virtue of the will of God
and not by consent of the people.

Elite.   The best; in political terms, usually refers to that group of people in a
community that by virtue of training, prestige, or social class are regarded
as best suited to rule.

Enlightenment.   A philosophical movement of the seventeenth and eighteenth
centuries that believed in the value and power of human reason. The
Enlightenment brought about the reconsideration and reevaluation of
religious, political, and educational traditions that preceded the revolutions of the eighteenth and nineteenth centuries.

Entrepreneur.   A person who undertakes to organize or manage a business
enterprise.

Extraterritoriality.   The possession of political rights within a country by a
foreign power; as in China before the nationalist revolution.

Fabian Socialists.   Members of the Fabian Society, a group of moderate,
reformist British Socialists, founded in 1884.

Formateur.   An official designated by the president to preside over the
formation of cabinets under the 1950 Indonesian constitution.

Franco-Prussian War.   War between France and Prussia in 1870; it was
won by Prussia, ending the Second Empire of Louis Napoleon
Bonaparte.

French Revolution.   The revolution that began in 1789, overthrew the French
monarchy, and ended with Napoleon Bonaparte's seizure of power in
1799.

Gandhiism.   The principles of the movement of Mohandas Gandhi, particularly noncooperation and passive resistance, used during the drive for
Indian independence.

Gaullism.   The principles associated with the movement led by and supporting
Charles de Gaulle of France.

Genealogy.   A record of ancestry of an individual; important for monarchs in
traditional systems who acquire legitimacy according to their lineage.

General will.   Concept developed by Jean-Jacques Rousseau in *The Social
Contract* referring to the abstract will of the people to which government
should be responsible. Rousseau's "general will" was not based on
concepts of voting majorities; it was something like a Quaker "sense of the
meeting" on a communitywide scale.

Gotong rojong.   Mutual aid; the spirit by which councils under Guided Democracy were supposed to reach unanimous agreement.

Government.   The political direction and control exercised over the citizens of
a nation-state.

Great Leap Forward. Chinese attempt to invigorate the PRC economy by loosening restraints and implementing decentralization (1957-1960).

Great Proletarian Cultural Revolution. See *Cultural Revolution.*

Group. A collection of persons who are united by some shared interest or activity.

Guided Democracy. Regime led by President Sukarno (1957-1965) that ended elections and governed through large councils in which Communists, nationalists loyal to Sukarno, and the military were permitted representation.

Hierarchy. Any system of persons or things arranged in ranks from higher to lower.

High school, comprehensive. New educational institutions in Great Britain, introduced in the 1960s, that included facilities for academic and vocational training in the same building and that allowed students to choose their course of study at a later age than had previously been the case.

"Hundred Flowers Bloom" Campaign. A brief outburst by Chinese intellectuals in 1957 that led to political reaction and repression of criticism in the PRC.

Ideographs. Written symbols that represent ideas or objects directly, rather than their phonetic sounds; used in written Chinese.

Ideology. A system of beliefs and values that organize the manner in which persons observe and evaluate their political and social systems.

Industry, nationalized. An industry that has been brought under the ownership and control of the nation; i. e., a publically owned and managed industry.

Infrastructure. The basic, underlying features of a social system.

Intelligentsia. Intellectuals,considered as a specially endowed elite; term is most often used in the USSR.

Interest aggregation. The process by which many groups and interests are put together into national programs and coalitions by political parties.

Interest group. A collection of persons who share an interest and who are organized to make this interest known to other groups, to the government, and to the community at large.

Judicial review. The power of courts to determine the constitutionality of acts of the different branches of government and government officials; characteristic of government in the United States and India.

Junta. A small group ruling a country; term is especially used after a constitutional regime has been overthrown, and no new constitution yet substituted for it.

Katanga. Province in Zaire; rich in mineral deposits.

Kinship. Family relationship; a village with kinship ties has strong family relationships among its inhabitants.

Koran. The sacred text of Islam, regarded as the foundation of religion, law, and politics by devout Moslems.

Labor force. The group of workers that is employed in a country.

Laissez-faire. Free trade; an economic doctrine that opposes government interference in trade and commerce.

Law Lords.   The highest appeals court in Great Britain, consisting of sixteen
    law lords and all previous lords chancellor.
Leader, charismatic.   See *Charisma*.
Legislature, bicameral.   Two-house legislature; usually one house represents
    the people directly, while the other represents some regional or aristo-
    cratic principle.
Legislature, unicameral.   Single-house legislature.
Legitimacy.   The ability of a leader to have his power recognized and accepted
    by the important groups and persons in his community as proper and
    appropriate.
Lord Chancellor.   Highest judicial officer in Great Britain; presiding officer
    over the House of Lords.
Manchu Dynasty.   Last imperial dynasty to rule China (1644-1912); originated
    in Manchuria and known in China as the Ch'ing Dynasty.
Market, free.   An economic system that allows the setting of prices by the free
    interplay of supply and demand, without government interference.
Martial law.   Law imposed by national military forces when civil authority has
    broken down.
Mercenaries.   Hired soldiers serving in foreign armies; as in Zaire.
Messianism.   A movement pledged to support a leader as sacred or chosen to be
    a deliverer.
Mestizos.   Population of Latin American countries of mixed European and
    native Indian blood.
Monarchs, supreme.   Political leaders who inherited their positions by reason
    of birth and were able to rule their dominions absolutely; as in pre-
    revolutionary France.
Monarchy.   A system of government that vests undivided and absolute author-
    ity in one ruler, whose position is legitimized by genealogy.
Monolithic.   Characterized by massive, rigid uniformity.
Musjawarah.   The distillate of opinion or consensus; the traditional In-
    donesian village method of reaching agreement, resurrected for use at
    councils at the national level under Guided Democracy.
Nation-State.   A legal unit, defined by international law, as the basis for the
    international system. A nation-state has land, territory, population, a
    government, and independence.
Netherlands East Indies.   Colonial name for Indonesia, when under Dutch
    rule.
Nonalignment.   National policy, followed by India under Nehru, of refusing to
    participate in alliances with either the United States or the USSR.
Oligarchy.   A system of rule by a small selfish minority. Aristotle defined
    "oligarchy" as the corrupt version of "aristocracy."
Ottoman Empire.   Turkish empire founded about 1300 and collapsed after
    World War I; ruled most of the Middle East during its peak years.
Outer Islands.   Term referring to islands outside of Java in the Indonesian
    archipelago.
Panchayat.   Indian village, based on agriculture.

Pantheon.   The collectivity of gods in a particular religion or mythology; as in the Hindu pantheon.

Pariah.   Outcast; the lowest social status in the Hindu religious social structure.

Paris Commune.   Short-lived communist government established in Paris in 1871; was crushed by republican forces.

Parties, political.   Organizations concerned with national programs and policy that aggregate the interests of smaller groups, nominate candidates for election, and help run the government once their candidates are elected.

Peer.   Equal; refers to person holding a peerage or noble title in Great Britain.

Plebiscite.   A direct vote by an electorate on some important issue.

Policymaking.   The process by which government leaders make decisions and carry out activities that affect the entire nation.

Politics.   Actions taken by and behavior patterns of citizens in attempting to arrive at joint policies and decisions within the state.

Price system.   The system of interaction between supply and demand by which prices are established for all goods and services in a free market economy.

Proletariat.   The working class; defined by Marx as those people with no property and capital who depend on their labor to survive.

Purge.   The act of ridding a political organization of elements regarded as disloyal or undesirable.

Rajah.   A title used by traditional local princes and rulers in India and Indonesia.

Rank.   A specific level within a bureaucratic or social hierarchy. See *Status.*

Red Guards.   Student group active in the Chinese Cultural Revolution.

Referendum.   The practice of placing a legislative measure before an electorate to be accepted or rejected.

Regime.   A specific type of governmental system.

Rights of Man.   The doctrine enunciated in the French Declaration of the Rights of Man and in 'the American Declaration of Independence, referring to the rights of all people to be free, equal, and independent.

Shari'a.   Islamic law deriving from the Koran and tradition.

Socialization.   The process by which people learn the values and beliefs that make up the culture of their society.

Socialization, political.   The process by which people learn their beliefs and attitudes relating to politics; i. e., their political culture.

Socialization structures.   The institutions that teach people the values of their respective societies, including family, church, schools, and the media among others.

Social system.   The basic patterns of behavior that hold society together. See also *Society,, integrated.*

Society.   A fairly large mass of persons who share enough values and characteristics that they see themselves as a group, distinct from other groups of people.

Society, integrated.   A society, though composed of many different groups, that is still united into a cohesive unit.

Sphere of influence.   A geographic area in which one nation dominates another; as China before the nationalist revolution was divided by Western powers into spheres of influence.

Stagnation, industrial.   A situation in which an economic system is not growing (in terms of jobs and new industry) rapidly enough to provide employment and reasonable increases in living standards for its population.

State.   See *Nation-State.*

Status.   The position of a group or individual in relation to other groups or individuals within a social hierarchy. Status accrues to an individual because of his personal qualities, in contrast to rank, which comes as a result of an office he might hold.

Subnationalism.   A feeling of national loyalty to a group that is not a nation but only part of a nation; as with tribal subnationalisms in Zaire.

Suez Canal.   Egyptian canal connecting the Mediterranean and Red Seas.

Suffrage, universal.   The practice of permitting all citizens (male and female), regardless of property qualifications or education, the right to vote.

Syndicate.   Congress party political leaders who split with Indira Gandhi and were defeated by her.

Synthesis.   The higher truth, in the philosophy of Marx and Hegel, that results from the dialectical conflict of a thesis and its opposite, the antithesis.

T'ai P'ing Rebellion.   Rebellion in China (1851-1864) that attempted to overthrow the Manchu Dynasty but failed.

Thesis.   Term used by Hegel and Marx in the dialectic method in which one proposition (the thesis) is confronted by its opposite (the antithesis) to yield a higher truth (the synthesis).

Treaty of Versailles.   Treaty signed by the world powers ending World War I in 1919.

Tsar.   Emperor of Russia.

Ulema.   Teachers and leaders in the Islamic religion.

Union Miniere du Haute Congo.   Belgian mining combine that was powerful in running the Congo during its days as a Belgian colony.

Universities, "red brick."   New British universities designed to admit students from all classes and backgrounds as opposed to the distinguished, socially eminent universities of Oxford and Cambridge (the latter sometimes referred to as "Oxbridge").

Utopia.   An imagined perfect or ideal system; as Marx's vision of communism.

Warlord.   Chinese general, generally who has seized power at the decline of one dynasty but before the erection of a new state; as the regime of Yuan Shih-kai, 1912-1916.

Glossary of Names

Adoula, Cyril (1921-   ).   Political leader in early years of Zaire's independence.

Alexander II, Tsar (1818-1881).   Reformist, modernizing tsar of Russia; noted for freeing the serfs.

Allende, Salvador (1908-1973).   First Socialist ever elected president of Chile; was president of Chile, 1970-1973, until overthrown by a military coup.

Aristotle (384-322 B.C.).   Greek philosopher, noted for his writings on *Politics*.

Beria, Lavrenti P. (1899-1953).   Head of Soviet secret police under Stalin; executed for treason after Stalin's death in 1953.

Bonaparte, Louis Napoleon (1808-1873).   President of France, 1848-1852; dissolved the republic and became emperor of France, 1852-1870.

Bonaparte, Napoleon (1769-1821).   Conqueror of Europe and emperor of France, 1802-1815.

Brezhnev, Leonid (1906-   ).   Soviet political leader; first secretary of the CPSU, 1964-   .

Burke, Edmund (1729-1797).   English political writer and statesman, noted for his conservative philosophy; born in Ireland.

Castro, Fidel (1927-   ).   Prime minister of Cuba, 1959-   .

Chiang Kai-shek (1887-   ).   Chinese political leader and general; president of the Chinese Republic, 1943-1950, until driven off the Chinese mainland; has since been president of the Republic of China (Taiwan).

Chou En-lai (1898-   ).   Chinese Communist leader; premier of the PRC, 1949- .

Churchill, Winston S. (1874-1965).   Conservative party leader and wartime prime minister of Great Britain, 1940-1945, and again, 1951-1955.

Darwin, Charles (1809-1882).   English naturalist and author of *The Origin of Species.*

Douglas-Home, Alexander (1903-   ).   Conservative party prime minister of Great Britain, 1963-1964.

Eden, Anthony (1897-   ).   British prime minister, 1955-1957; member of the Conservative party.

Faruk (1920-1965).   King of Egypt from 1936 until his abdication in 1952.

Frei, Eduardo (1911-   ).   President of Chile, 1964-1970.

Freud, Sigmund (1856-1939).   Austrian doctor; founder of psychoanalysis.

Fuad (1868-1936).   First king of modern Egypt from 1922-1936.

Gaitskell, Hugh (1906-1963).   English economist and political leader; Labour party leader, 1955-1963.

Gandhi, Indira (1917-   ).   Prime minister of India, 1966-   ; daughter of Jawaharlal Nehru.

Gandhi, Mohandas (Mahatma) Karamchand (1869-1948).   Hindu religious leader, social reformer, and leading nationalist of the Indian independence movement.

Gaulle, Charles de (1890-1970).   French general and leading politician of the Fifth Republic; president of France, 1958-1969.

Gibbs, Sir Humphrey (1902-   ).   British governor-general in Rhodesia when Rhodesians declared independence.

Giscard d'Estaing, Valéry (1926-   ).   French political leader, member of the Independent Republican party; president of France, 1974-   .

Hammarskjold, Dag (1905-1961).   Swedish statesman; secretary-general of the United Nations, 1953-1961.

Heath, Edward (1916-   ).   Conservative party leader and prime minister of Great Britain, 1970-1974.

Hegel, Georg (1770-1831).   German philosopher.

Ibañez del Campo, Carlos (1877-1960).   President of Chile, 1952-1958.

Kasavubu, Joseph (1917-   ).   President of the Republic of the Congo (Zaire), 1960-1965.

Khrushchev, Nikita S. (1894-1971).   Soviet political leader; premier of the USSR, 1958-1964.

Kosygin, Alexei (1904-   ).   Premier of the USSR, 1964-   .

Lenin, V. I. (1870-1924).   Russian revolutionary leader; premier of the USSR, 1918-1924.

Liu Shao-chi (1898-   ).   Chairman of the PRC, 1959-1966, until the Cultural Revolution.

Locke, John (1632-1704).   English political philosopher.

Louis Philippe (1773-1850).   King of France, 1830-1848.

Lumumba, Patrice (1925-1961).   Premier of the Republic of the Congo (Zaire), 1960-1961.

Luther, Martin (1483-1546).   German theologian; leader of the Protestant Reformation.

Mao Tse-tung (1893-   ).   Chinese Communist political leader; chairman of the CCP, 1943-   .

Marx, Karl (1818-1883).   German economist, philosopher, and early socialist.

Mendès-France, Pierre (1907-   ).   French political leader of the Fourth Republic; premier of France, 1954-1955.

Menon, Krishna (1897-   ).   Indian politician and close adviser to Prime Minister Nehru; was Indian ambassador to the United Nations.

Mobutu, Sese Seko (1930-   ).   Congolese general; president of Zaire, 1965-

Naguib, Mohammed (1901-   ).   Egyptian general and political leader; premier of Egypt, 1952-1954; president, 1953-1954

Nasser, Gamal Abdel (1918-1970). Egyptian political leader; prime minister of Egypt, 1954-1956; president of Egypt (and the UAR), 1956-1970.

Nehru, Jawaharlal (1889-1964). Prime minister of India, 1950-1964; father of Prime Minister Indira Gandhi.

Nicholas II, Tsar (1868-1918). Last emperor of Russia; executed in 1918.

O'Higgins, Bernardo (1778-1842). Liberator of Chile from Spanish colonial rule.

Peter the Great (1672-1725). Powerful, modernizing Russian tsar; ruled from 1682-1725.

Plato (427-347 B.C.). Greek philosopher and mathematician; famous for his dialogues, particularly *The Republic*.

Podgorny, Nicolai V. (1903-). Soviet political leader; president of the USSR, 1965- .

Prasad, Rajendra (1884-1963). Indian political leader; first president of the Republic of India, 1950-1962.

Rousseau, Jean-Jacques (1712-1778). French philosopher and social reformer; noted for his writings on education and for *The Social Contract*; born in Switzerland.

Sadat, Anwar (1918-). Egyptian political leader; president of Egypt since the death of Nasser, 1970- .

San Martin, José de (1778-1850). South American revolutionary leader, born in Argentina; was a leader in winning independence for Argentina, Chile, and Peru; was protector of Peru, 1821-1822.

Smith, Adam (1723-1790). Scottish economist, noted for the laissez-faire concepts presented in his book *The Wealth of Nations*.

Stalin, Joseph V. (1879-1953). Soviet political leader; secretary-general of the CPSU, 1922-1953; premier of the USSR, 1941-1953.

Suharto (1921-). Indonesian general and political leader; president of the Republic of Indonesia, 1967- .

Sukarno (1901-1970). Indonesian revolutionary leader and president of the Republic of Indonesia, 1945-1967.

Sun Yat-sen (1866-1925). Leader of the Chinese national revolution and early leader of the Chinese nationalist Republic; president of the Republic of China, 1921-1925.

Trotsky, Leon (1879-1940). Russian revolutionary; was minister of war, 1918-1925; went into exile when Stalin seized power.

Tshombe, Moise (1919-1969). Leader of the province of Katanga and early leader after independence in Zaire.

Webb, Beatrice (1858-1943). Along with her husband, Sidney Webb (1859-1947), was well-known author and economist; supporter of the British Labour party.

Wilson, Harold (1916-). Leader of the British Labour party, 1963- ; prime minister of Great Britain, 1964-1970 and 1974-

Yuan Shih-kai (1859-1916). Chinese general and warlord; president of China, 1912-1916.

Index

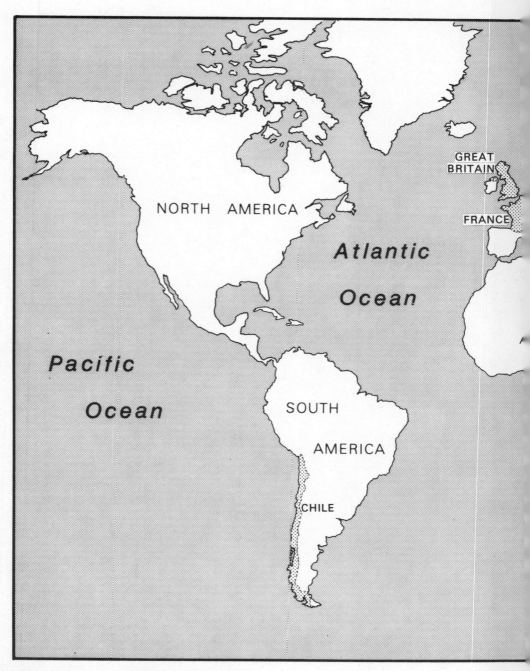

THE WORLD